A ROYAL PASSION

A ROYAL PASSION

The Turbulent Marriage of King Charles I
of England and Henrietta Maria of France

KATIE WHITAKER

W. W. Norton & Company
NEW YORK · LONDON

For information about permission to reproduce selections from this book,
write to Permissions, W. W. Norton & Company, Inc.,
500 Fifth Avenue, New York, NY 10110

For information about special discounts for bulk purchases, please contact
W. W. Norton Special Sales at specialsales@wwnorton.com or 800-233-4830

Manufacturing by Courier Westford
Book design by Iris Weinstein
Production manager: Andrew Marasia

Library of Congress Cataloging-in-Publication Data

Whitaker, Katie, 1967–
A royal passion : the turbulent marriage of King Charles I of England and
Henrietta Maria of France / Katie Whitaker.
p. cm.
Includes bibliographical references and index.
ISBN 978-0-393-06079-9 (hardcover)
1. Charles I, King of England, 1600–1649—Marriage. 2. Henrietta Maria,
Queen, consort of Charles I, King of England, 1609–1669—Marriage.
3. Married people—England—Biography. 4. Interfaith marriage—England—
Case studies. 5. Great Britain—History—Charles I, 1625–1649—Biography.
6. Great Britain—Kings and rulers—Biography. 7. Queens—Great Britain—
Biography. 8. Princesses—France—Biography. I. Title.
DA396.A22W47 2010
941.06'20922—dc22
[B]
2010003158

W. W. Norton & Company, Inc.
500 Fifth Avenue, New York, N.Y. 10110
www.wwnorton.com

W. W. Norton & Company Ltd.
Castle House, 75/76 Wells Street, London W1T 3QT

1 2 3 4 5 6 7 8 9 0

FOR ELIZABETH AND ALEXANDER

And in memory of
VICKI HARRIS

1967–2008

Contents

PART THREE · ENDINGS

List of Illustrations

Acknowledgments

I wish wholeheartedly to thank my literary agents on both sides of the Atlantic, Peter Robinson and George Lucas, who helped the book take shape in its early stages, and Maria Guarnaschelli, my editor at Norton, whose comments were invaluable in the final stages of the process.

In the intervening years I have been truly grateful for the able research assistance of Eric Langley, Stewart and Becky Mottram, Chris Richardson, Jill Ramshaw, and Vicki Harris. I would also like to thank the staff of the British Library, the Public Record Office, Cambridge University Library, Leeds University Library, The Royal Collection, The National Portrait Gallery, and my local branch of the North Yorkshire Libraries Service, who were all most helpful.

My husband, Weem, has been unstinting throughout in help and encouragement, and the boundless energies of my children, Elizabeth and Alexander, have provided most welcome distractions.

Family Tree

Henry Stuart, = Mary Stuart,
Lord Darnley   Queen of Scots
1545–1567   1542–1587

King Henry II of France = Catherine de Medici
1519–1559   1519–1589

Francis II   Charles IX   Henry III

King James VI of Scotland = Anne of Denmark
and I of England   1574–1619
1566–1625

Henry,   Elizabeth = Frederick, Elector Palatine   King Charles I = Henrietta Maria
Prince of Wales   1596–1662   and King of Bohemia   1600–1649   1609–1669
1594–1612   1596–1632

[others died young]

Charles Louis,   Prince Rupert [others]   Sophia   Charles   King Charles II   Mary
Elector Palatine   1619–1682   1630–1714   1629   1630–1685   1631–1660
1618–1680   = Ernest August,   = Catherine   = William,
                                               Elector of Hanover   of Braganza   Prince of Orange
                                               1629–1698   1638–1705   1626–1650

King George I,   [others]   King William III = Queen Mary II
Elector of Hanover   1650–1702   1662–1694
1660–1727

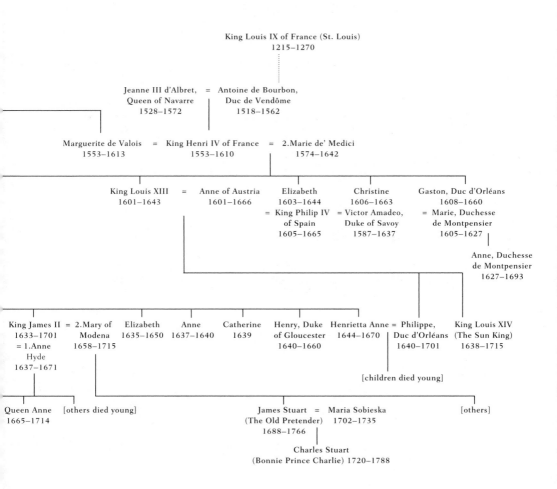

King Louis IX of France (St. Louis)
1215–1270

Jeanne III d'Albret,   =   Antoine de Bourbon,
Queen of Navarre   Duc de Vendôme
1528–1572   1518–1562

Marguerite de Valois   =   King Henri IV of France   =   2.Marie de' Medici
1553–1613   1553–1610   1574–1642

King Louis XIII   =   Anne of Austria   Elizabeth   Christine   Gaston, Duc d'Orléans
1601–1643   1601–1666   1603–1644   1606–1663   1608–1660
                                          = King Philip IV = Victor Amadeo,   = Marie, Duchesse
                                          of Spain   Duke of Savoy   de Montpensier
                                          1605–1665   1587–1637   1605–1627

Anne, Duchesse
de Montpensier
1627–1693

King James II = 2.Mary of   Elizabeth   Anne   Catherine   Henry, Duke   Henrietta Anne = Philippe,   King Louis XIV
1633–1701   Modena   1635–1650   1637–1640   1639   of Gloucester   1644–1670   Duc d'Orléans   (The Sun King)
= 1.Anne   1658–1715   1640–1660   1640–1701   1638–1715
Hyde
1637–1671

[children died young]

Queen Anne   [others died young]   James Stuart = Maria Sobieska   [others]
1665–1714   (The Old Pretender) 1702–1735
                                                       1688–1766

Charles Stuart
(Bonnie Prince Charlie) 1720–1788

Foreword

On September 23, 1642, in a riverside meadow a hundred and thirty miles northwest of London, the cavalry of King Charles I of England charged into the camp of their parliamentarian opponents, routing them utterly. The Battle of Powick Bridge, as it came to be known, was the first encounter of the English Civil War—a conflict that would kill thousands and last, with some intermissions, until King Charles I's son was defeated in battle on almost the same spot nine years later. This "cruel and unnatural" war, as both sides described it,[1] forms one of the bloodiest and most dramatic periods of British history, but its true significance reaches far beyond the shores of that little island nation on the northeastern edge of the Atlantic Ocean.

For this was a war unlike any previous one in the modern world—a confrontation not between rival claimants to a nation's throne, contesting questions of dynastic succession, but between an autocratic king and his rebellious subjects, who insisted they had essential rights and liberties that could not be overridden. England's parliamentarians broke new ground in taking up arms for their ideals: to combat both religious repression and political injustices, the most intolerable of which was taxation imposed by the king's authority, without parliamentary representation. In the resulting maelstrom, radical ideas rose to orthodoxy: a monarch ruled not by absolute, God-given right, the parliamentarians declared, but only "with a limited power . . . according to the laws of the land, and . . . for the good and benefit of the people." If he abused this trust, if his government was unjust, if he sought despotically "to overthrow the rights and liberties of the people," then it was the people's right to abolish his rule and set up a new government.[2] As the Civil War drew to its bitter end and King Charles I was defeated and then executed as a traitor to his people, his opponents formed a grand resolve. The very existence of a king, they declared, was "unnecessary, burdensome, and dangerous," utterly incompatible with "the just freedom and liberty of the people."[3] And so they created a new nation-state, "the Commonwealth of England": the first modern republic, established "without King or House of Lords,"[4] governed by the people, for the people.

In Britain this great new political order was short-lived. The republic proved unworkable; in 1653 Oliver Cromwell was appointed Lord Protector, a king in all but name; following his death five years later, the struggling British nation invited King Charles I's son, Charles II, back from exile to be its king. But the world had been changed forever. The parliamentarians' new ideals of liberty and republicanism, once raised, could not be laid to rest. Puritan settlers, fleeing from Charles I's repressive rule during the 1630s, had already carried their values into North America. A century later, when another British king sought to impose taxes there without parliamentary representation, the stage was set for these ideals to revive. The result was the American Revolutionary War and the foundation of "a new nation, conceived in liberty," as Abraham Lincoln put it.

For years, scholars have argued over the origins of that early English republic and the nature of the civil war that produced it. Was the conflict a "noble revolt," driven by the nation's tiny but powerful aristocracy, or was it a necessary consequence of vast social changes—"the rise of the gentry" and "the decline of the aristocracy"? Was it a Marxist-style revolution, or was the war driven primarily by religious divisions? Was it an outgrowth of numberless local family rivalries that grew to engulf the entire English nation? Or was it part of a wider, pan-British conflict, inseparable from the contemporary troubles of Scotland and Ireland? Each theory has had its enthusiastic exponents. Yet to me it seemed that there was a great, untold story at the heart of this conflict: the story of the love between King Charles I and his wife, Henrietta Maria of France.

Theirs was one of the greatest romances of all time: dramatic, emotional, and of vast historical importance. During the 1630s, Charles and Henrietta's love defined British court culture, driving an exceptional flowering of the arts. For the royal pair this was a period of blissful happiness. Careless of popular disapproval, they instituted vigorous repression of their puritan and parliamentarian opponents. It was a course that would lead ultimately to revolution. As resistance to their regime organized, the royal couple's passionate devotion kept them close, plotting together to preserve their power in the face of Parliament's radical reforms. Their story now becomes a dark political thriller, set in a chilling world of deception, plots and machinations, violence and death. Henrietta's prominent role in all the royal plans soon brought retaliation. Every day, it seemed, Parliament's investigations uncovered some "fresh conspiracy against the liberty of the state," and Henrietta was implicated in almost every one. Finally, on New Year's Day 1642, the parliamentary members decided that the queen must be charged with high treason. Determined to save his beloved wife, whatever the cost, Charles attempted a military coup—precisely what his opponents had long feared. When that failed, civil war soon followed.

Throughout the conflict, the couple's love fueled their desperate attempts to win back the idyllic life they had forged together. It drove them on through all the vicissitudes of fortune, yet in the end it brought them to isolation, downfall, and destruction. Even as the terrible strains of war tested their relationship to the limit, their letters still breathed with passion and loyalty. Every day or two a new letter passed between them, full of plans, hopes, fears, and confessions, and the undying devotion each felt for the other, which alone made all else bearable. "Thy love preserves my life," Charles told his wife, and Henrietta responded in kind: "I shall never have my health till I see you again"; "I cannot be happy."

As I read the couple's wartime correspondence, so intimate and impassioned, I was drawn at once into their world. The depth of their emotional attachment was irresistible. Though these events happened more than 350 years ago, the couple felt so close I could almost touch them. I was moved, but also surprised. The characters I saw here were worlds away from the Charles and Henrietta passed down to us by centuries of historical tradition. The old story tells of a cold, haughty king, shy, weak, and irresolute, and of a queen who metamorphosed from a frivolous teenaged bride into a bigoted Catholic termagant who domineered ruthlessly over her husband and children. Instead I saw a woman of tremendous courage, energy, and political insight, determined to protect those she loved. And Charles came to life as a man with a mission, who believed wholeheartedly in the justice of his cause and would never abandon his political and religious principles "whatever it cost me." This faith and his unshakable love for his wife were the twin stars guiding his course, although their conflicting demands sometimes pulled him almost in two.

My sense that I was confronting fresh, passionate characters was what really drew me to start writing this book. Who were these people who seemed so different from their conventional images? What bound them together so powerfully? One thing was clear. No conventional birth-to-death biography of either one of the royal pair could go to the heart of their characters: they were too closely involved with each other, too devoted and mutually dependent. My quest, I realized, was for a joint biography: a biography of a marriage, in all its intimacy of detail.

The task was a long one and full of surprises. Determined to bypass the traditional story of the marriage and get under these people's skins, I sought out the original, primary sources from the time and based my account only on them. Charles and Henrietta's own letters, memoirs, and speeches were vital, of course, but so too were the reports of foreign ambassadors stationed in London, and especially the secret missives of the pope's diplomatic agent, who was welcomed at Henrietta's court in defiance of English puritan public opinion. British government state papers, the private diaries and let-

ters of the couple's friends and enemies, the literary outpourings
of their courtiers, political tracts, international treaties, clergymen's
sermons, doctors' prescription books, portraits and prints, financial
accounts, and inventories all played their part.

Among these I found manuscripts that had barely been looked at
by historians in the centuries since they were first written: papers
that revealed astonishing undiscovered stories that went far beyond
the sketchy summaries, assumptions, misrepresentations, and bow-
dlerizings passed on by the occasional Victorian scholar who had
been here before me. A handful of manuscripts in the British Library
in London were particularly telling, for they utterly discredited the
memoirs written by Henrietta's grand chamberlain, the Comte de
Tillières, which historians have always followed unquestioningly in
their accounts of Charles and Henrietta's troubled first year together.
Tillières, I now saw—writing with his own agenda for the consumption of the French government in 1626—was the first origin of that
old, established view of Henrietta as a willful, tantrum-prone teenager, and Charles as almost a nonperson, entirely in the power of his
advisers. But the British Library manuscripts—letters written by the
French ambassadors present on the very first day that Charles and
Henrietta met—disproved Tillières's version of events, displaying
Charles as decisive, self-motivated, and considerate, and Henrietta
as poised and eager to please. Freed from Tillières's now all-too-
obvious fabrications, I was able to use other sources and look afresh
at the couple's first year of marriage, building up a nuanced story of
the strains forcing them apart—divisions of nationality, religion, and
alien groups of friends, rather than the personal incompatibility and
inadequacies alleged by Tillières. This then allowed an explanation
of how, three years later, Charles and Henrietta so easily resolved
their difficulties and fell in love suddenly and thoroughly, to produce a marriage famed as the happiest and most affectionate in all
Europe.

Even in published sources, widely available in any major library,
there were discoveries to be made. I was eager to recover the fresh-
ness and reality of the couple's lives, and make the events of history
feel immediate and contingent, like our own experience of everyday

life. So I paid scrupulous attention to the dates of the events I followed, often on a day-by-day basis. This careful collation of material paid off, revealing new facets to the marriage. Especially it showed how, in the last period of political turmoil before the war, Charles and Henrietta worked together as a unit to resist parliamentary opposition. It was not a case of Henrietta bullying and browbeating Charles, as commonly thought, but rather a genuine collaboration.

Along the way there was a host of smaller discoveries, each one a telling detail, adding new depth to the couple's complex relationship. In an Italian ambassador's letter home to Florence lay the horrifying revelations of the pioneering forceps delivery of Henrietta's first, premature child. It was a story carefully concealed by the Victorian scholar who alone, it seemed, had read this manuscript before me. Other Italian manuscripts, hardly less neglected, painted in glowing colors the happy affection of the royal couple among their children at Richmond Palace, and the pleasure of their eldest son when Henrietta took him to mass contrary to her husband's orders. This second manuscript was almost impossible to find in the Public Record Office in London, since only two scholars claimed to have seen it before me and one of them cited no manuscript volume number while the other gave an incorrect volume. Even once I tracked it down, the actual volume had no page numbers. Elsewhere I uncovered a charming vignette of royal family life in an obscure seventeenth-century book of court poems. An illustration here showed Charles and Henrietta's third child, James, the eager sportsman, out on the tennis court dressed in a specialized tennis kit: a costume that historians knew existed but for which no visual evidence was thought to survive. Much earlier in the marriage, I found, again by collating sources chronologically, that Charles and Henrietta's supposed great reconciliation after two tense years together—a reconciliation portrayed by numerous earlier biographers—was in fact only by mail: the couple were 70 miles apart at the time and had not seen each other for weeks.

These and many other discoveries combined to reveal the rich fabric of Charles and Henrietta's marriage and brought the pair to life as fascinating, complex individuals, whose relationship was by turns intimate, passionate, and tempestuous. After their first years of quarreling the pair shared everything. Surmounting their differences in religion and temperament, they became lovers, devoted parents, political allies, hard-pressed conspirators, and finally comrades in arms who had to endure the bitterness of defeat. Theirs was a love that shaped the course of British and world history; a love that was, as one of their contemporaries put it, "beyond expression."

A ROYAL PASSION

Prologue

WINTER 1649

Around noon on February 9, 1649, Queen Henrietta Maria sat down to dinner in the Palace of the Louvre. Here, in her ground-floor apartments looking out over the River Seine, she was just a few rooms away from the bedchamber where she had been born almost forty years earlier.[1] As a girl of fifteen, seated on a throne in another nearby state chamber, Henriette-Marie, as she then was, had received her first love letter from the English prince she was to marry. Everything about her then had been French: her exquisitely tailored silk dress, her hair in tiny curls, her witty conversation, her whole outlook on the world. But now, after twenty-three years of marriage, Paris was merely "a sad place of exile."[2] Her love for her husband and her children—three sons and three daughters still survived of the nine babies she had borne—tied her to England, as did a real affection for the country and its people. Visitors to the Louvre Palace were regaled with praises of the land she had been forced to leave. For ten or twelve years, they heard, she had been "the happiest princess in the world."[3] Her husband, King Charles I—*"mon cher* cœur," "my dear heart"—was the best of men: "good, just, wise," "a king, a husband, and a friend" all in one. The love between them was "the admiration of all Europe."[4] In those years, the continental mainland had been torn apart by the "fury . . . miseries and desolation" of the Thirty Years' War. Britain alone had flourished "in entire peace and universal plenty":

> Tourneys, masques, theatres better become
> Our halcyon days. What though the German drum
> Bellow for freedom and revenge? The noise
> Concerns not us, nor should divert our joys.[5]

But now all that was past. In the south wing of the Louvre, Henrietta inhabited some of the most splendid rooms in France. Rebuilt by a succession of her ancestors in the previous century, this section of the palace was in lavish Renaissance style, with classical columns and statues, and ranks of huge rectangular windows allowing the light to flood through. Inside, the walls were smothered in paintings, tapestries, and mirrors; the ceilings were elaborately molded in plaster and richly painted. The furniture was of the finest: Henrietta's state bed was upholstered in silks and velvets, embroidered with gold and silver. But none of this was hers. She had no personal mementos: the jewels she had brought from England were gone; her family portraits had been left on the palace walls at home. Everything here came from charity, lent by her brother's widow, the French queen regent, Anne of Austria, who had moved Henrietta into the vacant palace four years earlier.

Then she had fled to France not just for her own safety but also for her husband's. "As your affairs stand, they would be in danger if you come to help me, and I know that your affection would make you risk everything for that," she wrote to him from her sickbed in Exeter, doubled up with "cruel pains" and struggling to breathe. With parliamentarian forces advancing to besiege her, she fled westward into Cornwall. "Adieu, my dear heart," she wrote from Truro.

If the wind is favorable, I shall set off tomorrow. . . . I am hazarding my life, that I may not incommode your affairs. . . . If I die, believe that you will lose a person who has never been other than entirely yours, and who by her affection has deserved that you should not forget her.[6]

Crossing the English Channel under fire from a fleet of Parliamentarian warships, Henrietta's sole fear was of capture and imprisonment: the captain, she ordered, was "to set light to the powdermagazine" and blow up the ship if he saw she could not escape. It was one of those moments of wartime heroism her followers celebrated, the queen "one moment saved, another moment almost taken, . . . relying only on God and her unshakable courage."[7]

In November 1644 she entered Paris in triumph, sharing a gilded carriage with the French queen regent and six-year-old King Louis XIV. The king's guards rode before them; the French nobility followed in their coaches. Trumpets blared, church bells rang, bright hangings adorned the streets. At the Louvre, dignitaries galore made flattering speeches. But Henrietta's visitors were shocked at the pale shadow they encountered. Madame de Motteville, a French lady-in-waiting who now became Henrietta's frequent companion, gives the clearest portrait of her, "much disfigured by the greatness of her illness and her misfortunes," "so pierced with her sorrows that she wept almost all the time." The enchanting queen painted by Anthony Van Dyck in former years—a glorious brunette, elegant and poised—was all but gone. Just a few traces remained: "beautiful eyes, a good complexion and a well-made nose." But the dominant impression was of a woman, "thin and small," who stooped a little, "and her mouth, which was not naturally beautiful, had become large in the emaciation of her face."[8] That was the sympathetic version. To less partial observers, Henrietta seemed positively ugly: a "little woman with long lean arms, crooked shoulders, and teeth protruding from her mouth like guns from a fort," as her niece Sophia put it.[9] But this impression did not last long. Henrietta's charm was irresistible. "She had an infinity of wit, that sparkling wit which pleases beholders," Madame de Motteville recalled, adding:

> She was agreeable in society, courteous, pleasant and easy to get along with; living without the slightest ceremony among those who had the honor of being near her. Her temperament was inclined toward mirth; and among her tears, if something amusing occurred to her, she would somehow stop crying to entertain the company.

All in all, "she made herself loved by everyone." Even the young Sophia was won over after a few minutes' conversation, and "from that time forward I considered her quite handsome."[10]

Briefly that winter, Henrietta seemed a queen once more, with "numerous ladies-in-waiting, maids of honor, carriages, guards, and footmen." But within months this great French court had gone, for Henrietta would not pay them. Instead, she sent almost all her government stipend to her husband, keeping for herself only what "seemed absolutely necessary for her subsistence." By 1648, she was nearing destitution. The French royal family, in conflict with the Paris Parliament, had stopped her stipend. One by one, Henrietta sold her fine clothes, her furniture, and the last of her jewels, just "to be able to subsist a few days longer." She showed Madame de Motteville "a little gold cup from which she drank," swearing she had no other gold or silver.[11] She could no longer pay the few English courtiers who continued in her service, so they too were dressed in old, worn clothes, without jewels, struggling to survive on credit that the Parisian tradesmen were reluctant to give. As violence escalated on the streets of Paris that winter, the French royal family fled to the castle at Saint-Germain-en-Laye, ten miles to the west, while their army laid siege to the city. Left behind at the Louvre, Henrietta saw "a lasting civil war" approaching, much like the English Civil War she had left behind. Paris was completely cut off. Already people were going hungry, "for the price of all things doubles and trebles upon us."[12]

Yet still Henrietta's little band of courtiers kept up the proprieties. The British court before the war had been the most ceremonious in

Europe and now, at that midday dinner on Friday, February 9, 1649, Henrietta was served with full royal etiquette. Her table was covered with an Oriental carpet topped by a white cloth. A large saltcellar and a platter of freshly baked bread stood in its center. On a side table were basins and ewers for the queen to use to wash her hands. When Henrietta was seated, one of her chaplains—a Capuchin monk in a plain brown habit—said grace in Latin. Then a procession of gentlemen entered, with swords at their sides and lace collars around their necks, each bearing a platter of meat or fish. At their head, the sewer, on bended knee, set down each dish on Henrietta's table, where her carver bowed and then cut some meat from each. The first pieces were tasted by the courtiers who had carried them in. Then it was time for Henrietta to eat, while her cupbearer stood by a sideboard of glasses and decanters, ready to present her wine, on bended knee, whenever she wanted to drink.

The rules were strict. No one was to come too close to the queen, nor turn their backs toward her: if they had to walk away from her, they did it backward. And no one sat down with Henrietta, since no one there equaled her rank. Instead, her English ladies and gentlemen stood in a semicircle behind her chair. Meanwhile, the queen had to eat with the greatest delicacy. She was to cut her bread, not break it with her hands. She had to take salt from the saltcellar using her knife, wiped clean on a piece of bread, not on her napkin. She had to try some of every dish and wipe her mouth on her napkin before drinking. When finished, she had to clean her cutlery on a piece of bread and set it down on the table, not in her dish. Then, after another Latin grace, she would wash her hands in a basin of fresh water.[13]

But today Henrietta was hardly eating. She had slept badly, as so often recently. Though she kept up a brave face by day, "yet," her ladies noted, "her nights are more sad than usual." The emerging French civil war, so similar to her recent experience, doubtless weighed on her spirits, as did the utter destitution facing her. But these anxieties were light, she said, compared with her desperate worries for her husband, who faced a far "greater calamity."[14]

Since Henrietta's arrival in Paris, King Charles I had lost his war with Parliament. For two years he had been a prisoner, cut off from those he loved, striving vainly to negotiate an agreement with his captors or to escape to his wife in France. Occasionally Henrietta's letters got through to him, carried by loyal supporters who risked imprisonment and even torture if discovered. Once it was "a handsome lady, and wondrous bold," who slipped a letter behind the hangings in his apartments, where his guards discovered it, but Parliament could make nothing of the cipher in which it was written. Another time a former Royalist army officer, disguised as a peasant, stood with a fishing rod on a narrow bridge and passed up Henrietta's letter as the king crossed over. Caught by Charles's guards and questioned vigorously, the officer revealed what he knew: most important, that Henrietta urged her husband "to accept any terms" his enemies offered and save himself, even if it meant she could never return to England.[15] Charles found great comfort in these letters, seeing his wife's "sympathy with me in my afflictions"—true proof "that she loves me, not my fortunes." Though driven away "by my own subjects," she was still present in "my own heart."[16]

But otherwise he was unutterably alone. True, he was treated with full royal ceremony, just as before the war, but none of his former followers or friends were allowed access to him. Instead, his guards and servants were new men, "appointed by Parliament."[17] Worst of all was the religious repression.[18] Charles was devoted to the grand religious ceremonies that he and his archbishop, William Laud, had enforced during his years of glory. For him, these were "nearest to the practice of the Apostles"; the only true way to approach God.[19] He detested the Puritans, with their rejection of ceremony and use of extemporaneous prayers. Their religious freedom was merely a cover for rebellion, he believed. And of all the Puritan sects, he particularly loathed Presbyterianism as being utterly "incompatible with monarchy." He had learned this principle from his father, King James, who had hated the preachings forced on him as the young king of Scotland. "Scotch Presbytery," James had famously declared, "agreeth as well with monarchy as God and the devil." And now Charles himself had "too dearly bought the certain knowledge of it."[20]

Back in the 1630s, Charles had deprived English Puritans of their ministers. Now the tables were turned. All his requests for Anglican clergymen to "perform the usual offices about his person" were refused; only Presbyterian chaplains were provided for him and his attendants.[21] Sometimes Charles engaged these men in debate. In previous years, he had delighted in tying his wife's Roman Catholic priests in knots with his ruthless logic and profound knowledge of the Bible and the Church fathers. Now he allowed his Presbyterian companions to be "very earnest" in their opinions, while Charles replied with jokes, very "pleasant and merry," finding some entertainment and relief from the solitude of his captivity and often having the best of the encounter.[22] But he would never conform to their religious practice. At mealtimes, these chaplains stood ready to say grace, but Charles would not listen to them. Instead, standing under his cloth-of-state, he prayed by himself before sitting down to eat. Every Sunday he absented himself from their chapel ceremonies. Alone in his bedchamber, having ordered that no one enter "until he called," he occupied himself in "private devotion." Even on weekdays, he spent several hours every day "in reading and other pious exercises." He had become, he said, "my own chaplain."[23] He wrote his own prayers, confessed his sins to God, and begged forgiveness for three lapses in particular: once when he had "suffered innocent blood to be shed by a false pretended way of justice"; again when he had "permitted a wrong way of Thy worship to be set up in Scotland"; and again when he had "injured the bishops in England." "O Lord," Charles prayed, "I have no excuse to make, no hope left, but in the multitude of Thy mercies." Looking back over recent years, Charles set pen to paper, seeking meaning in all that had happened to him. This was his consolation now: that everything had been God's will, a judgment on him for his sins, to which he must humbly submit in hopes of forgiveness.[24]

It was this religious faith as well as his political faith that gave Charles his inner strength. He would abandon neither "for any extremity or misery that may befall me." In the last resort, he was sure, the British nations could not manage without him: the Parliamentarians would "ask so much and use it so ill" that finally the people would be "glad to relodge the power they had taken from the Crown."[25] So Charles remained "patient and cheerful" throughout his troubles.[26] It was a matter of pride: he was "above complaints or bewailings," he said. *Dum spiro spero* was his motto now: "While I breathe I hope."[27]

For a time he had his children's company. "Do you know me, child?" he asked seven-year-old Henry, whom he had last seen five years earlier, when the boy had been left behind as Charles and Henrietta fled from London: "I am your father, child; and it is not one of the least of my misfortunes that I have brought you and your brothers and sisters into the world to share my miseries."[28] Through the summer of 1647, Charles often saw Henry, Elizabeth, and thirteen-year-old James, who remained in England, prisoners like him. He was full of forebodings, instructing them carefully "how to behave themselves, if the worst should befall him," when their eldest brother, Charles, Prince of Wales, would be their king, to whom they must show "unshaken . . . affection and duty." To little Henry, Charles was especially insistent. He was "never to be persuaded or threatened out of . . . the [Anglican] Church," and he must never be made a puppet king by his Parliamentarian keepers "whilst either of his elder brothers lived." This Charles repeated every time they met, "with all the earnestness and passion he could express."[29]

Still Charles found great solace in his children. Sometimes they dined together, with James in the place of honor on the king's right hand: "His majesty is very fond of him, and loving to all the children; he bears the young lady often in his arms," the news reported. At other times Charles expressed "much joy," watching them "running and playing" in the garden.[30] But all too soon, Charles was in strict confinement once more, as his opponents grew ever more extreme. The king "was so great a dissembler, and so false a man, that he was not to be trusted," Oliver Cromwell declared. Parliament resolved to negotiate no longer, but work instead "toward the settlement of the kingdom without having further recourse to the king." In Paris, Henrietta begged the queen regent for aid "with her tears," but to no avail.[31] Hope only revived in the summer of 1648, with a flurry of Royalist uprisings. Eagerly Henrietta sold the last of her jewels, giving the money to her eighteen-year-old son, Charles, Prince of Wales, who left Paris to take command of the main English war fleet, which had mutinied in favor of the king. Under the combined threat of English, Scottish, and Irish forces, Parliament agreed to reopen talks. Their armies were soon victorious and Prince Charles's fleet retreated to Holland, but at Newport on the Isle of Wight, the talks continued nonetheless.

Everything depended on Charles's decisions now. He could expect no further military support, Henrietta wrote; France was too disturbed by its own internal divisions. And so, she implored, he must "embrace all such counsels and consultations that may tend to the peace and tranquillity of his three kingdoms."[32] By October, Charles was offering greater concessions than ever before. He would dismiss the bishops and allow Presbyterianism for three years. He would give Parliament control of the nation's armed forces for twenty years, and the government of Ireland would be settled however Parliament preferred. "Censure us not for having parted with too much of our own right," he begged his eldest son and heir. It was a great price, but one aimed at a great gain: "security to us, peace to our people." Later, another Parliament "would remember how useful a king's power is to a people's liberty."[33] But Charles was full of regrets. He wished there was only himself to consider. Then, like Job, "I would willingly have rather chosen misery than sin." Once he cried—"the biggest drops that I ever saw fall from an eye," his secretary noted—though Charles turned his head away, "loath to be discerned," and quickly recovered himself.[34]

But his offer to Parliament came too late. Even as the offer was being carried to London, where many Members of Parliament (MPs) favored accepting it, the army took matters into its own hands. The king—"that man of blood"—had caused the Civil War, they said. Now he had to be tried for high treason, to "account for that blood he had shed, and mischief he had done to his utmost, against the Lord's cause and people in these poor nations."[35] At dawn on December 1, soldiers pushed their way into Charles's bedchamber and carried him off to the bleak fortress of Hurst Castle on the south coast. The following day, the main body of the army marched into London. When

Parliament resumed four days later, soldiers stood at the entrance to the House of Commons, turning away MPs who favored negotiating with the king. Just eighty or so MPs remained in the "Rump Parliament," as it came to be called—all of them were army sympathizers who voted that Charles's offer was "highly dishonorable to the Parliament, and destructive to the peace of the kingdom."[36] On December 15, 1648, the army's Council of Officers ordered the king to be brought to Windsor Castle, ready for his trial.

In Paris, Henrietta was "struck to the heart with amazement and confusion."[37] Shivering in her apartments at the Louvre—for she could no longer afford firewood and it was so cold she would not allow her daughter Henrietta Anne out of bed—the queen swiftly wrote letters to Parliament and to the army's general, Lord Fairfax, asking for safe-conduct to come to "see the king my lord." She wrote secretly to Charles, too, promising to "use her utmost power . . . by all ways imaginable to help him," wishing even "that she might die for him, without whom she cannot, nor will not live." Then began the desperate wait for a reply, knowing that "so little of what I desire succeeds."[38]

It was at this time that the French royal family fled from Paris. Their army outside the walls stopped all letters coming in "by the ordinary way of the post." Not until the middle of January was there news from England, and even then there was no reply to Henrietta's letters.[39] In fact, their recipients had refused to open them, as they came from a person whom Parliament had voted "guilty of high treason."[40] Instead, Henrietta learned, the House of Commons had voted to put the king on trial.

Yet still there seemed room for hope. In Holland, Prince Charles told the Dutch government of the "great and imminent danger" threatening his father and persuaded them to send an ambassador "to save at least his life." The prince wrote to the English Parliament, too: if they killed their king, he threatened, it would "be resented by all the princes and states of the world."[41] Meanwhile, Henrietta got a messenger through to Saint-Germain, where the French court promised to send an ambassador "with the object of staying the execution." Forty thousand French troops might also go "for the relief of innocence." In England there was only limited support for the king's trial, even among Parliamentarians: of the 135 commissioners appointed to preside over the trial, only fifty-two were present when the court met.[42] As February began, Henrietta heard that Charles had been condemned and brought out for execution but had been rescued by the common people. Some of the queen's companions suspected this story was concocted by Henry, Lord Jermyn, Henrietta's most intimate confidant, hoping thus to prepare her gradually for the blow he expected would soon come. But Henrietta never guessed. Briefly she believed the tale. When she found it untrue, she "wept many tears," before finding consolation in the hope that the English people would yet save her husband.[43]

Finally she could bear the agonies of suspense no longer. It was still impossible for her to leave Paris—the Parliament's guards on the gates would not permit "any person of quality . . . to stir out of the city"[44]—but one of her gentlemen could get through to Saint-Germain to hear the latest news from England. Seated at dinner on Friday, February 9, the day after he had left, the queen was anxiously expecting his return. Behind her, the courtiers in their accustomed semicircle struggled to maintain a semblance of normalcy. Many of them knew that Henrietta's messenger had already returned, bearing news that "made me shudder all over," her chaplain, Father Cyprien de Gamache, remembered. But no one could bear to tell her yet. For a whole hour they delayed the terrible moment, laboring to keep up a "variety of conversation . . . on indifferent matters." But Henrietta was not really listening. Her mind was with her husband, and with the messenger she thought would have returned by now. Finally she cut across her courtiers' uneasy talk to complain "of his being so long in bringing her an answer."

At this, Henry, Lord Jermyn began very gently to break the news. The messenger was "faithful and prompt" in her commands, he said; certainly he would have returned sooner "if the news had been favorable." Henrietta did not miss the hint. "What is it then?" she asked. "I perceive plainly that you know." But still Jermyn could not say the words. As Henrietta pressed him, he circled around and around with "several evasions and many ambiguous expressions," hoping to prepare the queen "by little and little for the fatal intelligence." At last he told her everything.[45]

On Friday, January 19, 1649, the prisoner-king had returned to London for the first time since he had fled seven years earlier. The next day, his trial opened in Westminster Hall, the largest room in England, three hundred feet long, spanned by a vast arched ceiling of dark oak beams. Here, eight years earlier, Charles had watched Parliament try his most trusted minister, the Earl of Strafford, for high treason. Now the king himself was conducted under heavy guard to the high-sided wooden box assigned to the accused. In front of him, the court's president sat on a high-backed chair, while the rest of the commissioners were on tiered benches behind him. Not one rose to his feet or took off his hat, as etiquette demanded. Rather, Charles was supposed to remove his own hat, out of "respect to the court," which of course he would never do. Instead, he looked sternly at the commissioners: sixty-eight were present that day, "members of the House of Commons, officers of the army, and citizens of London": all "high-flown Parliament men."[46] Before sitting down on the crimson velvet chair in his box, Charles cast his eyes over the wealthy and privileged audience in the galleries above them. Then he stood up to stare around behind him, where soldiers separated him from the "multitude of spectators" who filled the space to the great arched doorway at the hall's far end.[47] When he was seated again, his charge was read aloud: that he, being king with only "a limited power" to rule "according to the laws of the land," yet "out of a wicked design to erect . . . an unlimited and tyrannical power . . . and to overthrow the rights and liberties of the people," had "traitorously and maliciously levied war against the present Parliament and the people therein represented." He was "the occasioner, author, and continuer of the said unnatural, cruel, and bloody wars," and so was personally "guilty of all the treasons, murders, rapines, burnings, spoils, desolations, damages, and mischiefs to this nation, acted and committed in the said wars."[48] Now he had to answer: guilty or not guilty.

But Charles refused. "By what lawful authority am I seated here?" he demanded.

Remember, I am your king, your lawful king . . . think well upon it, before you go further from one sin to a greater. . . . I have a trust committed to me by God . . . I will not betray it to answer to a new unlawful authority.

He stood firm all that day and the next. The courtroom bristled with hostility: "Justice! Justice!" the soldiers shouted, with a "hideous cry." The president overrode the king repeatedly:

Sir, I must interrupt you . . . you appear as a prisoner . . . you are to give a punctual and direct answer . . . you are not to dispute our authority . . . you stand in contempt of the Court . . . you ought not to interrupt while the Court is speaking to you. This point is not to be debated by you; neither will the Court permit you to do it.[49]

But still Charles kept his composure. Dressed all in black, with the Order of the Garter star shining on his long black cloak and his hat firmly on his head, he spoke without anger or hesitation. His lifelong stammer was gone in this moment of resolution:

For the charge, I value it not a rush; it is the liberty of the people of England that I stand for. For me to acknowledge a new court that I never heard of before, I that am your king . . . indeed I do not know how to do it. . . . There's no law for it, to make your king your prisoner.

At last the court would hear no more. It was not for Charles "to dispute the jurisdiction of the supreme and highest authority of England," its president told him. Charles's failure to answer the charge was recorded, and he was taken away.[50]

For three more days the court met in private, while Charles waited at St. James's Palace. All the old ceremonies of kingship were gone. His food was brought in by soldiers, with no tasting, no cup offered on bended knee—a proceeding so "uncouth" to Charles that he now ate alone. On January 27, the court summoned Charles once more. "Justice!" "Execution!" the crowd shouted.[51] The king made a last attempt to propose negotiations with Parliament, but the court would not hear him. They were already "resolved to proceed to sentence and to judgment," the president said. Then the clerk read aloud from his parchment: ". . . that he, the said Charles Stuart, as a tyrant, traitor, murderer, and public enemy to the good people of this nation shall be put to death by severing of his head from his body."

"Will you hear me a word, sir?" the king asked.

"Sir, you are not to be heard after the sentence," the president responded.

"No, sir?"

"No, sir; by your favor, sir." Then, turning from the king: "Guard, withdraw your prisoner."

"I may speak after sentence. By your favor, sir, I may speak after sentence, ever. By your favor—hold. The sentence, sir—I say, sir, I do—" But already Charles was being hustled out by the soldiers. "I am not suffered for to speak. Expect what justice other people will have," he ended, as the soldiers renewed their shouts of "Justice! Justice!" laughing and blowing their tobacco smoke over Charles, "a thing very distasteful unto him." "Poor soldiers, for a piece of money they would do so for their commanders," some heard him say.[52]

Back at St. James's Palace, Charles knew he had only a short time to prepare for death. At last he had the permission of the Commons to summon an Anglican clergyman, and he chose William Juxon, Bishop of London. During the 1630s, Juxon had served him as a bishop and as Lord Treasurer, in charge of the nation's finances. Yet still he had not alienated Charles's Parliamentarian opponents, for even they admired his "meek spirit," noting how, in his "mighty place and power," he had always shown "an equal moderation and humility."[53] During the Civil War years, while other bishops were prosecuted, imprisoned, or even executed, Juxon had lived quietly as a country vicar. But in moments of need, Charles always turned to him, seeking his advice in his negotiations with Parliament. What the king respected even more than Juxon's "solid and steady judgment" was his outstanding "sincerity and integrity." For, like Charles himself, Juxon was a man of conscience who believed that one's sense of right and wrong should be put before every other consideration. Back in 1641, as Charles agonized over Parliament's bill declaring the Earl of Strafford guilty of high treason, Juxon alone advised against approving it, for Charles knew Strafford was innocent. Yet at last his other counselors had persuaded the king "to choose rather what was safe than what seemed just; preferring the outward peace of my kingdoms with men, before that inward exactness of conscience before God." So Strafford had died, and Charles had regretted this "act of so sinful frailty" ever since. From that moment, he had determined "to prefer . . . the peace of my conscience before the preservation of my kingdoms," and Juxon had become his most "esteemed and favored" clergyman.[54]

Now, on Sunday, January 28, Charles welcomed Juxon "very open-facedly and cheerfully." As the bishop began expressing sympathy, Charles interrupted him: "Leave off this, my lord, we have not time for it. Let us think of our great work, and prepare to meet that great God to whom ere long I am to give an account of myself." All through that evening and most of the next day, the two remained alone together, "in prayer and other pious exercises of devotion." "My time is short and precious," Charles said, ordering that no visitors be allowed to enter. Even his nephew, the Elector Palatine, was turned away, departing "full of sorrow."[55] Only a messenger from Prince Charles was admitted, bearing the prince's "sorrowing letter," asking for news and begging his father's blessing, which the king answered at once. On Monday, Juxon preached in Charles's chapel: although God's judgments might be delayed, he said, they would come in the end to all men. Then he gave Charles Communion.[56]

There were only two other people the king wanted to see: Elizabeth and Henry, who still remained in Parliament's custody after helping their brother James to escape. Now, with the permission of the Commons, they came to "take their sad farewell of the king their father." Thirteen-year-old Elizabeth burst into tears at once, followed by her eight-year-old brother, who knelt beside her to beg their father's blessing. Lifting them, Charles kissed them and sat them on his knees while he spoke of the duty they owed to their mother and to Prince Charles, who would succeed him as king.[57]

They must not grieve for him, Charles said, for "it would be a glorious death that he should die, it being for the laws and liberties of this land, and for maintaining the true Protestant religion." Afterward, he was sure, God would restore his eldest son to the throne, and they would all be happier than if he had lived. In the meantime, he had already forgiven his enemies, and he urged his children to do likewise.

Charles asked Elizabeth to deliver his last message to Henrietta: "that his thoughts had never strayed from her, and that his love should be the same to the last." To Henry he reiterated his old commands: "Sweetheart . . . they will cut off my head, and perhaps make thee a king; but mark what I say, you must not be a king, so long as your brothers, Charles and James, do live." "I will be torn in pieces first," the boy replied.[58] Then Charles gave them the last of his jewels, all except the few he still wore on his person, and they said their farewells, the king kissing them in tears and "praying God Almighty to bless them." Elizabeth wept bitterly, while Charles stood at a window to hide his grief. As his bedchamber door opened to let the children out, he came back quickly and kissed and blessed them once more. Then Charles returned "immediately to prayer." After Juxon left late that evening, he still continued "reading and praying," preparing for his last day on earth.[59]

He slept for only about four hours. Around 5 a.m. on Tuesday, January 30, 1649, Charles opened the curtains of his bed and called to Thomas Herbert, the only one of his Parliamentarian servants to whom he had become close, and the only one still left to help him. Herbert was a congenial spirit: cultivated and well read, a courtier before he fought for Parliament in the war. Gradually he had fallen under the spell of the tragic, lonely king; the memoir he later wrote provides a touching portrait of Charles's last years of "solitude and sufferings."[60] "I will get up," Charles said to him now, "having a great work to do this day." So Herbert helped him into his clothes: a blue satin waistcoat and a lavish lace collar over two embroidered white linen shirts. "Let me have a shirt on more than ordinary," Charles told him:

The season is so sharp as probably may make me shake, which some observers will imagine proceeds from fear. I would have no such imputation. I fear not death! . . . I bless my God I am prepared.

Herbert combed the king's shoulder-length brown hair and then handed him his two watches, one gold and one silver, which he always wound himself. Around the king's neck went the broad sky-blue ribbon he always wore, with its oval pendant of the Order of the Garter: a figure of St. George slaying the dragon, carved in onyx, surrounded with "twenty-one fair diamonds."[61] On the pendant's back, twenty-one matching diamonds encircled a miniature portrait of Henrietta, "set in a case of gold, the lid neatly enameled with goldsmiths' work." Below the king's left knee, Herbert fastened the dark blue velvet Garter ribbon with its motto, *Honi soit qui mal y pense*, embroidered in 412 diamonds, and in one ear Charles hung a large pearl-drop earring. A black hat and mittens and his black cloak, emblazoned with its bright silver Garter star, were placed ready for the cold walk to Whitehall.[62]

It was still dark when Bishop Juxon arrived. As the sun rose, he performed the Anglican service of morning prayer. Then Charles continued "in prayer and meditation"; "ready to resign himself into the hands of Christ Jesus."[63] Around 10 a.m., guards conducted him out to St. James's Park, where several hundred infantrymen stood in two parallel ranks all across the park, their colors flying and drums beating loudly. Between them, Charles walked amid his guard of halberdiers, with Juxon on the king's right side and Thomas Herbert following. Mounting a wooden stairway between classical columns, Charles entered Whitehall Palace, his home before the Civil War. The windows here looked out over the tiltyard where, twenty-three years earlier, he had jousted to celebrate Henrietta's first arrival in England. Crossing the bridge over King Street, he passed on through another long gallery to his own bedchamber, hung with portraits of his closest family and friends. Here he remained with Juxon and Herbert for more than three hours while the House of Commons rushed to pass a final piece of legislation before he died: an "Act for prohibiting the proclaiming of any person or persons to be King of

England or Ireland, without consent of Parliament."[64] Meanwhile, Charles prayed and took Communion. He ate a little—a few mouthfuls of bread and a small glass of claret, to keep up his strength—and he chose a white satin skullcap to wear on the scaffold.

Shortly before 2 p.m., the colonel of his guards came to call him. Juxon and Herbert knelt weeping, and Charles gave each of them his hand to kiss. "Go," he told the colonel, "I will follow." And so he set off through the palace once more, with his halberdiers, until they reached the Banqueting House. Here, in 1625, he had ratified his marriage treaty, then kissed his new wife "in the presence of the whole people."[65] Now Charles passed quickly through the room, out through a hole broken in the wall, and onto the black-draped scaffold where he would die.

The executioner's newly sharpened axe rested on the wooden block where Charles would lay his head. Beside it stood the headsman and his assistant, masked and wearing false beards to further conceal their identity. In the street below, several hundred soldiers were packed around the scaffold's foot: infantrymen with iron helmets and ten-foot pikes held upright at their sides. Beyond them pressed "the multitudes of people that came to be spectators"—men, women, and children, stretching to the palace's great gateway on Charles's left, to the tiltyard wall in front of him, and far up the street on his right toward Charing Cross.[66] Among them was the future diarist Samuel Pepys, at this point only a fifteen-year-old schoolboy, playing truant to witness the death of the tyrant he hated. If he preached a sermon on the king, Pepys bragged to his friends later that day, he would take as his subject the biblical text, "The memory of the wicked shall rot."[67] Beyond the crowd, hundreds more troops were stationed in the street, both in the direction of Westminster and toward Charing Cross.

Charles walked once around the platform, examining everything. Near the block, heavy iron staples had been driven into the floor, with ropes and pulleys attached, to restrain him if necessary. But Charles merely smiled when he saw them, "without being any way daunted."[68] Then he began the speech he had prepared. Again, as at his trial, he spoke fluently, without a stammer and without any written text, "save only a few heads in a little scrap of paper."[69] The crowd was too far off to hear a word: even the infantrymen below the scaffold could not hear, Charles thought. And so he spoke to the handful of men who stood on the platform with him: soldiers from his guard and a few secretaries or newsmen taking notes, as well as Bishop Juxon.

Charles protested his innocence, "for all the world knows that I never did begin a war with the two Houses of Parliament": they had first encroached on his political privileges, not he on theirs. Yet it was right he should die: with this "unjust sentence," God was punishing him for the injustice he had committed in allowing the Earl of Strafford's execution, eight years earlier. Charles had already "forgiven all the world, and even those in particular that have been the chief causes of my death." Yet they were following "an ill way," he admonished. "Believe it," he advised the men in front of him, "you will never do right, nor God will never prosper you, until you give God his due, the king his due (that is, my successors), and the people their due."

Here Charles broke off, noticing that one of his listeners was touching the executioner's axe. "Hurt not the axe," he said, "that may hurt me." He wanted no painful, undignified death, hacked repeatedly with a blunt weapon. Then he picked up his thread once more. "For the people," he said, "truly I desire their liberty and freedom as much as anybody." Yet they were mistaken if they thought liberty came by "having share in government." Rather, their happiness came from fair laws, "by which their life and their goods may be most their own." It was for this political principle that Charles was going to die as "the martyr of the people."

There Charles would have ended, but Juxon intervened, reminding him to make a public statement of his faith. "I thank you very heartily, my lord, for that," Charles replied. "I had almost forgotten it." Then, turning back to his little audience: "Sirs, . . . I declare before you all that I die a Christian, according to the profession of the Church of England, as I found it left me by my father. And this honest man I think will witness it," he said, pointing to Bishop Juxon. "I have a good cause, and I have a gracious God; I will say no more."

Next he addressed his executioner: "I shall say but very short prayers, and when I thrust out my hands—" But Charles could not bear to say what followed. He took off his hat and handed it to Bishop Juxon, receiving in return his satin skullcap, which he put on his head. "Does my hair trouble you?" he asked the executioner, who said he should put it all under his cap. "I go from a corruptible to an incorruptible crown; where no disturbance can be, no disturbance in the world," Charles said to Juxon. Then, "Is my hair well?" he asked the executioner again.

He took off his cloak, handed it to the bishop, and lifted the Garter pendant with its portrait of Henrietta from around his neck. "Remember," the king said as he handed it to Juxon. After removing his doublet with its fine lace collar, he put on his cloak again. "You must set it fast," he said to the executioner, looking at the block. "It is fast, sir." "It might have been a little higher," Charles complained, hating to bow so low in front of his enemies. "It can be no higher, sir," came the reply. "When I put out my hands this way," Charles instructed once more, holding his arms out wide, "then—" For a few moments he stood and prayed, "with hands and eyes lifted up." Then he knelt and put his neck on the block. "Stay for the sign," Charles commanded again, as the executioner put the king's hair back under his cap. Then, "after a very little pause," Charles stretched out his arms. The swinging axe separated his head from his body at a single blow.[70] As the head rolled and blood spurted from the severed neck, there came one vast, spontaneous groan from the crowd, "such a groan by thousands then present as I never heard before, and desire I may never hear again," the Puritan minister Philip Henry remembered years later. The executioner lifted the dripping head high for everyone to see, and at this signal the waiting troops began to march "to disperse and scatter the people." "I had much ado among the rest to escape home without hurt," Philip Henry recalled.[71] The whole drama up there on the scaffold had been played out in no more than a quarter of an hour. "*Sic transit gloria mundi*," gloated the Parliamentarian news-sheets: thus passes the glory of the world.[72]

PART ONE

LOVE'S TRIUMPH

1

STRANGERS

On the afternoon of Sunday, December 12, 1624, the British court gathered in the long, paneled gallery of St. John's College, Cambridge. On the throne at the head of the room sat King James I—a bulky figure in clothes thickly padded against an assassin's dagger. Though only fifty-eight, James already saw himself as "an old king," and his looks confirmed his words. Large, tired eyes were deeply sunken in his long, creased face. His hair and wispy beard were flecked with white. Now, as so often, he was stiff with pain from gout, which swelled the joints of his feet, knees, elbows, and hands.[1]

Beside him stood his twenty-four-year-old son, Charles, Prince of Wales, bareheaded in honor of his father. Courtiers and nobles massed beneath them, summoned for a ceremony of "the utmost splendor." The French king's ambassador had just arrived in England, accompanied by a train of some eighty people. Now they entered for their first royal audience, bringing the "great treaty" that Louis XIII had signed in Paris in November, which James was now to ratify.[2]

Few people knew exactly what the treaty contained; many of its terms would be hated by the English public, and the long months of negotiations had been conducted in the utmost secrecy. So, once the elaborate greetings demanded by royal etiquette were completed, the ambassador retired for a private session with the king, the prince, and their two most trusted courtiers. Here, after last-minute discussions, Prince Charles signed the treaty and its associated documents, while James, his hands too swollen to hold a quill, watched his own signature being stamped on the pages by his secretary of state. Now, finally, it was agreed. The English prince was to marry the last available French princess, Henrietta Maria, the youngest sister of King Louis XIII.[3]

For twenty years, James had been planning such a marriage. When he inherited the English throne in 1603, he had become the first monarch of a united England, Scotland, and Ireland, and James was hugely proud of his new kingdom—"Great Britain," as he called it. A marriage alliance to one of Europe's two Catholic superpowers—the Hapsburgs of Spain or the Bourbons of France—would prove to the world the true greatness of the king and his new realm. It would also be a chance to play an important part in the great game of international diplomacy. Acting out his preferred role as King Solomon the wise, the peacemaker, James would use his own family's marriages to reconcile Protestant and Catholic Europe and achieve his long-held ambition for the union and "peace of Christendom."[4]

In 1605, negotiations had begun, aimed at securing the Spanish Infanta for Charles's elder brother, Prince Henry. But Spain demanded that Henry convert to Catholicism as a condition of marriage, so by 1612 James's hopes had moved to France. Royal marriages were primarily political tools, and the English princes had been brought up to acquiesce. "My part . . . is to be in love with any of them," Henry commented on his father's shifting plans.[5] But that same year, Henry died at the age of eighteen, leaving Charles to fulfill their father's matrimonial ambitions. By 1619, James was again determined on a Spanish marriage, so for the next four years he ignored repeated French proposals that Charles marry Henrietta Maria. It was Charles himself, together with the Duke of Buckingham, who chose the French marriage and then put James into "a state of siege," depriving him of all pro-Spanish company so that he would be "practically compelled to depend upon their wishes."[6] All through the summer of 1624, the king had resisted, but Charles and Buckingham had outmaneuvered him. In November, with the treaty terms agreed by the English ambassadors in Paris, James had finally been forced to comply.

The king had been angry then and he was still sulking now. Later that day, when his court celebrated the treaty with a "magnificent feast," James declared himself too ill to attend and remained in bed, "extremely melancholy."[7] His place at the head of the table was taken by Prince Charles, who was served with all the ceremony normally reserved for the king. Then, as the musicians played, the company stood up to dance, all men together since no ladies were present. James had little interest in women. His real attachments in life were all to men—especially those with "handsome persons and . . . fine clothes"[8]—and the courtiers dancing on this night clearly reflected the king's tastes. Gorgeously dressed in rich, brightly colored doublets, smothered in jewels, with fancy lace at their necks and wrists and high-heeled shoes on their feet, they wore tight silk stockings that showed off their legs right up to the thighs.

Dancing with the rest, the newly engaged Prince of Wales was the reason for all this jollity, yet he was an inconspicuous figure. Charles was a slight young man, just five feet four inches tall. Preferring to appear "sober . . . clean and neat" rather than "gaudy and riotous," he habitually wore dark colors and dressed "absolutely without jewels, more modestly than any gentleman soever."[9] Tonight, as always, he was far outshined by the Duke of Buckingham, the king's longstanding favorite. Buckingham was the most dazzling man at court: tall, handsome, stunningly dressed, an exquisite dancer, poised, confident, a delightful conversationalist, and a master of conspicuous consumption. Though he had started out as almost nobody—the younger son of a minor gentry family—Buckingham was now the most powerful man in the kingdom, his "entire engrossing of the prince's favor, as well as the king's" enabling him to do whatever he wanted in matters of government.[10] Charles had probably never noticed, but the French marriage had originally been Buckingham's idea, not his.

Charles had always lived in the shade of a more glamorous older rival. Born on November 19, 1600, the prince had been a sickly child who was not expected to live to adulthood. His legs were crooked and he still could not walk well at the age of four. He began to speak only as he approached his third birthday, with a stammer that lasted the rest of his life. It was his dashing brother Prince Henry—six years Charles's senior, handsome, athletic, clever, and strong willed—who won the hearts of the people, though neither he nor Charles could gain their father's affection. Lonely and insecure, Charles clung to his older paragon brother. "Sweet, sweet brother," he wrote to Henry, "I will give any thing that I have to you; both my horse, and my books, and my pieces,* and my crossbows, or any thing that you would have. Good brother, love me, and I shall ever love and serve you."[11]

Charles copied Henry in everything. He dressed like him. He followed him into the new continental fashion for collecting antique medals, books, paintings and *objets d'art*. He shared his passion for manly sports: hunting, fencing, and shooting with crossbows, muskets, and cannons. He especially loved to ride with his brother in the joust and the artful displays of the manège. Exercising constantly, Charles gradually grew fit and strong. By his twenties, he was recognised as one of the most accomplished horsemen of the age.

But by then he had also lost his beloved brother. In November 1612, two weeks before Charles's twelfth birthday, Henry died of typhoid fever and Charles was thrust into all the responsibilities of the heir to the throne. Dressed in black, he led his brother's funeral procession through the streets of London. The following February, he conducted his sixteen-year-old sister, Elizabeth, to her wedding to the handsome young German Protestant hero Frederick, Elector Palatine.† Three years later—in an investiture ceremony that was kept low-key to save money and avoid arousing painful memories of

---

* I. e., guns.
† Ruler of the Palatinate, now part of Western Germany.

Prince Henry—Charles formally succeeded his brother as Prince of Wales.

As he entered his late teens, Charles spent much more time with his father, joining him in state functions and in the hunting expeditions they both loved. It was only out in the field, however, that Charles won real approval from the king, who often said that in this he was "a true and worthy son." But the two remained emotionally distant. Charles was "excessively afraid of his father," whose hot temper often exploded in fits of ferocious foul language and even physical violence; James was always more attached to the handsome young men he took up as court favorites.[12] The last and greatest of these arrived in London in 1614, at the age of twenty-one. George Villiers was the handsomest man in the kingdom, everyone agreed, and his experience at the French court had given him a polish and wit that immediately charmed the king. Soon the newcomer was appointed the king's cupbearer, then gentleman of the bedchamber, sleeping in James's bedroom at night.

Whatever occurred there in private can never be known, but certainly the two men kissed and flirted shamelessly in public. "My sweet Steenie," the king nicknamed his new favorite, because of his resemblance to the angelic beauty of St. Stephen. Steenie was his "only sweet child," his "sweet child and wife," and James was "his sweet boy's dear dad."[13] In return, Steenie played up to the older man with a mixture of cheeky presumption and groveling self-abasement. He was, he repeatedly assured the king, "Your Majesty's most humble slave and dog." But the dog was rapidly becoming the master. Spoiled by the king like a favorite son, Steenie was showered with money, lands, and honors: "Never any man in any age, . . . rose in so short a time to so much greatness of honor, fame, and fortune, upon no other advantage . . . than . . . the beauty and gracefulness and becomingness of his person."[14] He advanced to the best positions at court: Master of the King's Horse, then Master of the Wardrobe, Lord Warden of the Cinque Ports, and Lord Admiral of England. From gentleman to knight, baron, viscount, and then Earl and Marquess of Buckingham: he had soon outstripped most of the ancient English nobility in riches and titles. By 1616, he owned estates that gave him an income of £80,000 per year—roughly £2,000,000 in modern money. Lord Buckingham was "without a rival," and he used his power to advance his impoverished relatives to wealth and influence, much to the other courtiers' annoyance.[15]

At first Charles resented the new favorite, and there were some bitter quarrels—over a jewel of Buckingham's that disappeared, and over a tennis match, when Buckingham told the prince to "kiss his arse" and threatened "to strike him."[16] Charles could never win these battles, for James always took his favorite's side—scolding his teenage son to the point of tears on one occasion, boxing his ears on another. Soon the prince learned to play second fiddle. He cultivated insignificance, moving around the court "like a planet in its sphere, so naturally and quietly that one does not remark it." He was reserved, even sullen, keeping his opinions to himself and rushing to agree with whatever his father or Buckingham said. Indeed, he behaved more "as if the favorite were prince and himself less than a favorite." Observers were shocked. Charles was either very cowardly or very clever so to flatter a man he must actually hate, they thought.[17]

But Charles grew to like his father's favorite. Realizing that the king could not live forever, Buckingham began to cast his charm over "Baby Charles," as both he and James called the heir to the throne.[18] Ever adaptable, Steenie treated the serious, shy young prince with none of the mingled insolence and sycophancy that so delighted James. There was respect and affection in his tone—"my dear young master," he called him. And Charles, lonely and insecure, eagerly accepted the proffered intimacy. "Steenie, there is none that knows me so well as yourself," he told his new companion.[19]

To Charles, Buckingham became "like a brother"—a leader, role model, and much-needed friend. He provided a buffer in the difficult relationship between father and son, pacifying the king when Charles angered him, flattering and cajoling James into doing what his "baby" asked. By 1621, an intense relationship had grown up. Charles was "yours more than can be expressed," he assured Buckingham.[20] The two were together all the time. Discarding the constraints of royal ceremony, Buckingham provided an easy camaraderie that Charles never otherwise experienced. Steenie came and went freely when others were denied access. He wore his hat in the prince's presence, he sat with his feet up, he appeared only half dressed. In his role of older brother, he drew Charles out into public life. Together the two young men gadded about town, often making a foursome with Buckingham's wife and the Duchess of Lennox and Richmond, a young widow "much courted and respected by the prince."[21] And together, in James's increasing periods of illness, the pair worked to put royal policy through Parliament. Encouraged by Buckingham, Charles threw himself into this new business with energy and enthusiasm. He regularly attended the House of Lords, where he spoke confidently, despite his stammer, and for the first time he began to gain public popularity.

With Buckingham, Charles also discussed the vexing question of his marriage plans. James had long been locked in inconclusive negotiations with Spain, but now there was a new urgency. On the Continent, the religious conflict that would be known as the Thirty Years' War had begun. In November 1619, Charles's sister, Elizabeth, and her husband, Frederick, had been crowned King and Queen of Bohemia, but within a year they had lost everything. Their home territory of the Palatinate was invaded by the Spanish, and they were forced to flee to Protestant Holland. James and Charles both vowed to help, but the royal government had no army or money for action.

So Charles and Buckingham abandoned their original plans for a European land war and began, like James, to hope that the prince's marriage could secure foreign aid for Elizabeth. Charles hated the never-ending stalemate of the Spanish marriage talks, so he and Buckingham hatched a plan. "How gallant and how brave a thing it would be," they thought, for the prince to travel secretly with Buckingham to Spain and court the Infanta in person. By their presence, the pair would speed up the marriage negotiations and persuade the Spanish to restore the Palatinate to Charles's sister and brother-in-law. Then Charles, like his grandfather and father, would triumphantly bear his bride home with him.[22]

When Charles, on his knees, told James their plan, he hated the idea. Their absence "would break his heart," James said. Charles risked becoming a hostage, forced to accept whatever terms the Spanish dictated before he could return home. "I am undone! I shall lose Baby Charles," James cried. But the king was no match for the combined forces of his son and his favorite. If he could not go to Spain, Charles said, he would never marry at all. If James denied this small request, Buckingham threatened, he could lose his son's love.[23]

And so, in February 1623, Charles dashed off on his great romantic adventure, riding incognito across Europe to save his sister and to woo the teenage princess with whom he soon pronounced himself "deeply in love." In Madrid he watched the Infanta "as a cat does a mouse."[24] He repeatedly threw himself in her path. He jumped a high orchard wall to talk to her when she was out gathering flowers. "No one loved a lady more ardently than he did the Infanta," Charles professed; "distance and other obstacles would never lessen it."[25] But the Infanta said she would rather enter a nunnery than marry a Protestant infidel. In the six months Charles spent in Spain, he was never allowed time with her alone. And far from the Spanish yielding to his charms, Charles found them insisting on ever more stringent terms in the marriage negotiations.

Most problematic were Spain's demands for toleration of Britain's Roman Catholics. Since the reign of Queen Elizabeth I, this hated and feared religious minority had suffered severe persecution. Catholics were barred from public office; they could not inherit or purchase property; their children could be taken away for Protestant upbringing; their church ceremonies were illegal, and they were fined for every Sunday that they did not attend an Anglican service; their priests were liable to the death penalty.[26] Though harsh, these laws were only intermittently enforced, but now Spain required that they never be imposed again, and that James and Charles must swear to allow Catholics public freedom of worship in perpetuity.

Charles was staggered. Such a treaty would be hugely unpopular in England: Parliament would never agree to repeal the anti-Catholic penal laws. But the Spanish refused to compromise, and Charles was eager to marry. That summer, he and James signed the

treaty, which promised the prince's marriage to the Infanta and toleration for British Catholics but contained no word of Spain aiding
the Elector Palatine, or the Infanta's large dowry—without which,
James said, "both my baby and I are bankrupts for ever."[27] Far from
improving matters, Charles's journey to Spain had resulted in total
British capitulation.

Yet still Spain delayed, demanding next that Catholic toleration
had to be put into effect in Britain before the wedding could take
place—which would delay the marriage by at least a year. Charles
and Buckingham lost all patience. The Spanish had "negotiated
with cunning and fraud, and their object was the acquisition of the
Palatinate," they now believed. They even intended to trap Charles
in an unconsummated marriage and deprive Britain of royal heirs.[28]
Though Charles "dissimulated to a great extent and said nothing"
to his hosts, both he and Buckingham were thoroughly "offended
and disgusted . . . with Spanish perfidy and deceit." In October they
returned to England, determined to arrange a French marriage for
the prince instead.[29]

By February 1624, the prince and the duke—as Buckingham had
now become by James's favor—were once again determined on a
British military campaign on the Continent, to defeat the Spanish
and recover the Palatinate. But first they needed to secure parliamentary funding. Sidestepping the king's opposition, they presented
their case directly to Parliament. Attending every day, Charles spoke
"so bravely and judiciously" and "with such prudence" that he gained
"universal applause." Expressing their disgust with the Spanish, he
and Buckingham delighted the anti-Catholic, anti-Spanish MPs,
who rushed to do what was asked of them.[30] Within weeks, Parliament demanded that the king "must abandon all dealings with Spain
both upon the marriage and the Palatinate": only then would they
grant any financial subsidies. James was furious and left London for
the country, "cursing and swearing."[31] But finally, in desperate need
of parliamentary money himself, he had to comply. In April he told
the Spanish he had to abandon the marriage plans, and that same
month Parliament voted to pay the largest subsidy ever for military
preparations. But with the vote came a new demand: James and

Charles must swear that, in the French marriage now being planned, there would be no toleration of English Roman Catholics, such as the Spanish had required. Readily the king and the prince gave their word. Charles in particular, still bitter at the Catholic duplicity he had encountered in Spain, spoke to Parliament "very strongly on the subject," promising to "abandon all thought of a marriage with France if they claimed what was granted to the Spaniards."[32]

An English ambassador had already arrived in Paris to sound out the French court. Henry Rich, Lord Kensington, was ideally qualified for the job: handsome, winning, witty, a fluent French speaker, every inch the courtier. He went everywhere, saw everyone, and was soon sending enthusiastic reports back to England. The French were eager for a military alliance with Britain, he said, for they feared "the power and usurpation of the Spaniards," who now encircled their borders from the Netherlands down through Germany to northern Italy and Spain itself.[33] Soon Lord Kensington was joined by a more senior diplomat, James Hay, Earl of Carlisle—another "very fine gentleman and a most accomplished courtier"—empowered to discuss detailed terms with the French.[34]

All that summer and on through the autumn, intense negotiations continued across Europe. In Paris, Carlisle and Kensington met "day and night" with the French king's ministers, thrashing out what the treaty would do for British Catholics and "for the restoring of the Palatinate." Meanwhile in Rome, a French envoy pressed the pope to grant the dispensation needed for Henrietta Maria to marry a Protestant. In England, the French ambassador was "in perpetual movement and . . . agitation," meeting regularly with the Duke of Buckingham and, when he could, the king.[35] But James, still privately hoping for a Spanish match, now "detested business . . . more than ever." During the summer, he was away in the country, where he spent "all his days hunting except Sundays." When the French ambassador finally caught up with him, he found the king only "dealt seriously with him about hunting and such trifles, but trifled with him about the main business."[36]

Throughout England, the marriage was "opposed by infinite passions." People feared Catholic oppression in general and the French in particular. It was expected that, once Parliament met again, it would "break this match even more than the Spanish one." Yet, driven on by Charles and Buckingham, the talks continued in the greatest secrecy. Always the question of religion was the "old stumbling block."[37] In July, the French offered to accept a mere private letter from James promising toleration of Catholics, but in August a crisis arose when Louis's new chief minister, Cardinal Richelieu, demanded that toleration be put into the treaty. Charles raged at "so scurvy a trick." If it were not for his respect for Henrietta Maria, he "would not care a fart" for the French, he ranted. "If they insist upon these new grounds, let them go hang themselves, rather than treat with them any more."[38]

All involved expected the match would be broken off, but Richelieu needed the British alliance, so he offered concessions. James and Charles could promise toleration of Catholics in an *Escrit secret*, separate from the treaty itself. By means of this "Secret Writing," the toleration might be hidden from British Protestants, who need never know how the king and the prince had violated their anti-Catholic promises to Parliament that spring. Yet the French still flatly refused to sign any military alliance to aid the Palatinate. Their king would simply give his word, they offered. Indignant, James refused to allow the marriage on such terms, but when he suggested reopening talks with the Spanish, Charles stood his ground. He "would never match with Spain," he said.[39] Bullied by his son and defied by the French, James finally backed down. Angrily, he ordered his ambassadors to sign whatever the French demanded and "terminate the matter in any event." Then he withdrew from the whole affair, refusing to see anyone "on the pretext of suffering from the gout."[40]

Hurriedly, Louis and his ministers signed the treaty before James could change his mind, and Paris erupted with "every sign of joy"— "bonfires, illuminations, fireworks," a cannonade at the Arsenal, and a grand ball in the Louvre. London, too, was ablaze with light, glowing "in every part" with the bonfires ordered by the government. At the Tower of London, they fired the guns while organs played in the city's churches and their bells rang out.[41] Charles was elated. Although the treaty contained no mention of the Palatinate, the

French were effusive in their verbal promises, swearing they would do "ten times more than we expect . . . and they will never abandon us in that action." Soon, he hoped, there might be a pan-European alliance against Spain, with the Italians and Germans also joining "to overthrow that colossus."[42]

At the end of November, Charles sat down to write his first letter to the fifteen-year-old girl he was engaged to marry. He had never met Henrietta Maria, but he had seen her once—fleetingly, from "afar off, and in a dark room"—when he and Buckingham had stopped in Paris on their way to Spain in 1623.[43] Disguised in wigs, the pair had visited the French court, where, Charles reported to his father, they saw "nineteen fair dancing ladies" rehearsing for a masque. Among them was Henrietta, playing the part of Iris, handmaiden to Juno, queen of the gods. But the tiny princess, just into her teens and small for her age, had made no impression on Charles. It was Juno herself—the plump blonde queen, Anne of Austria, wife of Louis XIII and sister to the Spanish Infanta—who had struck Charles as the most beautiful woman present, inspiring him with a still greater desire to reach Spain and court her sister.[44]

But now all that had changed. Since February, Charles had been swamped with praises for Henrietta Maria, sent back by Lord Kensington. As "wooing ambassador,"[45] Kensington had the task of stirring the royal pair into love, and he had performed this romantic role with enthusiasm. Henrietta was "the most admirable sweet creature in this world," he enthused to Charles. "Both my eyes and judgment never considered a person of that wonderful loveliness." "More wit, good nature, honor, and discretion were never seen."[46] Henrietta danced "as well as ever I saw any creature," he raved. No "man or woman in France or in the world sings so admirably as she. Sir, it is beyond imagination; that is all that I can say of it."[47]

Hardly surprising, then, that Charles was now "passionately in love."[48] Yet, bound by the rules of etiquette, Charles had not dared to write to Henrietta until the treaty was concluded. Only now, he told her, could he finally express "the impatience with which my soul has been tormented during my long wait for the happy accord of this treaty." Wound up to fever pitch by the overblown accounts from his ambassador, Charles was building romantic castles in the air. The fame of Henrietta's virtues "blazed out everywhere," he assured her. Even his own memories of watching the dance rehearsals in Paris had swelled, until now he thought it his "crowning happiness" to have seen her great beauty then. Charles's letter has a tortured quality, a sense of repressed emotions that escape awkwardly onto the page. So far he had managed just a single, long, complicated sentence. Then he despaired, signing off with: "I cannot express in writing the passion of my soul."[49]

A week later, Thomas Carey, Charles's most trusted gentleman of the bedchamber, entered the great gateway of the Louvre Palace in Paris, accompanied by the two English ambassadors. Across the courtyard, lighted by torches through the dark winter evening, they entered the apartments of Henrietta's mother, Marie de' Medici. Three paces in front of her, the Englishmen stopped and bowed deeply. Approaching closer, they went down on one knee and carried the hem of her dress to their lips. Then Marie, giving each one her hand to kiss, raised them up. The ambassadors then introduced Carey, who formally begged permission to take Charles's love letter to her daughter.

As *Madame de France*, the senior remaining royal daughter, Henrietta had her own grand suite of rooms in the palace. Seated on a throne in her grand salon, Henrietta received Carey and the ambassadors. She was still small for her age—a slender brunette whose pale oval face was squarely framed by tiny tight curls that took hours to prepare. With a careful curtsy, she accepted Carey's two letters—one from James and the love letter from Charles—saying that she "thanked the King of Great Britain for the honor of his notice, and Monsieur the Prince of Wales for the testimony he gave her of his affection." Then she hurried through the palace, carrying the unopened letters to her mother's apartments.[50]

Marie de' Medici had always been a strict authority figure in Henrietta's life. Proud, majestic, addicted to the grandeur and trappings of monarchy, Marie was a woman of "a commanding and high spirit," well able to "cause herself to be obeyed."[51] Even her closest associates acknowledged her coldness and lack of feeling, which extended to her own children. It was their father who was the affectionate parent, playing with the princes and princesses, kissing them, teasing them, perching them on his knee at meals. By his orders, the royal children were brought up at the country chateau of Saint-Germain-en-Laye with their half-brothers and half-sisters, the king's children by his mistresses. Five legitimate and five illegitimate children made up what was fondly called the *troupeau*, the little flock of Saint-Germain. They ate together, studied together, played together indoors and out. They particularly loved to stage little entertainments for their parents and the courtiers: ballets or comedies with elaborate costumes and sets. As a toddler, Henrietta was already joining in with a will—dressing up, singing, dancing, and running about with the others. Her years in the *troupeau* had a defining effect on her character, and she grew up highly sociable, lively, witty, loving informal companionship and a country life of retirement, but also every inch the princess, well schooled in all the ceremony of seventeenth-century royalty.[52]

When Henrietta Maria was only six months old, her father, King Henri IV, was assassinated by a Catholic fanatic. To his youngest daughter he became a heroic figure, "Henri le Grand"—King Henry the Great—as the French were already calling the man who had ended thirty years of religious civil wars and given France unity, religious toleration, and prosperity. In later life, Henrietta would be proud of such a father, collecting his wise sayings and proposing his statecraft for her husband to imitate.[53] But now it was her mother who ruled France as queen regent, with absolute political power during Louis XIII's minority. Busy with state affairs, she was a distant figure in her children's lives, visiting Saint-Germain only rarely. Her main role was to lay down rules for their household and be the ultimate disciplinary figure, ordering beatings for misbehaving boys and sending little notes and presents to children who were good. It was Madame de Montglat, the governess in charge of the whole *troupeau*, who provided the day-to-day maternal presence in the children's lives. "Mamangat," they called her affectionately—Mother Montglat—and even in adulthood they continued to write her letters under this affectionate nickname. Mamangat's daughter,

Jeanne, became a close friend and was nicknamed "Mamie" by the royal children—short for *Mon amie*.

As the years passed, the flock at Saint-Germain diminished. In 1610, the eight-year-old king, Louis XIII, departed for the Louvre, where he joined his mother in state functions but was still regularly beaten for disobedience. Five years later, Henrietta's eldest sister, Elizabeth, age thirteen, parted from her family in tears, leaving France forever to marry the future King Philip IV of Spain. In return, the fourteen-year-old Spanish Infanta, Anne of Austria, married Henrietta's brother Louis. In 1619, twelve-year-old Christine left too, to marry the future ruler of the Duchy of Savoy.

By now, Louis XIII was king in reality as well as name, having seized power from his mother in a bloody palace coup. While the young king watched from a window, his royal guards murdered Marie's favorite adviser, Concino Concini, who had accompanied her from Florence at the time of her marriage. Concini's wife, Marie's companion from childhood, was arrested and later burned as a witch. Marie herself was arrested and sent to the castle of Blois, a hundred miles south of Paris.

For three years, Marie de' Medici remained in the political wilderness, but there was a public reconciliation between mother and son in 1620, and she returned to Paris, where she lived magnificently once again. Over the following years, the young Henrietta Maria was often in Paris, and from her mother in particular she acquired all the cultivated and expensive tastes of continental monarchy: for music and the theater, architecture, garden design, paintings, *objets d'art*, and precious stones, a particular love of Marie's. By 1624, driven on by her "passion . . . to make her daughter a queen," Marie had become the principal force behind plans for Henrietta's British marriage.[54]

Henrietta had always known she would have an arranged marriage, chosen by her relatives "for her honor and advancement, and likewise for the advantage of . . . [the French] crown and kingdom." Now, under orders from Marie, her courtiers eagerly pointed out the advantages of marrying the British prince. She would be a great queen one day, no mere duchess like her sister Christine, and she would rule over three kingdoms: England, Scotland, and Ireland. In the meantime, she would have the grandest household any Princess of Wales had ever had, as the French were carefully ensuring in their negotiations. Life in England would be full of delights. As a keen horsewoman, Henrietta would find real companionship there, for the English ladies loved riding far more than the French did.[55] And Charles was "the most complete young prince and person in the world"—"a wonder," a man of "infinite merit."[56] All the court ladies had seen his handsome portrait, which Lord Kensington wore around his neck, and their admiring comments soon stirred Henrietta's "passionate desiring" to see the portrait herself. But it was not yet proper for the princess to show an interest in her suitor. So while the other ladies tantalized her, repeatedly opening the portrait's case and examining it closely, Henrietta remained apart, daring only to cast glances from "afar off." Unable to bear the suspense, she sent a secret message to Kensington, asking to borrow the portrait. Retiring into the private cabinet beyond her bedchamber, "blushing in the instant at her own guiltiness," she kept the picture in her hands for a whole hour before returning it, with "many praises of your person," the ambassador reported to Charles.[57]

By now Henrietta was thoroughly sold on the marriage. Good news of the negotiations brought "blushing, modest sweet joy" to her looks. But more often, as the talks seemed to founder, she suffered from melancholy and sleepless nights. "My God, why is there no news from England?" she demanded.[58] In May, with Charles's Spanish match officially broken off, she was acknowledged publicly as the British prince's "mistress"—"a title she is not a little proud of." At last she could openly send a message to Lord Kensington, saying she "desired infinitely" to borrow Charles's portrait.[59]

All through the summer, Kensington spent hours at a time with Henrietta at the Louvre, enthusing about her future life in England. With Marie de' Medici's permission, he relayed formal little lovers' speeches from Charles, professing the prince's "passionate service" and his admiration for "as well the beauties of her mind as her person," which Henrietta "received with all the joy that can be both by countenance and language expressed." Curtsying low, she replied, trembling, "that she was extremely obliged to his Highness" and looked forward to "meriting the place she had in his good graces."[60] By the autumn, Henrietta was proudly calling herself "bride of the Prince of England." "Impatient of all delay," she pestered her mother and brother to complete the treaty. The day she heard that it was finally settled was "the happiest day that ever she had," she told her brother Gaston, Duc d'Orléans.[61]

Yet Henrietta had been long schooled in hiding her feelings in public, and none of this passion showed in December, when she arrived in Marie de' Medici's apartments and surrendered the two unopened letters from England to her mother. Marie broke the seals and read the letters, professing herself delighted that they were "filled with so many courtesies that nothing could be added."[62] Only then was Henrietta allowed to read the letters. The one from Charles was the first love letter she had ever received; after reading it, she carefully tucked it away inside the bodice of her dress, against her heart—a sure sign of her love. As 1624 drew to an end, Henrietta composed a short reply to Charles, in courtesies that soon became as convoluted as the prince's own. Even if she was not truly worthy of all "these testimonies of your affection," she promised, still she would try to prove that she was not ungrateful: "I am and will always be, monsieur, your very humble and very affectionate servant."[63]

The British court was impatient for Henrietta's arrival, not daring to reconvene Parliament before the marriage was performed. Once she arrived, James and Buckingham were sure, Henrietta would charm everyone with her "graces and virtues," preventing "the exorbitant . . . motions that might otherwise be made in the House of Parliament." But January passed and still Henrietta remained in Paris, while the French and British squabbled over toleration of Catholics—James agreeing only to sign promises of "favor" to his Catholic subjects, while the French demanded "liberty."[64] The pope's dispensation for the marriage had already arrived in Paris, but it was being held by the papal nuncio until the treaty had been changed to include new demands from His Holiness. When the French reopened negotiations, the English were outraged at "the infidelity of these base perfidious monsieurs." As people began to talk of the marriage being broken off, Marie de' Medici was in a state of "distraction and passion," weeping whenever her daughter was mentioned.[65] Everyone assured Henrietta there was no danger to "the main business," "yet she fears all is not right, though she knows not what is amiss," reported Lord Kensington. Her ladies "never saw so great a perplexity as they find to be in her."[66]

Henrietta's only consolation lay in Charles's "most welcome" little love letters, which flowed across the Channel "to revive and comfort her, in . . . her fears." Charles was "eternally" hers, he promised; he would "be always happy to hazard his life to do you service."[67] There were gifts, too, including a collection of jewels of "very great price and remarkable beauty." "Do me the honor of accepting this little present," Charles implored, "although it be very unworthy of you."[68] Henrietta professed herself overcome, unable to express "how much I cherish the honor of your friendship." Hearing the English court was planning a tournament, she sent the prince her colors to wear "in the noise and breach of lances"—leaving James and Charles "infinitely satisfied . . . with Madame's kind reception of the present, and the demonstrations of her affection upon that occasion."[69]

But still James angrily refused to renegotiate the treaty "in the smallest degree." At last, in March, King Louis XIII saved the match by decreeing that if the pope did not issue the dispensation within thirty days, the wedding would go ahead without it. Charles was delighted. "At this time I think of nothing else but of hastening by all means the day on which I shall have the honor of kissing your hands," he assured Henrietta.[70] But in fact other matters were already preoccupying him. King James was ill with a recurring fever. After eleven sharp attacks—the last of them "very serious and accompanied by fainting"—the king was growing weak, his mind wrapped up in "a whirl of a thousand fears." On Sunday March 27, 1625, having confessed "the errors of his life" and forgiven "all men that offended him," he died of "a violent dysentery . . . the very bed exuding the excrement."[71]

That same day, Charles was proclaimed "King of Great Britain, France, and Ireland, [and] Defender of the Faith."[72] Some people noticed disturbing omens—thunder boomed "presently upon the proclamation, and 'twas a cold season"—but it was a time of hope for most. Charles was "the new sun," whose "wise government" would take the country into a popular war against Spain, and mourning for the old king was "swallowed up in joy of so hopeful a successor."[73] Charles spent his first week as king grieving privately in his bedchamber. Only then did he make his first public appearance, attending a sermon in the royal chapel at Whitehall, dressed in a black cloak that reached to his ankles. His subjects approved of Charles's seriousness. In his father's louche court, with its drunkenness and sexual impropriety, Charles had been a misfit—"sober, grave, sweet . . . without any evil inclinations." Now he promised his subjects "constancy in religion, sincerity in action and that he will not have recourse to subterfuges in his dealings."[74] At once he began to reform the royal household, aiming to remove not only the debauchery he abhorred but also the casual etiquette of his father's court. A king should "be approached with respect and reverence," he believed; there had to be "state and order in his court."[75] The new style suited Charles's reserved character, but in years to come it would often make him seem arrogant, high-handed, and supercilious, out of touch with the ordinary world around him.

Determined to be an "active, resolute" king, Charles spent April energetically involved in the war preparations he and Buckingham had long desired. He issued orders to hasten on the "great fleet . . . of above one hundred sail of ships." Sailors were press-ganged by royal proclamation and Charles went with Buckingham, Lord High Admiral of England, to inspect the forty ships already lying in the Thames.[76] With Parliament still delayed until Henrietta's arrival in England, there could be no proper funding for war, but Charles had high ambitions—to be "the arbiter of the Christian world"—and he would not be held back. On the strength of a loan from the City of London, he ordered vast new expenditures—on extra provisions and armaments and on new copper sheathing for the ships' hulls.[77]

In France, the pope's dispensation had been delivered, and they were preparing for the wedding. Henrietta visited a fashionable spa resort "to take the waters and medicines to recruit herself"; back in Paris, tailors, dressmakers, embroiderers, and jewelers were hard at work.[78] Outside the west door of the Cathedral of Notre Dame, a specially erected wedding stage was hung with tapestries, while a huge gold awning provided protection from the sun. At its center, the dais where Henrietta would be married was covered with purple velvet embroidered with gold fleurs-de-lys. A huge wooden walkway was built to carry the royal party from their dressing rooms in the archbishop's palace, and this too was adorned with yards and yards of the same purple-and-gold material.

Henrietta spent the day before the wedding in religious retreat with the Carmelite nuns at the Convent of the Incarnation, just outside Paris's city walls. She had often gone there during her childhood, sharing the nuns' austere life on the orders of her mother, who had founded the convent in 1604 with the help of her religious mentor, Father Pierre de Bérulle. Henrietta had come to love the place and formed a close bond with the prioress, Mother Madeleine, who served as her spiritual guide. Now, in Mother Madeleine's company, she prepared for the coming change in her life.

On Sunday, May 1, it rained all morning as the wedding guests arrived in reverse social order—the least important first, to suffer the longest wait. At 11 a.m., Henrietta entered the archbishop's palace to dress for the ceremony. Six hours later, the rest of the court arrived from the Louvre, and King Louis ordered the wedding procession to set out. First along the velvet-hung walkway marched a hundred royal guardsmen, flags flying and drums beating, followed by the trumpets, drums, and oboes of the king's music, all playing loudly. Then came the gentlemen of the French court—chevaliers, seigneurs, marshals, counts, and dukes, "their clothes strewn with diamonds, and wearing robes of inestimable value."[79] Next were the two English ambassadors and then the Duc de Chevreuse. A prominent French courtier and Charles's "nearest kinsman" in France, Chevreuse was to be Charles's proxy in the marriage—to "act the part of the bridegroom up to the point of getting into the bed," as the Venetian ambassador put it. He was dressed in black velvet, with a scarf "that dazzled all beholders, being literally covered with diamond roses."[80] Behind followed Henrietta Maria. Her gold crown was covered in huge diamonds, topped by a pear-shaped pearl "of inestimable price." Her velvet train was so long and so heavily embroidered with gold that it required two princesses and a countess to carry it, assisted by a page who walked beneath the train, supporting it on his head and arms. Leading Henrietta on either side were her two brothers: King Louis XIII in a velvet suit so smothered in gold embroidery that the cloth could not be seen at all, while Gaston, Duc d'Orléans was permitted nothing more than silk embroidery. Then came Marie de' Medici, wearing black as she had done ever since her husband's death, and then the French queen, Anne of Austria, and all the ladies of the court.

Outside the cathedral, Louis and Gaston delivered their sister into the hands of the Duc de Chevreuse. Standing side by side, he and Henrietta made their marriage vows. With the sign of the cross, Cardinal de La Rochefoucauld pronounced them man and wife, according to the Catholic rite. Immediately the two English ambassadors approached to offer their congratulations. To the French king they bowed deeply as usual. But when they turned to Louis's fifteen-year-old sister, they knelt down on the ground, with all the respect that English etiquette required. Henrietta was now queen of a country she had never seen, whose language she did not speak. She was also married to a man she had never met.

2

FIRST IMPRESSIONS

In Paris, the celebrations continued for days, with "infinite acclamations" from the people. Every night, fifty cannon were fired
outside the Louvre, and "very beautiful fireworks" were set off
over the River Seine.[1] Meanwhile, in London there was "great ringing
[of bells] and bonfires making." The young king was ecstatic about
"the greatest felicity which could happen to me in the world."[2]

But just as Henrietta was due to leave Paris for London, Louis XIII
fell ill. Henrietta chafed at the delay, telling the English ambassadors
of her "desire to cast herself into your Majesty's arms."[3] Charles also
fretted constantly, but more than husbandly eagerness was involved.
All his political plans—including funding for his long-cherished war
preparations—depended on the meeting of Parliament, which he
was still putting off until Henrietta's arrival. A week after news of
the marriage, finding the delay "too insupportable to bear," he dispatched the Duke of Buckingham to France "to hasten and facilitate
the journey of my dear wife."[4]

Buckingham traveled "in great haste." After just three days he arrived in Paris, to the astonishment of the French, announcing that "the king was dying with impatience and love" for Henrietta, and "he could not live long if he did not see her."[5] But the duke's best efforts produced no results. Louis remained as ill as ever, and no one would leave without him. Instead, Paris turned itself over to pleasure once again. A week passed in a whirl of "feastings and rejoicings," processions and fireworks.[6] Greatest of all was the feast given by Cardinal Richelieu "in honor of Madame's marriage." The whole of Parisian high society gathered at the Palais du Luxembourg for a "magnificent collation of sweetmeats," presided over by the three queens— Marie de' Medici, Anne of Austria, and Henrietta Maria. "All kinds of music" played in the "superbly prepared" rooms, followed by fireworks in the garden—the best and most imaginatively designed that had been seen in Paris for a long time.[7]

Throughout, Buckingham dazzled them all. The French were renowned for their expensive tastes, yet the duke—wearing clothes as "rich as invention can frame, or art fashion"*—managed to outshine "all the bravery that court could dress itself in."[8] With his "noble spirit" and his exquisite dancing performed "to great applause," he captivated the ladies of the French court, filling them "with joy (and something more than joy)." But the men disliked him.[9] Worst of all was Buckingham's dalliance with Anne of Austria, whose beauty Charles himself had admired in Paris two years earlier. Soon everyone was aware of Buckingham's "so dangerous and blameworthy desires," and Louis and Marie de' Medici were infuriated. But even they dared not offend the man known to have "all power over the mind of the [British] king."[10] Far from it: the French royals heaped "honors and civilities" on Buckingham and showered him with expensive gifts. Yet to all his urgings that they enter the alliance against Spain that Charles "so anxiously desired," the French remained politely evasive: his proposals "were very important and required mature consideration." All they would offer was limited

---

* Just one of his suits, smothered in diamonds, was said to be worth "four score thousand pounds."

funding for the little army that the English had sent in December to fight for the Elector Palatine.[11]

On Saturday, May 21, Henrietta spent a last day at the Carmelite Convent of the Incarnation. In the refectory she served the nuns with her own hands, and when it was time for her to leave, she told them how sorry she was that she could not take any of them with her to England and give them a convent there, close to her palace.[12] The next day, "amid shouts of applause and a countless throng of people," she left Paris. With her went the French royal family with their courts, plus the entourages of the three English ambassadors: Carlisle, Kensington, and Buckingham, bound for home. There were also two new French ambassadors—Secretary of State Sieur de la Ville-aux-Clercs and the Duc de Chevreuse—under orders to go to London "to obtain the ratification of the [marriage] treaty . . . and to see that the terms are carried out in every respect."[13]

So vast was the cavalcade that carriages smothered the roads like ants on an anthill, the French news reported.[14] Henrietta was taking an entire French court with her to England—from counts and countesses right down to cooks and chamberwomen. There were cupbearers and carvers to serve at her table, and valets and wardrobe-keepers to look after her clothes and jewels. A bevy of young maids of honor were to wait on the queen through the day, while additional maids waited on the maids of honor. She had her own treasurer and secretary, as well as a physician, a surgeon, and an apothecary. She had a specialist *pâtissier* as well as a baker; a starcher, a laundress, a clockmaker, and a jeweler. A master of horse took charge of her stables, with their esquires, grooms, and coachmen, and she had her own band of French musicians. In charge of them all was the queen's grand chamberlain, Comte Tanneguy Leveneur de Tillières, accompanied by his wife, the Comtesse de Tillières, while the female side of the household was headed by the queen's *dame d'honneur*— Henrietta's childhood friend Mamie, now Madame Saint-Georges. Also going to England were twenty-eight Catholic priests: a bishop, two abbots, chaplains, clerks, and, at the core of the mission, twelve Oratorian priests led by the founder of their order, Father Pierre de Bérulle, who would be Henrietta's confessor.[15]

Zealous, articulate, and enthusiastic, Bérulle and his Oratorians had long been dedicated to rebutting Protestantism and spearheading a Catholic revival in France. At court, Bérulle had grown ever more influential, becoming confessor to Marie de' Medici and winning a great reputation for his saintly life, his theological acumen, and his skills as a statesman. He had also become a strong advocate for Henrietta's marriage: a "holy" affair that would bring "the relief of the poor English Catholics, greatly oppressed for their religion."[16] But Bérulle—and the Catholic Church in general—also hoped for much more: the conversion of Charles himself back to the faith of his ancestors, bringing all Britain with him. Such hopes did not seem unrealistic in the light of recent European history. Since the first zeal of the Reformation, many Protestant states had returned to the old faith. In the 1610s, the Spanish ambassador had thought it would be easy to contrive the same in England: "Everything here depends on the king's will"; James could "introduce the sect of the Turks and Moors if he pleases."[17] This was the Catholic hidden agenda that British Protestants most feared from their king's marriage, and it was with precisely this mission in mind that Bérulle handpicked the Oratorians who accompanied him. Some were learned theologians, prepared to defend Church doctrine against all comers in England. Others were courtiers and men of the world, ready to charm the king and his closest advisers. Two were Scots, knowledgeable about British affairs. All were model churchmen noted for their faith and virtue and fired with the evangelical zeal of their order.[18]

Already the pope had written to Henrietta, urging her to champion the Catholic cause in England. Now was her chance to join the "most holy queens" in history: women such as Esther, wife of Persia's King Xerxes, who had used her husband's love for her to save the Jews from massacre; or her own ancestor, St. Clotilda, the Frankish queen who had converted her husband, Clovis, to Christianity; or Bertha, who married the pagan Ethelbert, King of Kent, and paved the way for the conversion of England. So Henrietta too had to attack her husband's heart "with the sword of salvation and the arts of piety" and become "the rebuilder of religion in those waters where it has suffered a most wretched shipwreck."[19] At the pope's request,

Henrietta had solemnly sworn that she would do "everything that could be useful and advantageous to the Faith, and to the Catholics of the Kingdom of Great Britain."[20] But still he was concerned. As Henrietta's great entourage stopped at Amiens, where Marie de' Medici had fallen ill, a papal legate arrived bearing a letter for the British queen and a most important gift. The Golden Rose was an ornament of the greatest price and most holy significance, blessed each year by the pope himself and then given away, only occasionally, to the greatest and most devout notables of the Church. In his letter, the pope urged Henrietta to become like the rose—"a flower of the root of Jesse among the spines of Hebrew iniquity."[21] Henrietta treated the pope's legate with exceptional marks of respect, going out herself to greet him and conduct him into her presence chamber. When the Duke of Buckingham objected that her behavior was improper for the queen of Great Britain, Henrietta retorted "that it so behooved her to treat the representative of the head of her religion."[22] It was the first quarrel in what would become a very troubled relationship.

Meanwhile, Charles was in agonies of impatience. The Lords and Commons had already gathered, ready for Parliament, but without Buckingham to manage his political business, and without Henrietta to charm the members into accepting the marriage treaty, Charles would not let the session begin. All through May, the king was forced to put off Parliament from week to week.[23] Some MPs—complaining at the expense of this prolonged city living and at the "danger of the plague," which was growing frighteningly, even though summer had not yet begun—had already returned to their homes. Those who remained spoke openly against the marriage and expressed as much distrust of Charles as they had of James the previous year.[24] Rumors circulated that the French were demanding yet more changes in the marriage treaty, and there were wild stories of Henrietta's total subjection to the pope, who, it was said, had imposed "upon her I know not what penitential confession . . . for consenting to marry our king without the pope's dispensation."[25]

For weeks Charles had been in a state of instant readiness to leave London and meet his bride at the coast; finally he could bear the delay no longer. Early on Tuesday, May 31, he descended the Whitehall steps to the river, where he embarked in his royal barge and was rowed swiftly down to Gravesend. Charles's court and luggage had already gone on ahead of him, so he traveled light and fast— the romantic adventurer once again, as he had been on his journey to Spain two years earlier. He reached Canterbury that evening—a journey of fifty-six miles that normally took travelers three days.[26] Here the bulk of his court was assembled, waiting to receive their queen in style, and the king spent two nights with them before driving on to Dover, "accompanied by five or six only of his suite, of the highest rank."[27]

At Dover Castle, expensive building repairs had recently been completed and a suite of nine rooms was lavishly fitted out with Crown furniture for Henrietta's first night in England. Anxiously, Charles inspected it all, making sure it was "answerable to the dignity of the persons whom it must pay tribute of honor to," and giving further "directions of what was fitting for the queen's accommodation."[28] Then, satisfied with his labors, he mooned away an evening on the roof of the castle, looking out over the harbor to the sea beyond, where his bride would soon appear. A group of courtiers found him there at 9 p.m. and then had to stay for "two very cold hours," until the daylight finally faded and the king was ready to come down.[29] The next day, Charles had himself rowed out through the harbor, where his great fleet lay at anchor, "as strong for the number, and as beautiful for the equipage as possibly may be." He ate dinner aboard the flagship, the *Prince Royal*, which would carry Henrietta to England. Then he visited a couple of other ships, inspecting the preparations for her courtiers before he returned to shore.[30] For three more days he remained in Dover, writing yet again to Henrietta, urging her to hurry and "come straight to him." Finally, as his ships set off for France, Charles returned reluctantly to Canterbury: Marie de' Medici had expressed a "passionate desire" that he should not meet Henrietta on her first arrival, in case she was seasick and disappointed his great expectations.[31]

Meanwhile, in Amiens, the physicians had announced that it would take a month for Marie de' Medici to recover. And so, at

Buckingham's insistence, it was agreed that Henrietta would continue her journey without her mother. On Monday, June 6, she and her court rode out of the town, to loud artillery salutes. For the first league, Marie and Anne of Austria accompanied the great procession.[32] Then, at the final moment of parting, Marie gave Henrietta a letter of "last farewell," telling her to keep it always with her, to "speak for me when I can no longer speak to you myself."

Here was advice to guide Henrietta through all the difficulties of her new life. There were sections on the kindness she must show her British subjects, on the orderliness she must maintain in her large royal household, and on the high standards of virtue she must observe in a nation notorious for the liberty it allowed its women. To her husband, the letter said, Henrietta owed a duty of love, respect, humility, and patience. "Do nothing that could displease him even a little," Marie instructed. But the bulk of the letter was devoted to religious instruction, and here the real author was Henrietta's confessor, Father Bérulle, using Marie's maternal authority to prepare Henrietta for the mission the Catholic Church saw as the true purpose of her marriage. Her first duty, before even that owed to her husband, must be to "God and the religion He has established in the world." Each day she must give thanks to God "that He has made you Christian and Catholic"—a faith "that you must maintain much more dearly even than your own life." Again Henrietta was exhorted to "be an Esther" to the English Catholics: "God has sent you into this country for them, for they are His people, and His people who have suffered for so many years!" And it was also God's plan that she labor for Charles's conversion: "This must be your most ardent desire on earth." If Henrietta failed in her duty, Marie warned, she would be cursed by a mother who was "able to hold you for my daughter only so long as you remain the daughter of Jesus Christ and His Church."[33] On her knees, Henrietta asked her mother's farewell blessing, which Marie gave, adding "that if she changed her religion she gave her instead a thousand curses." Both were in tears, expecting never to see each other again.[34]

At Boulogne two days later, Henrietta's spirits revived as she saw the sea for the first time in her life. "Very merry," she rushed down to the shore, approaching the water "so near that it was bold to kiss her feet, so that her Majesty was over shoes." Back in royal grandeur the next day, she gave audience to the six "ladies of rank" dispatched by Charles to greet her, including the Duke of Buckingham's mother, sister, and niece.[35] Careful to please, Henrietta received these important courtiers with "strange courtesy and favor," and they were duly impressed. Their new queen was no mere child, as hostile English rumors had reported, but already on the verge of womanhood. Conversing through the Catholic courtier Sir Toby Matthew, who accompanied the Buckingham ladies as translator, Henrietta showed herself "full of wit," with "a lovely manner in expressing it." Sir Toby enthused:

> Upon my faith, she is a most sweet lovely creature, and hath a countenance which opens a window into her heart, where a man may see all nobleness and goodness; . . . she will be extraordinarily beloved by our nation, and deserve to be so.

If the new queen felt nervous, she concealed it well. Sir Toby noticed just "a little remnant of sadness" in her face, which he ascribed to "the fresh wound" of parting from her mother. Her dress was "very plain," he noted, such simplicity being the height of sophisticated French fashion: Henrietta was all set "to teach our country wit in this kind." Then the Buckingham ladies departed and Henrietta returned to girlish things once more, going "in a poor little boat in the company of her brother," Gaston, Duc d'Orléans, to the horror of the English courtiers. But even as they feared for their queen's safety, they admired her courage in venturing out "for mere pastime."[36]

That same day, Charles's fleet of twenty ships sailed into the harbor, firing off a hundred-gun salute. Three days later, with the sea calm and a fine southerly breeze blowing, Henrietta entered an English longboat and was rowed out to the flagship. Firing their cannon again in salute, the other ships followed her out to sea.[37] It was a magnificent sight—the sails swollen with wind while the ships plowed deeply through the strangely still water, their holds heavily laden with the palace-load of royal gear that Henrietta was taking to England: solid-gold tableware for her dining room; basins and curling irons and a big silver mirror for her dressing room; a crimson velvet bed embroidered with gold and silver and topped with white ostrich feathers, with a suite of bedroom furniture to match, plus tapestries and carpets. There were carriages—some heavily built for country traveling, others swathed in velvet for city use. There were litters for grand state processions, and six extra carriages for Henrietta's courtiers. Then there were mules to carry the litters, horses to draw the carriages, and a further forty riding horses—all with bridles, saddles, decorative coats, and feathers.

Everyone was provided for, with furniture graded according to social status—from a silk-embroidered velvet bedroom suite for Mamie Saint-Georges right down to mere mattresses on the floor for the lowest valets. For the lodgings of Henrietta's Oratorian priests, there were suitably austere provisions—pewter vessels, and a simple serge bed, wooden table, and chair for each of their twelve cells. But for the queen's chapel, where the Oratorians would say Mass, no expense had been spared. The crosses for the altars, the chalices for holy wine, the pyxes and monstrances for consecrated bread—all were of gold or silver. There were chandeliers and religious paintings, and five rich sets of vestments and altar cloths in different colors, plus a library of tomes of Catholic theology, to be used to convert the English heretics. Nothing was forgotten: six shrouds were even packed, for wrapping the bodies of courtiers who might die in England.

More chests were full of Henrietta's clothes: wraps and nightgowns, handkerchiefs, stockings, and linen caps by the dozen. There were perfumed gloves and embroidered shoes. Luxurious dresses and state robes were smothered with gold and silver lace, stitched with pearls or lined with fur, each one worth a fortune. And then there were her jewels: some ropes of hundreds of pearls, but mostly diamonds and more diamonds—in ear pendants and rings, in buttons and crosses and knots, and in chains of up to two hundred stones at a time.[38] The expense was vast. The total value of the trousseau stood at some £30,000—roughly £7,000,000 in modern money—

and Henrietta was bringing twice as much again in solid gold coins as the first installment of her dowry.[39]

Just six hours after leaving Boulogne, the English fleet dropped anchor beneath the white cliffs of Dover after an exceptionally calm crossing—a sign of "how much this marriage is agreeable to God," the French thought. On shore, a deputation of grand courtiers received their queen with "humble respect." Then she entered Dover "in most stately and magnificent manner," winding up through the streets of the town to the castle.[40] Months later, after everything had turned sour, the Comte de Tillières would say that even on that first night the queen had been "badly lodged, even worse equipped, and her train treated with very little magnificence." But at the time, the French were delighted with the fine royal furniture and the "magnificent supper" prepared for the queen: "Nothing was omitted which could mark her status," the ambassadors wrote to Paris that evening.[41]

Meanwhile, news of Henrietta's arrival had reached Charles in Canterbury. Honoring his bride's wishes, the king stayed put for the night. But early next morning, full of "wondrous impatience," he left for Dover "in the most private manner," romantically abandoning all royal ceremony "to see and visit his queen."[42] He arrived in the castle while Henrietta was still at breakfast. Abandoning her food, she rushed downstairs to meet him. It was a moment of real romance. Falling to her knees, the young queen kissed her husband's hand. "Sire," she said, speaking in French, in which Charles was fluent, "I am come to this land for Your Majesty, to be used and commanded by you." But Charles would have none of this submission. At once he lifted her, wrapped her tightly in his arms, and kissed her over and over, "with all the tendernesses which an immaculate and unspotted affection could express."[43] Everyone was moved by the couple's open display of affection, their "pure and unfeigned caressments." This was a true meeting of souls, they said: you could almost see the two young lovers' hearts flying out through "the windows of their eyes" to fix "themselves in each other's bosom."[44]

Briefly, the couple conversed in front of their courtiers. Henrietta begged Charles's pardon for her delayed arrival. Seeing him now, she "was most content," to which Charles replied with "dear expressions of a never changing love."[45] At the same time, the king examined his new wife closely. For months he had been worried by stories of how small she was. Even the Earl of Holland (as Lord Kensington had now become in reward for his success as "wooing ambassador") had had to admit that "her growth is not great yet," though he reassured Charles that "her shape is perfect." Nonetheless, Charles had continued to worry, and he had asked the Duke of Buckingham to obtain an exact measurement of his new wife's height.[46] Now, finally, he could see for himself. Henrietta was indeed rather small—"her head reached just to his shoulder," observers noted, so she must have been about four feet ten inches tall. But this was more than rumor had reported. So was she wearing high heels? Charles peered down at his wife's feet, trying to see past her long skirts, until Henrietta noticed. "Sir," she reassured him, "I stand upon mine own feet; I have no helps by art. Thus high I am, and am neither higher nor lower."[47]

Then the couple retired to spend some time in private. Later, Charles himself recorded the request Henrietta now made to him:

> that she being young and coming to a strange country, both by her years and ignorance of the customs of the place, might commit many errors, therefore that I would not be angry with her for her faults . . . and . . . to use no third person, but to tell her myself when I found she did anything amiss.

It was a formal speech, clearly prepared in advance, but Charles was charmed. Readily he granted his bride's request, asking in return "that she would use me as she had desired me to use her, which she willingly promised me."[48] Henrietta's modesty and eagerness to please were delightful, and she was attractive in appearance, too. "She is nimble and quick," the English noted, "black eyed, brown haired, and, in a word, a brave lady." If she seemed pale—"perhaps a little touched with the green sickness"—there was no need to worry: anemia was common in teenage girls, and contemporary medical practitioners agreed it was easily cured by a husband's attentions.[49]

After an hour together, the couple emerged and Henrietta introduced her French household to Charles one by one, in order of their status. Then the royal pair sat down to dinner, where Charles served his wife with his own hands, carving pheasant and venison. Concerned only to please him, she ate "heartily of both," ignoring her confessor's protests that it was a Catholic fast day and "she should take heed how she gave ill examples or scandal at her first arrival."[50]

Charles and Henrietta had hit it off perfectly, and that afternoon the queen readily agreed to her husband's request that he and some of the Buckingham ladies should travel in her carriage on the way to Canterbury. But members of the French household were furious when they heard there would be no room for Henrietta's *dame d'honneur*, Mamie Saint-Georges. The two ambassadors protested vigorously to Buckingham: it was a gross violation of French etiquette. Mamie's title was one of the best in France—a true ancient, aristocratic dignity, no mere novelty, conferred recently by the king (as all the Buckingham family's titles were). Buckingham retorted that Henrietta herself had given her consent, and it was the custom of England that no lady had any right to travel in the queen's carriage, where places were given only by her command. As the quarrel escalated, a new figure stepped in: the energetic young Bishop of Mende, grand almoner in charge of Henrietta's priests, "a man of ready wit," "highly esteemed" by Louis XIII, and a nephew of Cardinal Richelieu.[51] Eager to advance Richelieu's policy of alliance with England, he would repeatedly pour oil on the troubled waters of Anglo-French relations. Now he advised the French ambassadors to show moderation and at last they had to agree, seeing that they could not alter matters, "whatever remonstrance we made."[52]

So disgraceful was the arrangement in French eyes—so gross the violation of their native customs, so disgraceful the contempt for all their arguments—that when the Comte de Tillières and the ambassador Sieur de la Ville-aux-Clercs later wrote their memoirs, neither would admit what had actually happened. La Ville-aux-Clercs reported with self-satisfaction that his own firmness against Buckingham had won Madame Saint-Georges a place in the queen's carriage, while the Comte de Tillières embroidered the story much further. According to him, this was not a dispute between Bucking-ham and the French household at all, but rather a violent quarrel between Charles and Henrietta themselves. In his version, Henri-etta, not Mamie Saint-Georges, protested vainly against the king's command, desperate to have her friend with her in the coach but unable to obtain her wish, "whatever supplications she could make." Charles finally backed down and allowed Mamie into the car-riage only on the "solicitations of the French ambassadors," "which annoyed the queen extremely." In fact, "she evinced a little too lively a resentment of it, in my opinion," Tillières added with pompous self-righteousness.[53]

Tillières's story of this episode and his portrait of Henrietta as a willful, tantrum-prone teenager, lacking even the self-confidence to ride in a coach with her new husband and some English ladies whom she had mostly already met and charmed in Boulogne, has been reproduced by historians ever since. Yet both Tillières's and La Ville-aux-Clercs's stories are disproved by the French ambassadors' letters written at the time, which survive in manuscript transcripts in the British Library. In these, Chevreuse and La Ville-aux-Clercs excused their failure to enforce French etiquette and have Mamie Saint-Georges ride in Henrietta's coach, explaining that it had all been agreed between Henrietta and Charles before they knew any-thing of it. Their letters portray a bride at one with her husband: "She had no will but his," and was perfectly happy to neglect her own followers to please him.[54] To English eyes, it was so trifling a matter that none of the contemporary newsletters mention it. But this was not trivial for the courtiers, whose status rested on the privi-leges to which they were entitled. The French would neither forget nor forgive the insult.

As the royal carriages drove out of Dover, "a gallant volley of shot" came from the castle and from the fleet below; it was so loud that even the echo from the surrounding hills could be heard across the Channel in Calais. All along their route, the roads were "strewed with green rushes, roses, and the choicest flowers that could be gotten, and the trees loaded with people of all sorts, who with shouts and acclamations gave them a continual welcome." Village church bells rang and the gentry and militia of Kent turned out "to attend and receive the queen . . . in such solemn manner and equipage as beseemed . . . the quality of her person."[55]

Five miles outside Canterbury, on the open hilltop of Barham Down, the procession was met by Charles's courtiers—dazzling in their finery "like so many constellations."[56] Anxious to behave correctly, Henrietta had asked the English ambassadors in France about the correct etiquette for this occasion. As Charles presented all the lords and ladies in order of their rank, she performed her role perfectly. Each grand lady, "from a fitting distance," made three low curtsies and then approached and kissed her hand. Then the queen returned their kisses "with such good grace that she won the esteem and goodwill of everyone." "She hath eyes that sparkle like stars," the English enthused; her face was "a mirror of perfection."[57]

At last the ceremonies were over. Even the lesser court ladies, the wives of knights and gentlemen, had been presented—curtsying to the queen from a distance without any kisses—and Charles and Henrietta remounted into her carriage and drove on to Canterbury.[58] At a grand nobleman's house just outside the city walls, "magnificent preparations" had been made for their wedding night. In the medieval hall, the king and queen sat down to a state banquet in view of all. Again Charles offended Henrietta's courtiers— this time by arranging that he and the queen should be "waited on by the king's attendants only, to the disgust of the French."[59] Then Henrietta retired to her bedchamber, accompanied by the Duchesse de Chevreuse, who helped her into her nightgown and put her to bed. A little later, Charles joined his bride. Unwilling to endure the bawdy high jinks commonly practiced on newlyweds, the king bolted the doors of the room, allowing in just two of his gentlemen to undress him. Then he locked them out as well, and Charles and Henrietta were left alone.[60]

Next morning, they stayed late in bed. Charles, normally a rigorously early riser, did not emerge until 7 a.m., when his courtiers found him uncharacteristically lighthearted, joking about how he had cheated them of their amusements the night before. All that day he continued "very jocund." Meanwhile, the ladies of Henrietta's court, having made the necessary inspections and inquiries, sent letters off to Paris, informing the queen mother "that the marriage of their British Majesties had been consummated to their common satisfaction." All that day, the honeymooning couple and their courts remained in Canterbury, which "seemed for that little time a very Eden or Paradise, where nothing was wanting that might serve joy or delight."[61] Next morning, with her great cavalcade, Henrietta set off for London and married life.

3

QUARRELING

On June 16, 1625, the royal couple entered London in triumph, rowing upriver in their grand state barge, attended by thousands of boats bearing "an infinite number of lords, ladies, and other people." Along their route, two hundred warships, "decorated and beflagged," fired off their guns: a deafening thunder "of fifteen hundred great shot," which continued for "twelve or fifteen miles together, and the nearer the king and queen came to London, the greater and greater still the volley increased." Charles was elated: observers thought they had "never beheld the king to look so merrily," and talk of Henrietta's beauty and good nature passed round the watching crowd. As the barge approached the City itself just before 5 p.m., the Tower of London fired off all its guns: "Nothing could be heard for the terror of the noise." Proudly, Charles brought his wife out onto the deck so that "she might see the people and the city," but at once it began to rain—a heavy downpour that forced the couple back inside. Still, eager to be seen by the crowd, they had the barge's large windows opened and stood together just inside one of them, braving the violent weather in their matching green suits, a picture of mingled majesty and love.

While the great flotilla swept beneath the medieval arches of London Bridge and on past the City, the torrent of rain continued, but no one's enthusiasm was dampened. Bells rang out from the churches, and crowds in "infinite numbers" cheered and cheered from streets and wharves, gardens and house windows, and from boats moored along the banks of the Thames. Under the weight of a hundred eager spectators, one ship capsized and sank: it was one of the marriage's miracles that everyone aboard survived. And still the royal couple sailed on, past St. Paul's Cathedral and then the Strand, where the noblemen's houses stretched down in formal gardens to the river's northern bank. At the long pier that was Whitehall's Privy Stairs, the barge put in amid more "acclamations of joy," and Henrietta Maria saw her new home for the first time.[1]

It must have been a disappointment. Rambling roofs and chimneys, and blank walls irregularly scattered with small square windows, made Whitehall seem more "an assemblage of several houses, badly built, at different times and for different purposes," than a royal palace, noted another seventeenth-century European royal arriving there.[2] Yet this straggling Tudor tangle of some fourteen hundred interconnected chambers was the principal seat of Britain's royal court and national government. King Street, a public road, cut it in two. To the west lay an elaborate sports complex: tennis courts and a bowling alley, a cockpit and a jousting yard, with St. James's Park beyond. To the east, reaching to the river, was a hothouse world where royals, courtiers, and government officials ate, slept, worked, and played. Servants labored in kitchens, pantries, and stables, while grandees entertained in their halls and drawing rooms. Next door to the king's bedchamber, the Privy Council met to decide the nation's affairs, while secretaries hunched over their papers in scattered lodgings. Fountains played in gardens; choirboys sang in the Royal Chapel. And at the palace's heart, connected via their adjoining presence chambers, lay the two suites of apartments known as the King's Side and the Queen's Side. Charles's rooms extended westward, looking out over the Privy Garden, while the

Queen's rooms spread eastward, with views over the river. Here Henrietta retired with her French household, while the church bells rang on till midnight and "all the streets were full of bonfires."[3]

In the following days, the wedding festivities continued. In White hall's grand Renaissance Banqueting House—built by Charles's father for such state occasions—the royal couple sat side-by-side on their thrones for the formal ratification of their marriage treaty. Henrietta was proclaimed queen, an Anglican bishop gave his blessing—the closest thing to a Protestant wedding ceremony the French would allow—and Charles kissed his bride.[4] A banquet followed, then dancing, at which Henrietta distinguished herself, dancing beautifully yet "without losing any of the gravity which must be kept by persons of her rank." The next day there was jousting, where Charles "made himself as much admired in these exercises as the queen his wife had been at the ball." Then the Duke of Buckingham excelled himself, entertaining Henrietta's French courtiers "with such magnificence and prodigal plenty, . . . that the like hath not been seen in these parts."[5]

But still the English could not match up to French expectations. The Parisian court was the most splendid in Europe. Louis XIII had more courtiers than any other monarch; his palaces were "very huge and stately"; French clothes were richer, their furniture more costly and more comfortable.[6] Henrietta's courtiers complained bitterly at their reception, which lacked the "gallantries that are usually made on such occasions." There should have been a state procession through London's streets, stopping to see the citizens' "shows and pageants." At Whitehall, there should have been masques and ballets, with Londoners coming to entertain their queen.[7] Charles had in fact planned such entertainments, but they had been abandoned because the plague was spreading in the capital. In the previous week, ninety-one had died of it, making people "much afraid." But still the French felt insulted. Even Henrietta's great state bed seemed to them merely a leftover from the reign of Queen Elizabeth I, its design so passé that even the oldest of the French men had never seen such a thing.[8]

Even worse were Charles's manifest violations of his marriage promises. The treaty stated that only Catholics should serve in Henrietta's court, yet already some English Protestants had been appointed. The French angrily dismissed them. But in the matter of the Catholic chapels that Henrietta was supposed to have "within every one of the kings houses, . . . kept as Madame shall appoint," they were powerless.[9] At St. James's Palace, Henrietta's official London residence, work on a large Catholic chapel had begun two years earlier, when Charles was courting the Spanish Infanta. Yet it was still unfinished. And at Whitehall—as Henrietta found when she emerged from her bedchamber the first morning, going to Mass "in her petticoat, with a veil upon her head," holding the arm of the Comte de Tillières—there was no proper chapel at all, merely a room set aside "for ecclesiastical purposes," and that "only a very small oratory in which no privacy is possible."[10] When the French complained, Charles merely answered that if Henrietta's closet at Whitehall was inadequate, they should hold Mass in her great chamber, "and if the great chamber was not wide enough, they might use the garden; and if the garden would not serve their turn, then was the park the fittest place."[11]

Then there was the active persecution being inflicted on English Catholics, despite all of Charles and James's promises when they signed the *Escrit secret* back in December. Even some of Henrietta's own servants were arrested and brought before the justices, charged with recusancy for refusing to attend Anglican services. The French clergymen in particular were utterly disheartened, seeing their coreligionists "in fear of prison and of the hangman," unable "to seek God but while trembling." All their dreams for how the marriage would "profit the Catholic religion" were in tatters, their promises to the pope unfulfilled.[12] Yet Charles would do nothing: Parliament had begun now, and he could not risk offending the anti-Catholic MPs until they had voted for the war funding he needed.

Even so, the MPs were beginning "to mutter about matters of religion," noting that Charles had promised, as Prince of Wales, "that he would never contract a marriage with conditions derogatory" to their religion. Yet now the marriage treaty was being kept secret, making them "suspect the more."[13] Henrietta's priests, in particular, were an affront. For the first time since the reign of Queen Mary, nearly seventy years earlier, when Protestant martyrs had been burned at the stake, Catholic clergymen walked openly through Whitehall, dressed "in their clerical habits." Every morning, at the very heart of the nation's government, they performed the hated Catholic Mass, with its alien trappings of incense, holy water, and images of saints— a ceremony that was otherwise illegal throughout the country. Amid the euphoria of Henrietta's first arrival, there had been hopes she might convert to Protestantism. But now the reality was plain: "We have got a good and devout princess," Catholics gloated, overjoyed at "the confusion of the malignant [Protestants]."[14]

Yet despite all the animosities, the royal couple remained unaffected. Continuing their honeymoon from Canterbury, they treated each other with "the greatest respect and affection" and avoided talking of the Catholic persecution and Charles's disputes with the French ambassadors. "The king shows the greatest respect and affection for the queen," the Florentine ambassador in London commented, "and she, whilst sensitive to all that is going on around her, conducts herself with much prudence, and toward the king with every symptom of veneration and regard."[15] But their happiness was short-lived. As the plague spread relentlessly, killing hundreds every week, the couple fled from London with their courts. Again Charles ordered the exclusion of Mamie Saint-Georges from their coach, but this time Henrietta objected, "showing some resentment," though in her usual witty style, with "more of gaiety than bitterness." It was Charles's first experience of opposition from his wife, and he did not like it. Special orders from him now formally deprived Mamie of any right of entry to the royal coach, leaving her courtiers bitterly angry that they had "not met with that fair treatment which they were led to expect."[16]

The French were under siege, pressed by the Duke of Buckingham to appoint the ladies of his family to important positions at Henrietta's court. In the king's court, Buckingham reigned supreme: "Nothing is done without him."[17] Hardly surprising, then, that he desired a similar influence over the queen. Briefly Cardinal Richelieu dithered. Was it worth abandoning the treaty terms just this once to please Charles and Buckingham? The English might do even worse if they resisted. Perhaps the duke's wife and mother at least should have the posts they desired. But in the end, Richelieu decided that no compromise was possible: quite apart from breaking the promises the French had made to the pope, having Protestants around the queen could so easily lead to "incalculable evils." Only the duke's mother, Mary, Countess of Buckingham, could be appointed, for she was a Roman Catholic and so "not contrary to the treaty."[18]

But here Charles himself intervened. There would be no British Catholics in the queen's household, he insisted, for fear of papist plotting and rebellions. So Buckingham's mother also was rejected. Enraged, the duke "spoke bitterly to the queen," and he insulted the French ambassadors to the point where La Ville-aux-Clercs decided that the duke had to be challenged to a duel—only abandoned when Buckingham apologized abjectly the next day. For the French, the incident was unforgettable. "Strongly set against the duke," they would blame all their ills—all the rejections, insults, and disappointments that were still to come—on Buckingham alone.[19]

Still the plague pursued the court, forcing them to abandon Hampton Court and then Windsor Castle. "We do nothing but travel," Henrietta complained, as the French ambassadors left England, demoralized, having settled none of the treaty disputes.[20] Father Bérulle was especially dismayed. What would become of his young charge, trapped in so terrible a land, "which has more storms and tempests than the ocean itself"? He had hoped to see Henrietta happy amid the royal roses of England, but she now seemed to him like a solitary, fragile flower among the spines of heresy. Eager to keep up the young queen's spirits and resolution, he encouraged her to throw herself into special religious devotions and austerities. Soon she was eagerly confiding to Mother Madeleine in Paris: "We have here a Convent of the Incarnation just as much as you do." Here Henrietta and her ladies lived like the Carmelite nuns, though not as strictly. "Monsieur de Bérulle who is here dispenses us from it," Henrietta explained playfully.[21]

Gradually Bérulle began to steer the queen toward his great end.

His methods were subtle. "In order not to startle her, one must hold a light bridle to her," he wrote. "It is necessary to speak to her little, with gentleness and respect, and not to burden or press her." Soon his persuasions had their effect: en route to Oxford, where Parliament was to reconvene on Charles's orders, Henrietta spoke to her husband for the first time about the persecution of British Catholics.[22] But Charles could do nothing, even if he wanted to. He was desperate for his war funding now; massive sums had already been borrowed and spent on the fleet, but without more money, it could not set out. On August 4, he made a personal appeal to the assembled Lords and Commons, but to no avail: the MPs refused any payment unless the nation's anti-Catholic penal laws were fully executed. It fell to Buckingham to save the day. Persecution was quite possible, he told the Privy Council: Charles's marriage treaty had involved no real promise of toleration at all; the *Escrit secret* signed in Cambridge had been merely a ruse to deceive the pope into issuing a dispensation for the marriage. To Parliament he lied again, assuring them "that his Majesty had not entered into any engagements in favor of the Catholics." All their religious demands would be satisfied, he promised.[23]

Henrietta and her household were astounded. They had trusted in the *Escrit*'s promises of toleration, but now they saw that Buckingham was capable of any treachery. His persecution of the Catholics was an act of revenge, they believed, for their refusal to appoint his womenfolk to the queen's court.[24] Henrietta could restrain her resentment no longer. To everyone at the English court, "of whatsoever quality," she was cold and disrespectful. The Bishop of Mende tried to reason with her: she should "treat the king and the grandees of the state with more courtesy"; her role here was to be an ambassador, persuading her husband to cooperate with French policies. But his words had no effect. Instead, Henrietta and Mamie Saint-Georges approached the Earl of Pembroke, Buckingham's chief rival at court, proposing that he join them to make a party dedicated to "ruining Buckingham in Parliament and elsewhere."[25]

Their plot was soon discovered and, on Charles's insistence, there were public reconciliations all round.[26] But Buckingham had far more powerful enemies than Henrietta and her friends. Within days of Parliament's first meeting, the MPs had turned to investigating the government's military ineptitude. The fleet was unready, the troops fruitlessly inactive, the money previously granted all misspent. "Everything goes wrong," they complained, and it was clear where the fault lay. "The Duke of Buckingham is trusted," they pointed out, "and it must needs be either in him or his agents." As they began to draw up the formal charges, accusing Buckingham of incompetence and abuse of power, Charles was forced to act. His "passionate love for the duke" left him no choice.[27] Forfeiting his long-awaited funding, the king dissolved Parliament less than two weeks after the session had begun.

The court left Oxford hurriedly, for the plague had arrived. There was no question of returning closer to London, where the disease was now killing four or five thousand people every week. So Charles and Henrietta traveled south to the coast. No place was big enough to house both courts, so the couple separated to live fourteen miles apart, on opposite sides of Southampton Water.[28] The physical distance exacerbated their emotional divisions. While Charles "went almost daily out hunting," Catholic priests flocked to Henrietta's court at Titchfield, stoking her anger with tales of the horrors being inflicted on their English flocks. She said she wished "she might be the first martyr" in the common cause. When Charles visited, she "treated him coldly," full of "unkindnesses" and "neglects."[29]

Once again Henrietta established a religious retreat, living with her ladies as nuns. Mamie Saint-Georges was the abbess, empowered to "command . . . and punish"; the Comtesse de Tillières was her deputy. Beneath them, the rest lived "as young religieuse[s] in probation under discipline," sharing one long table at mealtimes, eating and drinking from earthenware vessels "to show the love of poverty and mortification." "Lowest of all" was the queen herself, so "that better she might forget her queenly majesty." Unlike Henrietta's earlier, lighthearted, Carmelite-inspired convent, this was a serious matter, modeled on the extreme austerity of St. Elizabeth of Hungary. Catholic priests boasted of the ladies' remarkable "religious discipline," which included "perpetual prayers," fasting, going barefoot, kissing the ground, and even flagellation. The English were horrified at these "vulgar and lowly exercises," so inappropriate for a queen. Worst of all was what Charles delicately referred to as Henrietta's "eschewing to be in my company." The retreat's sexual abstinence, imposed by Henrietta's priests with "their feigned mantles of piety," was threatening the very succession to the British throne.[30]

On one occasion, Charles complained in person to Henrietta: his courtiers assured him that if she was their wife, they would use their marital rights much more often than he did, yet, "for the little I require from you, you make yourself difficult." But usually it was the Duke of Buckingham who entered Henrietta's quarters, even late at night, to berate the fifteen-year-old for her misdemeanors. The king was "very displeased," he told her. If she did not change her ways, "the time of affliction had come for her"; in the end, "she would no longer be treated as a queen, but as she deserved."[31] Henrietta found no support from France: Marie de' Medici had sent "private letters" ordering her to behave with more moderation. So when Bérulle suggested that he return to France to explain matters, the queen agreed, though reluctantly. "I envy your happiness in seeing Monsieur de Bérulle," she wrote to Mother Madeleine in Paris, "but it will only be for a month at most," she consoled herself.[32]

In the meantime, Bérulle chose another Oratorian to replace him as the queen's confessor. Father Sancy was highly qualified: he had been a courtier, soldier, and statesman before becoming a priest, and he knew at least some English. But Sancy was also hot-tempered and obstinate, and his incendiary behavior soon created new troubles for the royal marriage. One incident occurred when Charles was dining with Henrietta at Titchfield. As the king's chaplain began to say grace as usual, Sancy stepped forward and would have begun prayers of his own, "but that Hacket [the chaplain] shoved him away." So Sancy went to stand by Henrietta, where his prayer was prevented only by the king "pulling the dishes unto him, and the carvers falling to their business." When the meal was over, Sancy again tried to jump in, but Charles's Anglican chaplain started first. So Sancy loudly began his own grace, "with such a confusion that the king, in a great passion, instantly rose from the table, and, taking the queen by the hand, retired into the bedchamber."[33]

The outrages continued on Sunday, September 18, when the Anglican vicar of Titchfield arrived to preach at Henrietta's court. In the midst of his sermon, Henrietta emerged from her apartments with the Comte de Tillières and all her maids of honor, making "such a noise" that they brought the preacher to a halt. His angry demand, "whether he might proceed or no," was ignored by the queen's party, who continued, apparently oblivious to the sermon, out through the hall with as much noise as ever. Before he finished, they returned, with an even "greater noise and disorder than before." The shocking incident filled the news. According to some, the queen and her ladies were merely "talking loudly." Others said she had brought her hunting dogs, passing through with "the loud cries usual in chasing hares." But everyone agreed that it was deliberate disruption, the result of Henrietta's "zeal in religion."[34] In the following days, the vicar received verbal abuse and death threats from the French. Then, while he walked in his garden, a gun was fired from the adjacent orchard, where two of the queen's valets were shooting birds. Miraculously, the clergyman was unhurt, but the shot clearly was directed at him: the hail of tiny balls landed all around him. Soon the culprit was arrested and charged with attempted murder, but far more was involved than just "the folly of a lackey." The fate of nations hung in the balance; the Venetian ambassador feared that the "evil results" of such incidents could "disturb forever cordial relations" between England and France.[35]

Charles was at Plymouth with the Duke of Buckingham, waiting to see his navy sail for Spain, but now he rushed to resolve the crisis. To his surprise, he found it hardly necessary. "My wife begins to mend her manners," he reported happily to Buckingham, though "I know not how long it will continue, for they say it is by advice [from France]." But for the moment, at least, Henrietta was "very gracious" to her husband, and the couple sometimes spent three hours together at night. Also pleasing was Henrietta's abandonment of her religious retreat: one of her court ladies had died, begging the queen to "take warning," for she believed "her indiscreet mortifications" in their nunnery had caused her death.[36] "Best of all," Charles told Buckingham, "the monsieurs desire to return home." The king seized his opportunity and paid off thirty or forty of those "of low condition." But still too many remained: "excitable French people who cannot be quiet," who continued to augment "the bad understanding between the two nations."[37]

As the plague eased that autumn, the royals moved back to Hampton Court, where a new French ambassador arrived. The Seigneur de Blainville-sur-Orne was a high-ranking courtier and a counselor of state, but he received scant respect from the English. His demands for the proper execution of the marriage treaty were met with intransigent refusal. "What had been done against the Catholics was only for the good of his state," Charles said. Besides, "their sufferings were not as great as people made out."[38] But Blainville also had a stubborn streak, and he would no more back down than Charles. For weeks, all court business was "confined to disputes with the French." By mid-November, the English were furious at Blainville's "violence and rude conduct," while the French were "full to the throat with disgust" at the English treachery.[39] Henrietta was desperate, seeing the ruin of everything she had been made to hope for from her marriage. "I receive every day new afflictions," she wrote to Bérulle.

> As for the poor Catholics, the persecution is greater than ever. The ambassador and all of us despair at it. He does all he can for the service of God and for my service. . . . Every day they promise to satisfy him and, an hour later, they do all they can to annoy him and they laugh at him. . . . I beg you very strongly to come back the soonest that you can. I have great need that you be here.[40]

But Bérulle remained in France. Richelieu distrusted his enthusiastic Catholicism and blamed Bérulle for setting Charles and Henrietta against each other for his own religious ends. With the French government determined to maintain the English alliance against Spain, Bérulle's complaints about the English went unheeded. Still, Marie de' Medici insisted that Henrietta tread the impossible line of

pleasing everyone, giving "honor and respect to the king, warm welcome to the nobility, protection to the Catholics, affection to all."
All Bérulle could do was resign himself to the will of God and offer
Henrietta consolation from afar: "No day passes when I do not think
of Your Majesty and the travails you endure."[41]

And soon a new battleground was opening up. With their return
to Hampton Court, it was time, Charles thought, to reform the laxity
of his wife's court, where the French approached the queen "without ceremony," sharing her conversation with "openness and freedom."[42] For Charles, proper court etiquette was the very basis of
monarchy, the best means to make "princes to be adored." But Henrietta was appalled by his demand that she follow the same rules
that had been used in "the queen my mother's house."[43] These regulations "wounded her maids whom she loved, and distanced them
from around her person." "She could not surrender her liberty," she
replied; she hoped her husband would give her leave to order her
house as she wished. Charles was bitterly resentful, not so much
at the refusal itself—which could be ascribed to ignorance of English court customs—but at the way his wife had given it, in public,
in front of all their courtiers. He could never have imagined "that
she should affront me so." Later he drew her aside and explained
her mistakes, both in making a "public denial" and in "the business
itself." But his reproof only infuriated Henrietta further. Far from
"acknowledging her fault," the queen launched at once into so long
a tirade of French, full of "so ill an answer," that Charles refused to
record it.[44]

Charles would stand no more. He had endured "the unkind
usages of my wife" for too long, thinking she was "but young" and
her manners might mend. Buckingham had encouraged such hopes,
eager to preserve the French alliance.[45] But now Buckingham was
away in the Netherlands, seeking new anti-Spanish treaties, and
Charles no longer trusted his assurances. He still believed in Henrietta's basic goodwill: all her "disrespects" were "not in her nature,"
but rather caused by "the maliciousness of the monsieurs." And the
worst of the offenders was Mamie Saint-Georges. Ever since he had
excluded her from Henrietta's coach, Charles thought, Mamie had

been set on ruining his marriage, stirring Henrietta up into "such a humor of distaste against me, as that from that very hour to this, no man can say that ever she used me two days together with so much respect as I deserved."[46]

So Charles decided. He would "cashier my monsieurs" and send them back to France, every last one. But he would not act without consulting his one true friend. "Steenie," he wrote,

> send me word with what speed you may, whether you like this course or not, for I shall put nothing of this in execution until I hear from you; . . . but I am resolute; it must be done, and that shortly.[47]

Yet, despite Charles's indignation, none of the French were sent packing. The duke himself, we can presume, prevented it. But Buckingham's dogged diplomacy was beginning to seem futile, as France abandoned its hostilities toward the Spanish and instead turned its military might against the Protestant Huguenot rebels at La Rochelle. When the last remnants of the Huguenots' fleet took refuge in England, Blainville demanded that they be handed over to the French authorities. But Charles refused; such a betrayal of his coreligionists would upset his fiercely Protestant subjects and spoil his own pretensions of leading the Protestant cause in Europe. The French were livid. Henrietta's match had been intended "to marry England to France more than to marry individuals," Richelieu declared, "but it has turned out the reverse." With Richelieu threatening to ally with Spain, England now risked an international disaster: simultaneous war with all of Catholic Europe.[48]

Despite the failures in his foreign policies, Buckingham received "a most affectionate welcome" from Charles when he returned to England in December 1625. "Grief is eased being told to a friend," the king confided to the duke. And Charles needed consoling, for his relations with Henrietta now grew "worse and worse."[49] First the couple quarreled over her refusal to attend the ceremonies of Charles's beloved Order of the Garter. "Scruples of conscience" prevented her presence at the Protestant ceremony, the queen explained, but the English took it as a deliberate insult. Then Charles insisted that her courtiers swear the Oath of Allegiance to him: if they refused, they would have to leave the country at once. There was "a great commotion," and Henrietta went down on her knees to the king and wept.[50]

Amid the quarrels, Henrietta's sixteenth birthday passed unremarked, but Christmas was another matter. With the plague almost gone, professional actors were summoned to perform at Hampton Court. The queen even braved the City of London herself, going Christmas shopping incognito in the Exchange, where she "went nimbly from shop to shop, and bought some [knick] knacks, till, being discovered, she made away with all the haste she could." In the season of goodwill, reconciliations were begun. Henrietta was trying "to appear more wise," she assured Louis XIII: though still feeling wronged, "I affect to do nothing by passion."[51] Pleased, Charles responded with a lavish New Year's gift to his wife: Somerset House, which had been his mother's London home. At last Henrietta would have "a noble palace" in Renaissance style, such as she had known in France. With it came "all the ornaments and household stuff" from Charles's mother's time, including a fine art collection—making a present that was "greatly appreciated and has led to a more intimate understanding between their Majesties."[52]

Buckingham also was anxious for reconciliation. His immense war fleet—"the greatest that ever England sent out"—had been utterly defeated by the Spanish at Cadiz; just a third of the ships had limped home, war-torn and storm-battered, in what the English public regarded as "a shameful return."[53] Now he needed money for more ships, but he had no desire to call Parliament. The second half of Henrietta's dowry still had not been paid by the French, but Buckingham would have to appease the queen in order to get it. So he set out to become "as intimate as possible" with her. He "humbled himself frequently, offering his services," and promised to settle the dispute about appointing English ladies to Henrietta's court "to her satisfaction." He even offered Henrietta a place on the king's Privy Council. But the queen politely declined, on Blainville's advice that this was some new English trick.[54] She and her courtiers would never trust Buckingham now. Even the pacific Bishop of Mende had abandoned hope. Dispatched to Paris, he delivered "a clear account of all the disturbances that took place in the queen's household," complaining "very highly and in often biting terms" about the duke.[55] At last Henrietta's side of the story began to gain some credence. Marie de' Medici had "her eyes . . . full of tears": "she would rather have given a finger off her hand than have married her daughter in England," she said. There would be no dowry payment now, Louis told Charles's ambassadors—not until "the queen enjoys the fulfillment of what was promised" in the marriage treaty.[56]

And so the English court was forced to call Parliament again. In hopes of placating the House of Commons, persecution of Catholics was stepped up. The king's officers searched Catholic homes, where they "robbed . . . and made good prize of their books, beads, images, and priest's vestments," as well as "money and other things" they were not authorized to take. The magistrates' courts summoned suspected Catholics to swear the Oath of Allegiance to the king— an oath forbidden by the pope. Those who refused were "thrown into prison and their goods confiscated." "No one is excepted, even barons," Blainville reported. He and Henrietta were in despair at the Catholics' sufferings. Nothing worse could be done to them now "except banishment or death": they had reached their "extreme unction."[57]

Yet still Buckingham sought Henrietta's help. As the besieged Huguenots of La Rochelle grew closer to starvation and surrender, he and Charles were desperate to save them and thereby placate Parliament. If the town fell, Charles would "recover it in person," he stated. With the English ambassadors in Paris doing all they could to broker a peace deal for the Huguenots, Buckingham asked Henrietta to write to her mother. She was only too ready to comply, fearing that war with France would cut her off from her family. In her own hand, "expressing her anguish at being involved in the quarrels between her brother and her husband," Henrietta begged Marie to persuade Louis to show "moderation toward La Rochelle."[58]

By now Charles was preparing for his coronation, and he was determined it would be perfect. On his orders, a committee of bishops and peers had readied an order of ceremony corresponding exactly to the coronations of the medieval kings of England, except that Charles's service would be performed in English, not Latin. The king himself "viewed all the regalia" and tried on the Saxon vestments worn since the time of Edward the Confessor. But his plans had a flaw: his ceremony was for "the crowning of the king and queen together," and the French had "scruples" about Henrietta's participation in this Anglican ceremony.[59] It would offend the pope, Louis feared, and the British Catholics would be disgusted to see their queen, "in whom they have put their hopes, on her knees in front of a Protestant bishop, taking from him oaths and a diadem and the other ornaments of royalty." Yet Louis knew there were strong arguments for Henrietta's coronation—especially "that in rejecting this honor she is wounding the kingdom and even the dignity and birth of her children," whose right to the throne might thereby be called into question. So the French suggested a compromise. Perhaps the Bishop of Mende could crown her, just outside the church, as Charles had been married outside the Cathedral of Notre Dame. Or maybe, after Charles's Protestant rites were concluded, Henrietta could enter Westminster Abbey and have the crown placed on her head "without any other ceremony." Then she could proceed to the coronation feast and the opening of Parliament, so she would be seen "by all the people with the crown on her head."[60] But Charles would not allow the slightest alteration in his meticulously planned ceremonies—with the result, the learned doctors of the Sorbonne decided, that "the queen cannot be crowned without offending religion." Henrietta would lose "many prerogatives and the affection and respect of the people." But at least there would be no "prejudice to her conscience." After all, Louis commented, "a heavenly crown is better."[61]

So, on Thursday, February 2, 1626, Charles sat alone, enthroned on the stage in Westminster Abbey. Dressed in the ancient robes of King Edward the Confessor, with King Edward's crown upon his head, he looked out over the crowd of "thousands within the Church" who now at last were truly his subjects.[62] Henrietta would not enter the abbey even as a spectator, and the curtained gallery prepared for her remained unoccupied throughout the five hours of religious ceremonies: from Charles's procession up the nave—bareheaded and clothed in white satin—through the anointing of his shoulders, arms, hands, and head with sacramental oil, to his departure, crowned, dressed in ermine-lined robes of black velvet. Instead, the queen went with Blainville and her courtiers to a nearby house, from whose windows she watched Charles's procession to and from the abbey, while—according to one hostile rumor—"her ladies [were] frisking and dancing in the room" behind her.[63] English public opinion, at first antagonistic only to Henrietta's priests, was now turning against the queen herself. "The people . . . rejoice that she is not crowned," noted the Venetian ambassador, and for a while the Duke of Buckingham gained some popularity when rumor reported that he had personally prevented her coronation.[64]

Charles bore Henrietta's absence with apparent good grace. He even made a joke when he met her afterward, "putting his two hands to his crown and lifting it a little," like a gentleman doffing his hat to a lady. But it must have rankled, and just four days later Charles and Henrietta were enmeshed in their bitterest quarrel yet. It was the opening of Parliament, and Henrietta was again taking no part in the ceremonies, "from the same religious scruples."[65] Instead, on Charles's suggestion, she was to watch the king's procession to Parliament from the apartments of the Countess of Buckingham, whose windows at Whitehall looked out onto Charles's route. Carefully dressed and coiffed, Henrietta set off from her chambers to join the countess. But when she reached the Privy Garden, a space some hundred yards across, Henrietta found it was raining. Could she not go back and watch from her own windows? she asked Charles. Perhaps it was only drizzling, for Charles retorted that it was not raining at all. Henrietta contradicted her husband: the ground was wet and muddy, and her clothes would be dirtied; the rain and wind would disorder her hair; if she went out now, she would have to dress all over again for the evening. After some dispute, the king allowed his wife to return to her apartments.

But the Duke of Buckingham's prestige was also at stake: it would be a great honor for the queen to visit his mother. So now Buckingham headed for Henrietta's apartments and told her she had deeply offended her husband by refusing to go where he wished, just because of a little rain. Concerned, Henrietta consulted Blainville, who persuaded her to go at once to the Countess of Buckingham's chambers, despite the rain. But this displeased Charles more than ever: his wife was doing for the hated French ambassador what she had refused to do for her husband. And so, soon after Henrietta had joined the countess, the Duke of Buckingham appeared, saying the king wished her to leave. By now Henrietta was enjoying herself in the company of a large group of ladies, so she sent the duke back to Charles, begging to be allowed to stay. For Charles it was yet another affront: he had already expressed his desires. He sent Buckingham back again: Henrietta must leave at once, by his absolute command; if she refused, he would postpone his procession to Parliament rather than allow her to watch it from where she was. Henrietta was astonished at his rudeness and especially upset because it was done in public, in front of her own courtiers and many English observers. She had to obey the king's direct command, but she made no effort to restrain her tongue. As she left, she told Buckingham that she was most unfortunate: obedience seemed to be a crime in England. She was treated in a way very different from her due, and she would never have believed they would have mistreated her so in front of the English court just for having said the weather was bad.[66]

That night, the queen was still fuming. When Charles joined her in bed, she complained bitterly about his public offense to her, "and at the duke acting as messenger on this occasion." She was the most unhappy princess in the world, she said. She would rather die than offend him, but since she had done neither, she begged him not to treat her in that manner in front of the whole court, making everyone think he did not love her. In return, Charles explained his anger. Henrietta had offended him in four ways: first she had said it was raining, then that she would be dirtied, then that her hair would be spoiled, and finally that she did not want to do what she was told. Henrietta flew off the handle, retorting that she was innocent of all blame. She would never have believed that such words as hers could be considered faults, but from this time forward she would take great care not to say them. And so on. Charles got up from the bed. He would torment Henrietta no longer with his visits, he said. Then he left the room.[67]

The next day, the king retaliated. This disgraceful quarrel was yet another result of Blainville's pernicious influence over the queen, he believed.[68] So Blainville was banned from the English court, while Charles wrote a letter to France to complain. When Buckingham informed Henrietta that she could no longer allow the French ambassador to enter her presence, she was up in arms. For hours, Buckingham "pressed her for a promise," but she continued her retorts. She was astonished at the duke's insistence: "She would rather die than shut out her brother's ambassador." She was sorry for Charles, who already had too many foreign enemies without offending France as well. If Blainville came to her door, she would certainly let him in, and Charles should be grateful to her for it, since his own ambassadors in France would receive the same treatment that he gave Blainville. But despite the queen's tirades, Buckingham persisted. Finally, under his "constant pressure and the king's commands," Henrietta declared that "if his Majesty absolutely wished it, she would obey." In any case, she consoled herself, she would never be put to the test, since Blainville would do nothing indiscreet.[69]

For two nights now, Charles and Henrietta had not slept together. Her husband would visit her no more, Buckingham told the queen, unless she begged his pardon with due humility. If she had not done so within two more days, Charles would treat her as a person unworthy to be his wife, and he would expel Madame Saint-Georges and all the French household. Astonished, Henrietta replied with her usual spirit. There was only one fault that could make her unworthy to be the king's wife, and she was certainly too well bred to commit adultery. If the English expelled the French, they would damage their own honor by breaking the marriage treaty. As for asking for pardon, the incident had taken place so publicly that everyone had seen it, and all the English lords and ladies had praised her obedience to the king's commands. She could hardly beg pardon for a fault she had not committed. Nevertheless, if the king formally commanded her to do it, she would obey. But she would also have to say that she begged his forgiveness only out of obedience to his orders, having actually offended him not in word or deed or even in intention.[70]

But Henrietta in fact was eager for reconciliation. The next day, she asked to see the king alone, and at last the couple talked it over. She had been very surprised by what Buckingham had said, she began, for she was sure she had never committed any offense against her husband. If Charles thought she had, she begged him to forget it. When Charles again demanded that she ask his pardon, the queen replied she could not, since that would mean she would be wrongly accusing herself. Instead, she begged her husband to tell her what he thought she had done wrong. For a moment, Charles was astonished. Then, recovering, he answered, "You assured me that it was raining when I had told you that it was not." Surprised, Henrietta replied that she would never have thought that offensive, but if her husband thought it was, then she would try to think so too, and she begged him to think of it no longer. For Charles, this was close enough to an apology. After embracing his wife, he graciously conducted her back to her chamber, talking to her all the while, as lively now as he had been gloomy before.[71] That night, the royal couple resumed sleeping together, and court observers noted "the complete and sincere affection which subsists between the king and queen."[72]

On Shrove Tuesday, Henrietta and her ladies performed the pastoral play they had been rehearsing since before Christmas. *L'Artenice*, written by the French poet Racan, was a story of love among shepherds and shepherdesses. Henrietta appeared in the lead, while her ladies took the remaining parts, some even "disguised . . . with beards" for the male roles. Unlike English court masques, where the genteel performers danced and acted but never spoke, this continental-style entertainment gave the French ladies extensive speaking parts. Henrietta herself "repeated, it is said, six hundred French verses by heart." When news got out, English Puritans were scandalized, especially at "the first part being declaimed by the queen."[73] But Charles and his courtiers loved the show. The imaginative sets and costumes produced a "beautiful" effect. To honor the occasion, the court's surveyor of works, Inigo Jones, had built the first perspective stage scenery ever seen in England. And there was "remarkable acting" from the queen in particular, "surpassing all the others" with her "youthful grace."[74]

For four months, all remained quiet in the royal marriage while Charles and his ministers focused on their business with Parliament. The MPs were angry at the government's failures—especially the navy's defeat at Cadiz and the ruinous peace terms negotiated in Paris for the Huguenots—and they blamed "that great man, the Duke of Buckingham." The accusations against him came thick and fast—incompetence, nepotism, corruption, even sedition and treason.[75] Charles was incensed. It was not their role "to question my servants, much less one that is so near me," he told the Commons in person, but he merely inflamed the MPs' opposition: "They came not thither, either to do what the king should command them, or to abstain where he forbade them," they replied.[76] Soon the Commons was preparing to bring the duke to trial. So once again Charles dissolved Parliament without receiving any war funds. In desperate straits, he and his Privy Council sought their money elsewhere: increased customs duties, melting down the royal plate, pawning the Crown jewels, a forced loan from the unwilling English counties. Then, at last, Charles turned once more to his wife.

After a year in England, Henrietta could still speak no English, and she remained "thoroughly French, both in her sentiments and her habits." It seemed clear to Charles that her household was to blame: making "a little republic" all by themselves, they "wholly captivated his wife's will and affections."[77] English personnel were needed if he were ever to draw the queen closer to his country and himself, so now he named three great ladies to serve in Henrietta's bedchamber. Henrietta was aghast. All of them were Buckingham's protégées, and they were Protestants. And even worse: Lucy, Countess of Carlisle had an undesirable reputation. A great court beauty, she was already the Duke of Buckingham's mistress, and now, it was said, she was setting her sights on the king, encouraged by both her lover and her husband. "I hold her in great aversion," Henrietta tried to explain to Charles; if she had to take some English ladies, perhaps Buckingham's wife could be substituted, for she was a "most upright" lady.[78] But Charles would not compromise. Even Henrietta's French household urged her to comply: the king was clearly determined, they said, and it would be better to yield with good grace. So at last Henrietta agreed: Charles "was master," she told him, although "she would never have confidence with those ladies."[79]

Almost at once, however, a new quarrel erupted. One night, when the couple were in bed together, Henrietta gave Charles a list of the officials she had chosen to manage the lands he was giving her as part of the marriage settlement. But Charles bridled: he was the one who should name her jointure officials, and he refused to allow any French ones. When Henrietta objected that Charles's mother, Anne of Denmark, had chosen all her own officials, Charles replied that "his mother was a different sort of woman from her."

An exchange of insults followed, with Henrietta claiming preeminence as a "daughter of France" over a mere Danish princess, while Charles dismissed her status as "nothing very great." "Besides," he added, "she was the third and last" of Henri IV's daughters, "and therefore of less account."[80] Enraged now, Henrietta launched into one of her great tirades—"a passionate discourse" on "how miserable she was." All business only went the worse for her the more she was involved, she complained. Her most ordinary actions were taken as crimes. It was disgraceful for her "to be used so ill." At last Henrietta ran out of breath, or perhaps Charles could stand no more. In any case, the king ended the matter in no uncertain terms. The French courtiers were behind it all, he declared, but "I shall put them to rights." On that note, he went to sleep. For three days, Charles avoided his wife's company. Only then did he revisit her bed: "not for love of her," he told Henrietta, but only "for the love of his people," for whom he had to produce an heir.[81]

And then came the very last straw. For months the queen's religious practices had been causing scandal. At Easter, she had again retired to live with her ladies like nuns, performing "spiritual exercises" and singing the hours of the Virgin. They even went on foot through the streets of London from her "monastery" at Somerset House to St. James's Palace, where Henrietta's chapel was almost completed.[82] For Henrietta this was all normal Catholic devotion, but English public opinion was shocked: Henrietta's priests had humiliated the nation's queen, making her "dabble in the dirt, in a foul morning, from Somerset House to St. James's, her Luciferian confessor riding along by her in his coach." And if they "dare thus insult over the daughter, sister, and wife of so great kings, what slavery would they not make us, the people, to undergo?" Charles bitterly resented her priests, too, for ruining his sex life. Every day almost seemed to bring a different saint's feast when, they told the queen, "You must not let the king approach." And by these means, Charles complained, "the happy conversation that ought to pass between him and his dear wife, which is the principal comfort of marriage, hath not only been interrupted but wholly quenched or perverted."[83]

Now, as Charles's anger still festered after his latest quarrel with Henrietta, he heard of a new affront. Henrietta had gone into another religious retirement, to observe "the most holy Jubilee" that the pope had declared for 1626.[84] Amid a welter of Catholic observances, Henrietta and some thirty of her courtiers set out one afternoon to "walk afoot"—and perhaps even barefoot—across Hyde Park to the public gallows at Tyburn. Here London's condemned criminals were brought for torture and execution, including many Catholic priests who had "shed their blood in defense of the Catholic cause." At this "holy place," the queen and her courtiers went down on their knees in the public highway and prayed before the gallows. Henrietta asked that, if necessary, God would "give her grace with the like constancy to die for her religion."[85]

London public opinion was scandalized. Henrietta's so-called martyrs were common criminals and traitors. There were even rumors that she had prayed specially for the Jesuit priest Henry Garnett, who "had suffered cruel torture and death on that spot" for his involvement in the Gunpowder Plot twenty years earlier.[86] To Charles it was an abomination: Garnett was a ruthless traitor, convicted of attempting to assassinate Charles's own father and his whole Parliament. He could "no longer bear it," Charles said. Yet still he believed it was all due to "the ill crafty counsels" of Henrietta's servants "for advancing of their own ends." Now, he decided, he would "deliver" his dear wife from these most undesirable attendants.[87]

Back in November, the Duke of Buckingham had dissuaded Charles; but since then, France had made peace with Spain, ruining the duke's grand foreign plans. Angrily, Buckingham ranted against "the inconstancy and faithlessness of the French."[88] And Henrietta's household created nothing but trouble. They encouraged the English Catholics and sheltered illegal priests in Whitehall itself while the government's pursuivants sought them all over London. They "thwarted and censured" whatever the government did, and they made "cabals" against him in particular.[89]

So Charles's plan went ahead, unimpeded. On July 31, he and his Privy Council arrived at the queen's apartments. Finding Henrietta in her bedchamber suffering from a toothache, Charles ordered everyone else to leave. Locking the door behind them, he turned to his wife and explained. "For the good of herself and the nation," he had to "cashier all her attendants, priests and others." In future, he promised, she "would be better served and with more decorum."[90] For once Henrietta was speechless, taken unawares. Then, "seeing herself deprived at one blow of all those in whom she had any confidence, she began to weep bitterly."[91] From the other side of the door, the Comtesse de Tillières heard it all. "Never could a similar affliction be seen," she reported: "She almost died, crying out, despairing, demanding us back with such prayers and tears that if it had been another [man than Charles] assuredly we would have been called back." On her knees, Henrietta begged her husband, "with words that would have moved stones to pity," to let her keep her poor servants. They had never advised her contrary to his service, she swore. If the king had too great an aversion for Madame Saint-Georges, perhaps he might allow her at least the Comtesse de Tillières. But Charles was unmoved. All had to leave, at once.[92]

Meanwhile, in the anterooms outside, Charles's secretary of state, Lord Conway, informed the French that, "without reply or impertinent strife," they had to leave Whitehall at once for Somerset House, from there to leave the country as soon as possible.[93] As the queen's maids peered from the window, trying to see what was happening in her bedchamber next door, she rushed to her own window to say a last farewell. In her urgency, she broke the panes and, when the king followed to prevent her, she seized the iron bars beyond the shattered glass. As Charles pulled her away, her dress was torn and her hands bloodied.[94] The household could do nothing. When Mamie Saint-Georges spoke for them all, refusing to leave, Lord Conway called in the guard, who "thrust them and all their country folks out of the queen's lodgings," while the women "howled and lamented, as if they had been going to execution."[95]

4

NEW BEGINNINGS

Henrietta was devastated. That evening, she wept without cease, refusing to eat or drink unless some of her servants returned to her. Finally Charles summoned back one of her dressers, her cook, her baker, her pantry-keeper, and her dress-maker. Two of the Oratorian priests were also allowed to return, to say Mass in her chapel in accordance with the marriage treaty.[1] But the great court ladies and gentlemen, Henrietta's friends and companions from childhood, had to go. When they objected that they had no money for their journey—since their salaries had gone unpaid for months and they had lent what cash they had to the queen—Charles flew into a fury. "Steenie," he wrote to Buckingham from Nonsuch Palace in Surrey, where he had retired with his wife,

> I command you send all the French away tomorrow out of the town.
> If you can, by fair means (but stick not long in disputing), otherwise
> force them away; driving them away like so many wild beasts, until
> you have shipped them; and so the devil go with them.[2]

Evicted by Lord Conway and his yeomen of the guard, Henrietta's servants were carried downriver by barge to Gravesend. On August 12, 1626, they sailed for France from Dover.

Left alone, Henrietta felt "a complete prisoner," surrounded by Buckingham's relatives, "persons who had shown themselves her enemies since the moment she landed in England." They were always with her, spying with their "Argus eyes." Even at night she was never alone, for

> the duke's niece sleeps constantly in her chamber, nor does she ever quit the queen's presence, unless her place be taken by the duke's mother, wife or sister, who wait on her Majesty alternately.[3]

Henrietta's "tears and displeasure" were "continuous"; "she hardly sleeps anymore and eats very little." Several times Henrietta protested to Charles, leading to "angry discussions" between them.[4]

Desperate, Henrietta wrote to her mother: "Consider that I am your daughter and the most afflicted there be in the world; if you do not take pity on me, I am in despair." She begged to be allowed to return to France: "I cannot be happy without that." Letters went to Louis XIII and Cardinal Richelieu, too, imploring them "to succor me in my woes."[5] Henrietta's former household filled Paris with vivid stories of injustices "of the worst possible description." The Bishop of Mende, "having great access to Richelieu, told him at all hours the nature of the affront and incited him to vengeance."[6] And at Richelieu's request, the Comte de Tillières wrote a lengthy memoir of his year in England. Henrietta was perhaps a little too young for her role, he admitted. She might occasionally have been too passionate, too obstinate, too carried away. But her household was blameless. Everything was the Duke of Buckingham's fault. From the beginning, he had hated the French and determined to be rid of them. All the royal couple's quarrels had been caused by his total power over the English king—a pitiful creature, according to Tillières, without a mind of his own.

Tillières's story of the triangular relationship of Charles, Henrietta, and Buckingham has dominated historians' accounts ever since, yet it is a web of fabrications. In his eagerness to blacken the duke's name, Tillières created a melodrama of improbably souped-up emotions and reasonless prejudices. His endless circumstantial stories of what people said behind closed doors, of their inner motivations and secret evil designs, are the stuff of Dumas and Scott historical novels—dramatic and exciting, but obviously beyond the real knowledge of Tillières or anyone else, and completely unconfirmed by any other historical source. The memoirs are full of errors of fact and internal inconsistencies—some probably just misremembered but others deliberately falsified to promote his own partisan position. (My own account of the marriage's first year has used Tillières's memoirs only when they are confirmed by other sources, resulting in a story that is substantially different from any previously told.) But Cardinal Richelieu was persuaded, and he later reproduced the essentials of Tillières's story in his own memoirs, authorizing and perpetuating this version of events for the benefit of history. And in Paris that summer, Louis and his court were furious with the English, and with Buckingham especially. Marie de' Medici wept, denouncing the English as hypocrites who "habitually spoke fair and acted ill." "We shall be avenged," a Parisian courtier vowed.[7] But the French were not ready for war with England. Their navy was too weak, and their troubles with the Huguenots preoccupied them. And so they opted to negotiate, ready to "yield upon some points [rather] than come to blows."[8]

Two ambassadors were chosen for the delicate talks in London: the Comte de Tillières and his brother-in-law, Maréchal François de Bassompierre. Henrietta was delighted. The comte had always been her champion—"the English have great fear of him," she told her mother—and she had known Bassompierre from childhood. A cultivated courtier and experienced international diplomat, the maréchal had been close to her father and mother and was now her brother's trusted counselor. But Charles utterly refused to receive Tillières. Even Bassompierre was unwelcome.[9]

When he arrived in London that September, Bassompierre received none of the usual honors. On Charles's orders, no house was provided for him, and he had to pay all his own expenses. His first

meeting with Buckingham descended rapidly into mutual recriminations. Four days later, there was a tense audience at Hampton
Court, where Charles allowed Bassompierre only "a brief exchange
of civilities," fearing that any more than that would push him or
Henrietta into some violent outburst "in front of the whole world."[10]
At Somerset House two days later, Bassompierre found Henrietta
in a dreadful state, "so stirred by the outrage they have done her by
the distancing of her domestics that I could not in any way compose
her." When he finally had his private meeting with Charles, it was
more of the same: the king ranted bitterly about his grievances, and
it took all Bassompierre's courtly tact to soothe him.[11]

The next three weeks passed in a frenetic round of meetings with
courtiers, civil servants, and royals. It was a wearying, discouraging
process. Bassompierre reported:

> The king has spoken to me with such resolution . . . that if I had
> had permission to go back [to France], I would have taken leave of
> him at that same audience. I am so scandalized and angry to see this
> little queen, so good and pretty, in danger of losing her religion that
> I despair of it. I hear nothing every day from all the ministers of state
> but complaints that they make of the misbehaviors of the French; I
> answer them back sometimes, but in the end I grow angry or tired of
> it and I leave them alone.[12]

But still Bassompierre persisted in his policy of "prudent and amica-
ble approaches," thrashing out the possibilities for mutual compromise. He saw Henrietta almost daily, finding her exasperating as she
oscillated between bouts of depression and outbursts of "youthful
passion," quarreling bitterly with him and her husband.[13] Her formal
reconciliation with Buckingham, which Bassompierre engineered
"with a thousand pains," lasted a mere twenty-four hours before the
quarrels began all over again.[14] But at last an agreement was reached.
Instead of her previous four hundred or so attendants, Henrietta
would now be allowed forty or fifty French courtiers and servants,
including a doctor, a secretary, gentlemen ushers and waiters, and
two ladies of the bedchamber for companionship. For her chapel,

there would be a bishop and twelve priests, who had to be neither Jesuits nor Oratorians, the English insisted. And all these personnel had to be newly appointed, for Charles would allow none of her old household to return, except the physician.[15]

The next day, everyone was happy. It was the day of the Lord Mayor of London's procession, and Henrietta and Bassompierre took Buckingham and the Earl of Dorset with them in the queen's coach to Cheapside to watch. While they waited, the four of them played cards—a revolution in Henrietta's relations with Buckingham that delighted Bassompierre.[16] But just three days later, the royal couple quarreled once more, over Henrietta's religious devotions for All Saints' Day. Annoyed that his wife was yet again "shut up in her monastery" at Somerset House "without decorum," Charles demanded that Bassompierre make her desist. But the ambassador found Henrietta both "obstinate and very determined."[17] Losing patience, he threatened to return at once to Paris and tell her brother and mother that everything was her fault. It was several days before he and Henrietta were reconciled.

For two more weeks, Bassompierre remained in London to celebrate the successful conclusion of his negotiations. In the whirl of dinners, balls, plays, and musical soirées, all previous disagreements were forgotten. The Duke of Buckingham entertained king, queen, and ambassador with "the most superb feast" that Bassompierre had ever seen. Each course was accompanied by a separate ballet, with its own scenery and music, and then the three guests of honor joined the rest of the company to watch a grand masque, representing the French royal family sitting among the gods and making peace for all Europe, each figure so lifelike that Henrietta could name them. The dancing afterward lasted until four in the morning, when the party closed with "a splendid refection of sweetmeats."[18] Buckingham's reconciliation with the queen was apparently complete, and on Henrietta's birthday he joined in the "very fine assembly" she arranged at Somerset House, performing with other prominent English courtiers in a masque for the company's entertainment.[19]

At last Bassompierre departed for France, "very well satisfied." But in Paris he had a rude awakening. Henrietta's former confessor, Father Sancy, had accompanied him to London and now told tales behind his back. "Little had been gained for the satisfaction of his sister," Louis fumed, and Cardinal Richelieu "found a thousand objections" to Bassompierre's treaty.[20] So the French king refused to ratify it. New negotiations had to be opened, he insisted, "to win more"—both for Henrietta herself and for the poor English Catholics, whose persecution continued unabated, despite Charles's promises to Bassompierre.[21]

The English court was disgusted. Charles complained that "he was treated contemptuously." He had already yielded more than he really wanted to, "out of consideration for his brother-in-law," and "he could not go a step farther."[22] Hostilities between the two nations grew. When the French confiscated the entire English wine fleet in Bordeaux—two hundred ships, with their sailors and guns and some sixteen thousand tons of Gascony wine—Charles ordered his navy to embark on a campaign of organized piracy, intercepting French merchantmen and bringing them into English ports, where the ships and goods were impounded, the sailors imprisoned.[23]

Amid the drama, Henrietta began to build a new life for herself. She bought a lute and started lessons with "a certain Monsieur Gouttier, a Frenchman and a famous performer." All through December, she was busy "with fourteen ladies of her court" rehearsing a new masque, to be performed on Twelfth Night.[24] Christmas Day was a religious occasion, which Henrietta and Charles celebrated apart, but the next day they were together at Whitehall to begin "the festivities of Christmas," culminating in Henrietta's masque, which was "very pretty."[25] Led by "His Majesty, with the duke and fourteen others of the noblemen and knights," everyone danced until four in the morning. "Doubtless it cost abundance," a jealous Londoner commented: "It was said one Mr. Chalmer sold one thousand yards of taffeta and satin towards it."[26]

But neither Charles nor the French royal family were content to leave Henrietta in peace. Marie de' Medici and Father Bérulle sternly warned Henrietta against her new courtiers. "My most dear daughter," implored Marie, continue your exercises of piety, and do not listen to those who wish to divert you from them, under the pretext of gaiety. Their counsel is pernicious and will bring you to terrible miseries. . . . I am sorry to see these people close to you. But I would be much more sorry if their words entered your heart. . . . Remember, each day, that Jesus Christ Our Savior died to give you life.[27]

Meanwhile, Charles's hostility to Henrietta's French attendants flared up once more. All along, there had been rumors that her servants were spying. Now, suddenly, Charles had her lute teacher arrested and sent to the Tower of London. Three more servants soon followed him there, and threats were made that all her remaining French personnel would be "got rid of like the first, their conduct being so unsatisfactory."[28]

Still angry, Charles left to go hunting in the country. Weeks passed, and from their separate little enclaves the couple exchanged cold letters containing nothing but "dry, ceremonious compliment." When Charles planned to visit his capital, he dreaded a renewal of their quarrels, so he asked Buckingham to see Henrietta first to "set her in tune."[29] Charles spent a mere couple of days in London, but his reunion with Henrietta must have been a success. Inviting her to join him at Theobalds Palace, he "bestowed a dinner upon her." Later that day, on Henrietta's invitation, he rode with her back to London, where "Her Majesty gave him a supper" at Somerset House. There Charles "lay all night" with his wife, before returning to his hunting the next afternoon.[30] Neither knew it then, but it was a turning point in their relationship.

Gradually Henrietta was settling down. At Somerset House, the remnants of her French household provided some of the comforts and sophistication of home. In the end, Charles had allowed twenty or more servants to remain, including twelve musicians to play both for her entertainment and in her chapel.[31] He had also appointed three English Catholic ladies-in-waiting, who accompanied Henrietta to chapel each morning. There her two remaining Oratorian priests, Fathers Philip and Viette, said Mass with all possible ceremony. These two would be the queen's lifelong companions. Henrietta was particularly devoted to Father Philip, her confessor, a Scottish priest who had joined Bérulle's Oratorians after fleeing persecution in his native land. He was a learned man: he had headed the Oratory's theological college at Lyon for five years before Bérulle selected him to join the English mission. He was also notably moderate, warning Henrietta to "live well toward the Protestants" and never allowing her "to be pressed to any passionate undertaking under pretense of doing good for Catholics." Perhaps this was why Charles had chosen him to remain in England.[32]

With her natural warmth and lively wit, Henrietta was beginning to befriend the Buckingham ladies, who were now her constant companions.[33] Highest in her favor were the duke's mother and wife. The first was a passionate Catholic convert whose Whitehall lodgings were a notorious safe haven for "the most active papists in England," while her daughter-in-law, Katherine, Duchess of Buckingham, was a lifelong Catholic at heart who publicly practiced Anglicanism only to bolster her husband's position. She was also a woman of "very great wit and spirit," and generous as well, who now "presented the queen with a costly coach and six horses valued generally at twenty thousand crowns."[34] But dearest of all the Buckingham party to the queen was a little boy named Jeffery Hudson, whom Buckingham's mother had presented to Henrietta a few months earlier. Emerging from under the crust of a cold pie, Hudson had made an instant impression: at eight years old, he stood a mere eighteen inches high— "a marvelous sight, and the most perfect imperfection of nature that ever was born."[35] Henrietta was enchanted by "Little Jeffery"—or "the queen's dwarf," as he came to be called—a youngster who was fearless and full of fun, throwing himself into all the court pleasures of dancing, hunting, and acting. In fact, so attached did she become that when he fell out of a window at Somerset House that summer, "the queen took it so heavily that she attired not herself that day," even though the boy was not seriously hurt.[36] All in all, Henrietta was "very happy and cheerful" with her new English companions— so much so that in May she accepted Charles's formal regulations for her court, which she had so angrily refused at Hampton Court eighteen months earlier.[37]

But already new challenges were emerging for the queen. England and France were on the verge of war. Charles was preparing a fleet to aid the La Rochelle Huguenots, whom Louis and Richelieu were determined to destroy. During her husband's war with Spain, Henrietta had been happy to play the part of patriotic English queen, celebrating one of his naval successes with a dinner aboard the flagship and then riding in state through London with "a fair white feather in her hat."[38] But the prospect of war with her French family appalled her. She longed to mediate with all "the tenderness of a wife and sister," but she feared her intervention would only offend her husband.[39] So, at her suggestion, one of Louis's courtiers arrived in England. Once he had opened talks, she hoped, she would be able to play her part. But Charles had no sympathy for her predicament. Louis's messenger was suspected as a spy, and when Henrietta finally plucked up the courage to speak to her husband, offering "to mediate for a reconciliation," he flatly "forbade her to do so."[40]

Instead, Charles harkened to Buckingham's eager determination for war. For the duke, it was a matter of personal revenge: the French had twice refused to receive him as an ambassador, leading him to exchange "some very sharp notes" with Cardinal Richelieu, his opposite number in France.[41] All through the early months of 1627, Buckingham devoted himself to preparations, organizing the fleet and army and battling to enforce the king's unpopular fundraising policies, which saw droves of English gentlemen imprisoned for refusing to contribute to the forced loan. When the Royal Treasury failed him, Buckingham rented out his own houses and sold his jewels to raise money "for the use of His Majesty's Navy."[42] He even talked of commanding the expedition in person. Both his mother and his wife went down "upon their knees to dissuade him," but the prospect of revenge was too sweet and the hope of regaining his popularity at home too appealing.[43] Appearing in military costume—"with an immense collar and a magnificent plume of feathers in his hat"—Buckingham posed now as a Protestant hero, the defender of the Huguenots, promising to "spend his strength in the advancement both of religion and state."[44] But his trip had rather the air of a pleasure jaunt. An entire "great collier-ship" was loaded up with his personal provisions: fine food and wine, clothes, jewels, furniture, books, even his coach and litter.[45] Every day, farewell dinners were held in his honor. Buckingham himself arranged two separate extravaganzas for Charles and Henrietta, with masques heroizing his great mission in Europe. Charles's ardor was thoroughly roused, and for two weeks he personally supervised the final preparations at Portsmouth, "in continual action, visiting the soldiers, and seeing them exercised" and going "aboard every ship, great and small."[46] Finally, at 4 a.m. on Wednesday, June 27, the fleet set sail "with a very favorable wind": some thirty warships and forty transports laden with "soldiers, horses, war materials, provisions, and every kind of baggage."[47]

Henrietta put on a brave public face, writing to Buckingham "most heartily and cheerfully" with "her best wishes." But she was profoundly upset. Amid the escalating hostilities, she had not heard from her mother for months, "just as if they had entirely forgotten her in France," she complained.[48] The French diplomatic agent in London was her last link with home, but Charles sent him back to Paris, leaving Henrietta in tears. As Charles set off for his usual summer hunting tour of the Home Counties, she left for Northamptonshire. After more than two years of marriage, she had still failed to become pregnant, leading to widespread public comment on her "sterility" and "barrenness." Now she traveled to the small country town of Wellingborough, noted for its mineral waters, "which facilitate generation."[49]

For six weeks, Charles and Henrietta were apart, and during all that time Charles visited his wife just once, for no more than a couple of days—hardly a recipe for successful "generation," whatever the powers of Wellingborough's water. For all Charles's reconciliation with Henrietta, it was Buckingham who occupied first place in his affections. All that summer, the king worried for his friend, "praying for your good success in all things," and "hoping and longing for your safe return." Even when there was no business to discuss, Charles wrote eagerly to "Steenie," simply "to assure you, that upon all occasions I am glad to remember you, and that no distance of place, nor length of time, can make me slacken, much less diminish my love to you." Charles signed himself, as always, "Your faithful, loving, constant friend."[50]

Weeks passed without news from the duke, leaving the whole nation in suspense. Finally, word came that Buckingham's troops had captured the Île de Ré. It was only a qualified success—the French fort on the island still held out—but Charles was overjoyed.[51] Henrietta, still at Wellingborough, eagerly told the Buckingham ladies of "her love and good wishes" for the duke: she hoped his action would soon win him "the hearts of many." When Charles wrote to her, ponderously "expressing his regret at having to embark in a war with his brother-in-law, solely for the honor of himself and the nation, which the French have slandered," the queen returned a model reply, "expressing equal regret," but adding "that she wished him all success, being more interested for him than for anyone else."[52] Charles was thrilled by her support, and he eagerly informed the Duke of Buckingham:

> My wife and I were never better together; she, upon this action of yours, showing herself so loving to me, by her discretion upon all occasions, that it makes us all wonder and esteem her.[53]

By mail, at least, the couple were growing closer, but they would still have to test it out in person.

For a time, the news from La Rochelle continued to be good. But as summer turned to autumn, and the fort on the Île de Ré still held out, English optimism faded. Buckingham's womenfolk especially were in despair. Her husband was risking his life for nothing, the duchess complained, for "by this action he is not any whit the more popular man than when he went." And Buckingham's mother, the Catholic countess, was more outspoken:

> The kingdom will not supply your expenses, and every man groans under the burden of the times. . . . This is not the way; for you to embroil the whole Christian world in war, and then to declare it for religion, and make God a party to these woeful affairs, so far from God as light from darkness.[54]

Even Charles's exuberance was gone. "Grieved and ashamed," he apologized abjectly to his dear Steenie "for our slowness here in giving you supplies." "For God's sake be not disheartened," he begged, "for, by the grace of God, it is all past."[55] But it was too late. Early in November, the duke and his remaining troops landed at Plymouth, defeated ignominiously in their attempt to storm the fort at Ré. Buckingham insisted that his losses had been slight—just four or five hundred men—but hostile English reporters announced a "great slaughter," "a rout without an enemy," with "great numbers . . . crowded to death, or drowned."[56] Never had Buckingham been so unpopular. The government, in "fear of a rising," issued orders "to refrain from speaking of him, and of the retreat from Ré," which only further increased popular hatred against the duke.[57]

But Charles was still thoroughly enamored. "In this action you have had honor," he assured his friend. "All the shame must light upon us here remaining at home," for failing to send reinforcements in time.[58] At Whitehall he received Buckingham "most joyfully and graciously," treating him "more familiarly and kindly than ever." The two men passed a whole night alone together, while the duke made his report. The next day, Charles summoned his Privy Council, determined to send out a new expedition as soon as possible.[59] Over the following weeks, Buckingham sped between London and Portsmouth, attending to everything himself.

Meanwhile, in Paris, Louis laughed at the English king. "'Alack,' said he, 'if I had known my brother of England had longed so much for the Île de Ré, I would have sold it to him for half the money it hath cost him.'" Further degradation was heaped on the English when the French king ordered their captured guns and standards to be paraded through Paris in a public day of triumph.[60] But Louis had not forgotten his little sister in England, and in December, "of his own accord, without being asked," he released the numerous English prisoners from the Île de Ré and sent them home "as a present" to Henrietta Maria, to bolster her position at the English court.[61] Henrietta seized the opportunity to communicate with her family after the long months of silence. Desperately, she begged them to end "this war between her husband and brother." She knew that Tillières and Bérulle were fomenting the war with stories of her unhappiness in England, and she assured the court that they were "most false." "On the contrary," she enjoyed "complete liberty" in every aspect of her life and received nothing but "good treatment" from her husband.[62] There was certainly no need for the war to continue on her behalf. But for the moment, her appeals fell on deaf ears.

All through the spring of 1628, Charles stayed in London to manage the Parliament he had summoned in a new search for war funding, and the royal couple spent much of their time together. "Hot speech" even went around London "of the queen's being quick with child," although the unfounded rumor soon passed.[63] Despite his own shortage of funds, Charles lavished generosity on his wife: a clear sign of his new warmth. He ordered Henrietta's debts to be paid off, to the tune of £30,000. He gave her some of his own lands, worth £6,000 per year, to increase her income to the level of "the late Queen Anne." At last, in his eyes, Henrietta was coming to deserve the same status and respect as his own beloved mother. The king's gift even included Greenwich Palace, a favorite country resort of Anne's, where she had begun building the luxurious, Italianate Queen's House to designs by Inigo Jones.[64]

To please his wife, Charles even turned a blind eye to the English Catholics who illegally attended Henrietta's chapel, coming in such numbers that it was commonplace to hear people ask, "Have you been to Mass at Somerset House?" Parliament protested vigorously at such "connivance at popery": through the government's toleration, the number of Catholics "increases daily," a "very perilous" situation. Indignant at a whole raft of government abuses, the MPs drew up a formal remonstrance, laying the blame on "the excessive favor, authority, and power of the Duke of Buckingham."[65] Charles responded angrily. "He never expected that the Members . . . would have thus proceeded to intermeddle in questions of religion and state," he told them; "he always supposed that they knew little about them, but he now realizes that they knew nothing at all." Again he dismissed Parliament, and when Henrietta asked him not to approve the new anti-Catholic bill they had just passed, the king readily agreed.[66]

That July, the royal couple parted to spend the summer in their own separate ways. Henrietta revisited Wellingborough, "to facilitate childbearing," and stayed on there for weeks with her courtiers.[67] She had a new special friendship now with Lucy, Countess of Carlisle. It was an unlikely alliance—the devout Catholic queen and the loose-living court beauty—but Lucy was a charming woman, vivacious, witty, and intelligent. A glamorous twenty-eight-year-old, she easily assumed the position of role model for the teenage queen, introducing her to the use of makeup, as the English news reported, murmuring dark fears that Henrietta "in time . . . may by her example be led unto more debaucheries." Lucy's influence was even more resented by Buckingham's mother, wife, and sister, who "do hate her even to death . . . for that she hath the queen's heart above them all."[68] But they had to resign themselves to it: Lucy would remain Henrietta's favorite for the next fourteen years, until she finally betrayed her mistress on the eve of the Civil War.

Meanwhile at Portsmouth, Charles and Buckingham labored to get their great army and navy out to sea. While the king lodged a few miles away in the country house of Southwick, the duke stayed at the Greyhound Inn in Portsmouth itself, taking charge of day-to-day preparations. The business was vast and multifarious—ranging from quelling mutinous sailors, who demanded their pay and shouted "Death to the duke," to providing tapestries to hang in the duke's private cabin.[69] On Saturday, August 23, 1628, Buckingham was still not ready to sail. That morning, as always, his lodgings were thronged with people: courtiers, soldiers, sailors, relatives, servants, hangers-on. It was sometime after 9 a.m. and the duke was on his way out to see the king, "very jocant and well pleased," bearing a report that the starving populace of La Rochelle had been unexpectedly relieved.[70] But as he left the parlor where he had been breakfasting and crossed the crowded hall, a man stepped forward and struck a single knife-blow, "with great strength and violence," deep into his left breast. Buckingham pulled out the dagger at once. "Villain!" he shouted, starting to follow his attacker, whom no one else had seen.[71] But after just a few paces, the duke staggered and fell to the ground. The knife blade had passed through his lungs and into "the very heart itself," and the blood spurted "with much effusion" from his mouth as well as from the wound. Almost at once, without uttering another word, "that noble great person," the Duke of Buckingham—"the greatest and most remarkable favorite whom the world has seen for many centuries"—was dead.[72]

5

NO OTHER FAVORITES

The news about Buckingham reached Charles almost immediately. He was at morning prayers in chapel when the messenger whispered in his ear. Reverently religious and proud in
the sight of his courtiers, the king remained "unmoved, and without
the least change in his countenance," until the service was finished.
Then he fled to his chamber, where he fell on the bed, "lamenting
with much passion and with abundance of tears."[1] Later he summoned his privy councillors for an emergency meeting that lasted
into the night. But Charles would see no one else. All the next day,
he remained in his bedchamber alone, "profoundly afflicted" not
only by his friend's loss but also by "the horrid manner" of his death.
His only other thought was for the widowed duchess. To her he sent
his condolences, promising that he would "extend the protection of
a husband and father to her and to her children."[2]

But Charles and Buckingham's family were the only ones who
mourned. Throughout England, there was "extraordinary joy." In
London, they drank toasts to the murderer; elsewhere it was "very

difficult . . . to prevent bonfires and other rejoicings."[3] One of the first to hear was Henrietta Maria, a hundred miles away at Wellingborough. A long letter reached her from Dudley, Lord Carleton, one of Charles's most trusted councillors, who had witnessed the murder. "Madam," he wrote, "you may easily guess what outcries were then made . . . when we saw him thus dead in a moment, and slain by an unknown hand." Hearing the commotion, the Duchess of Buckingham had emerged from her bedchamber with another lady, and they stood looking down at "the blood of their dearest lord gushing from him." "Ah, poor ladies," Carleton wrote, "such was their screechings, tears, and distractions, that I never in my life heard the like before, and hope never to hear the like again."

In the confusion, the murderer could have escaped easily. But instead—as Buckingham's friends rushed around the inn, shouting, "Where is the villain? Where is the butcher?"—he had drawn his sword and walked out among them. "I am the man, here I am," he said. "With much trouble and difficulty," Carleton and some others prevented the crowd from killing him. As they waited for the king's musketeers to carry away the murderer, Carleton questioned the man. His name was John Felton, and he was a lieutenant in Buckingham's army. Eighty pounds in pay was due to him from the last campaign, and he had been unfairly passed over for promotion, but this was not why he had murdered the duke, he insisted. His only aim had been to "do his country great good service." Expecting to die in the attempt, he had stitched a note into his hat, explaining it all.[4]

Wholeheartedly, Henrietta turned to comforting the "many distressed ladies" in her court—all with Buckingham connections. Her profound sympathy at "the fatal blow" touched everyone, and it was "kindly taken by the king" when he heard. Then she rushed to see Charles, whose "melancholy and discomposure of mind" were clear to everyone, though he did all he could to behave "both manly and princely."[5] All his feelings—anger, frustration, bitterness, desperation—the king now poured into completing the fleet preparations begun by his dead friend. He appointed a new admiral and personally attended to the provisioning of each ship. Amid the delays, Charles fretted and fumed, chivvied and chased, and his subjects were impressed: "The king, they say, in fourteen days after the duke's death, dispatched more business than the duke had done [in the] three months before." At last the fleet sailed: more than eighty ships, heading for Plymouth to rendezvous with some seventy more.[6]

A week later, the Duke of Buckingham was buried in Westminster Abbey. It was a quiet affair: lack of funds and fear of riots put a stop to Charles's plans for "as ample and sumptuous a funeral as could be performed." Instead, hardly more than a hundred mourners accompanied the coffin through the dark evening streets, while the city's militia beat their drums and the crowds behind them murmured ominously, a "noise, more like joy than commiseration."[7] Neither Charles nor Henrietta was present. Already they had left London, on country travels together for the first time. They were inseparable now, Henrietta doing all she could "to comfort and console" her husband.[8] From Hampton Court they rode out together regularly, "enjoying the pleasures of the chase" or making quick visits to London. They visited Buckingham's widow in Chelsea. For Charles, there was therapy in it: he talked constantly of his old friend—"his martyr"—repeating that "the world was much mistaken in him": he had been a "most faithful and obedient servant in all things."[9]

But now others had to be found to fill Buckingham's shoes. More and more every day, people noted, it was Henrietta who received all "the favor and love that were previously divided between her and the duke."[10] Basking in his wife's sympathetic attention, Charles began to draw her into his own political world. Together they orchestrated the return to favor of the aristocrats who would take over Buckingham's responsibilities at court. The Marquess of Hamilton, who had spent six years in Scotland after refusing to consummate his arranged marriage to Buckingham's niece, was now summoned back to become the Master of the King's Horse. That first night of his return, when Hamilton still refused to bed his bride, Henrietta sent him spiced wine and Charles lent him a nightshirt of his own, "and would not be satisfied till he had seen them both in bed together." A few weeks later, the royal couple rehabilitated the duke's old enemy, Thomas Howard, Earl of Arundel, driving in state to his London house to view his famous art collection.[11]

That November, Charles celebrated Henrietta's birthday in style, riding in the joust, an icon of romance and chivalry. The royal couple behaved like young lovers: "You would imagine him a wooer again, and her gladder to receive his caresses than he to make them," a courtier reported. When Charles left London for a few days of hunting, Henrietta was desolate: "Her Majesty can take no rest . . . but sighs for his return." Her only consolation was Charles's portrait, "his shadow at her bedside."[12] By Christmas, there were signs that Henrietta was pregnant: she had conceived just a few weeks after Buckingham's death. Thrilled, Charles was "always with her," and he did all he could to please his wife. First he suspended the execution of the penal laws against the English Catholics. Then, realizing that Henrietta was still being pestered by "clamorous" tradesmen, he reissued his previous year's order that her vast debts should be repaid.[13]

Eagerly the royal couple began to prepare for their "long-desired" new arrival, appointing courtiers to the baby's royal household and making arrangements for the birth and christening.[14] Throughout the nation, in every parish church, prayers were said "for the safe childbearing of the Queen's Majesty": "Lord, . . . keep her safe . . . that there may be strength to bring forth her joy and our hope. And make her a joyful mother of many children." Public celebrations were ordered: bonfires were lighted and bells were rung, and all London's foreign ambassadors came to congratulate the royal couple, "much to their satisfaction."[15] But much of the population was far from pleased. What if Charles were assassinated? Then Henrietta, as a papist queen regent during her baby's infancy, "might mar all." Wild rumors circulated of her pernicious influence over her husband, even that she had taken him to Mass—a story that stirred one loyal Englishman into murderous desires to strike "another Gunpowder [plot] blow."[16] When Charles dissolved yet another Parliament, disappointed as always in his hopes for funds, Henrietta, like Buckingham before her, got the blame. The king had been "well inclined to the Parliament," the rumor went, "but lying with the queen all night, the next morning, his mind was changed," and that very day he sent the MPs home. The government acted fast to suppress the story.

One female servant was arrested for repeating it and saying "that she wished the queen were ducked in the midst of the sea . . . with a millstone round her neck."[17]

Henrietta's power was growing. By her intervention with the king, a condemned Jesuit priest was "not only reprieved, but pardoned." Boatloads of captured French fishermen were released after she "exerted herself with much warmth" on their behalf.[18] But there was one project that mattered more to her than any other: making peace between England and France. Her great ally in this was the Venetian ambassador in London, Alvise Contarini, whose government desired an Anglo-French alliance against Spain. Already, just weeks after Buckingham's death, Contarini had drafted a treaty. Having seen the king, who said he would "think about it," Contarini went straight to Henrietta, who promised "with great joy and readiness" to speak to Charles that night.[19] "She did not pretend to interfere in state affairs," she assured her husband, "yet the reconciliation with her brother concerned her greatly," and Charles had to "excuse her if she dared to recommend to him the negotiation" begun by Contarini. Charles readily yielded to her entreaties: that same evening, he sent word to Contarini that he would begin talks.[20]

Still Charles was unwilling to desert the Huguenots, but then came the "most heavy and bitter news." Despite the presence of the English fleet off La Rochelle, the Huguenots had been forced to surrender.[21] Many thousands had starved to death waiting for English help that never came, and the survivors looked more "like ghosts than men." The French king had ordered them fed, but, too starved to eat, they died "with the meat in their mouths." All England was shocked and shamed, and Charles, powerless, was now "entirely in favor of peace."[22] But there was one topic on which he would never compromise: his wife's household. When the French demanded that he honor Bassompierre's treaty of two years earlier, Charles refused point-blank. "The king knows that the French made trouble," his courtiers explained, "and for the future he means to be master here."[23] Even Henrietta was unenthusiastic, fearing that new French courtiers would only stir up more disagreements. Instead, she sent word to her mother that she was "perfectly satisfied" with her court.

She was being well treated in religious matters, too, so there was no need for the French to make treaty terms on her behalf.[24] Still Louis would not back down, so, in the end, the peace settlement between the two nations was merely a "cessation of arms," leaving all important matters to be settled by an exchange of ambassadors. Nonetheless, on Sunday, May 10, 1629, at Greenwich Palace, peace was ceremoniously proclaimed "by sound of trumpet and four heralds," while the royal couple watched in satisfaction, standing together "in a window of the gallery."[25] Henrietta by now was almost seven months pregnant.

The next day, she went to Somerset House, "where she had the 'Te Deum' solemnly chanted" in thanksgiving for the peace.[26] But as she returned in her barge to Greenwich that evening, she suffered a fall. It was from this, many people thought, that "the child was turned and dislocated in her womb." Others blamed a fright she had had two days earlier, when she came upon "two great dogs" fighting in her gallery at Greenwich, one of which "did snatch at her and pull her by the gown." Others spoke of the unnatural "violence of her exercises," for Henrietta loved to go out walking, climbing the hill above Greenwich, with its magnificent views over country and river to London itself.[27] But whatever the cause, on the night of Tuesday, May 12, about midnight, Henrietta began to be "oppressed by the pains of childbirth."[28] Nothing was prepared: the French court ladies summoned "to wait on her in childbed" had not yet arrived, nor had the French royal midwife, Madame Peronne, whom Marie de' Medici had promised to send. So unexpected was the labor that there were not even English court physicians or midwives at Greenwich.[29]

Instead, behind the shuttered windows and guarded doors that tradition required for royal births, it was the king himself who hovered in "constant attendance at the bedside," defying the custom that normally excluded all men from the delivery room. On the white linen sheets, with all her rings, laces, and buckles removed—according to the superstition that this would ease her labor—Henrietta was in agonies of pain, with her baby in the wrong position, "turned overthwart in her belly."[30] The local Greenwich mid-

*King Charles I and Henrietta Maria in the early years of their marriage,
ready to go out hunting together. Henrietta's dwarf, Jeffery Hudson,
holds one of the dogs. Such joint expeditions
were a regular part of the couple's married life.*

George Villiers, Duke of Buckingham, and his family. During the 1620s, the duke was the handsomest man at court and Charles I's greatest favorite. On her arrival in England, Henrietta detested him, but Buckingham's wife and daughter later became her close friends.

Charles I and Henrietta Maria with their two eldest children. Two-year-old Prince Charles, wearing a toddler's gown and cap, stands by his father, while Henrietta holds baby Mary in her arms. Crown, scepter, and orb rest on the table beside the king, who stares authoritatively toward the viewer. But there are hints, too, of a more domestic life: a lapdog sports at the couple's feet; the prince's hands rest gently on his father's knee, while the king extends his right arm protectively behind his little son.

One of the grandest portraits of Charles I produced by his favorite painter, Sir Anthony Van Dyck. Here Charles appears as a victorious emperor, riding under a triumphal arch bearing a general's baton. In his pose of effortless superiority, he lords it over his surroundings and over us as we view him from below. The painter has erased all traces of the king's social and physical awkwardness. Charles had this portrait hung at the end of the Long Gallery at St. James's Palace, dominating paintings of the Roman emperors, by Titian and Giulio Romano, that lined the gallery's long side walls.

*Henrietta Maria as painted by Van Dyck: divinely beautiful and
remote, a queen indeed, the true object of Charles's "heroic love and
regal respect." Van Dyck's numerous portraits of the queen give no
hint of the fun-loving woman in her twenties who had "an infinity
of . . . brilliant wit" and passed much of her time in "frivolous
but innocent things."*

Charles and Henrietta Maria out walking on the hill above Greenwich
Palace, with their eldest son, Prince Charles, and their courtiers. The royal
couple loved their country life at Greenwich and spent a month
or two there at the start of every summer.

*Charles and Henrietta Maria dining in royal state. Their most important
courtiers stand in a semicircle behind the royal pair, while dinner is borne in
by a procession of gentlemen, and a royal cupbearer serves wine from
a separate table. No one except other royalty was allowed
to sit down in the presence of the king and queen.*

Lucy, Countess of Carlisle—the most beautiful and witty of all the court ladies, and Henrietta Maria's great favorite. Lucy was notorious for her love affairs, and she caused much suspicion when she introduced the teenage queen to the use of makeup in 1628. In the political crisis of 1642, she betrayed the king's plans to visit Parliament and arrest traitorous MPs. The English Civil War soon followed.

wife, summoned to face the emergency, "swooned with fear" when she realized she was supposed to minister to the queen. In fact, there was little she could have done, for the seventeenth-century midwife came armed with little more than sponges, poultices, and ointments. Realizing that both his wife and child were in "the greatest danger," the king summoned a London specialist: the fashionable surgeon Peter Chamberlen.[31]

Normally surgeons were called in only as a last resort, for the hook they used to extract the baby killed the child if it was not already dead. But Chamberlen was known for his unusual success, gained by using a trio of revolutionary iron instruments—forceps, vectis, and fillet—which would remain a secret of the Chamberlen medical dynasty for another hundred years.[32] But "the queen was at such an extremity" that the surgeon could only offer Charles the stark choice: "They could save either her or her child." For Charles, the decision was clear. "He could have other children, please God," but Henrietta was irreplaceable.[33]

The vectis was probably the first instrument that Chamberlen used—as a lever to turn the baby's head down into the normal delivery position. Then, pulling with the forceps or the fillet—a long-handled noose looped around the baby's head—Chamberlen, "with his own hands, removed the creature from her belly" at around three in the morning.[34] Despite the surgeon's dire predictions, the baby emerged alive: a boy, the first royal heir to be born in England since Henry VIII's son, Edward VI, more than ninety years earlier. But Charles's long-cherished christening ceremonies were abandoned. There would be no processions of richly dressed nobility, no tapestries and swathes of cloth of gold and silver, no anthems, drums, trumpets, and thundering cannons. The child was failing fast. In the rush to make sure he did not die unbaptized, the tiny Prince of Wales was carried unceremoniously to the font, where Dr. Webb, "then chaplain in attendance" at court, christened him Charles, after his father. Within an hour or so of his birth, the boy was dead.[35]

The court was devastated, and Charles, "more than anyone else, showed himself most affected by it." If only the pregnancy had lasted a little longer; just a few more weeks, the physicians said, and this "hopeful prince" might have lived. But now "the fruit of their desires has been cut off."[36] The premature delivery, especially given Chamberlen's intervention, could easily prevent Henrietta from having more children, it was believed—a thought that left Charles "very greatly distressed." Yet Henrietta herself "was doing well, and was full of strength and courage." A flock of medical personnel attended her now—"physicians, surgeons, midwives, and others"—and the ladies of the court paid the customary calls.[37] While she remained at Greenwich with her bedchamber windows covered and the fire burning, as tradition demanded for her lying-in, her baby was carried to London for burial. Beneath a black velvet canopy, six earls' sons bore the tiny coffin to Westminster Abbey. Behind the children and their little burden followed a grand procession of noblemen, bishops, judges, and court gentlemen, who saw the little prince laid to rest beside the body of his grandfather, King James.[38]

For more than a month, the royal couple remained quietly at Greenwich. Henrietta quickly recovered her health and Charles began to hope there would soon be another pregnancy. Early in July, they left to spend the summer "away hunting, passing from one country house to another": Nonsuch, Windsor, Theobalds, Oatlands, Woodstock.[39] They parted only briefly: once when Henrietta visited Tunbridge Wells to drink the waters for her health, and again in September when she stopped at Somerset House to celebrate the Exaltation of the Cross, "being a great day of devotion with her."[40] But otherwise they were together. In fact, the king spent so much time in his wife's apartments, his privy councillors complained, that it was impossible to speak to him except when he was out hunting. Charles, oblivious to the courtiers' disapproval, kissed Henrietta repeatedly in front of them, congratulating himself on how happy his marriage was. "You do not see that at Turin [where Henrietta's sister, Christine, was married to the Duke of Savoy]," he boasted to the new French ambassador, "nor at Paris," he added, referring to Louis XIII's notoriously loveless and childless marriage. "I wish that we could be always together," he told his wife, "and that you could accompany me to the council." But that he knew was impossible, for "what would these people say if a woman were to busy herself with matters of government?"[41]

With others, Charles remained as reserved and unbending as ever, "a prince of few words" who "obliges no one, either in deed or word."[42] But in Henrietta's company he was a different man, as full of wit and fun as she was. He teased his wife for her long morning lie-ins; she should at least try to get up in time to attend Mass with her priests before noon, he scolded. Her lavish extravagance, despite his court's dire financial straits, provoked nothing more than indulgent joking: "She is a bad housekeeper," he confided loudly to the French ambassador within Henrietta's hearing.[43]

This new ambassador, the Marquis de Chateauneuf-sur-Cher, was empowered to negotiate all the outstanding disputes between the two nations. Henrietta had to have twelve priests for her chapel, he insisted, with a bishop as grand almoner, as well as a French *dame d'honneur* and physician. But Charles was unyielding. The Buckingham ladies were quite sufficient; there would be no French physician, and certainly no bishop, he insisted, still smarting from the affronts of the Bishop of Mende. Twelve priests he would allow, but not the Oratorians.[44] After three months of fruitless labors, Chateauneuf was furious. He had expected that Henrietta's "great influence" would make Charles "concede everything by courtesy" to her.[45] But she had refused to lift a finger. Seeing nothing beyond her own present happiness, she was incapable of any sustained effort, Chateauneuf complained. She had even obstructed him, insisting that Father Philip remain with her, contrary to the French government's wishes.[46] They had selected Capuchins to serve her now— another order much favored by the French royal family—and wanted Fathers Philip and Viette to return to France so there would be "no diversity of tempers and conducts" among her priests, whose rivalry might weaken their mission in England. But Henrietta stood firm: the two Oratorians would stay on beside the Capuchins—an awkward mishmash of orders that pleased no one but her.[47]

She was, however, readier to aid Chateauneuf in his attempts to prolong England's hostilities against Spain. Charles was now desperately poor—he could "hardly find the means to provide for the daily needs of himself and the queen," let alone fund a war[48]—so he decided to open formal peace talks. When Chateauneuf failed to change the king's mind, he turned to Henrietta. But even she found it difficult to influence Charles in a matter so vital to his financial and political interests. When she warned her husband "that the Spaniards would only deceive him once again," Charles "retorted that that was only her opinion." In a fit of pique, she snubbed the new ambassador leaving for Madrid, telling him "she would have nothing to do with Spain, nor with any person there."[49] "She shed tears in anger," but still "she could not prevail with his majesty" to cancel the embassy—even though Charles and his courtiers were now delighted, "in practically certain hopes," that she was pregnant again. By November, Henrietta had missed two periods, and her craving for mussels—for which she "sent all about the town"—alerted the English public to her delicate state.[50]

It was not an easy pregnancy. "Owing to her tender age and delicate constitution, she suffers some discomfort," the Venetian ambassador reported in January 1630, when Henrietta was five months pregnant.[51] But preparations for the new arrival continued, much as the previous year. Again public prayers were offered up. Again London's ambassadors congratulated the royal couple. Further expensive purchases were made: £2,000 for "linen for the queen's lying-in," and more than £600 for embroidery for her bed. And again Henrietta expected her mother's midwife, Madame Peronne, and some nurses from Paris "for the coming confinement."[52]

Amid it all, a new French ambassador arrived in London. The Marquis de Fontenay-Mareuil came to replace the Marquis de Chateauneuf, bringing with him the Capuchin priests who were to serve in Henrietta's chapel. The Capuchins were one of the most successful missionary orders of the time, even more severely devoted to poverty and simplicity than the Franciscan order from which they had emerged. The twelve handpicked friars arrived in London fired up not only to serve the queen but also to "promote the glory of God in the assisting of Catholics and in the conversion of Protestants." Certainly they expected to accomplish more than Henrietta's old Oratorians, who had "quitted England, without any advancement of the Catholic religion," they thought.[53]

After four years with just two priests, Henrietta was delighted to see the full ceremonial rituals of the Catholic Mass return to her chapel. The sermon on the Capuchins' first Sunday gave her "wonderful satisfaction," and their appearance, on her orders, in their simple habits and sandals caused a sensation. London's Catholics flocked to Henrietta's chapel "in hundreds and thousands," seeing her priests "as men sent by Heaven" and dreaming of a new era of religious freedom. Protestants came too, to gawk and laugh at the Capuchins, "clothed in dresses so extraordinary and so strange," though at least one in the crowd, a convinced Puritan, stayed on, impressed, to be converted.[54]

Charles, away in the country hunting, was appalled when he heard of the flagrant appearance of the Capuchins, "very conspicuously, preaching in their habit," causing "a great stir among all the Puritan party." In a bid to win back public popularity, he announced, despite the terms of the marriage treaty, that in his new baby's nursery "there should neither be nurse, rocker, nor any other officer . . . save only Protestants." He also issued orders that "none of his subjects shall go any more to Mass in the queen's chapel"; guards would be posted there, and at all the foreign ambassadors' chapels, to arrest any of his Catholic subjects trying to get in.[55] Despite Henrietta's anger at these orders, Charles stood firm: it was against the terms of her marriage treaty "that her chaplains should be used by any but by herself and her own servants." In the following weeks, there was bloodshed outside the houses of the French and Spanish ambassadors, whose servants issued forth "with their naked swords" to defend their coreligionists, but still the arrests continued.[56] For Charles it was a public relations triumph. He was a true defender of the nation's faith, the news reported: his subjects had to "live in the religion that I profess and my father before me," he had told his wife. But behind the scenes, Charles did his best to appease Henrietta, releasing many of the arrested Catholics.[57]

In March, the queen passed the point where her previous pregnancy had ended prematurely. This time she was taking things carefully. There were no strenuous country walks; instead, she rode out in the sedan chair her mother had sent from Paris. It was a wonderful thing, "handsomer than I deserve," she wrote to Marie. A little heart that Marie also sent was even more treasured. Henrietta wore it around her neck all the time, "for I fancy it brings me such good fortune that I am always afraid when I am without it." Charles also sent his thanks, especially for the sedan chair, for on Henrietta's "preservation, and on this new hope that God has given us, depends my content."[58]

Soon the French midwife and nurses arrived in London; their tangle with Dunkirk pirates while crossing the Channel, which "moved the queen to tears," was safely over.[59] Henrietta wanted to give birth at Greenwich, and, with the plague increasing, the whole court was eager to leave London. But soon Greenwich was infected, too. And so, afraid to travel farther with the queen very close to her time, the royal couple stayed on in St. James's Palace.

> The place proves very agreeable to both their Majesties . . . the king having his recreations near, and the queen her entertainments and devotions, for which the new-built chapel is decently adorned, and the new-come Capuchins lodged commodiously beyond the austerity of their rule.[60]

On Friday, May 28, 1630, Henrietta received another "most beautiful present" from her mother, "of divers linen and other things" for the new baby.[61] Around dawn the next day, the labor began. Again there were the shuttered windows, the guarded doors, the burning fire, the queen in pain on her linen sheets. The surgeon Peter Chamberlen was in attendance, as a precaution, but this time the birth was managed by Madame Peronne, and everything went as well as could be wished. By noon, the twenty-year-old queen found herself, "(God be thanked) . . . in good estate," "the happy mother of a Prince of Wales."[62] Charles was overjoyed. A year after the death of his first baby, he now had a healthy son: "a fair prince" showing every indication that "he will be very strong and vigorous."[63] At St. James's that day, a handful of privileged callers were ushered in to see Britain's "great joy and expectation" lying in his cradle, while his happy nurses told and retold the story of how "he had never clenched his fists, but had always kept his hands open"—a sure sign "that he will be a prince of great liberality."[64] Charles received the visitors' congratulations "with much joviality and with demonstrations of great pleasure." In his excitement, he even reversed his former strictures about the baby's household: to his wife's great pleasure, he now named the Catholic Countess of Roxburghe as governess in charge of the prince's household.[65] For the king, the whole day had to consist only of joy. By his orders, prisoners were released from jail and public prosecutions were abandoned, and that night the whole city came alive with bonfires burning and bells ringing and every possible expression "in the language of public rejoicing." Even the heavens themselves seemed to join in England's bliss, for the next day, as Charles and the nobility rode in state to St. Paul's Cathedral for a special service of thanksgiving, a new star appeared in the sky, visible even in bright daylight, promising good fortune.[66]

PART TWO

PARADISE LOST

6

THE COURT OF LOVE

Twenty-seven days after the birth of her son, Henrietta Maria knelt, holding a lighted candle, just inside the door of her chapel at St. James's, while one of her priests recited from the Psalms. Holding a corner of the priest's stole, she advanced to the altar, where he sprinkled her with holy water in the form of a cross. It was the Catholic "churching" ceremony, purifying and blessing a woman after a birth and readying her to bring up her child in a Christian manner.[1] But all was not as it seemed. In normal practice, this ceremony was performed only after the baby's Catholic baptism. But the rule had had to be waived for Henrietta. Charles had insisted on an Anglican christening for his son, and two days after the queen's churching, the ceremony took place. Rich tapestries swathed the walls of the king's chapel at St. James's. The Lord Mayor of London wore his velvet, the city's aldermen their scarlet gowns. Lords stood on the left, ladies on the right. Buckingham's niece, the teenaged Marchioness of Hamilton, carried the baby to the baptismal font, walking beneath a canopy borne by six barons.

The nation's foremost nobles were proxies for the boy's royal god-parents: Louis XIII and Marie de' Medici of France and Charles's brother-in-law, Frederick, Elector Palatine. William Laud, Bishop of London, dipped water from a great golden basin and named the boy Charles. Then heralds pronounced the prince's full royal titles, to cheers from "the crowding multitude" outside, while drums and trumpets sounded and cannons thundered from the Tower of London and the ships on the Thames.[2]

Henrietta's priests were outraged, protesting that the rearing of the royal children in their own faith had been promised in the marriage treaty. Historians ever since have repeated this charge, but in fact the English and French negotiators had left the treaty deliberately vague, stipulating only that the children be brought up under their mother's care until the age of thirteen.[3] If Henrietta herself felt disappointed, she showed no sign of it. Neither she nor Charles was present at the font: the Anglican liturgy of the time gave parents no role in the christening ceremony. Instead, Charles watched from a window while Henrietta waited in her bedchamber. There the royal couple received the returning christening party in state, before their son was carried back to his nursery.[4]

That night, bonfires filled the city again and church bells rang out. But many Puritans thoroughly regretted the birth. The children of Charles's sister, Elizabeth of Bohemia, were more suitable heirs to the throne, they thought, for they had been "brought up in the Reformed religion; whereas it was uncertain what religion the king's children will follow," since they would be "brought up under a mother so devoted to the Church of Rome." One Puritan was so incensed that he asserted that Henrietta had been precontracted to another man before she married Charles, which made the prince a bastard—a claim so seditious that the culprit was "like to be hanged, drawn, and quartered."[5]

As June ended, the whole nation was in terror of the plague, which spread with the summer heat. Soon Charles and Henrietta left London, first for Nonsuch and then on to the remote New Forest and Titchfield, their refuge during the plague year of 1625. But the couple's two-month-old baby, too small and vulnerable to travel, was left behind at St. James's. There the tiny Prince of Wales had a household of more than thirty people. There were eight rockers for the baby's cradle, and eight more maids to wait on them. There were nurses, a physician, an apothecary, a laundress and her maids, and a wet nurse whose breastfeeding would be the baby's only source of food for his first year.[6] In charge of them all was the prince's lady governess—not the Catholic Countess of Roxburghe whom the elated father had named on the day of the birth but rather the Anglican Countess of Dorset. The appointment forced Henrietta to break solemn oaths she had made before her marriage to "select none but Catholics to nurse, bring up and serve the children which may be born." Yet now, eager to keep her husband's favor and well aware of the futility of protesting, Henrietta gave way with good grace. Besides, the Countess of Dorset was well known to the queen and had family members who were Catholics. The countess's husband, now Henrietta's grand chamberlain, was even suspected of secret Catholic sympathies.[7]

The plague that summer was nothing like the epidemic of five years earlier, but still the city emptied, the theaters closed.[8] St. James's remained in strict isolation, but from Nonsuch Palace, Charles and Henrietta made day trips to see the prince, "who prospereth exceedingly, to their great joy." When the royal couple moved farther away, daily letters kept them abreast of the boy's progress. "He thrives well," his physician reported on Sunday, August 15: "He has neither sucked nor wakened but once all that night." And twelve days later: "The Prince's favor, likelihood, strength, mirth, and night's rest increase daily. The lady governess is most careful and diligent."[9] By late September, the king and queen were back near London. Henrietta doted on her little boy. "He is so fat and so tall that he is taken for a year old," she wrote to Mamie Saint-Georges, "and he is only four months: his teeth are already beginning to come." "I wish you could see the gentleman," she enthused again, "for he has no ordinary mien; he is so serious in all that he does, that I cannot help fancying him far wiser than myself." Proudly she dispatched portraits of her baby to her far-flung family.[10]

That autumn was a happy time, with the whole family reunited and Henrietta suspecting she was pregnant again. For Charles's birthday on November 19, 1630, there were unprecedented celebrations—all the church bells ringing "and above a thousand bonfires kindled that night."[11] A few days later came news that the long-desired peace treaty with Spain had been signed in Madrid. With the Spanish refusing to restore the Palatinate to his sister's family, Charles had had to be satisfied with a mere promise that they would "be mediators" in the matter. But still he was delighted. He was determined now to follow his father's precepts and stand back from the religious and political conflicts of Europe. With no expensive foreign wars, he would be able to fulfill his longtime dream of governing the nation without calling Parliament.[12]

It was the beginning of a new chapter in British history. For Puritans, it would be an era of oppression, but Charles and his courtiers looked forward to a "time of universal quiet and peace" both at home and abroad.[13] That Christmas, the royal couple expressed their high expectations in two specially created masques: dramatic extravaganzas, one performed by the king and his gentlemen for the queen's entertainment, the other by the queen and her ladies for the king. Written by Ben Jonson, with Inigo Jones as designer of the spectacular visual effects, the two dramas shared a single theme: the nature of true love—chaste, rational, noble, aspiring—and its power to reform the world. On the stage, Henrietta was the goddess Chloris—"queen of the flowers and mistress of the spring" and "the top of paramours"—whose love and flower power banished the goblins of hatred, jealousy, and fear and established an era of peace and happiness. In the king's masque, Charles played the heroic lover whose band of "perfect lovers"—modest, courteous, and valiant— drove away all the enemies of Callipolis, the city of beauty. "Joy, joy to mortals," the masque proclaimed, "whilst love presents a world of chaste desires."[14]

That winter, Henrietta's hopes she might be pregnant proved unfounded, but no one was too disappointed, for "the youth and vigor of their Majesties affords unquenchable hopes of good fortune in the matter of the succession." And in the New Year of 1631, the queen conceived again. Her new baby was born in the early hours of Friday, November 4, "after a few hours' travail."[15] The little girl, three weeks early and "very weak," was christened at once, without ceremony, and named Mary after her mother and grandmother. But, despite her parents' fears, the tiny princess did well, "so . . . nothing is wanting to make this joy entire."[16]

As the years passed, the royal family grew steadily. In 1633, another boy was born, "a goodly, lusty child," named James after Charles's father and given the title Duke of York. Two years later came another daughter, Elizabeth, and in 1637 there was another "new princess for the kingdom," named Anne after Charles's mother.[17] Each new child was a joy, but Henrietta often found the pregnancies difficult. The pregnancy with James, in particular, brought a host of ailments, including vomiting and spells of exhaustion. Then, at seven months, her right arm was almost paralyzed, and her physicians feared she would lose the use of that side of her body. Charles abandoned his hunting break and rushed to join her at Somerset House, but already she was "out of danger and bettering hourly."[18]

For each birth, Henrietta retired to St. James's Palace, believing that only there, where her first surviving son had been born, would all turn out well. Even in 1637, with the plague raging, the queen insisted on returning from Hampton Court for Anne's birth.[19] As Henrietta waited through the last few weeks for her labor to begin, Charles was always there, a solicitous husband, never failing "to procure for her all suitable comforts." Each time, the birth was managed by Madame Peronne and her French nurses. Then Henrietta remained for three weeks in her bedchamber, "recovering from the trials of her delivery," while Charles sat by her "the greatest part of the day."[20] Afterward came her churching ceremony and reemergence into public life.

Each royal child had his or her own establishment of servants, although none was waited on as grandly as Prince Charles, the heir to the throne. Instead of his thirty personnel, ten or fewer became the norm for the others, including a single nurse and a mere four rockers. As the babies grew into busy little toddlers, their rockers were in constant attendance, holding them up for a last look out the window at bedtime, making sure they were properly dressed in hat and neckerchief against any chill evening air. Then, as the children grew, the wet nurse and rockers were replaced by a band of watchers and a dry nurse. Over them all was the lady governess, caring for the child as well as managing the entire household and its finances. For James, as for Prince Charles, this was the Countess of Dorset, but for the girls, less politically sensitive, Charles went back to his original plan, appointing the Countess of Roxburghe.[21]

The children began early on the courtly training that was all-important for royal life. Even before his second birthday, Charles, Prince of Wales, was receiving foreign ambassadors with his parents. By the age of four, he was giving audiences of his own, in company with his little sister and brother—James had only just passed his first birthday. The children's behavior on these occasions was closely scrutinized: Charles reproved the six-year-old Prince of Wales, the Venetian ambassador reported, "for having received me too stolidly when I kissed his hand."[22] There were other grand events, too. Prince Charles accompanied his father to the annual Garter ceremonies, and at eight was himself installed as a Knight of the Garter— an honor the boy desired "exceedingly."[23] Sometimes the children dined in state with their parents in front of a watching crowd, and they joined the adults on stage to perform in court masques.

Academic education, by contrast, was a low priority. The children were tutored in French and the girls learned to sing, but even at the age of nine Prince Charles was still learning to use a pen, his large letters smudged and painstakingly formed on paper that had been specially ruled with guidelines. As the prince grew older, Brian Duppa, Bishop of Chichester, was made his tutor—not so much for his scholarship but because he was a perfect gentleman, who

> hath no pedantry in him, . . . reads men as well as books . . . and in a word strives as much discreetly to hide the scholar in him, as other men's follies study to show it.[24]

Just as in Henrietta's childhood *troupeau*, now all her children grew up together. St. James's Palace was their London residence, with its extensive gardens and orchards and a fine library and art collection containing more than 550 paintings and 300 pieces of sculpture. For the boys, there was an armory with model forts and soldiers, a riding house, and an artillery house with child-size cannons. But much of their time was spent at Richmond Palace, the traditional home for the royal children, "upon account of the unusual wholesomeness of the air."[25] Here a jumble of stone and brick buildings towered picturesquely over the River Thames, enclosing several courtyards, which made the rooms "very light and pleasant." In the gardens and the various "houses of pleasure" were facilities for bowls, tennis, archery, and billiards. There were houses for pigeons and other birds, and in the 1630s King Charles created a great new deer park, covering much the same area as modern Richmond Park.[26]

Though etiquette decreed they should live in separate palaces, Charles and Henrietta loved to be in their children's company. In London they joined them at St. James's for supper, and at Richmond they visited for days at a time. A Catholic priest accompanying the royal couple on one of their visits experienced firsthand "the happiness of those little princes [and princesses] at the arrival of their majesties." Then,

> in the evening they all ate together, the prince and the Duke of York at the king's side, and the Princess Mary at the queen's; the Princess Elizabeth, being still very small, did not appear at table.

Their private family life, he noted, was full of "reciprocal affection." Instead of the royal ceremony and hauteur that would have been expected, there was "a courtesy as singular as could be found in the house of any private well-bred gentleman."[27]

Prince Charles was particularly close to his parents, and the historical record provides glimpses of the life they shared. In 1633, we see the king ready to leave for Scotland, spending his last evening walking in St. James's Park with his nearly three-year-old son, and staying out "a little too late," as the boy's physicians thought when he fell ill. Two months later, the prince welcomed his father home "with the prettiest innocent mirth that can be imagined."[28] In 1636, he performed on stage as Prince Britomart, with a band of "little cavaliers," for his mother's entertainment.[29] Two years later, we see him admiring a new, beautifully bound book of his father's and asking for one himself, which the king arranged, to the boy's delight. Later again, he is an agile eleven-year-old out riding with his father. Seeing a hare, the king took a shot and wounded it, at which the prince "skipped off his horse, and ran after her" through a couple of water-filled ditches, caught her, "and laughing showed her to the king."[30]

Of course there also were moments of exasperation. Three-year-old Mary embarrassed her mother by refusing to sit still to have her portrait painted. "I shall have another done of her, which will be better," Henrietta had to promise her sister Christine.[31] Three years later, Prince Charles annoyed his mother by obstinately refusing to follow doctors' orders. "Charles," Henrietta wrote,

> I am sore that I must begin my first letter with chiding you, because I hear that you will not take physic. I hope it was only for this day and that tomorrow you will do it, for if you will not, I must come to you and make you take it, for it is for your health.[32]

Often Henrietta would rush to be with her ill children, excusing herself from royal business.[33] When the king was away in Scotland, Prince Charles suffered a gastric infection, with days of evil-smelling, blood-spotted diarrhea, "the like whereof I did never see come from a child of his age," one of his doctors commented. It was potentially fatal, and Henrietta, "so troubled . . . that I was not myself," stayed constantly with her son at St. James's, consulting physicians and approving their remedies: milk enemas "to refresh his intestines and suage his pain," followed by a gentle purge of senna and rhubarb.[34] As the boy began to recover, Henrietta had him moved to the healthier air of Greenwich, where she supervised his diet and brought him out from the sickroom into lively company. Throughout, the queen was a marvel of solicitude. "A more truly virtuous, noble, wise, sweet young lady did I never behold," a courtier enthused; "also the best wife and mother in the world."[35]

For the royal couple—Charles progressing through his thirties,

Henrietta in her twenties—the 1630s were certainly a golden age, with the years passing in an idyllic round. Later—battered by the Civil War, bereaved, impoverished, exiled—the Royalists looked back with the greatest nostalgia on the glorious days of spring and summer. Lovingly they painted their memories of an "enchanted island" untouched by the ravages of war: of dappled light beneath ancient oaks, of meadow grass so lush it reached to the cattle's bellies; of hares lying in their forms all day, and stags venturing from the woods to eat the sweet marjoram on the hills. The country scents were vivid, too—cows' breath, "a field of beans when newly blown, or . . . a meadow being lately mown"—and the people in the landscape with their simple pastimes: playing tabors and pipes; tying cowslips into a ball for a lover's gift; dancing. Then too there were the delights of "most innocent convenient country houses," with their "shady walks and close arbors," which made one exiled Catholic courtier "sigh to be again . . . in little England, where time slideth more gently away than in any part of the world."[36]

Charles and Henrietta enjoyed this idyll to the utmost. Each year, as the weather warmed, they left London for "the pleasant position and the more healthy air" of Greenwich, five miles down the Thames.[37] They spent up to two months there, still close enough to London for government business to continue amid the place's many rural pleasures. There was hunting, of course, and there were long walks up the hill above the town, where sheep grazed and huntsmen walked with their dogs. The prospect from here—across rich hedged fields to the silvery bends of the River Thames scattered with shipping and London beyond—was the most admired view in England, painted by a succession of artists. Just a short distance from the splendors of their palace, they could be deep in the countryside, where they might suddenly come across "a shepherd and his little boy reading . . . the Bible to him," or the milkmaids returning home "in pomp with their milk" while musicians played before them. Henrietta in particular was well known for "her taste for the country," where "the dances of the peasantry amuse her."[38]

And Greenwich was only the beginning. In July began the summer progress itself, sometimes with a stay at Oatlands—Henrietta's palace in Surrey—or else a stop at Theobalds, "one of the most charming places belonging to the Crown near London and especially enjoyable for every kind of hunting."[39] Then they went on farther, staying in royal hunting lodges—Woodstock, Newmarket, and Royston were all favorites of Charles's—and in the houses of the nation's leading aristocrats. Mostly these stops were short—just a few nights spent by the court in a gentleman's house were enough to exhaust most private pockets. But at Wilton, a hundred miles west of London, the wealthy Earl of Pembroke was lavishly hospitable and even redesigned his house and grounds according to Charles's tastes: "all *al* Italian," with a "magnificent garden and grotto." Charles loved Wilton "above all places: and came thither every summer."[40] Then, as September drew on, the court returned closer to London for extended stays at Windsor Castle and Hampton Court.

It was a huge production: two entire royal retinues traveling through the English countryside. Everyone and everything went with them: Henrietta took her dwarfs, monkeys, lapdogs, even "the billiard boards," as well as her priests and chapel choir, who performed "with most beautiful music" wherever she stopped.[41] An army of servants went before them, making everything ready. The county authorities repaired the roads, and "extraordinary stages for posts" were arranged to make sure the king received important correspondence promptly.[42] But Charles paid little attention to business during these summer months. Ambassadors grew desperate, unable to fulfill their masters' "repeated instructions," because he was "far away hunting or else engaged in other recreations," "grown drowsy . . . in the charms of peace." Even if they managed to catch up with him, their attempts to talk business were often skillfully diverted by Charles into talk of "hunting, pictures, and the like." "Immersed in the delights of banquets, in his affection for his wife and in the pleasures of the chase," the king "would never come to any decision of consequence."[43]

Sometimes the royal couple took a company of professional actors with them from London, with a large tent for their performances. Or else the queen and her courtiers appeared on stage themselves in masques created for special occasions.[44] One summer night in 1634, Henrietta even "consented to sing . . . in hearing of the [Savoyard] ambassador and, after supper, danced with him and others, both French and English dances till after midnight." The queen's singing was a rare and special pleasure, as a court poet enthused:

> Never any earthly thing
> Sung so true, so sweet, so clear;
> I was then in Heaven, not here.[45]

That summer, the royal pair made their longest journey together, a six-week tour northward as far as Nottingham and Welbeck Abbey, where they were received by the Earl of Newcastle, one of England's wealthiest aristocrats. It was a "stupendous entertainment; which (God be thanked) . . . no man ever after imitated." There was also a masque, Love's Welcome at Bolsover, performed at one of New-castle's nearby houses. The six-night stay cost some £15,000, more than £3,000,000 in modern money.[46]

In 1636, a plague year, the royal couple left London early. There was no stop at Greenwich, for the infection was already there, so they went to Hampton Court, Henrietta in particular feeling "very nervous about the plague." In July the couple parted, Henrietta staying at Oatlands while Charles hunted from Bagshot to Salisbury. But he then fled in haste, even abandoning his baggage, after one of his guards died. At the end of August, they were reunited in Oxford, which was still plague-free.[47] The university excelled itself. The city's streets were specially cleansed "of dirt, filth, rubbish, and all manner of uncleanness," and students and dons alike were ordered "not to wear long hair, nor any boots . . . nor to wear their gowns hanging loosely."[48] At Christ Church, the nation's rulers were welcomed with gifts: a velvet-covered Bible for Charles and gloves for Henrietta. Two days passed in festivities. The magnificent dinners and suppers consumed seventy deer, five oxen, and seventy-four sheep, plus "melons, grapes, fish, poultry, and so forth." There were Latin speeches, music, a visit to the university library, and plays performed by the students. Then the royal couple parted, Charles hunting in the New Forest while Henrietta remained at Oatlands, three months pregnant with Anne.[49]

The couple's longest separation was in 1633, when Charles traveled north for his Scottish coronation. At first he had hoped to avoid this troublesome and costly commitment, asking that the Scottish crown be brought to London "to save him from so long a journey," but the Scots had replied that "he must not be so false to his country"; if he delayed too long, "they might, perhaps, be inclined to make choice of some other king."[50] Finally Charles agreed. The preparations were immense. His entire court was going—councillors, clergymen, musicians, and all—much of it by sea: a ship was even hired "to transport his Majesty's buckhounds." Fifty carts were ordered, "with necessary provisions, to attend the king in his journey."[51] Henrietta, four months pregnant with James, remained behind with a skeleton Privy Council to manage the affairs of England. All along the way, the nobility and gentry greeted their king with deference and honor. The hospitality was stupendous, and Charles stopped frequently for hunting, too. The two-hundred-mile journey to York took more than two weeks, an average of just fourteen miles a day. But as Charles crossed the border into Scotland, he began to feel more urgency. Missing Henrietta, he was "determined to make the shortest possible stay in that kingdom."[52] Meanwhile, at Greenwich with her children, Henrietta found "singular contentment" in her husband's frequent letters, "whereof we had no small need considering how disconsolate she hath been." She was "well in health though sad for the most part," spending too much time over her needlework, "which gives her overmuch leisure to muse."[53]

On June 15, Charles entered Edinburgh triumphantly, with pageants and music, speeches and poems, and the cheers of the populace. Three days later, he was crowned with all the church ceremony he loved. Scots Presbyterians were horrified to see the bishops in their golden copes, the altar and wax candles, and especially the crucifix to which the bishops bowed, which "bred great fear of inbringing of popery."[54] But Charles and his courtiers were "highly delighted" by the crowd outside, whose "affection . . . surpassed all belief, and extended to all ranks," Charles reported to Henrietta. Two days later, he opened the Scottish Parliament, intending "to hasten the dispatch of the remaining business." Within ten days he was finished, and full of "extraordinary satisfaction": the Parliament even "offered spontaneously" to pay most of his travel expenses.[55]

Henrietta was more cheerful too, with the promise of Charles's imminent return. Out on a river trip from Greenwich, she challenged Lord Goring, one of her favorite courtiers, "to race over a long course of the Thames," watched by "a large number of ladies and cavaliers." The queen won, and Goring paid her "the stakes arranged beforehand": some £30,000 in modern money.[56] Meanwhile, Charles came south in a "very hurried and almost flying journey," with coaches and relays of fresh horses ready all along his route. The 360 miles from Berwick to Greenwich took him just four days—he hoped "to take the queen by surprise, so as to make his return more welcome to her when she was not expecting him." But Henrietta was perfectly prepared, and she came out from Greenwich "as far as Stratford Bow" to meet him. Then the normal summer pleasures recommenced.[57]

Of all his pastimes, Charles's greatest passion was for hunting. He had a pack of "harriers and beagles" for hare coursing, as well as gun dogs ("slug hounds") for when he went wildfowling. The queen had her own pack of hounds under her Master of the Bows and String Hounds, and the king's hawks were kept in the royal mews.[58] But it was deer hunting that filled Charles's time for weeks on end. For this, he had thirty-two buckhounds, their keepers all in royal livery. Often the king would get up, attend morning prayers in chapel, then go out "before five in the morning." Yet still he might not be back until dark.[59] The day's sport was vigorous in the extreme. Charles was "below the average height," even in an age of small people, but he was very fit, "well proportioned and strong," and he rode with "untiring energy." Bad weather was no deterrent: "This morning, his Majesty and all that hunted with him in the forest were soundly wet." In the rush of the chase, he fearlessly endured many falls from horses. Sometimes there were minor injuries, such as "a blow in the face" or an injured leg during a "grievous fall."[60] But in September 1636, he "came near losing his life" when, "following a stag at full speed," his horse ran headlong into a deep bog. The beast, "completely submerged," was left "dead on the spot," but Charles, buried so deeply that "only his head and the top of his shoulders remained above ground," was saved by his followers "at the risk of their lives." Unperturbed, he changed his clothes and mounted a new horse to continue the hunt.

But if Charles led a charmed life, some of his courtiers were less fortunate. Just two weeks later, one of them lost two fingers when his knife slipped during the killing of a stag.[61] Another had died after his leg, broken during "a fall out hunting with the king," turned gangrenous. Perhaps the thrill of real danger, combined with the exhilarating outdoor exercise, was the true appeal for a man whose indoor life was so rigidly controlled by etiquette. And his contemporaries admired him for it:

> *Hunting, it is the noblest exercise,*
> *Makes men laborious, active, wise . . .*[62]

Certainly the king thrived on this vigorous lifestyle. Even the smallpox, that feared killer and maimer, left him unscathed. His first ten days of illness he dismissed as just a passing fever, "after he had heated himself at tennis." When the first spots appeared, he refused to believe his doctors' diagnosis and would not stay in bed: "All the day long he is . . . merry, and eats and drinks heartily, and recreates himself with some game or other." Henrietta insisted on sleeping with her husband, despite the risk of infection, and in the daytime she was "never . . . out of his company." Just five days after the first spots appeared, Charles was already "in a good way of recovery."[63]

Each year in October, the court returned to London. At Whitehall Palace, everything proceeded "with great pomp and splendor even to excess." Each room of the royal apartments had its regulations about who could enter and what they should do there. Royal meals were borne in state by gentlemen wearing swords, the food served on bended knee while the assembled courtiers stood in their semicircle. Some two thousand people were employed to serve the royal couple—a similar population to that of a reasonable-size town in the period—and their maintenance cost £250,000 per year, roughly equivalent to £60,000,000 in modern money.[64]

But behind closed doors, in Henrietta's apartments, the atmosphere was relaxed and informal. The queen was happily surrounded by her family and friends and her beloved pets: small birds and monkeys and especially lapdogs, whose clever exploits were a favorite conversational subject. Henrietta's wit was irrepressible and rather sharp, and her court was often filled with laughter, especially at the expense of outsiders, such as when a luckless foreign ambassador mistook Henrietta's dwarf, Jeffery Hudson, for her eldest son. "Becoming aware of this error too late, he apologized, which only made her Majesty and the others who were standing by laugh the more." Two years later, the court ladies laughed "for all the rest of the day" after another ambassador held forth pompously to the queen in Latin for more than an hour. Failing to understand a word, Henrietta could only give him "a very concise and almost voiceless answer."[65]

At Whitehall the royal couple enjoyed the many pleasures of London's winter social season. In the palace's tiltyard were jousting and bear-baiting: a stake was set up for tethering the beast, and rails protected the spectators during the bouts arranged by Charles's Sergeant of the Bears. There was an indoor alley for bowls, and outdoor greens next door in St. James's Park. Whitehall also had three tennis courts—two roofed over and one open to the sky. Tennis was hugely fashionable: every royal palace had at least one court, and government business was often delayed by "the king's going to tennis." The sport was fiercely competitive—there was certainly no question of flattering Charles by letting him win—and vast sums of money changed hands in bets: a French visitor of Henrietta's left England in 1631 with £3,000, "which he had won of the king at tennis."[66]

Theater was a passion for both Charles and Henrietta, and actors were summoned into Whitehall to perform: in 1632 alone, three professional companies performed at least fifty plays there. The plays of Beaumont and Fletcher were great favorites, as were those of Shakespeare, Jonson, Davenant, and a host of minor contemporary writers now largely forgotten. There were performances at court even in Lent and on Sundays, despite a 1625 law forbidding it.[67] Further entertainment came from trips to see the latest rarities—manuscripts, books and art works—brought home by England's foremost collectors from their European travels. There were feasts laid on by their courtiers, and dancing in the great hall at Whitehall. The reveling rose to a particular height in 1635, when Charles's nephew, Charles Louis, the new Elector Palatine, arrived in London: "Comedies, festivities and balls are . . . indulged in every day at court for the prince's sake."[68]

Each year, at the end of October, all London joined to watch the Lord Mayor's procession, "the greatest that is made for the reception of any municipal magistrate in the world." Then came the two royal birthdays: Henrietta's on November 15 and Charles's on the 19th, celebrated with parties at court, each time a little different. One year, Charles laid on a jousting display for Henrietta. Another time, Henrietta arranged a feast and a play at Somerset House for Charles and a selection of favored courtiers.[69] The Christmas holidays formed the climax of the year. After their separate religious observances on Christmas Day, the Twelve Days of Christmas began, filled with feasting, dancing, and plays in abundance, comedies especially. All London's ambassadors came to congratulate the couple on each New Year, and this, not Christmas Day, was the time for presents to be exchanged. The culmination of it all occurred on January 6, Twelfth Night, when Charles and his principal courtiers performed a masque for Henrietta and the rest of the court.

On those nights, the court was always crowded, with the eager audience jostling at the door of the masquing chamber. Many came without invitations—women hoping to charm their way in with a pretty face and "extreme brave apparel," men relying on bribery, even risking "the danger of a broken pate" from the doorman's staff.[70] The room beyond was full to bursting, everyone dressed in their finest, men and women alike smothered in jewels and vying for the best seats closest to the queen. At last came the call to be seated, and the wonders of the masque began: "Heavens and hells, their gods and devils, and clouds, sun, moon, and stars . . . cities, castles, seas, fishes, rocks, mountains, beasts, birds, and what[ever] pleaseth the poet, painter, and surveyor."[71] Everything here was the brainchild of the court's surveyor of works, Inigo Jones. Artist, architect, and engineer, trained by years of continental travel, Jones was the ideal man to produce these masterpieces of Renaissance design. Under his direction, perspective scenery—with its ranked wings of classical ruins, palaces, or forest trees framing the hazy painted backdrop beyond—was first introduced to England for royal masques. He even introduced the use of a stage behind a curtain. For each event Jones created a new set of stage machinery, with pulleys and wheels to work the moving ships, floating clouds, growing trees, and other contrivances that so provoked the audience's wonder. By 1638, his techniques were so refined that he even staged a complete aerial ballet. He also designed the costumes, consulting continental books of emblems and *commedia dell'arte* figures to create designs loaded with classical symbolism, each one a confection of opulent fabrics, gold, silver, jewels, and ostrich feathers.[72]

The main body of the masque was performed by professional actors and musicians, speaking and singing the lines that a court poet had written under Jones's direction. First came the antimasque, a riot of disorder demanding to be resolved, leading up to the summoning of the heroic, godlike figures of Charles and his courtiers, whose mere approach, silent and grand in some fantastic stage machine, was sufficient to set the world to rights. After the king and his lords performed a final triumphal dance specially choreographed for the occasion, the masque was over. Then everyone present danced far into the night, with a banquet to finish.

With Christmas over, Charles and Henrietta left to hunt in the country. Sometimes, however, the weather was just too dreadful: one winter's hunting trip to Newmarket was cut short "on account of the cold of that place." Henrietta, prone to catching colds and overtiring herself, grew less enthusiastic, and in 1635, when Charles left for Newmarket as usual, she remained "doubtful because of the inconveniences of that country."[73] In any case, these January trips never lasted long, and the royal couple always returned to London for Shrovetide in February, the traditional carnival season, when the court again abandoned business and threw itself into a whirl of "dances, comedies and other pleasant diversions," chief of which was a masque presented by Henrietta and her ladies "for the gratification and pleasure of the king."[74] Henrietta was so passionate about her masques that rehearsals often began before Christmas: twice a week to start with, then every day as the great event approached. This time the king sat in the place of honor, enjoying himself immensely, and then joining the dancing afterward "until near daybreak."[75]

Occasionally the season went without a masque. In January 1633, as Charles prepared to leave for Scotland, his usual Twelfth Night masque was replaced by a pastoral performed by Henrietta and her ladies. *The Shepherds' Paradise*, written by one of Henrietta's courtiers, was partly an exercise to improve the queen's English: the performance went on for seven or eight hours, during which Henrietta alone spoke some eight hundred lines of English verse.[76] But usually there were the "year's double masques," playing out the royal couple's fantasies of superhuman love and godlike power. Henrietta's roles made her the image of female perfection—pure in virtue, innocent in her love, glorious in her beauty, calming and nurturing, a softer counterpart to Charles's appearances as an all-powerful personification of masculine "heroic virtue."[77] The result was a heady mix of romance and nationalism, as the titles of the masques themselves make clear: *Albion's Triumph*, *The British Heaven*, *The Temple of Love*.

These early months of the year were also the season for fashionable society weddings—marriages made not in heaven but at Whitehall, where Charles and Henrietta were tireless matchmakers. It was no frivolous matter. With these marriages they were joining the nation's aristocratic leaders in one close-knit, dynastic web loyal to the king and each other, creating a stable and powerful government. Charles was prepared to offer prospective grooms some strong incentives: "a princely addition" to brides' dowries, with the promise of more favors in the future. The resulting weddings often took place at Whitehall, where Charles sometimes gave away the bride himself; afterward, "a most sumptuous banquet was given to the flower of the nobility."[78]

With the warmer weather of spring, the royal couple would begin to spend more time outdoors. Again the historical record provides us with glimpses: of Henrietta canceling all her official audiences and going out on an impulse, "the fairness of the day calling the queen abroad"; of Charles at his jousting exercises in St. James's Park, receiving two crimson-dressed horses from the Spanish ambassador, whom the king then took back to Whitehall, where he "showed him his statues as he passed through the Privy Garden."[79] There were pleasure drives into the City too, such as when the couple "spent some time at Ludgate Hill," examining a favored shopkeeper's wares, before going on to the asylum at Bedlam

> to see the mad folks, where they were madly entertained. . . . Two mad women had almost frighted the king and queen, and all their attendants, out of the house, by their foul talk.[80]

April brought the annual ceremonies of the Order of the Garter, performed with great pomp at Whitehall or Windsor Castle, attended by Charles and sometimes also by Henrietta. Then came the festivities of Maying. One year, Henrietta drove out at the head of a vast procession of coaches, leaping down to gather the season's first branch of white May blossom. Another time, Charles rode with her "on Maying . . . through Hyde Park to Kensington, where a collation was prepared for them by the Earl of Holland," one of Henrietta's favorite courtiers.[81] The royal couple were often seen at this season driving "in Hyde Park all the day in all state,"[82] where fashionable London came in their coaches to join them. Then, in the middle of May, Charles and Henrietta left for Greenwich and their summer country progress.

Wherever they went, the couple indulged their passion for all that was fine and beautiful. They redecorated their palaces at vast expense, with tapestried walls and furniture covered with pure gold leaf, or upholstered in silks and velvets and cloth of gold. Gorgeous clothes and jewels were irresistible: in fifteen years, Charles spent some £20,000,000 in modern money on his personal wardrobe.[83] They redesigned their gardens in the latest fashion, with sundials and fountains and arbors. At St. James's, Henrietta laid out a French formal garden of embroidery parterres, and Charles displayed the bulk of his statuary collection: more than 250 pieces, "the rarest wonders of Italy," transported miraculously into the heart of England.[84]

Together the royal couple amassed one of the greatest art collections in Europe—more than seventeen hundred paintings were spread among the royal palaces.[85] Their agents scoured the Continent and made vast purchases. Even as he struggled to fund Buckingham's expedition to La Rochelle in 1627, Charles was arranging the largest single art purchase yet seen in Europe: the treasures of the Duke of Mantua, "so wonderful and glorious a collection the like will never again be met with."[86] Art arrived as gifts as well. Especially impressive was a collection of sixteenth-century Italian paintings sent to the queen from Rome by Cardinal Barberini. When they arrived, Charles rushed to join her, "the boxes were opened . . . and the pieces viewed one by one with singular pleasure." Charles was so delighted that Henrietta predicted, only half in jest, that "she would not be able to keep them, as the king would steal them from her."[87]

The royal couple were also enthusiastic commissioners of new works, and their court attracted leading continental artists. Foremost among them was the Flemish painter Anthony Van Dyck, who arrived in 1632 and spent most of his remaining years in England, producing vast numbers of royal portraits: Henrietta sat for him at least twenty-five times. It is not hard to see why he was so favored. In earlier paintings by Daniel Mytens, Charles had appeared stiff and coarse-featured, dwarfed by his elaborate clothes and surroundings; Van Dyck transformed the king into an individual of effortless superiority, his expression remote, his whole figure utterly elegant and poised. Somehow Van Dyck imparted not just majesty to these pictures but something mythical. Henrietta, too, has metamorphosed into a figure both more mysterious than Mytens's doll-like rendition and more authoritative: unutterably beautiful but also remote like her husband, with an enigmatic "Mona Lisa" smile just turning up the corners of her lips. Van Dyck's portraits have become the definitive images of Charles and Henrietta, yet they were deliberate constructions. Here, as in their masques, the royals are godlike beings, monarchs by divine right, above common mortals "as far . . . as they are above beasts."[88] We see no hint of the queen who declared, based on her own self-appraisal, "that women could not be beautiful beyond the age of twenty-two." Nor do we see the vivacious young socialite, naturally "inclined toward gaiety," who loved "frivolous but innocent things."[89] Van Dyck's Charles comes closer to contemporaries' descriptions of a king who was "very majestic . . . and would be approached with respect and reverence." But we could not guess that Charles was a small man who admittedly rode with skill, "but not very gracefully."[90]

The couple's most costly taste of all was architecture. Charles's ideas were on the grandest scale, with plans for razing Whitehall to the ground and building instead a vast rectangular block of buildings enclosing almost a dozen huge courtyards. There would be endless columns and classical statues, pediments, urns, and balustrades, all designed by Inigo Jones and his pupil John Webb, following ancient Roman and Renaissance Italian models. The resulting building would have filled much of St. James's Park and dominated that end of London.[91] But here the reality of an English king ruling without the support of Parliament finally made itself felt: Charles could never fund so grand a scheme. Henrietta was the more effective builder of the pair. Her Whitehall apartments were under almost continuous alteration throughout the reign. At Greenwich in 1630, she resumed work on the Italianate Queen's House that had been left unfinished by Charles's mother. The building work alone took five years, and the interior decoration continued until 1639. There were marble floors, carved stone fireplaces, and painted ceilings— the most important being Orazio and Artemisia Gentileschi's *Allegory of Peace and the Arts under the English Crown*.[92]

But the project that undoubtedly meant most to Henrietta was at Somerset House, where she spent four years in the mid-1630s creating a new Catholic chapel and a monastery for her priests. The monastery would be simple, as required by the Capuchins' vows, but the chapel was planned on the grandest scale, paid for by Charles to the tune of some £4,000, as agreed with Bassompierre back in 1626. Inigo Jones designed a stylish Renaissance building, its interior lavishly decorated with arches, columns, and carving. At 100 feet long and 30 feet wide, this chapel obviously was intended to hold far more people than just the queen and the handful of Catholic courtiers allowed to attend Mass with her by the terms of her marriage treaty. In fact, a special chamber was included at one end, behind a carved screen, to hold the queen's court.[93] The vast space beyond, as far as the altar, was a reflection of Henrietta's rising ambitions for her faith. Here, in the heart of London, she would have "a public church," where her priests would "celebrate Mass, preach, and hear confessions"—not just for herself but "for the benefit of the other Catholics."[94] Secure in her husband's love, she was ready to revive all those grand Catholic visions that had been the original *raison d'être* of her marriage.

7

QUESTIONS OF FAITH

The time was ripe for Henrietta to advance her plans. With no need now to pander to Parliament, Charles could please his wife and offer his long-persecuted Catholic subjects a lenient rule. Even before her new chapel was completed, London's Catholics flocked to the room in Somerset House where she held her religious services. On Sundays, there was "a continual ebb and flood of people from six in the morning till twelve at noon," as the Capuchins said one Mass after another, while Charles, "looking at them from a window of the queen's palace," made no objection, so that he seemed "by his silence [to be] approving of their devotion."[1]

The penal laws were now enforced only rarely, and those who did suffer under them could appeal to Henrietta for assistance, which she was always ready to give. She carried individual cases to Charles, arguing their merits and winning him over. For her sake, he ordered that an imprisoned priest was "to go freely abroad for the benefit of his health"; another time, "merely at the queen's suit," he pardoned fourteen Catholics condemned to death at Newgate sessions. When

Henrietta raised the case of four lay Catholics, "old and simple and extremely poor," imprisoned for years in York Castle for unpaid recusancy fines, Charles ordered the release not just of them but "all such as were detained for matters of conscience."[2] Then Henrietta proceeded to the king's crypto-Catholic secretary of state, Sir Francis Windebank, informing him of Charles's desires, which Windebank translated into written orders. But the secretary was afraid. Knowing the hatred these measures would stir up if they were discovered, and seeing so many orders signed on his own authority, he finally begged the king for a written warrant "for my safety."[3]

Under Henrietta's patronage, the royal court gained an increasingly Catholic character. It was not just the queen's ladies who were practicing Catholics now: two of her favorite male courtiers— Walter Montagu and Henry Jermyn—converted in the mid-1630s. And some of Charles's closest advisers were sympathetic to Catholicism: men such as Lord Treasurer Weston and Chancellor of the Exchequer Francis Cottington, who both publicly practiced Anglicanism to advance their careers but became Catholics before they died. In Charles's chapel at Whitehall, Anglican preachers denounced the Puritans as "a most pernicious sect, and dangerous to a monarch," but spoke mildly or even warmly of Catholics and much of their doctrine. And many Catholics were already beginning to hope for more: the conversion of Charles himself and ultimately all of Britain. Henrietta herself saw the Anglican Church as a mere historical aberration: the result of Henry VIII's infatuation with Anne Boleyn and his determination to have a son, perpetuated by Elizabeth I only because the pope did not recognize her mother's marriage and thus her own right to the throne. Anglican liturgy was in essence similar to her own, Henrietta thought, with its "altars, burning candles, priests, surplices, bishops."[4]

Charles did much to raise Catholic hopes. In addition to his "princely goodness" to British Catholics, there were his well-known hatred of Calvinism and Presbyterianism; his frequent description of himself as a true Catholic (though not a Roman one); his expressions of goodwill for the sitting pope, Urban VIII; his belief in the necessity of confessing sins to a priest; and his acceptance of fifteen hundred years of Roman Catholic doctrine, which he felt had gone astray only at the Council of Trent, ninety years earlier. When an English Franciscan priest at Henrietta's court published a book arguing that the English creed could be reconciled almost entirely with Roman doctrine, Charles was delighted, declaring that he "would willingly have parted with one of his hands" so that the English break with Rome might never have happened.[5]

Keen to discover whether Charles and his bishops were as ripe for conversion as they seemed, the pope dispatched an envoy to England in 1634. Gregorio Panzani, an Italian priest, was soon gathering intelligence: most of the Anglican bishops were "moderate" men sympathetic to Catholicism, he reported hopefully; a few were even "almost Catholic." Panzani had been warned that Henrietta would be little help to him: she was a frivolous young woman, too much occupied with dancing and balls. But gradually, working with her confessor, Father Philip, he began to involve the queen in his schemes. She was the one who persuaded Charles to see Panzani, after he at first refused. Then she was present at the "very remote and unsuspected place" where Charles welcomed the envoy "with a very cheerful countenance, taking off his hat, while Panzani kissed his hand" and assured him of the pope's affection and gratitude for his kindness to his Catholic subjects.[6]

One of Panzani's most important pieces of business was to arrange a formal exchange of diplomatic agents between the papal court and Henrietta's: the first official connection between England and Rome since the death of the Catholic Queen Mary I in 1558, and an important step toward achieving the pope's ambitions for Britain. Again it was Henrietta who approached the king. Charles was not unwilling, but he stipulated that the agent had to be a layman and not a priest, and he had to be officially accredited only to the queen and not himself. He could not afford to associate openly with the pope. But Charles had great hopes from this new diplomatic contact with the Holy See. He wanted the pope's help to negotiate with the Hapsburgs and restore his sister Elizabeth's family to the Palatinate. He also wanted the pope to remove his prohibition against British Catholics swearing the Oath of Allegiance to their king.[7]

For Rome, the choice of agent was vital. Drawing on his intimate knowledge of the English court, Father Philip warned that the pope's man had to be a perfect courtier: "noble, rich, handsome, and affable in conversation," charming with the ladies and especially with Henrietta, who at twenty-five took great delight in fine clothes and witty conversation. But at the same time, he had to be "grave and reserved . . . the king and queen being strictly virtuous, and professed enemies to immodesty." He also had to be exquisitely tactful, never reproaching Charles for his persecution of the Catholics, and he had to bring rare presents of art and jewels and other "Italian curiosities," so everyone would be "enticed by proper baits." Such a man could bring all England back to Catholicism in just three years, Father Philip predicted.[8]

It was a demanding brief, but the pope found the perfect man. George Con was Scottish born, like Charles himself, but he had spent the last thirteen years pursuing a successful career in Rome. Author, cardinal's secretary, diplomat: Con was a clever man, "which may be read in his face." Widely respected for his piety and learning, he also "knew men and business well" and was "graceful in his person, . . . affable in conversation."[9] Although she had never met him, Henrietta had long taken an interest in Con's career and had recently asked the pope to make him a cardinal. The matter was important to her: the appointment of a British cardinal by her intercession would increase her prestige among Europe's Catholic monarchs and win her greater loyalty from England's Catholics. But Rome remained evasive. Such grants were allowed only to monarchs who "had performed some remarkable service for the church," the pope's cousin, Cardinal Barberini, told Henrietta. But if she and Con secured "liberty of conscience for the Catholics," it would be sufficient.[10]

Con arrived in England in 1636, fired up to make "great impressions there."[11] Catholic toleration and even the nation's conversion and reunion with the Roman Church were all on his agenda. Joining Panzani, who was attending Henrietta during her summer's country progress, he thought there was every reason for hope. "In every place where the queen goes, her chapel is set in order, which stands open and is visited by all in the neighborhood with much reverence."

Even in Northampton, a town "considered most puritanical," the local people were eager to see the chapel for themselves. "Once we had these beautiful things in our churches," some sighed; others even stayed to hear Mass.[12] Con was impressed by Henrietta, too. Every day or two, he went to see her, finding her "exemplary" in her religion and virtue. Her devotion at Mass "moved all those who were present," and she was "full of incredible innocence"—so much so that Father Philip told him "she has no sins except those of omission . . . as to sins of faith, or of the flesh, she is never tempted."[13] Clearly such religious feeling could be turned to Con's purposes, but Henrietta had a long way to go before she would be the powerful political instrument he desired:

> She thinks little of the future, trusting wholly in the king. She must be more concerned to gain the ministers of state, whose mistress she could be if she wished.[14]

In line with Father Philip's advice, Con arrived armed with presents. For Henrietta there was a cross of diamonds from the pope, which she immediately fastened around her neck. She wore it all the time, showing it with pride to her visitors: "See there . . . the treasure that His Holiness has sent me: . . . I consider this cross the most precious thing that I have." Con also brought her a portrait of St. Catherine, which he intended to have framed; but Henrietta, too thrilled to wait, "gave orders that the picture should be fastened to the curtains of her bed."[15] Rosaries were handed out to her Catholic court ladies—an occasion enlivened by Jeffery Hudson, who, eager for a gift himself, called out to the queen, "Madam, show the father that I also am a Catholic." But there were gifts for Henrietta's Protestant courtiers too, and more still en route from Italy, including "valuable pictures" for Charles's trusted ministers Windebank and Cottington.[16]

The Italian Panzani, speaking no English and poor French, had had only limited connections at the English court. But Con, a native Briton with all the culture of twenty-four years' residence on the Continent, was welcome everywhere. He even dined with William

Juxon, Bishop of London, to the amazement of Henrietta and London's public opinion. Gradually he was building his own party at court. Accounts of what went on in Henrietta's private apartments reached him via her Catholic ladies, especially Katherine, Duchess of Buckingham—"Fond Kate," as Con called her affectionately. Following the duke's death, she had publicly returned to her childhood religion: "[I] would pour out my life in defense of [Catholicism]," she protested. "Nothing can frighten me from my faith."[17] Even Protestant ladies succumbed to Con's charms: Henrietta's favorite, Lucy, Countess of Carlisle, showed him such loyalty that she was suspected of popery herself, although, Con remarked, "the poor lady has never thought of any other religion than that of beautifying herself." More significant was the Countess of Arundel, wife of the famous art-collecting earl. Fluent in Italian, she had already built up close ties with Panzani. Like her husband, she was "Catholic in all but [public] profession," Con enthused, and she was a valuable asset, bringing him reports of the secret transactions of Charles's Privy Council. The earl, too, was soon coopted into Con's faction: "I have made him several discourses of the disadvantages which the king has in not being a Catholic, with which he has been moved."[18]

Francis Windebank also aided Con; and Endymion Porter, one of Charles's grooms of the bedchamber, gave him access to the most sensitive information. But two men in particular the agent counted as vital to his plans. Walter Montagu was an enthusiastic Catholic convert whom Charles had angrily banished from court. Having been secretly ordained as a priest abroad, he now returned to England after Con placated the king. "The presence of Montagu, which I have earnestly desired, will be serviceable, and I hope much from it," Con told Rome.[19] Then there was the queen's confessor, Father Philip, who had incredible influence over her. It was said that just a single look from him was enough to tell her what she should do. Ever present in Henrietta's chambers, Philip was on familiar terms with all who went there: "The king and queen do love him, and so do all the courtiers."[20] But beneath his mild exterior the priest was an energetic Catholic missionary—one day discussing theology with the Prince of Wales's tutor in hopes of winning him over to Rome,

another talking to the king himself, urging "that it was directly opposite to the whole design of the Gospel, that there should be more
churches than one; whence he inferred the necessity of a reunion."
He even hinted that, for this great end, Rome might make concessions on doctrines to which Charles particularly objected.[21]

Galvanized by Con and Father Philip, Henrietta was proud to be
the leader of the newly fervent Catholic party at court, devoting herself to the job "with enthusiasm." She established two devotional
societies—the Confraternity of the Holy Rosary and the Third Order
of St. Francis—whose rites she led in person. Every Saturday, the
devotees gathered in her chapel to hear the litanies "sung with great
solemnity" by her Capuchins; on two Sundays every month, they followed the queen and her priests in "solemn procession" to confess
their sins and receive Communion. The ceremonies were "so striking, and made such impressions on the heart," that both societies
grew swiftly. Even Protestants came, "some of whom . . . sought
conferences [with Henrietta's priests] and were converted."[22]

Henrietta had some of the ideal qualities for a party leader. Her
generosity was celebrated, and "she was staunch in her friendship,
secret and trustworthy to those who confided in her." She was also
persistent and determined for her cause, and profoundly influential
where it mattered. Once more she pressed Charles to permit a Catholic bishop to come to England. When he refused, she was unde-
terred and began to beg as well as argue. At last Charles relented: he
would turn a blind eye to a bishop, he promised, if the pope allowed
English Catholics to take the Oath of Allegiance.[23]

In Henrietta's apartments, where George Con and Charles met
almost daily, a friendship began to form. Con was precisely the kind
of cultivated, well-traveled, and intelligent man whose company the
king most enjoyed. The two men sat down together to play cards:
on one occasion, when many of the stakes were Catholic trinkets
such as crucifixes and relic cases, Charles refused to play; he would
not know what to do with them if he won, he protested. "Give them
to my daughter," Henrietta suggested, smiling. "No, no," Charles
replied, "I will give them to George here," pointing to Con, "and he
shall give me such of the other things as he wins."[24] Con joined the

royal couple on all sorts of occasions—eating supper in Henrietta's apartments; accompanying them to see their children at Richmond Palace, "to my infinite comfort"; sharing their visit to the London house of the Earl and Countess of Arundel, where their famous art collection was on view.[25]

He and Charles rapidly discovered a shared passion for art. As they talked, Con brought out small items from his pockets—carved antique gems and a miniature painting—which he gave to the admiring king.[26] Charles took great delight in these conversations: when the papal agent arrived at Windsor to watch the Garter ceremonies, Charles insisted on taking him instead to the Royal Gallery, "to conduct me through everything, showing me the pictures and speaking of various things." In the chapel, the Knights of the Garter already had their robes on, but Charles merely said, "They should have patience." Meanwhile, one of the pictures spurred the king to criticize the credulity of Rome: "The Pope ought to reform the fables that are written in *The Lives of the Saints*." Con's repartee was swift. If the pope "were able to remedy all the disorders of Christianity, he would begin with the removal of heresy"—a difficult matter, Con added pointedly, when there were still princes such as Charles who lent it their support. Charles took the reproof in good spirit, merely telling Con that such talk was more suited to Rome than to England. But the waiting knights were enraged, and Puritans among them even declared, Con heard, "that the king had committed sacrilege on each occasion when he had taken me by the hand."[27]

Charles had inherited his father's love of theological debate, and often he would challenge Con over some central tenet of Catholic faith: the invocation of saints, purgatory, the pope's infallibility. In Spain, he recalled one evening, he had seen a Catholic procession in which the people showed more reverence to the Madonna than to the image of the Son of God himself—a clear Catholic abuse. Everyone joined the dispute. Henrietta corrected someone's misquotation of St. Bonaventure, and then Con replied that the Church should not be judged by a few ignorant Spaniards: if Charles had been to Rome, he would understand Catholic practice properly—a rebuke that the king accepted. Con was often outspoken. He always referred to his Protestant opponents as "heretics," but Charles was not offended.[28] Whatever happened in their debates, Charles was always the embodiment of courtesy: "He seldom contradicted another by his authority, but by his reason." "By your favor, sir, I think otherwise," he would begin, before carefully giving his reasons. And, at least according to Con, when the king "saw that he was wrong, he very humbly fell silent."[29]

For Charles, it was really all a game. He even laid bets with Henrietta's Catholic courtiers about the true nature of their Church's doctrine, referring to Con for the answers, which the king then refused to accept. In one case, he even requested a written statement from the pope before he would admit he had lost his wager.[30] But for Con there was always the hope of much, much more. Whenever possible, he turned these sparring matches into serious discussions that might advance the Catholic cause. He urged Charles to reunite their two churches. He spent many hours discussing the disputed Oath of Allegiance. Charles even drafted a new version of the oath, which Con forwarded to Rome. It was a dangerous step. Charles's subjects denounced the idea as amounting to "absolute liberty of conscience," "by which one has often seen states consumed." But finally, seeing that no agreement could be reached, Rome ordered Con to close the subject.[31]

At the end of 1636, the Catholic cause received a further boost with the opening of Henrietta's new chapel at Somerset House. On Henrietta's orders, the first Mass there was performed with "all possible pomp and magnificence." When the congregation was seated, curtains opened to reveal a monstrance containing the Holy Sacrament, which, by a careful contrivance of lamps and candles—about four hundred in all—glowed red and appeared "all on fire." Around and above it was a vast painted stage set: "a Paradise of glory" with the dove of the Holy Spirit flying above seven layers of clouds, crowded with hundreds of angelic figures. An anthem began, performed by Henrietta's choir and musicians, hidden behind the altar so that the sound seemed to come from the painted angels themselves. As Mass proceeded, "sung in eight parts so melodiously that one must have had a heart of stone not to be moved by it," everyone was lost in "admiration, joy, and adoration": there were even tears in Henrietta's eyes. After midday dinner, there were vespers, compline, and a moving sermon preached by Henrietta's grand almoner on a text from the Psalms: "This is the Lord's doing, and it is marvelous in our eyes." Outside, so many people thronged at the chapel doors, "bent on forcing their way in to see the magnificence," that the congregation could barely get out. Over the following days, the crush continued—so great "that it was impossible to close the doors of the church." Charles did nothing to stop them from coming. In fact, he too wanted a look: after gazing on the altarpiece for a long time, he said he had never seen anything more beautiful or more ingeniously designed.[32]

With the Somerset House chapel as a base, the Capuchins set about proselytizing with redoubled vigor: "Not a week passed but there were two or three conversions." Directing it all was Henrietta's grand almoner, Jacques du Perron, Bishop of Angoulême. Spurred on by Con, he openly frequented the houses of Protestants "to dispute with them and with the women in particular, and to try and make converts." Secretly, he arranged meetings of leading Anglican clergymen in his own house, where he and Father Philip held "almost incessant disputes and conferences." And, with Con holding out the hope of cardinalships as rewards for their "labors and perils," Philip and du Perron had an even greater catch in their sights: the heir to the throne, Prince Charles.[33] For Henrietta, it would be a dream come true: the conversion of her children remained a burning concern throughout her life. She had herself begun steps toward the prince's conversion two years earlier, secretly taking him to Mass, "where he noted everything, and being asked which rites pleased him more, his own or the queen's, he replied the queen's." But she had been forced to desist: "On account of his tender age, he repeats whatever is said to him." Still, she had resolved that she would "instill Catholicism" in her son in due course.[34] Now Philip and du Perron set to work on the prince's tutor, Bishop Duppa: "As the enterprise is one of the utmost importance, it is necessary to spread the foundations widely."[35]

But that was the best they could all hope to achieve, Con had realized. Despite his initial hopes, the king was clearly beyond his reach, as "severe against the deviations of Rome . . . as any gentleman in Christendom."[36] In fact, Charles was an idealist with his own vision of how Protestantism should be practiced—a vision he was determined to impose on the nation's church. His great ally in this project was his old friend William Laud, whom Charles had promoted through a series of plum appointments, culminating in the top job in the Church of England: Archbishop of Canterbury. The two men were religious soulmates—Arminians in doctrine who believed, like the Catholics, in the existence of human free will, as opposed to the Calvinist doctrine of predestination adhered to by English Puritans. They envisioned an orderly, ceremonious British church that would inspire religious awe with its "beauty of holiness."[37]

In 1633, when Laud became Archbishop of Canterbury, he set to work at once to make their grand vision a reality. Intolerant, impatient, and hot-tempered, Laud "never abated anything of his severity and rigor." His opponents feared and hated him, and that year seven hundred Puritans fled across the ocean to New England, prompting fears that the old country would be depopulated and its trade ruined.[38] But still the reforms continued. By the summer of 1636, when Con arrived in England, the nation's churches had been transformed. Once more, as before the Reformation, the stone altar stood grandly at the east, separated from the congregation by a railing. Candlesticks stood on it for Communion, while priests in elaborate vestments set out the wine in golden chalices. Images of saints adorned the walls; priests bowed at the name of Jesus. In many places, the more zealous clergy had even begun to hear confessions, just as Catholic priests did.

For Charles, this was "the middle way between the pomp of superstitious tyranny [i.e., Catholicism] and the meanness of fantastic anarchy [i.e., Puritanism]." But to many of his subjects it seemed mere "popish superstition and idolatry."[39] The new ceremonies were detested "hardly less than the [Catholic] Mass itself." Some people even said that Laud and Charles were closet papists who planned to reintroduce Catholicism to England by stealth. Opposition grew. Previously loyal Anglicans, "from fear of falling into Catholicism," "abandoned themselves to Puritanism." And the Puritans became ever more extreme, clinging "to the bareness of their worship," "performed in its purity, as they put it." It was a "Puritan plague," the Venetian ambassador commented, and the more Charles tried "to extirpate them, the stronger they become."[40]

As 1636 closed, the opposition began to organize, encouraged by "many of the leading men of the realm." In the absence of Parliament, they had no public voice as yet. But Charles's government knew they were holding "secret meetings" throughout the country. They had a dual aim: to destroy Archbishop Laud and his ceremonies, and to change the nature of Charles's political rule.[41] For eight years now, there had been no Parliament. With considerable ingenuity, the king's ministers had researched ancient records to find ways of raising money on his royal authority alone. In accordance with a long-forgotten law of 1227, knighthood fines were exacted from wealthy Englishmen who had not attended Charles's coronation to be knighted. Forest fines were assessed on all those who had built their houses on royal forest lands, which technically included almost all the English countryside. Most unpopular of all was "ship money," an ancient property tax occasionally raised on coastal counties for the maintenance of the navy. "England without a fleet was a body without a head," Charles declared, and the Royal Navy needed expanding to keep up with other European powers. So in the mid-1630s, he began to claim ship money annually from the entire nation, not just its maritime borderlands. There was a public outcry: Charles was changing the very principles of government, aiming to achieve "absolute monarchy."[42]

In January 1637, the Earl of Warwick spoke to Charles quite frankly. The people would not put up with ship money, a tax on which they had been given no chance to vote in Parliament, and by which they

signed away the liberties of the realm, and . . . deprived their posterity of those benefits which had been left to them uncontaminated as a sacred treasure by their ancestors.

If only Charles would summon Parliament, Warwick suggested, he would discover the true loyalty of his people. Warwick was prepared "to stake his head that Parliament would readily consent to supply him with all that he might desire": England's populace would give "their substance, their blood and their children, if they saw it was done by the proper channels."[43]

But Charles was immovable. After the humiliations of the early years of his reign, he abhorred the very name of Parliament. In his eyes, it was a terrible monster, a "Hydra . . . as well cunning as malicious." To summon it now would destroy his years of work in establishing his own "independent authority," and even the needs of his nephew, the Elector Palatine, now in England to rally support, would not persuade Charles to do that.[44] His resolve was further strengthened by England's judges, who unanimously pronounced ship money to be legal: "His Majesty may, in times of necessity, impose what sums of money he pleaseth upon the subjects for defense of the kingdom"; and he alone was the one "to determine all those times of necessity." It was a blank check for Charles to take whatever he wanted from his subjects' purses, whenever he chose:

> at one stroke it roots out for ever the meeting of parliament, and renders the king absolute and sovereign. . . . If the people submit to this present prejudice, they are submitting to an eternal yoke and burying their past liberties, which will remain a memory only.[45]

So the collection of ship money continued through 1637, while Laud pressed ahead with depriving Puritan clergymen of their jobs. When three Puritan sympathizers came out in print, accusing Laud and his bishops "of undermining religion in order to erect popery on its ruins," the government acted severely. The public hangman cut off their ears, slit their noses, and branded their faces with the letters "S. L.," for "seditious libeler." The punishment sparked outrage. A huge crowd gathered around the scaffold that day, crying out at the injustice and "collecting the blood of the victims." New libels appeared against Laud, pasted up anonymously at night all around

London: "The Arch-Wolf of Canterbury" was "persecuting the saints and shedding the blood of the martyrs."[46] Just a week later, another antigovernment agitator, John Williams, Bishop of Lincoln, was condemned to be "shut up in the Tower of London without limit of time, besides a fine of £10,000." Again there was an outcry, with people accusing his judges "of the most unjust tyranny," while more libels came out against Laud. At every act of repression, the Puritan party seemed only to grow stronger, "and prudent people . . . are not a little afraid of it." Yet Charles remained largely oblivious. Still he thought himself the happiest king in Christendom.[47] Contemptuous of the opposition, he was determined to go even further.

That summer, he and Laud imposed an Anglican-style prayer book on the Scottish Church, to remedy what they saw as "the disorder and indecency" of its Calvinist practices.[48] Trouble flared immediately. In Edinburgh Cathedral, the congregation rose and interrupted the ceremony, tearing the rich vestments off the bishop and his clergy and trampling them underfoot, handling the religious men "so savagely that they barely escaped with their lives." Then the people in the rest of the city's churches attacked their own ministers; "they say even the women and children used their teeth and nails against them." When the news reached London, Charles and his ministers were dismayed: the Scots' example could easily "stir up revolutions among the people here, who are no less scandalized and discontented." Briefly Charles wavered and seemed "to incline to milder ways to pacify them." But in the end he would not back down. He sent orders to Edinburgh that all his "reforms shall be obeyed entire."[49] The royal proclamation was read out in a heavy calm, but violence erupted once more the next day. Again the women and children "were the special actors," attacking the Bishop of Galloway "in such a barbarous manner as the like has never been seen in this kingdom," so that only "with great difficulty was he rescued." Order was breaking down. "The entire people there refuse to obey the ecclesiastical ceremonies introduced." One bishop, terrified, "confined himself to his house . . . to observe . . . the trend affairs will take." Another was compelled by the populace to perform the usual Presbyterian service. In many places, the Laudian prayer book was publicly burned. Some people even talked of choosing a new, more Protestant king: "In fact the whole kingdom is in confusion."[50]

Meanwhile, Scottish propaganda spread throughout England, depicting Laud's new prayer book as part of a court Catholic conspiracy, designed to reconquer all of Britain for the pope.[51] Desperate to disprove the mounting accusations that he himself was a papist in the pocket of the greatest conspirator of all, George Con, Laud was engaged in a campaign of vigorous anti-Catholic repression. Almost every day came some new action: in Winchester a Catholic school was discovered and closed down; in London all the copies of an illegal Catholic book were seized "and burnt by the hangman." Prompted by Con, Henrietta complained to Charles about Laud's "proceedings," and soon his best efforts were getting him nowhere. When Laud acted against a priest who had performed a Catholic marriage, Henrietta intervened and "the king . . . commanded him to desist."[52] Her influence saved from destruction a popular Catholic pilgrimage site in Wales and overturned Laud's plan "to take away the eldest sons of all who were popishly affected, and breed them up in the [Anglican] religion established." Meanwhile, Henrietta's chapel continued as busy as ever: "No sooner one Mass is ended . . . than the chapel is full for the next, though it be a goodly and spacious room"; on Sundays, "no less than six thousand persons do hear Mass there."[53]

But at last Laud saw his chance to outmaneuver the queen and spur Charles's government into action. On October 21, 1637, one of Charles's courtiers, the Earl of Newport, went to Laud "in a high passion," saying that his wife had just converted to Catholicism.[54] The Countess of Newport was the most prestigious court lady that Henrietta's party had yet converted, and the next day Laud complained to Charles's Privy Council. He spoke freely against "the increasing of the Roman party," the freedom of worship at Somerset House, and the behavior of three of Henrietta's Catholic friends in particular—George Con, Walter Montagu, and Sir Toby Matthew, whom the Earl of Newport blamed as the chief "instruments in the conversion of his wife." On bended knee, Laud begged Charles to punish Montagu and Matthew. As for Con, Laud "knew not how he came hither, or what he did here," he said, "therefore he would say nothing of him." Everyone was in an uproar, and Charles was furious. "He would have these things remedied," he said, and he used "such words" of Montagu and Matthew that the pair were in terror, knowing the law prescribed the death penalty for such a crime.[55]

"I did my duty to the king and state openly in council," Laud stated proudly. But he too was a frightened man when he heard the news from Henrietta's apartments: "The queen [is] acquainted with all I said . . . and highly displeased with me, and so continues." He now had open enemies on both sides, Catholic and Puritan, "very like corn between two millstones."[56] Briefly he considered apologizing to Henrietta, but in the end he did not dare to: only recently, "a libel" had appeared, accusing him "of papism, and of having continual correspondence with the pope's nuncio [i.e., Con]." So Laud stood firm and begged Charles "to defend him against the violence of the queen." At the next Privy Council meeting, with "violent passions," he demanded the enforcement of the long-lapsed penal laws, and especially of "the accustomed edicts against the queen's chapel." He found many allies among the councillors—Charles himself was still "bitterly displeased"—so a new proclamation was drawn up, ordering "the severest penalties" for English Catholics.[57]

"Exceedingly afflicted," Con rushed to the queen. Complaining of "the audacious impudence of Canterbury, the danger to the Catholic religion, and to her majesty herself," he stirred her to a passion. In fact, "the queen's sentiments were so vigorous that I begged her to moderate herself, and to deal gently with the king."[58] With Henrietta calm once more, the pair embarked on a meticulously planned campaign. Every morning they met to decide what each of them, "partly in jest and partly seriously, ought to say to the king" that day, aiming at "deferring the proclamation, and gaining time." Soon Charles assured them he would "not let it be published until it has been modified, at least to some extent." He had to be seen to do something, but he would not proceed against the queen's chapel, he promised.[59] But Henrietta wanted still more. With Charles ill in bed, she kept him company "almost all the time," wheedling away until he ordered the Earl of Newport to moderate his behavior toward his wife, with whom he had been quarreling bitterly. Walter Montagu and Toby Matthew were soon rehabilitated at court. In fact, it emerged, they had not been involved in the Countess of Newport's conversion at all: it had been an entirely female affair, the work of the Duchess of Buckingham and the countess's sister, Olive Porter, one of the most energetic of Henrietta's proselytizing ladies.[60]

In the end, however, Charles had no choice but to publish the proclamation. The whole Privy Council judged it necessary, he explained to Con: public indignation at Catholic activities was just too strong, and Laud had to be protected from the Scots' accusations that he was "trying to subvert this kingdom to that faith." It was a blow for Con, disproving all his assurances to Rome "that through his efforts this kingdom is marching with great strides toward obedience to the Holy See." But, as Charles pointed out, the proclamation was far less severe than it might have been.[61] Granted, it expressly forbade new conversions, but it did not prohibit British Catholics from attending Mass, condemning only those "contumacious persons" who "give scandal by celebrating or hearing of any Mass." And there was no explicit prohibition against Catholics attending Henrietta's chapel or the chapels of London's foreign ambassadors, as Laud had originally demanded.[62]

If Con was dispirited, Henrietta was utterly undaunted. As the proclamation came off the presses, she was already making arrangements for the largest-ever Mass in her chapel. By her special command, the Countess of Newport was there, as well as other court ladies who had recently converted but had not yet attended Mass publicly. After leading them all to receive Communion, Henrietta retired to her chamber, triumphant.

"Have you seen the effects of the proclamation?" she asked Con, with heavy irony.

"I have seen the effect of Your Majesty's piety," he replied, "and I shall not fail to represent it to our lord [the pope], and to the lord Cardinal Barberini."[63]

All that Christmas, London's Catholic chapels were as busy as ever. "The reformed [i.e., Protestant] church loses openly," the Dutch ambassador reported. As the New Year of 1638 commenced,

Con informed Rome with relief that not a single Catholic had been harmed over the holidays.[64] On toward spring, it grew ever clearer that the proclamation had been mere empty words: a government public relations exercise designed to defuse Puritan agitation. To satisfy Catholic demand, there were now nine Masses on festival days at Somerset House, and a further eight at Con's private chapel every day. That February, Olive Porter brought in two new ladies— her mother and her sister-in-law—for Catholic instruction. And they were not the only ones: "Our great women fall away every day," came the news from the court that Easter.[65] All through Holy Week, London was filled with conspicuous displays of Catholic devotion. Replicas of Christ's sepulchre were set up in all the Catholic chapels, and many people made pilgrimages among them. The Countess of Arundel seized the opportunity for more good work, taking the Earl of Bath and other Protestant friends to see the sepulchre in George Con's chapel, at which the earl said he felt more devotion than in any Anglican church.[66] In the end, the Newport affair had only proved the Catholic party's real power at court. At the age of twenty-seven, Henrietta was a skillful political operator, capable of outmaneuvering even Archbishop Laud himself.

But if Henrietta was pleased by her successes, Charles's government soon saw the fearsome effect on public opinion. Libels and lampoons circulated freely. One letter made the rounds asserting "that the king's Majesty was a Catholic." "The queen was a whore," it was said. People spoke out against ship money "with the utmost freedom."[67] Everywhere payment was refused. When even members of Charles's own Privy Council began to protest against the tax, the king angrily declared that they were not to give an opinion on any question unless he asked for it. The councillors were astonished, foreseeing many "difficulties which may arise, but as he who commands wishes it, they must obey." And from Scotland came news that if Charles wanted the new prayer book enforced, he "must send an army of forty thousand men to defend the minister who must read it." But Charles would not listen. Instead, he sent back a declaration that anyone who persisted in antigovernment meetings would be "guilty of high treason."[68]

For the Scots, it was the last straw. On February 28, 1638, all the nobles and gentlemen in Edinburgh gathered at Greyfriars Church, where, one after another for four hours, they signed the National Covenant drawn up by the leaders of the resistance. Solemnly, the Covenanters swore to defend their own "true religion" against Charles's innovations, which

> do sensibly tend to the re-establishing of the popish religion and tyr-
> anny, and to the subversion and ruin of the true reformed religion
> and of our liberties, laws and estates.

This was not a rebellion, they asserted, merely "an unfeigned desire to maintain the true worship of God, the majesty of our king, and the peace of the kingdom."[69] The next day, Edinburgh's church ministers came to sign the Covenant, three hundred strong, and the following day the city's people—men and women alike—added their names.

Charles was "much distressed in mind," and Henrietta begged him to back down, urging "the fear of civil war, with danger to his royal person." But the king told her "not to alarm herself": "when he wishes he can reduce those subjects to obedience." Just a week later, news came that the Scots had taken over the government. Taxes "and every other mark of the royal authority" had been abolished; the bishops were to be expelled and their revenues distributed to the parishes. "If the Scots decide to choose another king, as they claim to have just and legitimate cause for doing, the whole power of England would never suffice to subdue them," the Venetian ambassador reported.[70] At last the king began to speak of compromise, offering to withdraw the new prayer book, provided that the bishops remained in place and "the rebels ask pardon for their past offenses." It seemed the only sensible course: he had neither money nor the support of his people, so any attempt to use force against the Scots would bring the "manifest danger" of losing England and Ireland as well, "which are unprovided with troops, fortresses, or anything else which might secure a state."[71] But Charles in fact had no thought of backing down. There was too much at stake: "Not only now my crown, but my reputation for ever . . . which is irreparable." "I will rather die than yield to these impertinent and damnable demands . . . for it is all one, as to yield to be no king in a very short time."[72]

And so he began preparing an army to march into Scotland. His plans were known only to a handful of trusted advisers. Bypassing the Privy Council completely, he spent hours in "long and secret interviews" with Archbishop Laud.[73] For some time, he had also been secretly consulting George Con about what to do "with those countrymen of yours," as Charles jokingly called them. Using the crisis for his own benefit, Con stirred up the king's resentment against the Covenanters: they were merely greedy, ambitious men whose supposed religious principles were a pretext for rebellion. Enthusiastically Con talked of the assistance Charles could gain both from his own Catholic subjects and from Catholic powers abroad. For many decades, British Catholics had been forbidden to bear arms, but now, under Con's urging, Charles planned to raise Catholic forces against the Covenanters. The Scottish Catholic nobles were already arming, while the Irish Earl of Antrim offered to bring over ten thousand of his Ulster clansmen for Charles's service.[74]

At Greenwich now for the start of the summer, Charles threw himself into frenzied activity, determined to prevail. Every few days, a fresh letter went off to the Marquess of Hamilton, his new chief man in Scotland. "My train of artillery . . . is in good forwardness, and I hope will be ready within six weeks," the king wrote:

> I have sent for arms to Holland, for 14,000 foot and 2,000 horse: for my ships they are ready. . . . I have consulted with the Treasurer and Chancellor of the Exchequer, for money for this year's expedition; which I estimate at two hundred thousand pounds sterling, which they doubt not but to furnish me.

"My resolution is to come myself in person," he added five days later. Meanwhile, Hamilton was instructed to draw out his negotiations with the Covenanters, "your chief end being now to win time . . . until I be ready to suppress them."[75]

In July, bad news came: the Covenanters refused to accept the terms Hamilton had offered and had enrolled forty thousand men "skilled in the use of arms," who could be mustered at a few hours' notice. Charles was alarmed. "His very face clearly betrays the passions within." He even informed his Privy Council for the first time about Scottish affairs, though the councillors made no reply, remembering that they were to give no advice "unless asked."[76] Hoping to gain more time for his military preparations, Charles offered further concessions to the Covenanters: the General Assembly governing the Presbyterian Church of Scotland could meet that November, he agreed, and then the Scottish Parliament. But as the king continued to wait anxiously, a new threat appeared.

For seven years, Henrietta's mother, Marie de' Medici, had been a political refugee in the Spanish Netherlands, following her failed coup against Cardinal Richelieu. All that time, she had been seeking refuge with her youngest daughter in England. A "very ardent" partisan of her mother's, Henrietta had urged her husband to do more for her, and Charles was full of assurances. But he was extremely unwilling to receive his mother-in-law. As the Venetian ambassadors put it, Marie would be an "unspeakable annoyance"—"one of the heaviest burdens" that could fall on Charles and his government, in terms of both expense and the danger of further popular unrest.[77] Charles also recognized the risks to his own domestic happiness, given Marie's well-known influence over her youngest daughter. Then again, Marie's political intriguing could push Charles into greater hostilities with France than he desired, especially given that Henrietta was still "very embittered" against Cardinal Richelieu.[78]

Already Charles had reluctantly received another prominent French opponent of Richelieu's. The Duchesse de Chevreuse had fled from France—first to Spain and then to England in April 1638— just as Charles issued his first conciliatory offer to the Covenanters. Henrietta was delighted: she had "a special affection" for the duchesse, one of her companions during her first year in England. The Spanish government was thrilled too, having "no small hopes of the good offices that Madame de Chevreuse may do for them."[79] In London, the duchesse lived in "noble and well-furnished" court apartments, supported by a generous stipend from Charles and Henrietta. "All the lords pay her court and she passes the time merrily." However, she was nothing but trouble for Charles. She "spends as if our treasure were infinite," Laud complained.[80] And her presence was a new provocation to Puritan public opinion. Riding around London in George Con's coach, dining with the French ambassador, spending long hours at the Spanish ambassador's house in secret negotiations, she was another controversial Catholic presence at the English court, raising suspicions of who-knew-what? All through the summer, she tempted the English royals with a Spanish proposal for marrying their eldest daughter, Mary, still just seven years old, to the heir to the Spanish throne. It was an idea that "pleases them greatly here," but Spain's enemies feared it was merely a ploy "to lull this crown to sleep."[81] The duchesse even ventured to take Princess Mary to Mass in Henrietta's chapel at Windsor, for which she was sternly rebuked by Charles. In sum, she was "a cunning and practicing woman," Laud complained, and "I would . . . we were rid of her."[82]

But instead, news came that Marie de' Medici was leaving Flanders for England. Driven on by Henrietta, who worked "to coax him to undertake this most expensive entertainment," Charles ordered preparations "to receive and entertain her properly." "The king yields to all the caprices of his wife," the news-writers complained.[83] Three thousand pounds a month would be paid for Marie's support, and Charles stopped all court salaries in order to raise the needed money. Expensively redecorated apartments were set aside for her at St. James's Palace.[84] Ships were sent out to seek her storm-tossed flotilla; the king and queen's coaches "and twenty more" were prepared to transport her; London's mayor and aldermen were ordered to prepare for her grand entry. Still Charles hoped Marie might change her mind, and he sent off a final messenger "under the show of compliment, in order to stop her coming." But on October 18, Marie's little fleet of ships was sighted off Harwich, and news reached London the next day that she had landed. "This is but a new beginning of evils," Laud noted.[85]

But still Marie was treated with the utmost honor. All along her route, townspeople turned out in welcome, and Charles himself rode out to accompany her on her state entry into London. The procession was immense: the queen mother had brought a suite six hundred strong, and there was Charles's court as well. Six thousand militiamen armed with pikes and muskets lined the streets, while the shops, balconies, and windows of the houses were filled with "an infinity of people." Cannons fired from the Tower of London, while Henrietta, six months pregnant, waited at St. James's Palace for the mother she had not seen in thirteen years. "I look forward to seeing her every day," she had just written to her nearest sister, Christine, Duchess of Savoy.[86] Trumpets blared amid the shouts of the crowd outside St. James's, and a messenger announced Marie's approach. With her four young children—two princes and two princesses—Henrietta descended the palace's great staircase, followed by her ladies. In the courtyard below, her mother's great state carriage came to a halt, and Henrietta walked to its door and threw herself down on her knees. No sooner had Marie raised her daughter in her arms and kissed her than Henrietta, "filled with joy," knelt again, to be lifted and kissed once more. "An extreme joy made mutes of everyone, as well as a great sadness."[87]

The two had changed immeasurably. From a girl of fifteen, Henrietta had become a wife, a mother, and a queen. Accompanied now by "all the grandest and most beautiful ladies of the court," she eclipsed them all in both "grace and . . . majesty, in which she never found an equal." But if Henrietta had grown, Marie had shrunk. Her portrait sketched by Peter Paul Rubens around 1625, when Henrietta had last seen her, shows a sturdy, contented matron, her authority clear in her heavy-lidded gaze and the slight smile that curls the corners of her mouth. But now, Henrietta wrote to Christine, tactfully glossing over the effects of their mother's sufferings, "I found her a little changed."[88]

After that first long silence, Henrietta and her mother and many others wept. "Truly," recalled one of Marie's courtiers, "I have never seen so much joy or so many tears together." Recovering herself, Henrietta presented her children to the grandmother they had never seen: kneeling like their mother, the boys and girls received her blessing. Then Charles stepped down, took his mother-in-law on his arm, and led the way upstairs, followed by Henrietta and the children and all the lords and ladies. That night, looking out from their windows at St. James's, Marie and her entourage saw the sky lit up with fireworks while crowds in the streets danced, sang, and drank around their bonfires. At court, the celebrations continued for days. Nothing was talked of but parties and balls and plays.[89]

Marie's influence at court was evident to everyone. Charles and Henrietta visited her almost daily—the king a picture of respect, taking off his hat to stand talking to his mother-in-law, while Henrietta displayed "the most filial reverence." As often as her health permitted, Marie returned their visits, having no greater "pleasure than that of being with them at every moment."[90] Her presence also strengthened the Catholics in Henrietta's court. The gift she brought her daughter from Flanders—"a beautiful image" of the Virgin Mary, "exquisitely carved"—provided a new focus for the devotions of Henrietta's Confraternity of the Holy Rosary at Somerset House. Mother and daughter often attended Mass together, sometimes at Marie's chapel at St. James's and sometimes at Somerset House, where Marie was delighted to see the crowds and experience firsthand "the great progress of their holy religion in the kingdom where it had formerly been so persecuted." She also met regularly with George Con, eagerly discussing his great plans for propagating their faith.[91]

On through the winter, Charles continued his military preparations. Money, munitions, and food were sent north to the Scottish border. Throughout England, the local militias were mustered, and Charles appointed the crypto-Catholic Earl of Arundel as Lord General in overall command.[92] Amid it all, Christmas passed without the usual court masques. Then, on January 20, 1639, the queen went into labor. All the signs were bad. Despite her superstitious preference for St. James's, she had been forced to remain at Whitehall for the birth: her mother's court of several hundred people left no room at the other palace. And soon the labor was in difficulty. In great pain and "in evident danger of death," Henrietta prayed "with great humility and fervor" to the Virgin Mary, her patron and namesake. Almost at once, the queen's pains were eased and her baby was born. The little princess was christened Katherine, but, "after only one hour of the miseries of this world," she died. Weak and ill and in "deep grief," Henrietta recovered only slowly.[93] Her doctors, afraid her condition might worsen, recommended she go to France "for the better air." But she was adamant that she had "no intention of undertaking this journey."[94] Her place was in England, where, despite her weakness, she was doing all she could to assist her husband in his political crisis.

For some months, she had been involved in the plans to raise Catholic forces in Ireland and Scotland, and now she also began to seek Catholic aid from abroad. Her miraculous survival in childbirth by the Virgin Mary's intercession provided the perfect cover for the secret missions of two Catholic priests who left England that February. One, Father Tresson, the superior of Henrietta's Capuchin priests, was ostensibly bound for the Santa Casa shrine of Mary at Loreto in central Italy, carrying "a very rich votive offering of gold and jewels" in thanksgiving for her recovery. But then he was to visit the pope, doubtless to discuss Rome's recent offers of aid against the Covenanters.[95] The second messenger-priest, Father George Gage, traveled to Flanders with another thanksgiving offering—for the shrine of Our Lady of Sichem—as well as secret instructions to open talks with the Spanish court at Brussels. It was all part of a plan devised by Gage and his brother Henry, a colonel in the Spanish army: the king, they suggested, could borrow an army from the Spanish, use it to defeat the Scots, and then bring it into England to "keep the Parliament in awe." The Spanish, though in principle willing, were busy fighting their own war against the Dutch and the French; they had taken such heavy losses that they had to reply that they could not send any troops.[96]

But already Henrietta was involved in a third set of negotiations. For months, the English, hoping to remove the financial burden of entertaining Marie de' Medici, had been working for a reconciliation between her and her son, Louis XIII. Marie was eager to return to France: she would "lay aside all her passion, and . . . be entirely submissive," she promised. But Louis refused, and he also rejected the English request for her to receive her own French income in England. She had to return to Florence—her birthplace and childhood home—if she wanted any money from France, he insisted. Refusing to go there, Marie stayed on in London, still costing Charles's government £3,000, paid promptly every month. Even Henrietta now saw the necessity of Marie's departure, so, hoping she might succeed where Charles had failed, she sent her own negotiator to Paris. Henry Jermyn, a Catholic convert in his early thirties, was fast becoming one of her greatest intimates.[97]

At this point, the king was almost ready to leave London for the North. Without calling an English Parliament, there was enough money only for a brief campaign, but Charles was optimistic. His "great army" would total thirty or forty thousand men, he expected. By invoking ancient feudal rights and summoning the nation's aristocracy "to attend our royal person and standard at York," bringing their own armed retinues, the king planned to raise much of his cavalry at no cost to the government. Already he was talking of being "in [a] short time in Edinburgh to settle that disordered government."[98] While most of his court and government went on ahead to York, Charles remained in London for one last week with his family. Then, on Wednesday, March 27, 1639, leaving half of his two-hundred-strong bodyguard "to attend the queen and [the] prince," Charles departed to lead his troops "against the Scottish Covenanting rebels," Laud wrote in his diary: "God of His infinite mercy bless him with health and success."[99]

8

LIBERTY AND RELIGION ALIKE

This time there was no leisurely journey to the North, hunting and dining along the way. In just three days, Charles was at York, where he was received with "every sign of devotion," he wrote to Henrietta.[1] But his army was a mess: poorly armed, ill-fed, undisciplined, even mutinous. For a month he remained in the city, gathering his forces, while his advisers voiced concerns about "how unsafe it was to venture the king's person among an untaught and inexperienced army." But they made no impression. Determined to quell the "intolerable insolency" of the Scots in person, Charles set off for Durham, Newcastle, and then the border.[2]

It was a bleak march northward from Newcastle in wet and windy weather, with "no towns nor trees fit for shelter . . . no fresh straw to litter a horse in all the way, nor means to lodge a Christian."[3] The soldiers walked in water up to their ankles and then slept at night beneath the open sky. The whole time, bad news kept coming in: the Scottish Catholic nobles had surrendered or fled without a fight; the Covenanters had taken Edinburgh Castle; their army was marching south toward England, forty thousand strong. But many, at least in the officer class, kept up their spirits with their hearty detestation of the enemy:

> those scurvy, filthy, dirty, nasty, lousy, itchy, scabby, shitten, stinking, slovenly, snotty-nosed, logger-headed, . . . villainous, barbarous, bestial, false, lying, roguish, devilish, long-eared, short-haired, damnable, atheistical, puritanical crew of the Scotch Covenant.[4]

Just west of the border town of Berwick, they made camp on a hilltop looking out over the River Tweed to Scotland. Charles—"the most active and vigilant prince . . . that I think lives"—supervised everything himself, "riding and viewing the place and giving direction for ordering the camp."[5] Men were set to work making trenches and ramparts, but morale was failing. The soldiers with their picks and spades "called and complained for want of bread and drink." Their position was perilous, they said: the river below them was "fordable [for] forty horse abreast," and there was "high and commanding ground" on the far side, a perfect place for the enemy to deploy their artillery. Even Charles's officers could not help being "a little daunted when we look upon . . . our own confusion and wants."[6]

Meanwhile, in London, Henrietta and her children were living at Whitehall under heavy guard, fearful of a predominantly Puritan populace that supported the Scottish Covenanters more than their own king. Seditious pamphlets appeared constantly, and rumors circulated like wildfire: the war was part of a "long-intended devilish plot" by Charles's corrupt advisers "to reduce these realms once more to subjection to the Roman Court"; the Scots were the instruments of God; they alone held back Archbishop Laud's "idolatry."[7] The archbishop went around in fear, his servants armed with swords. George Con, too, was accused of "perverting his Majesty's simple subjects" and spying for the pope, while the queen's priests, it was said, embezzled government funds to support their bastard children.[8]

Every week, on Henrietta's orders, London's Catholics arrived at her chapel for "solemn service and sermons," praying "for the king's happy progression in his designs, and for his safe return."[9] And she hoped for much more than their prayers. Letters went out from the queen and two of her leading Catholic courtiers, Walter Montagu and Sir Kenelm Digby, asking the nation's Catholics to express their "duties, and zeal to his Majesty's service . . . by some considerable gift," "freely and cheerfully presented" to help the war. They owed so much to her and Charles, Henrietta urged, for by her "extraordinary graces and protections" she had won them "the happy moderation" under which they now lived. Now was the time for them to show their gratitude and prove she had been right always to assure the king of their "loyalty and affection."[10] Charles was "exceedingly" gratified by the plan—a sum as large as £50,000 was hoped for—and soon Henrietta had a second scheme in the pipeline. She would write "to all the great ladies" in the land, "as well wives as widows," asking them "to contribute . . . toward the charge of the king's army." The sum she named was £100 each. With £10,000 from the ladies, plus £10,000 of her own money and the money from the Catholics, she hoped "to surprise his Majesty."[11] But she was to be disappointed. Apart from a few "court countesses," none of the ladies contributed, and in the end a mere £14,000 came in from the Catholics—barely enough to support the army for a week.[12] Even Rome let Henrietta down: papal aid for Charles could come only if he converted to Catholicism, Con reported. The only real hope now lay with the Spanish government in Brussels, where Henrietta's overtures had at last brought an offer of troops for Charles, though it was too late for this campaigning season.[13]

A few days into June, the Scots army suddenly appeared across the Tweed from Charles's troops and immediately set up two batteries of guns. The English were appalled. The force was far larger than imagined, and there was "great . . . murmuring" among the private soldiers, who blamed the scoutmaster general, a northern Catholic, for failing to gather proper intelligence. Amid the "hubbub," the Earl of Bristol, long an opponent of the court, spoke out publicly to the king, questioning "the ground of this quarrel" with the Scots and calling for an English Parliament: "Most of the lords here . . . were resolved to petition his Majesty for one," he said.[14] At other times, Bristol's outburst might have brought him a stinging put-down, such as Charles had delivered to his privy councillors regarding ship money a year earlier. But the king was too dismayed by the enemy and by his own men alike. In contrast to his earlier belligerence, he was now full of "hopes of an approaching agreement with the Scots," Henrietta heard in London.[15] It was the first of many about-faces that Charles would perform in the coming years: "The facility with which the king starts on an action and his lack of firmness in sustaining it" would exasperate his followers. Just six days after the Scots reached the Tweed, formal peace talks began. Six days later, it was all agreed: the armies would disband and there would be a General Assembly and Parliament in Edinburgh in August; Charles himself would attend.[16]

From London, Secretary of State Windebank begged the king to reconsider: "I cannot without horror think upon your Majesty's going into Scotland in person, and exposing yourself . . . to the mercy of a people enraged, [and] weary of monarchical government."[17] Henrietta and the privy councillors added their voices to his: the latest news from Edinburgh confirmed that "the people there are mad and mutinous."[18] Reluctant to follow their advice, Charles stayed on in Berwick, gathering intelligence and holding talks with the Covenanter leaders, while Henrietta awaited his return "with great impatience." But after everything Charles learned convinced him that the situation was hopeless, he decided to return to London to "take other counsels."[19]

It had been the royal couple's longest-ever separation, and Charles hurried south now, "impatient of remaining away from his wife any longer." After just three days' journey, he joined her at Theobalds. Driving in state with Marie de' Medici, they entered London to cheering crowds. They left Marie at St. James's Palace and walked together the last few hundred yards across the park to Whitehall.[20] But it was no happy homecoming. Charles "was very melancholic," seeing that "he had lost reputation at home and abroad," and the palace seethed with "factions and animosities."[21] Even among the couple's courtiers were Puritans, such as the Earl of Northumberland, Charles's Lord Admiral, who had all along opposed his Scottish policy. Informed of his master's war plans only as the final preparations were made, Northumberland had then joined other privy councillors in urging the king to summon England's Parliament, but Charles had "sharply" rejected their advice, leaving them dissatisfied and resentful.[22] In stark opposition to this Puritan faction stood Archbishop Laud, who denounced the Scots as "rebels and traitors," inflaming the king's anger even more against them. Their Covenant was "ungodly," "damnable," "treasonable," Laud said, and the peace treaty made at Berwick was "dishonorable," and fit "to be broken."[23] To men like Northumberland, who shared many of the Scots' religious principles, it seemed that Laud condemned anyone "who spoke well of the reformed [i.e., Protestant] religion."[24]

Henrietta and her pro-Catholic courtiers made up yet a third faction, resented and feared by Laud. "We are undone," the archbishop had complained, when Henrietta persuaded Charles to appoint two of her protégés to the Privy Council: "I am so full of indignation that I dare not let my pen go."[25] But there were divisions even within the queen's camp. The Earl of Holland, long trusted by Henrietta and used by her to "boldly speak for the Catholics" when no others dared—back before Con's arrival in England—was now falling rapidly from the queen's favor because of his too-Puritan sympathies. Holland's wife was already joining the popular calls for a Parliament, which was needed, she said, to destroy the "excessive power" of the Catholics.[26] Meanwhile, Henrietta's great favorite, Walter Montagu, vied with his old mentor, George Con, for the queen's nomination to a cardinalship. And many of her courtiers resented the rapid rise of Henry Jermyn. Noted for his courtly manners and "agreeable wit," he was now "more then ever in the favor of [the queen], and indeed to a strange degree."[27]

In September 1639, the balance of power among the various factions was dramatically altered when a new man arrived at court. In his late forties, Thomas Viscount Wentworth was ambitious, ener-

getic, and intelligent, in "every way qualified for [political] business."[28] For the previous eight years, he had served Charles as Lord
Deputy of Ireland. There the vast challenges of government corruption, military inadequacy, and a "very insolent" Catholic majority had been to him just "means to show his abilities."[29] Ruthlessly
playing off Catholics against Protestants, he had managed Ireland's
Parliament in triumphant style, gaining substantial tax grants for the
king. The Convocation of the Anglican Church of Ireland that he
summoned was just as successful, reforming the Protestant Irish
Church along Laudian lines. Laud and Wentworth became fast
friends in those years, collaborating to advance their shared ideal of
ordered, authoritarian government in church and state. And Charles
was delighted with his Lord Deputy's achievements: his letters to
Wentworth would become more "panegyrics than dispatches" if he
were not careful, the king confided.[30] By 1637, Charles was consulting Wentworth on some of the most significant decisions facing him—how to raise money at home, whether or not to go to war
abroad. A year later, Wentworth was one of the very few trusted with
Charles's secret plans for war with Scotland. Now, with the failure
of his Scottish policy, Charles wrote urgently "to desire your attendance and counsel."[31] His need was pressing. Fearful of popular
resentment, Laud had withdrawn from his private discussions with
Charles on Scottish affairs. George Con, long the sharer of Charles's
secret military plans, left England that summer, an ill man, and died
in Rome the following year. So Charles ordered Wentworth to join
him in London as soon as possible and in the greatest secrecy: "I will
not have you take notice that I have sent for you, but pretend some
other occasion of business."[32]

Still Wentworth went fearfully to London: "The nearer I come to
it, the more my heart fails me; nor can I promise myself any good
by this journey."[33] Henrietta's faction, he knew, regarded him with
"great animosity," and Henrietta had become more powerful than
ever. "She was never so well with the king," came the news from
court, and her men were rising to new power. George, Lord Goring, Master of the Queen's Horse, became the king's vice chamberlain and a privy councillor, while her new favorite, Henry Jermyn,

advanced to Goring's old post. Even Sir Kenelm Digby and Walter Montagu, Catholics long distrusted by Charles, were on the way up.[34] But Wentworth found a warm welcome from Charles. The queen's newly appointed men were primarily courtiers without real political experience, and so, in his hour of need, the king turned eagerly to Viscount Wentworth. Within a few weeks, he was the man who had "most influence with his Majesty."[35]

Already Charles had begun fresh military preparations against Scotland. Troops were sent to the frontier; the fleet was readying to sail northward. When the Scottish General Assembly and Parliament met in defiant mood, exiling the nation's bishops to England and threatening to expel the king's garrisons from all their castles, Charles's resolution for war hardened: the Scots had to be crushed to prevent "the same pernicious sentiments" of rebellion from spreading into England.[36] But money, as always, was the great stumbling block. Every day the king's ministers met to discuss the best methods for raising more, "but all involve inextricable difficulties." Some were too likely to raise popular resistance; others were "rejected as illegal." Charles considered cutting Marie de' Medici's allowance, but he was soon dissuaded by Henrietta's "influential offices."[37]

Wentworth, however, was sure he had the answers: twenty thousand soldiers could be sent from Ireland, funded by the Irish Parliament and commanded by officers of "devoted loyalty," and in England there had to be a new Parliament—the only way to gain the funds Charles needed.[38] Wentworth was an articulate and persuasive man, and throughout November he battled determinedly against the king's "inveterate objection" to Parliament.[39] His own recent successes in managing the Irish Parliament were undeniable, and he was confident that the English MPs, faced with an invading Scottish army, would rally wholeheartedly behind Charles. As the news from Scotland worsened, his arguments were also supported by Charles's intimate Committee of Eight, with whom alone he discussed Scottish affairs. All agreed that war "was visibly necessary." Yet there was no prospect of Crown money to fund it: Parliament had to be called. True, the previous Parliament, twelve years earlier, had been "mutinous." But since then, the "happy peace and universal plenty over the whole nation" surely would guarantee the people's goodwill toward Charles: only "sober men" would be elected to the House of Commons, and they would "provide remedies proportionable" to the king's need.[40] Recognizing his "extreme necessity," Charles could only agree. The war was "a public business and of great weight, and not to be undertaken but upon the public charge," he announced to his Privy Council, so it was "our own desire to meet our people, and to demand their assistance in the ancient and ordinary way of a Parliament."[41]

Everywhere people "expressed great joy" at the news. The political opposition, afraid that Charles might change his mind, were full of assurances "that they will arrange everything to please him." Only the Catholics were apprehensive, seeing "no talk of anything except against the Catholic religion."[42] As the New Year of 1640 began, the government pressed ahead with "huge preparations" for the campaign—mustering troops, preparing a fleet, and appointing commanding officers. Money was no problem: the Privy Council had agreed that its members would lend Charles what he needed from their own private resources, to be repaid once Parliament met in April and voted proper supplies. Substantial funds were also expected from the Irish Parliament.[43] And if the English MPs did "prove peevish" and refuse to pay up, there were fallback plans. Wentworth, fresh from autocratic rule in Ireland, promised to "find a way to obtain promptly from the people [of England] a fresh levy of £300,000." And Charles himself was rumored to have "secret intentions" to use his northern army to terrify Parliament into submission.[44]

He and Henrietta were in high spirits—relieved to be beyond their seemingly interminable indecision and full of hope that they would now leave behind the past financial, political, and military failures. At Whitehall on January 21, 1640, the couple appeared together on stage for the first time, expressing their robust optimism in the lavish fantasy world of a new court masque, more spectacular than any before, performed for the entertainment of Marie de' Medici.[45] Devised as usual by Inigo Jones, with the script written by Henrietta's courtier William Davenant, *Salmacida Spolia* carried a clear message for Scotland. Amid a fierce storm appeared the malicious, snake-haired fury Discord, come from the wars of Europe to disturb Britain's peace. But Discord's evil designs were short lived, as the Good Genius of Great Britain descended from the heavens in a silver chariot, imploring Concord to "ease the cares of wise Philogenes"—Charles himself, the Lover of his People. The masque proclaimed Charles's peaceful virtues: prudence, innocence, "forgetfulness of injuries," "affection to the country." "Without blood, without sweat"—like the ancient Greek colonists at Salmacis, referred to in the title—he would reduce the "turbulent natures" of the country's "fierce and cruel" barbarian inhabitants "into a sweet calm of civil concord." Finally, Henrietta and her ladies appeared from a cloud—all "in Amazonian habits," with helmets topped with ostrich plumes and curving swords at their sides—sent down from heaven to reward Charles "for reducing the threatening storm into the following calm."[46]

It was a last moment of peace and happiness. Henrietta, pregnant once again, was "in perfect health" and "very cheerful."[47] Despite all the military demands on the royal coffers, she was busy with building and gardening projects. At Greenwich, she was completing the interior of the Queen's House, ordering twenty-two paintings of the story of Cupid and Psyche for her cabinet there and eagerly awaiting the delivery of paintings of other mythological scenes for her bedchamber and the main hall.[48] She had a completely new project, too. Back in August, as Charles was returning to London, she had arranged to buy the manor of Wimbledon for £16,000. Situated atop a hill, the grand Elizabethan mansion had dramatic vistas over a "great orchard with walks" to the countryside beyond. Just three miles from Whitehall, it would make a perfect country villa, Henrietta figured, and she launched at once into building a new royal wing and laying out elaborate gardens. With sixty orange trees in tubs, fountains, summer houses, a maze, and a huge avenue of limes, elms, and cypress trees, this was the most ambitious of all her garden designs: a sign of optimism and determination to continue life as usual, even as the country turned against its royal leaders.[49]

In January 1640, in gratitude for his "prudent counsels" and multifarious labors, Charles made Wentworth the Earl of Strafford—

one of the most senior aristocrats in England. Almost alone among the government ministers, the new earl wholeheartedly advocated Charles's war against the Scots, and observers noted that he was "stepping quickly toward the entire control of this monarchy."[50] In March, he left for Dublin to manage the Irish Parliament. Under his coercion, they soon voted funding for a nine-thousand-strong army to be shipped to Scotland, while the Irish Church agreed to pay further substantial sums. The people there would "give all they possess" to support the king, Strafford enthused.[51] Then he rushed back to attempt the same in London. But the English elections had gone against the king. Angry at being "deceived in his hopes," Charles pushed forward with his military preparations, "ostensibly in order to subdue the rebellious Scots by force, but with the secret intention of using these arms to bridle the insolent demands of Parliament and make them do their duty." As the troops mustered, he planned "to scrutinize the quality of the men, endeavoring to have as few Puritans as possible in the companies"; Catholics, by contrast, were readily given military commands.[52]

On Monday, April 13, despite his misgivings, Charles rode in state to open the new Parliament. Henrietta viewed the "very glorious" procession from a stage in Whitehall's gardens, then moved into a private gallery in the House of Lords to watch as Charles, "arrayed in his regal robes, ascended his royal throne." "There was never a king that had a more great and weighty cause to call his people together than myself," Charles told Parliament.[53] Then the case for war was made by Lord Finch, his new Lord Keeper and a protégé of Henrietta's. Appointed after promising to "do every favor" for the Catholics, Finch was one of the couple's few true loyalists besides Strafford. Now he declared that the Scots had "taken up arms against the Lord's anointed, their rightful prince and undoubted sovereign": their actions were "foul and horrid treasons," leaving the king no choice but to send "a powerful army, to reduce them to . . . obedience and subjection." And so Charles asked his Parliament to "lay aside all other debates" and vote a sum of money "fit and convenient for so great an action."[54]

The MPs, unmoved, turned to denouncing the government's long-running encroachments on their rights, especially the collection of ship money, the Laudian reforms in the Anglican Church, and the illegal toleration of the nation's Catholic minority, "demons . . . full of subtlety, full of malignity." Within days, a new leader emerged in the House of Commons. John Pym was neither a stylish nor an entertaining orator. He read his speeches aloud from closely written pages of densely argued points, sometimes stumbling over his own handwriting. Yet his passionate conviction stirred his hearers beyond all else. "A good oration!" the MPs called, as he ended a two-hour, systematic and exhaustive analysis of the government's oppressions in church and state.[55]

For three weeks, king and Commons continued at loggerheads, as the MPs turned a deaf ear to all Charles's demands for money and his assurances that after that he would hear their grievances and "give just satisfaction to his people." They knew from earlier Parliaments just how little trust could be placed in his promises, so they devoted their time to drawing up a complete list of grievances to present to the king.[56] Meanwhile, feelings in London were running high. Talk of Charles's plan to use military force against Parliament was widespread. Handwritten libels circulated, justifying the Scots' rebellion and complaining about the political machinations of Hamilton, Laud, and Henrietta herself.[57] At last, desperate, Charles offered to abolish ship money if Parliament would vote for his supplies. But it was not enough. For eleven hours that day, the MPs continued with further demands and denunciations of the government. "It was in vain to expect longer . . . for no money would be had against the Scots," Charles's secretary of state, Sir Henry Vane, reported to Whitehall.[58] The next day, dressed in his crown and robes, the king addressed his Parliament, insisting that it was "some few cunning and some ill-affectioned men that have been the cause of this misunderstanding." As for himself, "no king in the world shall be more careful to maintain . . . the liberties of their persons, and true religion." Then Lord Keeper Finch pronounced the concluding formality: "My Lords, and ye knights, citizens, and burgesses of the House of Commons, the King's Majesty doth dissolve this Parliament."[59]

It was a devastating blow. "Tuesday, the Parliament ended, and nothing done," Laud noted in his diary. Fear and dissatisfaction were "in the hearts and words of every creature," Lucy, Countess of Carlisle observed.[60] When they met later that day, Charles's ministers stressed the insuperable difficulties of pursuing his "great designs" against the Scots; perhaps it was best "to do nothing and let them alone," the Puritan Earl of Northumberland suggested. Only Strafford remained confident "that there are yet ways left to make his Majesty happy."[61] Charles had done all he could by constitutional means, the earl argued. "Reduced to extreme necessity," the king was now "absolved from all rules of government," and free to do whatever "power will admit." There was no need to fear opposition at home; the only necessity was to "go vigorously on" against the Scots. "You have an army in Ireland you may employ here to reduce this kingdom," he pointed out. "Scotland shall not hold out five months. One summer well employed will do it."[62] Money seemed no problem to him, what with ship money and a £100,000 loan that Charles had demanded from the City of London. The Convocation of the Church of England had already voted to supply funds. And Strafford, "much interested" in Henrietta's idea of borrowing Spanish troops or money, was beginning meetings with their ambassadors to negotiate the deal.[63]

The next day, Strafford's policies for despotic government began to be put into effect. John Pym and other opposition leaders were imprisoned, and all their papers were seized. The king summoned London's Lord Mayor and aldermen before his Privy Council. Since they had failed to provide the £100,000 loan requested, "therefore he now required £200,000"; the names of rich merchants who could lend this sum had to be supplied by Sunday, or else "he would have £300,000 of the City." When they still resisted, Strafford proposed violent measures. "Sir," he told Charles, "unless you hang up some of them, you will do no good," and four of the most outspoken aldermen were committed to prison.[64]

By now, all Henrietta's past distaste for the earl was gone. Admittedly his face was plain, even ugly, she later recalled, but his manners were "very agreeable" and "he had the most beautiful hands in the world." More important, he was without doubt "the most capable and faithful of the king's servants."[65] But outside White-hall's walls, Strafford's draconian measures only further infuriated Charles's subjects. Within twenty-four hours of Parliament's dissolution, there were mutterings that the earl was "in danger to be torn to pieces or to have his throat cut." Laud, too, was blamed for "the breach of Parliament," and printed notices called on London's apprentices to turn out "for the hunting of 'William the Fox.'" Three days later, new notices went up, summoning "every class" to appear on Monday, May 11, in St. George's Fields outside Southwark and "secure . . . the death of many leading ministers, reputed enemies of the commonweal."[66]

The government ordered troops to occupy the fields throughout that Monday. But in the evening, after the soldiers had gone, crowds began to gather. By dark, "some thousands" were there: mainly apprentices, the city's most inflammable class, all of them armed. Shortly before midnight, they set out to march, "with drums beating . . . in a riotous manner," the half mile to Lambeth Palace, Laud's London residence, where they arrived "with the purpose of slaying him."[67] The archbishop had already fled to Whitehall, having "strengthened the house as well as I could." Shots came from the men inside, and a woman in the crowd was wounded, but still the "rascal routers," as Laud called them, stayed on for a "full two hours." Only when they were certain the archbishop was not there did they leave, threatening to "come back and visit the houses of other ministers in even greater numbers and better armed."[68]

Outraged at this "rabble of mean, unknown, dissolute persons" and their "infamous, scandalous, headless insurrection," Charles acted vigorously to prevent the violence from spreading. London's usual night watches were doubled; two hundred militiamen kept watch day and night over the royal children at Richmond Palace. Cavalry troops were ordered into London, four cannon were placed outside Lambeth Palace, and Strafford's house also was "well defended."[69] Some fifty suspected rioters were arrested and interrogated, in "great efforts" to discover whether they had Parliamentarian leadership. Meanwhile, "in great wrath," Charles pressed ahead with his efforts to force money from his subjects. He also approached the new papal agent, Carlo Rossetti, requesting aid from Rome.[70]

But on May 14, 1640, the rioters gathered in greater force than ever. Lambeth was too strongly defended now, but a mob of seven thousand proceeded to attack another of Laud's palaces at Croydon, while other bands assaulted the city's prisons, "knocked down the gates, slew the keepers, and released all the prisoners, especially those in custody for the riot of Monday." Alarmed, Charles reinforced the guards at Whitehall and ordered six thousand militia troops into London "to prevent fresh disturbances."[71] But his resolve was failing. Strafford had fallen suddenly and seriously ill. Lacking his bold counsels, and worn down by ten days "full of fears ever since the Parliament broke up," Charles made moves for conciliation. The imprisoned MPs and the London aldermen were set free. When the City again refused a loan, no action was taken. Charles even released three Scottish negotiators whom he had imprisoned a month earlier, sending one of them north to Edinburgh to try to reopen talks.[72]

But the rioters were not so fortunate. As a warning to others, one of the leaders from the first night was convicted of high treason at a hasty trial and hanged and quartered. Another man was tortured on the rack before being executed, but he still revealed nothing about the instigators of the riots.[73] What did emerge from the government's interrogations was the violent anti-Catholic sentiment of the mob. Laud was a papist who "had a crucifix on the Communion table in his chapel and . . . bowed toward the altar," they ranted. After demolishing his house at Lambeth, they threatened, they would destroy Marie de' Medici's residence at St. James's, and Henrietta's chapel at Somerset House, "because they were houses of popery." A confusion of rumors raced through the streets of London. "The queen went to the [Anglican] Communion with the King"; she was even considering converting, it was said. But Archbishop Laud had dissuaded her, and now "the king goes to Mass with the queen."[74]

Laud was terrified, knowing the power of such talk to stir the common people to violence. The government had to act at once against Catholics, he urged, to disprove the "most hateful" notion of his own and the king's defection. And Charles could no longer refuse. After years of frustration, Laud went to work with a will. Catholic books were burned in the streets. His agents searched suspect houses and seized Catholic devotional objects, books, papers, and printing machines. He ordered the arrest of forty-seven known priests and all English Catholics attending the chapels of the queen and the foreign ambassadors.[75] The effect was immediate. Rioting against the government ceased, but instead the mob turned all its fury against the Catholics. Outside Somerset House one night, a wild crowd gathered, issuing threats against Henrietta's Capuchin priests. A few days later, notices appeared, summoning the defenders of the purity of the Gospel to raze the papal agent's house and kill him. Carlo Rossetti fled to St. James's Palace, which, like Somerset House, was under heavy guard, but the houses of London's Catholics were freely looted that night. The agitation against Henrietta even reached Whitehall, where someone scratched on the window of the king's antechamber: "God save the king, God confound the queen and all her faction, and God grant the Palatine to reign in this kingdom." In a fury, Charles smashed the glass with his fist.[76]

As May ended, Charles and Henrietta were together at Greenwich to begin their summer holidays. But the crisis was now sparking discord even between the two of them. Distrusting Charles's policy of appeasement, Henrietta urged him, "with all her might . . . to pursue the war with spirit against the rebels until they are completely subdued." What he needed, she said, was Catholic money, and she hoped to obtain "large contributions" from his subjects and "some help from the pope."[77] At Rossetti's urging, she also spoke to Charles about the government's new persecution of the Catholics, arguing that it would only alienate these otherwise-most-loyal subjects and prevent them from aiding the king's cause. But amid continuing rumors that Laud "was turned papist" and that Charles himself "commonly went to Mass," the king could not afford to please his wife. The nation's penal laws remained in force.[78]

But not for long. On July 8, Henrietta's baby was born after an easy labor: a boy, named Henry after his mother and his French grandfather. Charles was effusive in his joy, enthusiastically granting favors to his wife. He placed Henry under the care of the Catholic Countess of Roxburghe, who was already governess to the three princesses. He also suspended the penal laws for the month of Henrietta's lying-in after the birth, and he ordered the release of all imprisoned Catholics. Charles was now as resolved on war as Henrietta could wish. "Deeply incensed" after the Scots Parliament met, contrary to his wishes, and approved all the decisions of the Presbyterian General Assembly, he had lost "all hope of settling affairs there by gentle means."[79]

But where would he obtain the necessities of war? The latest offer from the pope—six to eight thousand troops, ready to serve Charles "to the last breath," carried on ships from the Spanish Netherlands—would be available, Rossetti warned, only "to sustain a king who was a professed Catholic, and for the defense of our Holy Religion"—a state of affairs that Henrietta would have loved to see but that she admitted was profoundly unlikely.[80] And Charles's other requests for foreign aid were no more successful. The £300,000 offered to Strafford by the Spanish ambassadors never materialized, and the proposal of an alliance with France in return for a loan of £400,000 was also rebuffed. So Charles returned to his old policy of forcing money from his reluctant subjects. In a surprise move, his government seized all the gold and silver brought into the Royal Mint for coining by London's merchants, amounting to some £100,000.[81] The threat of replacing some of the nation's silver coins with copper was also held over the merchants, in an attempt to pressure them into a new loan. Even so, the City of London corporations refused, so at last Charles resorted to reducing by half Marie de' Medici's monthly allowance. This time, Henrietta made no objection and Marie was forced to dismiss many of her courtiers "and to arrange to live a more frugal life."[82]

Meanwhile, the English troops were desperately unready for war. Many, when they heard of Parliament's dissolution, refused to serve; the remainder marched northward only in the greatest disorder. Hundreds mutinied against their Catholic officers and the ungodly cause for which they were called to fight, or simply for lack of pay. Strafford's ten-thousand-strong Irish army, mostly Catholic, remained unshipped, again for lack of money. And still the northern

army had no commander-in-chief on the scene. The Earl of Northumberland, appointed on Strafford's advice, refused to leave London—due to illness, he protested, although many suspected that it
was no more than a "mendacious pretext."[83] Northumberland was
not alone in his disaffection. Henrietta's former favorite, the Earl
of Holland, had already secretly joined his half-brother, the Earl of
Warwick, as a leader of the opposition. The Earl of Pembroke, who
had entertained the king so lavishly each summer at Wilton, was
also fast falling out of sympathy with his master. Despite his luxurious tastes, Pembroke was at heart a godly Puritan who disliked Laud
and was disliked by Henrietta Maria.[84]

Still Charles remained optimistic. The Scots had sent their soldiers home "to save expense," he heard; they had no significant
forces on the border; divisions among their leaders would bring him
"considerable advantage."[85] But suddenly news arrived that their
army was mustered and marching south in force. Newcastle, lacking
both men and fortifications, could not hold out against an assault.
"Extraordinarily perturbed," the king decided to leave for the North
right away: his presence would confirm the wavering troops in their
loyalty and ensure that the Scots were halted at the border. When
his councillors objected, Charles remained adamant, determined
to act to "secure his wife and children."[86] The next few days were
crammed with preparations. The Earl of Northumberland continued to plead illness, so Charles appointed Strafford to command
the northern army, despite his lack of military experience. Then, on
Thursday, August 20, 1640, Charles left London. There was at least
this ground for hope, Strafford noted: "In my life I have not seen a
man begin with more life and courage."[87]

That same day, the Scots army entered England, more than
twenty thousand strong. Well disciplined and led by experienced
commanders, they were fearless of Charles's army of "debauched,
bragging, southern swingers," expecting significant resistance only
from a few northern Catholics, adherents of "that whorish religion"
of the "papist wench" whom the king had married.[88] Already they
had distributed their manifesto through Northumberland, professing that their "expedition" was "destined solely for the support of the

religion and liberty of both kingdoms" and demanding the punishment of Charles's "evil councillors": the Anglican bishops, the Catholics, Laud and Strafford. Their army would remain, they promised, until they saw the English Parliament assembled to end the nation's "prolonged disturbances."[89]

Charles's commanders, marching their outnumbered troops up to Newcastle as fast as possible, despaired; their only hope was that the king's presence would "remedy all." But when Charles reached York, there was little he could do. His army was small in numbers, "with no sort of order and by no means ready to engage the enemy." The Yorkshire militia, whose "vigorous support" Strafford had promised, refused to muster. The king's proclamation—declaring the Scots guilty of high treason and offering a pardon if they would "return quietly to their homes"—was merely "labor lost" as the Scots continued their advance.[90]

On August 28, the first battle occurred on the River Tyne just outside Newcastle. Charles's commander had taken out part of the town's garrison, to prevent the Scots from crossing the river, but, under fire from the Scots artillery, the English infantry threw down their weapons and fled. Fording the river, the Scottish cavalry charged the English cavalry, which retreated, "routed and in disorder," as far as Durham, twenty miles away. The next morning, the remaining English forces abandoned Newcastle. Strafford, advancing northward to meet them, still held out hopes to Charles: "Some of the troops are in very good order. . . . In a word, I believe as many of them [i.e., the Scots] were slain as of us." But privately the earl despaired. "Pity me," he wrote to a friend,

> for never came any man to so lost a business. . . . Our horse [i.e., cavalry] all cowardly; the country from Berwick to York in the power of the Scots; an universal affright in all; a general disaffection to the king's service, none sensible of his dishonor. . . . God of His goodness deliver me out of this, the greatest evil of my life.[91]

At Windsor Castle now with her children, Henrietta was "miserably cast down" by the news of Newcastle's fall: a "willful rout" by ill-intentioned men under evil commanders, she believed.[92] But the populace at large was delighted. Even though it was "forbidden under severe penalties to speak in favor of the rebels," London was full of talk condemning Charles and praising the Scots—"honest people" who "would do us no harm but rather good."[93] Rumors of terrifying Catholic plots spread like wildfire: the king was planning to bring Strafford's Irish army over "to gain satisfaction from his English subjects." Marie de' Medici also was implicated, with "seven thousand men and more in readiness to perform her designs," it was said, and London's Catholic foreign ambassadors were all plotting with the pope.[94] Notices again appeared in the streets, with threats to burn down Henrietta's chapel and kill Carlo Rossetti. Other notices called on the apprentices and the troops quartered around London "to fall upon" Laud. Five regiments of infantry mutinied, refusing to embark for the North. The courtiers were "in such distraction as if the day of judgment were hourly expected."[95] Guards were appointed for Henrietta and her children; Laud, terrified of "the popular wrath," withdrew to Henrietta's court for safety, only emerging "with circumspection." And at the Tower of London, orders came down to build new earthworks "and take steps to command the city with guns," in case of an uprising.[96]

Meanwhile, Henrietta was deeply involved in all of Charles's plans. Almost every day she received letters from him. She also saw all his official dispatches immediately after Secretary Windebank did. Only then was the Privy Council to be informed of "so much [of their contents] as you shall think fit," Charles ordered Windebank. Every week, the council reported to Henrietta on its business in London. Her advice to Charles, the councillors knew, was far more influential than their own.[97] Yet at last, "sad at heart," seeing the Scots fortifying Newcastle, taking Durham "without resistance, and . . . approaching swiftly to York," Charles sought guidance from his Privy Council. "You shall do well to think of timely remedies to be applied, lest the disease grow incurable," he wrote, "for I apprehend you are not much better in the South."[98] The council hardly needed telling. Windebank was already panic-stricken. "The danger is greater than any since the [Norman] Conquest," he thought; the only policy now had to be "conciliation of the disaffected lords, and redress of grievances"; Portsmouth had to be fortified "as a place of retreat, in case of the worst."[99] But despite their shared fears, when the councillors met they differed profoundly on what remedy to propose. Moderates and Puritans were eager for Parliament to be called, which was anathema to Charles's chief ministers, crypto-Catholics or high Anglicans all. But the Earl of Manchester proposed a new idea. Three hundred years earlier, King Edward III had summoned a Great Council of Peers to aid his war with Scotland; "they raised great sums of money without a Parliament, and assisted the king." Now was "a like occasion." A few councillors objected, but the majority supported his plan.[100]

Charles was delighted with their proposal. "It is thought most fit," he noted in the margin of their letter.[101] He had just received a petition from twelve opposition peers in London calling for a new Parliament; a second petition from the Scots was couched in such similar language that everyone could recognize "the secret communication" between the two parties, collaborating against the king's government. At first Charles had not known how to reply, but now he could say that he would discuss the matter with his Great Council of Peers. Commanding the Scots "not to advance further . . . and to await what will be decided," and setting a date of September 24 for the council's first meeting in York, gained him almost three weeks to make preparations in case of further Scots offensives.[102] Charles was pleased when he reviewed his army outside York: "Sixteen thousand foot, and two thousand horse, besides the trained bands of Yorkshire," which had finally agreed to muster. "Braver bodies of men and better clad have I not seen anywhere," Secretary Vane reported proudly to London. But the strength was only skin-deep. By this time, most of the troops were thoroughly disaffected, seeing the Scots not as the enemy but as "the redeemers of their religion and liberty." It was unlikely that they would stand and fight.[103]

Meanwhile, on Charles's orders, Windebank and the Privy Council were attempting to raise a new army in the South, ready to defend the king and queen "in case of disaster." But Charles was growing ever more frustrated with them: "I see ye are all so frighted, ye can resolve on nothing." Increasingly now, he sidelined even Windebank, and Henrietta was the first to hear the latest news from the North, sent to her directly "by his Majesty's special order."[104] It was in one of her replies that Henrietta proposed a radical plan. When the king met his Great Council of Peers at York, she proposed, he should not just ask their advice on calling Parliament; he must declare that he had already decided to summon Parliament of his own volition. Parliament was inevitable in any case; at least this way, the king might win some much-needed popularity.[105] Charles's councillors, alarmed at the continuing disturbances in London, wholeheartedly seconded Henrietta's advice. And Secretary Vane in York agreed: just the promise alone would be sufficient "to put the Scots out of the kingdom . . . [and] to cure all our sores."[106]

And so Charles began his Great Council of Peers by announcing that a new Parliament would meet in London on November 3—the earliest possible date, given the need for new elections. Charles spoke "freely and graciously" for much of the morning, making a remarkable impression. In more than twenty years, Vane reported, "I have not known his Majesty [to] express himself better." Charles was aiming to win popularity for Henrietta as well as for himself. She was the one, he said, who "had by a letter advised him to [do] it."[107] But any hopes of impressing the Scots were soon dashed. When Charles's negotiators arrived in Ripon, midway between the two armies, to open peace talks, they found the Scots confident "that they are on vantage-ground." Well aware that Charles could not fight them, the Scots insisted on their original demands, as well as the "immediate payment" of compensation for their "loss and expense" in the war.[108] They also required that any new treaty be approved by the English Parliament: until then, they would not leave. Charles was furious at the rebels' "audacity," but his negotiators could achieve nothing better. At last they returned to report that there would be no peace treaty for now. Instead, the Scots would send commissioners to Parliament, which would have the final word. In the meantime, there would be an armistice, but only on condition that the English paid £25,000 each month "for the maintenance of the enemy's army."[109]

So disadvantageous was this arrangement that many courtiers

suspected foul play. The English negotiators, they noted, were all Scottish sympathizers—disaffected courtiers such as the Earls of Pembroke and Holland, and some of the twelve opposition peers who had just sent in their petition to Charles, all "equally zealous for the calling of Parliament." The Scots had flattered these men with their talk of remedying "the excess of the queen's power" and removing Laud, Strafford, and other ministers from office, to be replaced with "persons . . . of honor . . . who are known to be zealous for the preservation and advancement of the Protestant religion." In fact, the Scots had insinuated, the English negotiators themselves were the ideal men to "be in most credit about the king."[110] So went the story, but Charles would have none of it. It was the Scots alone, he said, by their "cavil and delay," who had made it impossible to finalize the treaty at Ripon. "Therefore I can nowise blame the [English] Lords . . . but must thank them for their industry and pains."[111]

Yet as he left York to meet his new Parliament in London, the king could only be apprehensive. Despite his efforts to "sweeten" the opposition by releasing prisoners held for "matters that may raise disputes in the ensuing Parliament," and despite his careful nomination of Royalist MPs to constituencies under his control, still the elections had gone against him. The new Parliament was expected to be "most insolent" in demanding reforms that would amount to "a very considerable diminution in His Majesty's authority."[112] Charles had been desperate for the Scots army to leave England before Parliament met, fearing that their presence would encourage the MPs. But he had failed, and now there would be eight Scottish commissioners in London, ready to "sow ideas pernicious to the public quiet." Already the opposition was declaring that it would follow the Scots' lead and remove the bishops from the House of Lords, where they generally voted in support of the king.[113] "Total desolation" was facing the members of England's Catholic community, who firmly expected Parliament to demand "fresh severity" against them. Charles's most trusted ministers were in fear of "final ruin," with the real possibility of "most severe punishment" at Parliament's hands.[114] And in St. Paul's Cathedral, Puritan protesters, like the

Presbyterian Scots before them, "gathered in great numbers and violently . . . broke down the altar, and tore to pieces the books containing the new canons"; the Anglican ministers only escaped harm by fleeing. Everyone, it seemed, admired the Scots: it was to their "bold resolution" that the English would owe "the reestablishment of liberty and religion alike."[115]

9

EVIL COUNSELORS

Four days before Parliament opened, Charles and Henrietta met once more at Theobalds, just north of London. For weeks Henrietta had waited "with great impatience" for this moment, but now she was full of bitterness. Charles's agreement with the Scots was "full of indignity": he had set a dangerous precedent that would encourage his other subjects "to rebel without fear," knowing they would win not "merited punishment" but "rewards and other advantages."[1] So disappointed was she that, looking back in later years, she forgot her own role in advising the king to call Parliament. Instead, she laid the responsibility for the whole northern disaster on political malcontents among the lords at York, who were plotting the destruction of Strafford and ultimately of the king himself.[2]

But Charles, battered for two months by the harsh political and military realities of the North, could see no alternative to his policy of appeasement. There was no triumphal procession to the state opening of Parliament this time: money was too tight and Charles could not pretend having an enthusiasm he did not feel. Instead, he went privately by barge downriver to Westminster Stairs—a major opportunity lost for pleasing the crowds that always turned out for royal pageants. But inside the House of Lords, the king did his best to please. Concealing his anger, he made a careful speech, asking Parliament's help in satisfying the Scots and paying the English army, and offering in return to redress their grievances. Just one hint of his true feelings leaked out, when he referred to the Scots as "rebels," but his subsequent apologies were exemplary—"so effusive . . . showing so much submission that came ill from the mouth of a great prince" that his real terror of offending Parliament was plain to see. His speech was greeted with "universal acclamations," for the MPs well knew his weakness and thus their own ability to direct everything as they chose.[3]

Just as in the previous Parliament seven months earlier, they ignored the king's pleas and eagerly turned to discussing their grievances. Once more John Pym took the lead. Painstakingly, he expounded the whole sorry mess of government abuses—all due, he said, to a secret Catholic conspiracy: "the highest of treason," "a design to alter the kingdom both in religion and government." Already it was almost accomplished by an unholy alliance of foreign agents, the "papists' party," "the corrupt part of our clergy," and depraved government ministers: men who were ready to "further all bad things . . . [and] to run into popery." At Pym's urging, a committee was appointed "to find out authors and they to receive punishment."[4] Yet Charles showed not a single flash of anger at this denunciation of his long years of nonparliamentary government. Instead, hoping to prove himself "equally estranged from the Catholic faith," he promised to order "the departing and disarming of papists" from London and Westminster. The new fortifications at the Tower of London also would be dismantled, and the soldiers and their commander would be dismissed.[5]

But such easy concessions were not remotely enough. Again Pym stood up in the House of Commons, this time denouncing the Earl of Strafford: "a main instrument to provoke the king to make a war between us and the Scots" and so "bring in the papist party." The earl also had planned to bring his Irish army into England, "to suppress the laws and liberties of this kingdom," Pym charged.[6] That same day, the MPs voted to accuse Strafford of high treason. At their request, the Lords summoned the earl to hear his charge and then sent him immediately to prison, to wait while the Commons prepared the full details of his charge. Charles had no will to resist: "He was resolved not to protect anyone," he told Parliament, and would do what he could "for expedition in that business."[7]

Over and over again, Charles conceded to Parliament's demands. When they granted him money to pay his northern army, he accepted their condition that their commissioners would control the funds—a notable violation of the king's prerogative. He agreed to dismiss all suspected Catholics from his army. He even appointed the Puritan Earl of Essex to command the army in Strafford's place.[8] But still Parliament continued, unmollified, on its course. With "accusation and outcry" against Archbishop Laud coming in "from every quarter," and especially from the Scots negotiators, who charged that he was "an incendiary" who had "labored to set the two nations into a bloody war," the Commons set up a committee to investigate. Soon Laud was arrested on charges of high treason, for his alleged involvement "in the great design of the subversion of the laws of the realm, and of the religion."[9] Again Charles took it quietly.

Henrietta, however, fretted and fumed by turns, "much troubled at all the Parliament does," seeing their "great malignity to her."[10] Already their investigations into Pym's supposed popish plot had cast suspicion on her. A Catholic fast, arranged the previous summer "toward the queen's pious intentions"—which had really been nothing more than a prayer for Charles's success in the North—was now viewed as part of a plan for a bloody Catholic uprising. Pym whipped up the MPs' terrors with his talk "of the papists intending a day to cut the Protestants' throats," adding that "there was great danger to us all." Marie de' Medici was implicated too. According to Pym, an Irish priest in her entourage had said that if Charles would not accept this Catholic coup d'état, then he too would die with the rest of the Protestants.[11] At Somerset House the following Sunday, while a large congregation heard Mass in Henrietta's chapel as usual, a hostile mob gathered outside. Some had brought weapons, others had stones picked up in the street. As the service ended, they attacked the departing Catholics with fury, until a city official "quelled the tumult, with no little trouble."[12]

In desperate straits, Henrietta wrote to Cardinal Barberini in Rome. The Catholics had been banished from London, she told him; their priests were to be charged under the penal laws, "which go right to death." Her Catholic courtiers were now under investigation for attempting to convert Protestants, "and the pity is that the affairs of the king do not permit him to oppose all this violence . . . on the contrary he suffers now for his [former] bounty toward those of our religion." The only remedy, she urged, was money, with which she planned to bribe the opposition leaders and so "forestall a great part of their violence." Already she was preparing to open the necessary talks via old court favorites such as the Earls of Northumberland and Holland, and Northumberland's sister, Lucy, Countess of Carlisle, who were now intimate in the opposition camp. "I have so disposed my design that only the money is lacking," she told the cardinal. But raising such a sum was impossible in England. Could Rome oblige? A loan of £125,000 might be sent in small quantities, by bills of exchange, to ensure the utmost secrecy. "There is no one but His Holiness, you, and me who yet know of this," she added.[13] In the meantime, she responded vigorously to her opponents. If Parliament attempted to remove her Catholic servants, she would dismiss all the Protestants, she threatened, and appoint a new household composed entirely of "people of her faith."[14] From Paris, Louis XIII backed her up. "I do not want to meddle in Parliament's affairs," he said, "so let them keep off my sister's marriage articles. Otherwise I know well what I shall have to do."[15]

But Parliament was not to be bullied out of its anti-Catholic crusade. As new reports came in of "the number and danger of the papists," the Commons' newly formed Committee for Inquiry after Papists turned to examining the government's long-running policy of releasing Catholic priests from jail. Wary of attacking the royal couple directly, they avoided any mention of Henrietta's involvement and explicitly cleared Charles of all guilt: he had signed "very few" of the warrants releasing priests and he always ordered the priests to leave the country promptly, "such is his Majesty's care." Instead, the MPs vented their fury on Secretary of State Windebank. Detailed evidence was presented showing how he had issued most of the warrants without written authorization from the king or due legal process. But when the Commons summoned Windebank to appear before them, he fled to France, well aware that Charles and Henrietta could not protect him.[16] In this case, at least, Parliament had failed to bring its man to justice, but the MPs were not dissatisfied. Their primary aim was "to remove from the king all his most confidential ministers," and their project was advancing fast.[17] A fortnight later, Lord Keeper Finch also fled abroad to escape arrest on yet another treason charge. And with Parliament investigating "the pope's pretended nuncio," Henrietta was forced to ask Rossetti to leave the country "as soon as possible": neither she nor Charles could see any other way of ensuring his safety.[18]

Just seven weeks from the opening of Parliament, almost all of Charles's closest advisers were gone. Henrietta was outraged, and not just for her own sake and the sake of the Catholics. Even Laud's arrest infuriated her, as she saw "her husband not only deprived of his most faithful ministers, but so effectively despised by his own subjects." Ceaselessly she urged Charles "to throw himself into desperate courses," though so far he had not been listening.[19]

That Christmas of 1640 was a subdued affair. Just a couple of weeks earlier, Charles and Henrietta had lost their youngest daughter, Anne. While Windebank prepared to flee from London, the round-faced three-year-old princess lay in her bed too weak to move—feverish, coughing constantly, struggling for every breath. When one of her rockers reminded her to call on God, she replied, "I am not able to say my long prayer," meaning the Lord's Prayer, "but I will say my short one: 'Lighten mine eyes, O Lord, lest I sleep the sleep of death.'" Soon after that, she died. The doctors' autopsy tells us that the cause was tuberculosis: "a suffocating catarrh, with inflammatory disposition of the lungs, the roots of which ailments have been in her a long time." Despite their best efforts, "this princess could not be long-lived," they concluded.[20] Stricken with "intense grief," Henrietta retreated to Wimbledon for a few days, to see the work progressing on her new house and "take the air." When she returned to Whitehall for Christmas, there were none of the usual festivities. No masques were performed, nor were there any remarkable parties, dances, or feasts. Venison was eaten in quantity—109 dead deer arrived "for the consumption of his Majesty's household"—but this was a free commodity from the king's "several forests, chases, and parks," putting no strain on the royal finances.[21]

Meanwhile, Charles and Henrietta sought what support they could against their opponents. For more than two years, the Dutch had been asking for an English princess to marry their *stadtholder*'s son and heir, William, Prince of Orange. Marie de' Medici had first proposed the idea in 1638, when she stopped in the Dutch United Provinces en route to England. But the match promised no honor or gain to the English royals, so the matter had been dropped. But as Parliament began its furious assault on the royal government in November 1640, Charles and Henrietta reconsidered. Their second daughter, Elizabeth, five years old, might be suitable.[22] That would leave Mary, just turning nine, free for her long-mooted and more honorable Spanish match. But as soon as the marriage with Elizabeth was agreed to, the Dutch pressed to receive the eldest daughter instead, offering Charles "a first claim on the affections and interests" of the entire United Provinces. They would intercede with the Scots and "do all in their power to arrange a settlement," and if negotiations failed, they would be ready to provide more material assistance to the royal cause.[23] Early in 1641, three Dutch ambassadors arrived to negotiate the deal, and Mary's marriage was settled within a couple of weeks.

The alliance gave Charles and Henrietta new confidence and fighting spirit. Henrietta asked Carlo Rossetti to stay on in London after all. Charles, abandoning his former "hesitation and reserve," announced "that he will not permit Parliament to punish his servants," and he threw himself into efforts on Strafford's behalf, with "the greatest activity."[24] When Henrietta heard that a Catholic priest had been arrested and condemned to die, she thought nothing of asking her husband for a reprieve, as usual, and now he was happy to oblige. A priest would suffer a traitor's death—by hanging, disemboweling, and quartering—and this atrocious punishment had never been inflicted during Charles's reign.[25]

But the MPs were astounded. Father John Goodman had already been caught and imprisoned three times, "and banished [from] this kingdom," to no effect whatever. His reprieve now, "in this time of Parliament, when they expect a thorough reformation," was a shameless instance of the court's "great connivance at Jesuits and priests." They demanded an immediate investigation, to discover who had "dared to intercede." The danger to Henrietta was clear, and Charles acted at once. There had been no dangerous persons interceding on Goodman's behalf, he informed Parliament. Goodman had been convicted simply for being a priest, without any other aggravating offense, so Charles had reprieved him, just as his predecessors, Elizabeth and James, had often done. To satisfy the MPs, he offered to banish or imprison Goodman and take whatever measures they advised for expelling Catholic priests from the kingdom.[26]

But Parliament was unappeased. Father Goodman had to be executed to set an example, Commons and Lords alike demanded. It was clear to all that the case involved far more than the fate of just one man. Charles had the right to pardon convicted criminals, but now Parliament was pressuring him to abandon this royal prerogative. The question had become "whether the supreme authority lies with the king or Parliament."[27] Pulled between fear of Parliament's anger and dread of the consequences of surrendering to their power, Charles could not decide on Goodman's fate. Meanwhile, blocked for the moment over Goodman, the MPs shifted their attack onto Henrietta.

On Wednesday, January 27, a paper was produced in the Commons. Entitled "Motives for a Contribution from the Catholics to the King's Northern Expedition," it contained the letters that Henrietta and her courtiers had sent out seeking Catholic funding for Charles's war with the Scots. The MPs were profoundly alarmed. To them, it seemed proof of what they had long suspected: that Henrietta was involved in a dangerous Catholic conspiracy to enable Charles to govern without Parliament. The letters themselves described the king's war as "a Catholic cause" from which the Catholics might hope to gain "a suspension of the penal laws against them." Sir Kenelm Digby and Walter Montagu, it was alleged, had been "treasurers general to receive the collections," and both were summoned into the Commons for questioning. Both earnestly professed their innocence. None of the queen's current courtiers had been deeply involved, they insisted; it was the papal agent, George Con—now far beyond the reach of the law—who had masterminded the whole affair. But the Commons' suspicions only intensified, and soon new evidence was brought in, of Catholic troops being raised in England and Ireland at exactly the same time that Henrietta had been collecting her Catholic money.[28] Her contribution, it seemed, was part of a wider and yet more dangerous Catholic plot: for an armed insurrection to destroy the nation's Protestant government.

Charles and Henrietta were shocked at the paranoia, the rampant conspiracy theories, the witch-hunting fury of the Commons. In "extreme necessity" now, they held "long consultations" at Whitehall, until at last they hatched a plan for joint action to defend Henrietta from further Parliamentarian attack.[29] First came Charles's part. On February 3, by his order, the members of both houses of Parliament assembled in Whitehall's Banqueting House, where the king delivered a speech in state. He would put the penal laws into effect once again, as they desired, and would order all Jesuits and priests "to depart the kingdom within one month." As for Father Goodman, Charles still believed he had been right to reprieve him, and yet, to avoid "giving so great a discontentment to his people," he would leave Goodman's case to the decision of Parliament, though he asked them to be merciful.[30]

Charles had given away a lot; he had even set the precedent of abandoning his prerogative, and Parliament showed "great satisfaction."[31] Having proved their real power, the MPs had no further interest in Goodman, who was left forgotten in prison. But the royal couple believed they were soothing away Parliament's anger. Now it was Henrietta's turn to approach the Commons with further pacifications, as she hoped. She always had been "most willing to do all good offices between the king and his people," she assured them: in fact, she had written "expressly to persuade the king to the holding of a parliament." Now she was ready wholeheartedly to support her husband's measures against Catholics. She would send Rossetti "out of the kingdom" and restrict her chapel ceremonies at Somerset House, allowing in only those people "convenient and necessary for the exercise of her religion." In return, she asked a boon. She knew Parliament was displeased at her efforts to raise money for Charles's northern campaign, but she "was ignorant of the law" and had acted "merely out of her dear and tender affection to the king." So she asked Parliament to forgive and forget, "to look forward and pass by such mistakes and errors of her servants as may be formerly." This kindness, she promised, would "be repaid with all the good offices she can do to the house."[32]

Such "suave expressions," Charles and Henrietta hoped, would halt Parliament's "career of license." But they were quickly disappointed. The Commons received Henrietta's message coldly, with "a general silence."[33] A week later, they renewed their attack on her Catholic courtiers: "dangerous instruments" who were plotting with "Romish priests and Jesuits here, and . . . foreign states abroad" to raise a Catholic insurrection. These men must be banished from court, the MPs demanded; Strafford's Irish Catholic army had to be disbanded at once, and all English Catholics disarmed.[34] There was also a new assault on Charles's government: a bill passing rapidly through Commons and Lords required that Parliament meet at least every three years. The Triennial Bill was an outrageous violation of the king's "ancient prerogative" of calling Parliament "at his pleasure." When Parliament sent it in for his approval, Charles was "very angry," refusing to respond. There was an uproar in the Commons, where the MPs "loudly threatened the most extreme designs." Still Charles delayed "for many hours," balancing his loss of royal power against the violent uprising he feared his continued resistance could bring.[35] But Henrietta was all for conceding. With pressing "entreaty," she "used all means" to persuade her husband to sign.[36] They had particular need to please Parliament at that moment: Strafford's trial was approaching, the House of Lords would be his judges, and Strafford had to be saved. He was the most "able and loyal" of all Charles's ministers, Henrietta believed; while he served the king, the Parliamentarian opposition "could never succeed." Parliament's destruction of the earl was just the first step toward the "ruin" of the king himself.[37] Now Charles had to yield his political rights for the Earl of Strafford's sake. Then, if only they could survive for the present, there might soon be scope for successful resistance. Strafford's largely Catholic army was still undisbanded and available in Ireland, and Henrietta hoped for troops from her brother Louis as well as William of Orange. With their aid, the king could dissolve Parliament, free the Earl of Strafford, and restore a properly authoritarian royal government.[38]

Charles needed little urging. He had already promised to save Strafford, even if he had "to run the greatest risks."[39] So now he gave his assent to the Triennial Act. "You have taken the Government almost to pieces," he told the assembled Lords and Commons, "and, I may say, it is almost off the hinges." Like a watchmaker, he warned, they must soon think of reassembling the machinery: "Just remember [that] if you leave out one pin, the watch may be the worse and not the better."[40] The MPs were delighted, offering the king their "most humble and hearty thanks." At their request that night, there was "ringing of bells, and bonfires, through the whole City," all thoroughly resented by Charles. As the Venetian ambassador reported, "nothing is left to him but the title and the naked shows of king, and he does not know how to conceal the passions which naturally torture him."[41]

Fighting for survival now, the royal couple made desperate attempts to weaken their enemies' power. Henrietta's plans for bribing the opposition leaders with papal money had come to naught: Rome again replied that Charles had to convert before receiving aid. So instead she laid new plans: to win over their opponents with offers of career advancements. Prestigious and lucrative government jobs were now available, vacated by loyal courtiers who were in prison or exile; other courtiers could always be nudged out to make room for new men. Thus she began her tactful approach to her Parliamentarian enemies. Even John Pym and his closest intimates "do attend the queen in private," word leaked out from court.[42] Ultimately these Puritan crusaders remained true to their cause, but other prominent opposition members were more amenable, offering to support the royal couple in return for a share in government. On February 19, Charles gave out the first rewards to seven Parliamentarian lords— until this point "his most obstinate persecutors,"who had advanced Strafford's impeachment and the Triennial Bill and spoken against "the improvidence and evil counsels" of Charles's ministers.[43] Now, however, they were appointed to the Privy Council.

The results were immediate. When Parliament once more debated the dismissal of Henrietta's Catholic courtiers, three of these new men spoke up to defend her. Far from being a danger to the nation, the Earl of Bristol asserted, Henrietta was an eager friend to the Parliament. She had "furthered" both the calling of Parliament, the previous summer, and the passing of the Triennial Bill just now in February, when the king had been undecided. The Earl of Hertford confirmed Bristol's words: in the summer, the queen had "told him in discourse [that] a Parliament [was] the only way."[44] And in the House of Commons, the Earl of Bristol's son, George, Lord Digby, urged that, rather than suspecting and penalizing the queen, the MPs ought to send her "thanks for her furthering the calling of the Parliament and the passing of the Triennial Bill."[45] But these men spoke in vain. Urged on by Pym, the Commons voted "to desire the removal of all popish recusants from court"; soon the Lords joined them.[46] Embattled on every front, Charles acceded. The royal couple's new faction had failed its first test of strength, and already a far greater challenge was approaching.

On Monday, March 22, the Earl of Strafford's trial began. In Westminster Hall that morning, the accused man dropped to his knees in front of his judges and then stood up to wait—frowning and gloomy-faced, as he always was when not speaking—for the king's arrival. An unusually tall figure, "but stooped much in the neck,"[47] the earl was dressed simply in black, his only ornament being the bright star of the Order of the Garter on his cloak. All around the hall, ranks of seating ten tiers high were now crammed full. All the MPs were here, also the Scots negotiators, and crowds of the curious: five hundred spectators or more, predominantly hostile to the earl. In front of them were the Lords, dressed in their scarlet state robes, their broad-brimmed hats firmly on their heads to show their superiority over everyone else present. The king's throne was empty, for the Lords would allow him to attend only as a private observer, concealed in a lattice-fronted gallery. Here, around 9 a.m., Charles and Henrietta arrived with some courtiers, and then the legal proceedings commenced.[48] The accusation against Strafford was stated—high treason—and the charge was read in full: twenty-seven articles, ranging from embezzling government revenue and encouraging Catholics to inciting the king to fight the Scots, breaking the English Parliament the year before, and plotting to bring over his Catholic Irish army to use against the English. Strafford's written answer was read out, rebutting each article in turn. Then the court adjourned and Strafford returned to the Tower of London.[49]

The next day, the Commons' prosecution, led by John Pym, began to call its witnesses, whom Strafford cross-examined himself. He had the perfect qualities for a law court. "His memory was great," a contemporary recalled, "his elocution was very fluent, and it was a great part of his talent readily to reply, or freely to harangue upon any subject."[50] He showed up the weakness of the prosecution's evidence, discredited and humiliated its witnesses, switching effortlessly from impassioned self-defense to biting sarcasm that raised laughs in the audience, remaining always calm and collected under pressure. As the days passed, he began to win over many in the audience, in spite of themselves, changing "the universal hatred against him into compassion."[51] Soon the prosecution was forced to shift its ground, even abandoning some charges. As Strafford repeatedly argued that, even if he had done many of the things of which he was accused, his actions in no way amounted to treason, the prosecutors protested that the individual charges were irrelevant: it was the overall charge in its entirety that had to be considered as "constructive treason."

Charles and Henrietta, hoping to "give their servant courage," attended the trial every day. Carefully they listened to "all that could be alleged" against him, while Henrietta's court ladies took notes "all day."[52] Often they returned from the sessions with "their hearts gripped with sadness and their eyes full of tears," she later recalled. The evenings were spent in discussions and plans. Charles, leaving "nothing untried," sought out new witnesses to give favorable testimony on the most dangerous charges, while Henrietta intensified her secret talks with the opposition leaders.[53] Every night she went alone, carrying a torch in her hand, up the private back stairs to the apartment of one of her ladies who was away in the country. There she met "the most wicked" of the royals' opponents, offering them the nation's most important political offices. It was a perilous policy: "using honors as a reward for sedition" set an "evil example."[54] But there was still another more violent and final solution.

At Portsmouth, one of the best harbors in the country, new fortifications were going up, under the command of Henrietta's favorite, George, Lord Goring—the classic dashing cavalier, a man of "wit and courage and understanding."[55] Henrietta was funding the work herself: she took £1,300 in cash from her own income, for an undisclosed purpose, just two days after Strafford's trial began. Once well fortified, Portsmouth would be an ideal landing place for the troops she and Charles still hoped to bring in from overseas to save themselves and Strafford.[56] The couple also had a new military hope. Despite Parliament's efforts to raise money for the two armies in the north of England, both the Scots Covenanters and Charles's English troops remained largely unpaid. By March, the local people could support them no longer, "their cattle and victual being . . . exhausted and . . . their commodities . . . so dear, that no sort of victual is sold but at a double rate." Both armies urgently begged Parliament for relief, and rumors spread through London that the English army was "near a mutiny." Yet Parliament took no action, "so busy about the trial of my Lord Stafford we think of nothing else."[57] So Henrietta and her courtiers seized their opportunity. William Davenant, her servant and most favored playwright, author of the last triumphal royal masques of the 1630s, made contact with James Chudleigh, the captain who had come south to present the English army's grievances. Parliament was "so well affected" to the Covenanters that it would pay their army first, Davenant insinuated.

Then the captain was introduced to Henry Jermyn, who invited him to see the queen.[58]

Over the next few days, Henrietta's inner circle met repeatedly in her "drawing chamber" and "the little gallery in the q[ueen's] chamber" to discuss the possibilities.[59] What emerged was a plan to seize control of the English army in the north. The Earl of Newcastle, the governor in charge of Prince Charles's household and one of Henrietta's favorites, would be named Lord General. George Goring would be his deputy. Then the army could be brought south to Nottinghamshire, ostensibly to be entertained on their new general's estates but in fact to be ready to threaten the English Parliament should Strafford's trial go awry. In that case, the Prince of Wales himself would ride at their head, with a thousand court cavaliers. Strafford would be released from the Tower of London, by subterfuge or violence, Parliament would be dissolved, and the royal family would retire to Portsmouth. There, with the support of "a good part of the royal army," Charles would resume his proper political power "and impose laws on those who wished to destroy them"—with the further "assistance of Ireland and Holland . . . through the aforenamed port."[60]

As the first week of Strafford's trial ended, Henrietta took the scheme to Charles, who told her that he also had a group of plotters planning to approach the army, led by another of her old favorites, Henry Percy, the Earl of Northumberland's younger brother. The royal couple were excited but also anxious. While Charles advocated merging the two groups of conspirators, Henrietta feared discovery: if any one man fell, he would bring down all the others, and then "the king and she would be left with no one in whom they could trust." But in the end Charles prevailed: "They must risk all for so great a good."[61] On the king's orders, the two groups met at Whitehall, but irreconcilable differences emerged. Charles's men were planning a measure that was, in appearance at least, both peaceful and legal. A petition from the army would ask Parliament to grant the key concessions that Charles wanted: the retention of the bishops in the House of Lords, the continuance of Strafford's Irish army, and the restoration of the impoverished king's income. In this plan, the army's military force was merely to be an unspoken threat behind the petition. When they heard Jermyn's "extravagant discourses," Percy's men were appalled and afraid. Such "sharp and high" measures, "not having limits either of honor or law," would only bring disaster to king and country alike. To quell their protests and prevent untimely disclosure, Charles was forced to disavow all the plots: "These ways were vain and foolish, and [he] would think of them no more," he told Percy and Jermyn.[62] But Henrietta's plans continued in secret.

Captain Chudleigh, carefully schooled by Jermyn, was sent back to the North to win the army's loyalty. Meeting secretly with some of the most dissatisfied officers, he told them of Parliament's "dislike of their letter" of complaint. "The Parliament was so in love with the Scots that the army was not likely to be paid," Jermyn had assured Chudleigh, but "the king would pawn [his] jewels rather than leave the army unpaid." If they did take action, they would find plenty of support: "The best gentlemen would assist the army, and the French, and a thousand horse from the clergy."[63] Then Chudleigh produced a letter for the army officers to sign, inviting George Goring to become their lieutenant general. The next day, he returned to London. There, finding that Goring had left for Portsmouth, he took his letter instead to Sir John Suckling, another of Henrietta's plotters, who brought Chudleigh "to kiss the king's and queen's hands." Charles, despite his professions to Henry Percy, was obviously still deeply involved: it was at just this time that court observers noticed that Jermyn had gained "a strange interest" with the king. But Chudleigh's letter had only a handful of signatures. A few days later, another meeting of army officers refused to sign a declaration "of their readiness to serve his Majesty" and tore it up.[64] Despite the court's best efforts, the army would not support the king to the extent that had been hoped, so the army plot was set aside.

For the moment, at least, there seemed no need for armed intervention in London politics. By the beginning of April, the Earl of Strafford's defense was driving his enemies to distraction. Even the Commons' most damning accusation—that Strafford had planned to bring his Catholic Irish army to England "to reduce this kingdom"—was parried successfully by the earl in a court session that lasted for ten hours. As Strafford disputed the last few charges, Charles and Henrietta were full of "hope . . . that this minister so valued and beloved by their Majesties will be saved."⁶⁵ Saturday, April 10, was set for the final summing-up of the prosecution and defense cases, and Westminster Hall was packed with eager spectators: "'Tis worth a hundred-mile riding to see." But when the session opened, the prosecutors asked to bring in new witnesses to two of the earlier charges. Strafford parried with the request that he also "might be permitted to produce witnesses" on five of the charges.⁶⁶ When the judges agreed, it seemed the prosecution had merely played into his hands, and the trial would go on indefinitely, with the earl gaining ever more public sympathy. His opponents were aghast: the prosecution had to abandon its new evidence at once, so that Strafford could not present his. "Withdraw! Withdraw!" the Puritan MPs shouted to the prosecution, rising en masse from their seats. "Adjourn! Adjourn!" cried the anti-Strafford Lords. Determined to ensure the end of the session, they rushed out of the hall "in little better than tumultuous manner." Across the pandemonium, Charles and Strafford caught each other's eyes. "The king laughed . . . and the Earl of Strafford was so well pleased he could not hide his joy."⁶⁷

But their victory was short-lived. That same afternoon in the House of Commons, an MP produced a pre-prepared bill against the earl. The trial in Westminster Hall was clearly failing, so this bill of attainder instead would simply declare Strafford guilty of high treason and require his "punishment by death." As the House of Commons debated Strafford's case over the following days, Henrietta stepped up her talks with the opposition leaders. Charles saw Pym twice, offering him the newly vacated post of Chancellor of the Exchequer.⁶⁸ But to no avail. When the bill was put to the vote, only Lord Digby spoke against it. Almost half of the MPs were absent, too frightened of Pym's party and their supporters on the streets of London to attend that day. But the remainder voted resoundingly to pass the bill: 204 in favor, with just 59 against.⁶⁹

London waited with bated breath to see whether the House of Lords would follow suit. Charles promised that even if they did, he would never sign the bill into law. "Upon the word of a king you shall not suffer in life, honor, or fortune," he assured Strafford. But Strafford's friends had begun to fear "that his Majesty will be put to a very great strait, and in a manner necessitated to do that in the earl's case which is so much against his heart."[70] Popular agitation was vast. In the streets of London, posters went up listing all the MPs who had voted against the bill of attainder: "the Straffordians, enemies of justice, betrayers of their country." In response, Strafford's friends put out their own list of those who had voted for the bill: "the Anabaptists, Jews, and Brownists of the House of Commons."[71] A petition to Parliament, said to bear twenty thousand signatures, demanded Strafford's death. Mobs assembled outside London's Catholic ambassadors' chapels, attempting to "force the doors." And the City authorities notified Parliament that they could not pay for supporting the northern armies until Strafford was dead: the people were determined "not to contribute before they obtain this satisfaction."[72]

Once again Charles and Henrietta began to think of military action. Secretly, Charles sent "a sum of money to York to be distributed to the troops quartered there, with the idea of winning their favor." Henrietta reopened her negotiations for a papal loan, urging Rossetti to persuade Rome to accept Charles's promise of toleration of English Catholics rather than the king's own conversion. Charles already had enough men to stand out, the queen confided: all he needed was money.[73] Charles talked openly of going in person "to take command of his army"—ostensibly against the Scots, but everyone could see he was readying for action against "the more seditious of the English." At Whitehall, Henrietta was packing up, ready to join George Goring at Portsmouth "in the event of fresh disturbances." Her gold and silver was loaded into crates to accompany her, perhaps even as far as France, where it could be pawned or sold to pay for military action.[74] And there were secret plans for rescuing Strafford. His secretary had a ship on the Thames, ready to take the earl to Ireland, and Sir John Suckling had recruited a hundred men, enough to seize control of the Tower of London and set Strafford free.[75]

Meanwhile, in the House of Lords, the debates on the bill of attainder continued, "in long discussions and dangerous altercations." Many peers resented the Commons' interference in their own privileges, passing judgment on one of their own—ill will that Charles did "all in his power to encourage."[76] Amid vicious recriminations, crucial pieces of evidence against Strafford disappeared; when one turned up again, a letter "T" had been added, so that Strafford's alleged plot to use his Irish army *here* in England had become a perfectly innocuous plan to use it *there* in Scotland or Ireland.[77] Charles's newly won-over opposition Lords urged leniency toward Strafford, arguing that Parliament could gain any concessions it wanted from the king in return for allowing Strafford to live. But the other opposition Lords knew they could never trust Charles's assurances or Strafford's promise to retire from politics if acquitted. Charles's reliance on his old minister was simply too strong. "Stone dead hath no fellow," the Earl of Essex argued.[78]

On Saturday, May 1, Charles delivered a speech to Parliament. Presenting his own evidence in Strafford's favor, he pitted his word as king against the prosecution witnesses. "You know I must have part in the judgment," Charles reminded his auditors: any bill they passed would need his approval. And so, he urged, they must

> find a way to satisfy justice, and not press me against my conscience, considering what inconveniences may follow. I should do much to comply with both Houses, but I must let you know that no fear or respect whatsoever shall make me go against my conscience.

This was Charles's ultimatum: If Parliament passed this bill, they would precipitate a confrontation with unimaginable consequences. But he offered a compromise, too. "Although I cannot find my Lord of Strafford guilty of high treason, yet I cannot hold him clear of misdemeanors," and to this lesser charge Charles would accede willingly: "Therefore you may proceed to condemn him."[79]

Amid the furor, the fourteen-year-old Prince William of Orange had arrived in London. Despite it all, he was received with great ceremony. In Henrietta's privy chamber at Whitehall, he was greeted by his soon-to-be brother-in-law, Charles, Prince of Wales. Just approaching his eleventh birthday, Charles was a serious boy:

> So wise, grave, aged, he in youth appears,
> As if his age had twice out-stript his years—

but he was also a notably athletic and martial fellow. Taking an eager interest in his father's wars, he had used up several barrels of gunpowder and match in his artillery practice while the king was away in the North. He also took fencing lessons from his governor, the Earl of Newcastle, one of the foremost swordsmen of his day. Dark-haired and dark-eyed, the boy was, people hoped, another "valiant Black Prince": "that brave man of men" who had "made France shake."[80] Accompanying Prince Charles that day was his younger brother, James, Duke of York, a seven-year-old of boundless energy:

> He hates dull idleness, and loves to be
> In action, such as fits his high degree.

A portrait of this time shows the short-haired, chubby-faced James dressed for tennis and swinging his racket in front of a watching crowd.[81] But now, as they conducted the Dutch prince into Henrietta's withdrawing chamber, the two boys carried themselves with the smooth etiquette of accomplished courtiers. The king and queen received William "with great affection," although it was noted that Henrietta did not allow him to kiss her, on the grounds of his republican origin.[82] William, however, was unperturbed. Eager to meet Princess Mary—"He speaks of nothing but of seeing his bride"—he set out that afternoon to visit her at Somerset House. But Mary also denied him a kiss: she had expected to marry the Spanish heir and was as unhappy as her mother with her lover's lowly birth.[83] Day after day, William returned, bringing presents of "rich jewels" for his fiancée and her family, coming and going at Somerset House through a garden door to which he had been given a key.[84] Soon the young couple were beginning to seem more suited—"he is as good as he is pretty, which makes him more deserve so good a princess"—

and William gained his reward. Nine-year-old Mary—"mild, modest, affable, . . . discreet and debonair"—began to show him favor, "and with her mother's permission has sealed their affection with a kiss."[85]

On Sunday, May 2, 1641, the day after Charles issued his ultimatum to Parliament, William and Mary were married at Whitehall. Standing side by side, the two children made a handsome couple: William, with pink-flushed cheeks and long, curly brown hair, was every inch the elegant cavalier with a gold sword at his side; Mary, half a head shorter, was all in white, with ringlets and pearls in her hair; the huge diamond brooch William had given her was clasped on her bodice.[86] There had been no time to prepare the usual grand festivities. Instead, around 2 p.m., the royal family sat down to dinner in the king's withdrawing chamber, "with the greatest privacy that might be." That evening, the Dutch ambassadors joined them to "see the married couple bedded together." For the newlywed children, it was a mere formality, designed to ensure that the marriage could not be annulled; in the half hour they spent in bed together, nothing more was exchanged than a few kisses. Then William spent "the rest of the night in the bedchamber of the king of Great Britain, who looks on him most fondly."[87]

The next day, the political maelstrom recommenced. Though doubtless intended as an offer of compromise, Charles's speech to Parliament had done nothing but harm. Outside the House of Lords that Monday morning, a "tumultuous" crowd was waiting—"many thousands of the most substantial of the citizens." The Earl of Strafford was a traitor, they shouted, a public enemy, and he must die. "Justice, justice!" they yelled each time a lord arrived for the day's session, jostling those suspected of opposing the bill "with great rudeness and insolence," and "threatening the most violent measures against the state and against His Majesty's own person and all the royal house" if Strafford was not "condemned to death."[88]

Meanwhile, the members of the House of Commons, "in great passion and fury" at Charles's speech—"the most unparalleled breach of [parliamentary] privilege that had ever happened"—

reaffirmed their belief in Strafford's guilt and in the existence of "some great design . . . by the papists to subvert and overthrow this kingdom." To deal with the national emergency, all had to join together to sign a "protestation"—swearing, much as the Scots Covenanters had done three years earlier, "to maintain and defend . . . the true, reformed, Protestant religion . . . as also the power and privilege of Parliament, [and] the lawful rights and liberties of the subjects."[89]

Amid the whirl of fearsome rumors, John Pym began to make dramatic revelations. He had known of the court's plotting with the northern army for more than a month. George Goring had betrayed "the main [part] of the business"—whether from real disapproval, as he gave Parliament to understand, or from his fierce ambition, "uncontrolled by any fear of God or man," which had been bitterly disappointed when he was not appointed lieutenant general of the northern army.[90] Pym and his inner circle had kept the knowledge to themselves, waiting for the perfect moment to reveal it. Now, as the House of Lords vacillated over the attainder bill, that moment had come. There were "secret practices" at court, Pym announced on Wednesday, May 5, "to discontent the army with the proceedings of Parliament; and to engage them in some design of dangerous consequence to the state." His charges were still vague. "The Parliament hath not openly declared what the plot was," reported one of the Scots commissioners in London.[91] But Pym said quite enough to alarm his colleagues in Parliament. A committee should be set up at once to investigate, Lords and Commons agreed. Suspects must be apprehended. The king should be asked to ensure that "no servant of his Majesty, the queen, or the prince, may depart the kingdom, or otherwise absent himself"—a request Charles "very willingly granted." Most important, a new bill had to be passed to prevent "this present Parliament from adjourning, proroguing, or dissolving without the consent of both Houses." In effect, the Parliament was to become "perpetual." Drawn up overnight, the bill went through two of its three necessary readings the next day—such was the urgency of the MPs' plans.[92]

Meanwhile the courtier-plotters fled, despite Charles's assurances to Parliament. Henry Percy left Whitehall at once, carrying a passport that Henrietta had obtained from Charles. Henry Jermyn, who was out in London enjoying himself, received an urgent note in the queen's own hand, warning him not to return to the palace: he must go at once to Portsmouth and then escape to France. By the morning of Thursday, May 6, when the Commons summoned their suspects for questioning, Davenant and Suckling had also disappeared.[93] The MPs heard that Henrietta also intended "to take a journey to Portsmouth," about which they soon informed the House of Lords, who sent two of their members to Whitehall to ask the king "for the deferring of the queen's journey." They were concerned, they said, at "what danger her person may be in, if she go[es] there."[94] Then the House of Lords began the preliminary voting on the Earl of Strafford's guilt.

At Whitehall, Charles and Henrietta were distraught. Parliament had accused Jermyn not just of political crimes but also of "too great an intimacy with the queen." It was much more than an attack on Henrietta's honor: a queen's adultery was treason, and two of Henry VIII's wives had been executed for just that crime. So now, "in an unprecedented manner," parliamentary agents went rummaging through Jermyn's rooms in Henrietta's apartments at Whitehall, "without any respect for the place," in hopes of seizing incriminating papers and of giving further "offense to Her Majesty."[95] All chance of Strafford's escape was past. Parliament had reinforced the Tower of London with four hundred new troops; the city's gates and the banks of the Thames also were strongly guarded. With Jermyn and the others gone, the royal couple felt truly alone, "without servants or counsel."[96] But they had no thought of giving up. Henrietta was born of a father who did not know the meaning of fear, she said, and she came from a nation that never retreated. On her behalf, Father Philip made a last great appeal to France. "Can your good cardinal or can your king suffer a daughter of France with her children to be affronted?" he demanded. Could they allow England and Scotland to join together in one state, "as seems to be the present design," which would surely "be prejudicial to France"?[97] Meanwhile, Henrietta's packing continued faster than ever. By Friday, her carriages were standing ready for her departure, but the French ambassador urged her not to go: flight would only bring on the dangers she feared. So Henrietta remained in London, at least temporarily.[98]

That same morning, new revelations reached Parliament. Troops were massing in France, doubtless "designed for Portsmouth." This "design," and the courtiers' plot "to seduce the king's army," must be "united together" in one terrible master plan, the MPs agreed.[99] Public opinion was enraged at "the greatest treason . . . since the [Gun]powder Plot"; "Jesuits and priests conspiring with ill ministers of state, to destroy our religion." Rumors circulated like wildfire. The Scots were to be paid off and sent home, it was said, while the English army marched on Parliament and the court brought in French and Irish forces "for their assistance."[100] Henrietta's part was to supervise the French invasion and, "to this end, apparently the queen was going to Portsmouth." There was even a story that Charles and Henrietta had agreed to hand over Portsmouth to Louis XIII, in return for ten French regiments.[101]

Alarmed, Parliament ordered a deputation to be sent to Portsmouth "forthwith." They were to question the port's governor, George Goring, and send him back to Parliament if he seemed at all suspect. Then they were told to raise the local militias to secure the port and prepare the ships "for the defending of that town," under "commanders of trust and fidelity."[102] With this arranged, the House of Lords turned once more to the bill of attainder. Many peers had absented themselves, afraid "of having their brains beaten out" by the riotous crowds outside Parliament: of the eighty peers who had sat in Strafford's trial a month earlier, no more than forty-six were present.[103] Earlier voting had already established that Strafford was guilty of the Commons' charges. Now legal counsel gave the "unanimous" opinion that these crimes really amounted to high treason.[104] Then came the final vote. Charles's traditional supporters, the Anglican bishops, abstained en masse, happy to be persuaded by Laud's old enemy, the Puritan Bishop of Lincoln, that since they had not been present at the trial, they should not vote now. And the opposition peers whom Charles and Henrietta had worked so hard to win over did nothing either. Even so, the bill of attainder was passed by a vote of just 26 to 19.[105] But it passed. Now only the king's assent was needed.

At the Tower, Strafford was reduced to "utter despair."[106] Charles could not afford to save him, he was sure; the "evils which may happen" were too great. Earlier that week, as the riotous crowds demanded his death, he had urged Charles "to pass this bill," and so regain "that blessed agreement which God, I trust, shall ever establish between you and your subjects." "Sir," the earl wrote,

> to a willing man there is no injury done; and, as by God's grace, I forgive all the world, . . . so, Sir, to you I can give the life of this world with all the cheerfulness imaginable.

Secretly he had still hoped the Lords "would perhaps not have the effrontery to put him to death."[107] But now that hope was disappointed.

At Whitehall, Henrietta was "very angry," but Charles maintained a surface calm. "The king eats and sleeps well still," the news reported. When a deputation arrived from the Lords the next morning, asking him to assent to the attainder, he told them to wait. "At four o'clock this afternoon," he said, he would address the entire Parliament.[108] Meanwhile, the Lords put their time to good use, voting through the bill prohibiting the "adjourning, proroguing, or dissolving of this present Parliament." That afternoon, they presented Charles with this bill as well, "for the royal assent." But again Charles asked for time. He would give his answer in Parliament "on Monday morning, at ten o'clock."[109]

A nightmarish twenty-four hours followed for the royal family at Whitehall. Outside the palace, a mob of thousands gathered, crying, "Justice! Justice!" and making "great and insolent threats and expressions [of] what they would do if it were not speedily granted." The courtiers were horrified, expecting "the multitude would come the next day and pull down Whitehall, and God knows what might become of the king himself."[110] All of London was in "confusion and entirely under arms," it was said; Parliament was summoning troops from the county militias "with all speed," ready to "undertake any kind of audacious enterprise against the royal persons." Amid rumors of a popular uprising to massacre papists, the court's Catholics sought out Henrietta's priests and confessed their sins; then the Capuchins went into hiding in safe houses. On Charles's orders, guards were stationed on all the staircases. Panic-stricken courtiers secreted their jewels under their clothes, ready for flight.[111] When word came that the crowd was talking of moving on to attack Marie de' Medici at St. James's Palace, Charles ordered a hundred musketeers from the Middlesex militia to defend her, but they refused to go.[112]

Charles remained "in great anguish," battling with his conscience.[113] On Sunday morning, he consulted his Privy Council about how "to suppress these traitorous riots." But, terrified of Parliament and its mob, the councillors only pressed him to pass the attainder bill. "There was no other way to preserve himself and his posterity," they said; "he ought to be more tender of the safety of the kingdom than of any one person, how innocent soever." The violence threatening him now would be "a just excuse for whatsoever he should do." When Charles objected that their proposals were "in a diameter contrary to his conscience," they suggested that he consult his bishops, "who, they made no question, would better inform his conscience."

Accordingly, Charles summoned several leading churchmen. His conscience prevented him from condemning an innocent man, he told them—to which John Williams, Bishop of Lincoln, responded with a long speech, full of the fine distinctions so beloved by seventeenth-century academics and churchmen. Charles's "public conscience as a king might . . . oblige him to do that which was against his private conscience as a man," he said. "The conscience of a king to preserve his kingdom, the conscience of a husband to preserve his wife, the conscience of a father to preserve his children"—all these outweighed Charles's own private conscience. In fact, Williams concluded, Charles must pass the attainder "for conscience' sake."[114] Just one man spoke out against Williams's clever equivocation. Archbishop Laud's old friend, William Juxon, Bishop of London, told Charles he should not pass the bill "while his conscience scrupled at it as murdering the innocent"—a "heroic" lone voice, Charles later acknowledged.[115]

Still he held out. After all, it was not just a matter of his conscience. There was also his word—given to the House of Lords just eight days earlier—that he would not sign the attainder. And Strafford himself, recovered from his despair, was urging Charles to approach Parliament once more with defenses of the earl and offers of compromise. He could even, Strafford suggested, bring out his last letter, releasing Charles from his promise to save his life, in hopes that that would win Parliament's sympathy.[116] But with the crowd still baying for justice outside, Charles could see no hope in that. Instead he prayed, and he brought out the letter to scrutinize once more. It was Strafford's final undoing. When the king's advisers saw the letter, they argued: "This free consent of his own clearly absolved the king from any scruple that could remain with him." Charles need not authorize the bill in person, they proposed: he could simply sign a commission appointing some of the Lords to pass it for him. That way, "his own hand was not in it"—a small sop to his precious conscience.[117] Finally, at nine o'clock on Sunday evening, Charles caved in. It was not to save himself, he said, with tears in his eyes.

> If my own person only were in danger, I would gladly venture it to save Lord Strafford's life; but seeing my wife, children, and all my kingdom are concerned in it, I am forced to give way.

Charles felt utterly worthless and defeated: his conscience was abandoned; his honor shot; his promise perjured; his power as king proved nonexistent. "My Lord of Strafford's condition is more happy than mine," he said.[118]

On Monday, Charles's commission of Lords gave "the royal assent" to both of the bills: "one for the continuance of the Parliament, the other for the execution of the Earl of Strafford on Wednesday following."[119] "Now we have done our work," an MP shouted as he departed. On Tuesday, the angry crowds were gone, the London streets quiet once more: "The mouth of the people is stopped."[120] That day, Charles made one last attempt to save his friend. The Prince of Wales carried the king's message to the Lords, asking that Strafford might live out his days "in a close imprisonment," to be executed only if he attempted to escape or "meddle in any sort of public business." Charles hoped his ten-year-old son would win the peers' hearts, but his hopes were in vain.[121]

Around 11 a.m. on Wednesday, May 12, the Earl of Strafford set out for the place of execution. At first he had been angry: "Put not your trust in princes, nor in the sons of men, for in them there is no salvation," he is alleged to have said. But now he was resigned, forgiving his enemies and repenting his sins: "Never such a white soul returned to his maker," reported James Ussher, Archbishop of Armagh, who had spent the last two days with the earl.[122] On Tower Hill, people had been arriving all night, and a seething crowd surrounded the scaffold—two hundred thousand strong, it was thought. Strafford should go in his coach to the scaffold to avoid being torn apart, the Lieutenant of the Tower advised, but the earl would have none of it. "I care not how I die, whether by the hand of the executioner or by the madness and fury of the people; if that may give them better content, it is all one to me."[123] And so they set off. Archbishop Laud, himself a prisoner in the Tower, stood at his open window to bid farewell to his old friend at a distance. While the earl knelt on the ground, the sixty-seven-year-old archbishop raised his trembling hands to give his final blessing, but, overcome by emotion, he fainted before the words had passed his lips. "Farewell, my lord," Strafford said, "and God protect your innocency!"[124]

Beyond the Tower's gates, the crowd parted in silence to create a small passage for the earl. Dressed in black, carrying his hat in his hand, he walked erect—like a general marching to victory, it was said—accompanied by a small band of friends. From the scaffold, he addressed the crowd. "I do freely forgive all the world," he said.

I am not the first man that has suffered in this kind; it is a common portion that befalls men in this life; righteous judgment shall be hereafter; here we are subject to error and misjudging one another.

Having said farewell to his friends, Strafford knelt and prayed. When his brother wept, he offered consolation: at last he would have rest, he said: "No thoughts of envy, no . . . cares for the king, the state, or myself shall interrupt this sleep."[125] Refusing the cloth the executioner offered for covering his eyes, Strafford knelt by the block and spoke for one last time: "I do solemnly protest before God I am not guilty of that great crime laid to my charge." He prayed again and then placed his head on the block. The executioner raised his axe, Strafford stretched out his arms to show that he was ready, and then, invisible to most of the crowd, his head "was severed from his body at a blow."[126] As the executioner lifted the dripping head, the crowd went wild in a "universal rejoicing." "His head is off! His head is off!"—the news went out through London and the countryside. As dark came, bonfires were lighted and candles were put in every window: those without a flame were smashed by the crowd. With Strafford gone, the people trusted that "all should be well."[127]

At Whitehall, the royal couple mourned the passing of a hero. His last moments had displayed "the beauty of his mind and his admirable steadfastness," said Henrietta, paying earnest tribute. "The king suffered greatly from sadness, the queen shed many tears," a friend of hers later reported. But it was not just for Strafford that they grieved. Everyone could see now that Charles's authority was gone: he was "a king of foolish kindness, neither loved nor feared, without esteem, without respect, without obedience."[128] Charles now felt only "the hatred of the people, which is even stronger against the queen." As Parliament's investigations into the army plot tried to ascertain the involvement of "every person without exception, which means their Majesties themselves, if they appear guilty," it was clear that there were "secret intentions to lead these princes to the last calamity." The royal couple's names were being rendered "utterly odious to the people," it was said, all as part of the "ambitious designs" of the Puritans, "whose sole profession is to sweep away every kind of superior power." It was this, perhaps more than Strafford's death, that left the king suffering "the tortures of the deepest affliction." In signing the bill of attainder against Strafford, Henrietta later said, Charles had also signed his own death warrant.[129]

10

SHAME AND FEAR

That summer of 1641, the last of the royal couple's confidants were wrenched from them. Summoned for questioning by the Commons, Carlo Rossetti fled hurriedly from England. Marie de' Medici soon followed, after Parliament blamed her for having "instilled evil counsels into her daughter" and demanded that she "leave this kingdom" at once.[1] Meanwhile, the MPs pushed forward their Ten Propositions for reforming the royal government. Parliament's men must be placed at Charles and Henrietta's courts, the queen's Capuchins had to be "sent out of the kingdom," while Prince Charles's education was to be confided to "persons of public trust, and well-affected in religion." As the MPs began to implement their constitutional reforms, Henrietta feared that Charles would "soon lose his liberty as well as his crown."[2]

And still the investigations into the army plot continued, now singling out Henrietta as the real mastermind behind it. "We were sold to the French by the queen," one MP wrote in his diary.[3] Henrietta's courtiers were interrogated; her letters to the Continent were seized and opened; her nefarious deeds were exaggerated by "malignant invention." She spent those summer months in "the deepest affliction," and the whole court was "in a state of anxious expectation" as Parliament searched through its old records to find precedents for "what was done with other queens in like circumstances."[4]

By July, Henrietta was desperate to leave England. She hoped to get away to the Netherlands, ostensibly to drink the waters at Spa for her health and take Princess Mary to join her husband at The Hague. But her real aim, as Parliament could see, was to gain support for her husband. "Great quantity of treasure, in jewels, plate, and ready money," had been packed up, "to be conveyed away with the queen"—far more than she would ever need to cover her own traveling expenses. Even the crown jewels were to go, the Commons had heard.[5] And so they rushed to block her, alleging the risk of her being corrupted by the "great number of English fugitives" already overseas, army plotters, and others "who, by their late designs and practices, are known to be full of malice to this state." Henrietta resented Parliament's interference: "She was prepared to obey the king, but not four hundred of his subjects, as this did not befit her spirit or her birth," she told the Venetian ambassador. But in the end, as Charles presented "strong arguments" and Parliament stepped up the pressure, she had little choice but to comply.[6] "I swear to you," she wrote to her sister Christine, Duchess of Savoy:

> I am almost mad at the sudden change in my fortune. . . . Imagine my condition at seeing the king deprived of power, the Catholics persecuted, the priests scattered, our loyal servants removed from us and pursued for their life for having endeavored to serve the king, and me kept here like a prisoner, forbidden even to follow the king who is leaving for Scotland, and with no one in the world to whom I can tell my afflictions, and knowing withal that I must not show any resentment at it. . . . The king leaves the day after tomorrow if the Parliament does not restrain him by force; they threaten to. God help us: we have need of it.[7]

Charles's trip to Scotland was the couple's great new bid for power. He was going to meet the Parliament assembling in Edinburgh and to ratify the peace treaty that had finally been concluded after ten months of talks: the Scottish army would withdraw and disband. Then, Charles hoped, the English Parliament would "fall flat" without its greatest supporters. And he and Henrietta had even greater visions: of Charles winning the Scots over and returning victorious, "accompanied by the forces of Scotland, and by the remains of the English army stationed at York."[8]

Terrified of losing power, the Commons strove to prevent the king's departure, talking of massed demonstrations, twenty thousand strong, or even deposing the king, perhaps to "set up a democratic government."[9] But Charles departed unmolested. As he traveled northward, his hopes and Parliament's fears seemed confirmed. The Scots army at Newcastle was "full of obedience and zeal to his person," and in Edinburgh he was welcomed "with an incredible joy and acclamation of all this people." Such a demonstration "was never seen before," he wrote delightedly to Henrietta.[10] As Parliament commenced, Charles took "infinite pains" to please his subjects and "fulfill absolutely the expectations of everybody."[11]

Meanwhile, Henrietta managed affairs in England, corresponding with the king and issuing orders to Charles's Privy Council and his new Secretary of State, Sir Edward Nicholas. She organized meetings of loyal supporters and gathered intelligence: Lucy, Countess of Carlisle, in particular, brought her information and even written papers collected from John Pym and others of her friends among the opposition leaders.[12] As popular feeling swung back against Parliament during its adjournment that autumn, with people complaining about its new taxes and recent "unusual" actions, Henrietta worked to win back disaffected opposition members—of whom several, she noted, "evinced a desire to return to their duty."[13] Among them was London's Lord Mayor, who, like other wealthy citizens, was tired of Parliament's "long continuance," which was impoverishing the entire capital, they believed. With his help, Henrietta now planned to put on a magnificent, crowd-pleasing pageant for her husband's return. She urged the king to arrive in London before Parliament met once more, but Charles's Scottish business was still unfinished when Parliament reconvened, "with great ardor," on October 20.[14]

At once the MPs announced the discovery of "a fresh conspiracy against the liberty of the state." A committee was appointed, and Pym soon presented its report, noting that secret Catholic forces were massing for "some wicked design . . . still in hatching." Henrietta's confessor, Father Philip, was a "dangerous person," corresponding with English court fugitives overseas and contriving "new and mischievous plots." And the Prince of Wales was at risk, staying with his mother at Oatlands. Parliament ordered the boy's new governor, the Marquess of Hertford, to move him back to Richmond Palace and never let him out of his sight.[15]

Amid this anti-Catholic hysteria, London received terrible news of a "general rebellion of the Irish papists . . . and a design of cutting off all the Protestants in Ireland; and seizing all the king's forts there." Ten thousand Catholics were up in arms, it was said; as the days passed, the news grew "worse and worse." The Catholics controlled at least nine counties and were besieging Dublin.[16] The rebels' own statement—"that they remain obedient subjects of his Majesty and have taken action with the sole object of securing liberty of conscience and restoring the legitimate authority of their lawful sovereign"—made it seem that the uprising had been masterminded at the English court. Henrietta was again a chief suspect, and soon Parliament was seizing and opening foreign mail in search of evidence.[17] Father Philip was summoned to the House of Lords for questioning. When he stated that the Bible he was given for swearing his oath "was not a true Bible," he was sent to the Tower of London. Every day in London there were outcries about new Catholic plots: even a wild story of 108 Catholics being enrolled to assassinate 108 Puritan Lords and MPs, followed by a Catholic uprising.[18]

But still, with the Lord Mayor's help, Henrietta succeeded, after weeks of "very great preparations," in staging a triumphal event for Charles's return to London on November 25.[19] The streets were lined with City dignitaries. Huge crowds cheered, and Charles, on horseback beside his eldest son, thanked them "by gesture and speech, thus causing a renewal of the shouts of welcome." "Long live the king!" they cried.[20] The royals and their accompanying lords and ladies were feasted at the Guildhall, where Charles promised popular measures for the City's "honor, profit, and quiet." Then, through the winter dark, the royal party rode by torchlight to Whitehall, "always amid the same shouts and acclamations." Truly it seemed that the people, "grown tired of so much violence, are contemplating a return to their old loyalty and devotion."[21]

Heartened by his success in Scotland and his grand reentry to his capital, Charles was ready to confront his enemies. The very next day, he dismissed the Parliamentarian Earls of Essex and Holland from their command over the London militia. He also removed the guard that Parliament had appointed for its own safety during his absence. When the MPs protested, he sent his own men to watch over them, and his troops were soon threatening to fire their muskets on the crowds outside Parliament.[22] For months, the Commons had been preparing a "grand remonstrance," demanding yet again that the king dismiss his evil counselors and abolish the "immoderate power" wielded by the Anglican bishops, "which they have perniciously abused." On December 1, they at last presented it to Charles, but he was not intimidated. After picking holes in their accusations and laughing at their presumption, he told them he would consider their requests at his leisure.[23] Heartened by the king's tough stance, the loyalist party at court now talked big. There would "shortly be a great change in this kingdom," one of Henrietta's Catholic friends announced. Then everyone would see whether Charles was indeed "a king or no king."[24]

The MPs were infuriated. They would "live and die together in defense of the Protestant cause," they swore. Command of the nation's armed forces had to be taken out of the king's hands. Charles and Henrietta had to publicly proclaim "the rebels in Ireland to be traitors," to prove the queen did not "secretly . . . encourage the rebels."[25] But Charles remained on the offensive. Ever since Parliament's recess, many loyalist MPs had stayed at home, afraid of the opposition's power. Now the king ordered the 210 absent members to take their seats in January 1642. Then, on December 22, to clinch his control of London, he replaced the Parliamentarian Lieutenant of the Tower with a loyal army officer recently returned from the north: Colonel Thomas Lunsford. The next day, he sent the Commons a defiant answer to their "grand remonstrance." He saw no sign of the "corruption in religion" they alleged, for "no Church can be found upon the Earth that professeth the true religion with more purity of doctrine than the Church of England doth." As for evil counselors, "we know not any of our Council to whom the character set forth in the petition can belong," but if the Commons could bring "a particular charge and sufficient proofs" against any man, they could have "justice of the law."[26]

Members of the Commons were more alarmed than ever. Colonel Lunsford was "a debauched quarrelsome man, very desperate, and fit to execute any dangerous design," they protested. His appointment proved that there was "some dangerous design in hand against us." They needed to petition the king for his removal, they agreed. In the meantime, they asked Lunsford's superior, the Parliamentarian Earl of Newport, Constable of the Tower, to take personal "custody and guard of that place."[27] But this the king would not allow. On Christmas Eve, he dismissed Newport from his post, bringing the conflict to a flash point. Hostile mobs turned out, protesting against Lunsford. Order would never be restored while the colonel remained at his post, the Lord Mayor warned the king; the apprentices might even try to storm the Tower. Afraid now, Charles dismissed Lunsford. But his new appointee, Sir John Byron, was just such another loyal officer and thus "little better accepted" by the angry citizens.[28]

When Parliament reconvened after the briefest of Christmas breaks, there was a noisy crowd at its doors once more. "No bishops! No popish Lords!" they shouted.[29] It was a powerful rallying cry. For years, the bishops had been the focus of popular fear and anger, hated for enforcing Archbishop Laud's reforms and widely perceived as "papist"—a charge not so far from the truth, in many cases. One had even secretly converted, it had seemed six months earlier, when he refused to swear an oath of loyalty to "the doctrine and discipline" of the Church of England.[30] And now, Pym claimed, it was these royal supporters in the House of Lords who had prevented the peers from joining the Commons' appeal for Lunsford's dismissal.[31]

As the Lords arrived for that day's session, the crowd's mood was fierce, and soon some attacked John Williams, the former Bishop of Lincoln, whom Charles had recently made Archbishop of York in gratitude for his support for the episcopacy. Then Lunsford himself joined the fray, at the head of a party of disbanded army officers. "Chasing the citizens" around Westminster Hall with drawn swords, the officers wounded some of them before beating a swift retreat to Whitehall. But still the crowds remained. The next day, they moved on to Westminster Abbey, intending "to pull down the organs and altar" and destroy the royal tombs. But Archbishop Williams and his servants fought off the rioters: "divers of the citizens were hurt, but none killed."[32]

In the midst of all the violence, London's tradesmen closed their shops and gentlemen walked the streets well armed, "as in time of open hostility." Charles called out the militia: if the people refused to go home, the soldiers were to "kill such of them as shall persist in their tumultuary and seditious ways."[33] Even so, on the day after the assault on Westminster Abbey, the mob appeared outside Whitehall Palace, just as they had done for Strafford's attainder seven months earlier. This time, however, Charles was prepared. His courtiers were under orders to wear their swords, and they were reinforced by numerous officers from the disbanded northern army, who had "offered their services to his Majesty" and formed an unofficial body-guard.[34] As the crowd approached the palace's great gateway, carrying clubs and swords and shouting, "No bishops, no papist Lords," the defenders drew their swords and went over the railings toward them. To these men, the yelling mob was merely "the scum of the people," but they had no desire to kill them: it would only provoke "more dangerous disturbances." So they slashed with the flats or blades of their swords, rather than thrusting with the points, wounding forty or fifty but killing none.[35]

Whitehall was safe, but for how long? As rumors came in that the City's apprentices were mustering, ten thousand strong, "exasperated" at the wounds received by their fellows, Charles increased his army-officer contingent to 120 and ordered the local militia to watch "night and day" under their command.[36] A guardhouse was hurriedly erected just outside Whitehall's great gatehouse, while some four or five hundred more gentlemen submitted their names and addresses, ready to be called out at a moment's notice. Daunted, the apprentices stayed away from Whitehall, but angry crowds still ruled the rest of London. Charles's bishops were now too frightened to attend the House of Lords, having been "violently menaced, affronted, and assaulted, by multitudes of people . . . and put in danger of their lives." Archbishop Williams and eleven other bishops presented a "protestation" to the king and the Lords, demanding that everything passed by Parliament during their "forced and violent absence" be declared "null and of no effect."[37] It was a bold bid by these king's men not only "to overthrow all Acts passed" but also, if order could not be restored, "to cause a dissolution" of Parliament itself. But Pym's party was not so easily outmaneuvered. The bishops' protestation was "high treason . . . endeavoring to subvert . . . the being of Parliament," the Commons charged, and the archbishop and his eleven colleagues were arrested. Far from aiding Charles's cause, their protestation had merely lost him twelve votes in the Lords, about which he was "greatly perturbed."[38]

Once again his enemies were seizing the initiative. Pym whipped the MPs into a frenzy of alarm at Whitehall's warlike preparations, alleging "that there was a plot for the destroying of the House of Commons." The next day, the Commons asked the king for a guard from London's militia, commanded by the Earl of Essex—a Parliamentarian military force to rival his bodyguard at Whitehall. Unwilling to provoke further popular violence, Charles played for time. The MPs' petition contained "so many particulars," he replied, that "he could not remember what was delivered . . . and therefore desired to have it in writing."[39] But even his delaying tactics could be turned to the opposition's advantage. Hurriedly submitting their written petition to the king, the Commons appointed a committee to receive his reply the next morning: New Year's Day, when Parliament would not be sitting. But this was no ordinary committee meeting. It would assemble in the City, where the apprentices could be relied on to protect it. All the MPs were invited to attend, "and all that will come are to have voices at this committee." In effect avoiding the constraint that Parliament must meet at Westminster, where Charles's writ had summoned it, the committee would become a secret meeting of the Commons, with none of its business recorded in the official journal. And the committee members were given the broadest of remits: if no reply came from Charles, then they must "consider what then shall be fit to be done for the safety of the king, the kingdom, and this house." To advance this work, they were given "power to send for parties, witnesses, papers, and records."[40]

Early on January 1, 1642, the MPs marched "publicly" through the City to the Guildhall. Going "supplied with arms," as if there really were "a plot against the liberty of Parliament," they won "the affection of the ignorant people." There is no firsthand record of what then took place inside the Guildhall. Even the diarist-MP Sir Simonds D'Ewes, normally so meticulous in his recording, is silent about the business that day. Nonetheless, word leaked out. When no message arrived from Charles, the MPs' discussion ranged widely, "into the most important matters." They considered the king's recent actions and his obvious resentment against them. But still they could not believe that he was deliberately working against them: evil counselors surely were to blame. Yet every courtier of significance was already gone—executed, imprisoned, or self-exiled. Only Henrietta remained. So at last "they persuaded themselves that the actions of the king and his resentments proceeded from the counsels of the queen." She was the one who had to be charged with high treason, for "conspiring against the public liberty" and for secret involvement in the Irish rebellion.[41]

When word reached Charles, he resolved at once to take preemptive action. Other ministers he had been prepared to sacrifice, but he would not lose Henrietta. On Monday, January 3, when the MPs returned to the House of Commons once more, he struck. As the session opened, Lord Keeper Finch and Attorney General Sir Edward Herbert arrived in the House of Lords to charge six members of the Parliament with high treason. One, Viscount Mandeville, was there in the Lords; the other five, including John Pym, were MPs in the Commons. All of them were prominent opposition activists, and all were involved in the move to impeach Henrietta, but the king was not accusing them of that.[42]

Charles had planned this move for a long time. Returning from Scotland in November, he had brought back evidence that these same leaders had encouraged the Scots armies to invade England. But back then, even as the mob took control of London's streets, Charles had hesitated, fortifying himself at Whitehall instead of putting the City "into flames and blood"—as any other European monarch would have done, the French ambassador thought. It was Charles's fatal flaw, many observers agreed: his "tenderness and compassion," his excessive "clemency," his unwillingness to resort to violence until it was too late. One likened him to Julius Caesar, who had been "merciful to such an extent that he had been forced to repent of it."[43] But with Henrietta in danger, Charles was forced to act. Attorney General Herbert presented seven charges of treason, prepared by the king himself, and asked the Lords to "take care for the securing of the persons." But the Lords, though ready enough to imprison Archbishop Williams, and Laud and Strafford before him, on the Commons' bare accusation, were now reluctant. They insisted that a committee be appointed to consider the matter and to examine precedents and records. Meanwhile, when Charles's men sealed the six members' chambers and trunks so they could be searched for evidence, the Commons declared the action a "high breach of privilege of Parliament" and sent their sergeants to break them open again.[44]

Charles was furious; he knew he was in the right. He had good evidence against his enemies and needed nothing to bring them down "save only a free and legal trial, which was all I desired." With these agitators gone, he hoped, he could win back the rest of the Parliament and be once more "at peace in his kingdom." So, in the greatest secrecy, he and Henrietta made plans for "a bold blow," as she described it.[45]

Charles began his preparations that same night. Thirty or forty artillerymen were sent to man the cannons in the Tower of London, while the usual guard there remained without weapons. A message went to the Inns of Court, asking the gentlemen there to "be ready at an hour's warning, if his Majesty should have occasion to use them." Another message ordered the Lord Mayor to refuse the Commons' request for "strong guards" from the City's militia. Instead, if riots threatened, the Lord Mayor must order out troops "to suppress all such tumults and disorders." If the people refused "to retire to their houses peaceably," the soldiers were to open fire and "destroy such of them as shall persist in their tumultuous ways."[46]

All through the following morning, on Charles's orders, armed men mustered at Whitehall until the court was "thronged with gentlemen and officers of the army." "The House of Commons would not obey the king," they were told, so now they were to go with Charles himself and "force them to it." A watchword was agreed upon. If the Commons resisted the king's demand for the delivery of the five MPs, he would come back out to his men and give the word, and they would seize the five "by force and violence."[47]

Inside the palace, the royal couple dined as usual. Then Henrietta retired to the little cabinet behind her bedchamber, where Charles took leave of her, "resolved to change his destiny by the destruction of his enemies." He would be "the master," he told her as they embraced: he hoped in just one hour to return "with more power than he had at their parting." While Henrietta knelt at her private altar, "making prayers for this enterprise," waiting with all "the emotion and impatience that could be expected,"[48] Charles entered his coach and left Whitehall at the head of "a great multitude of men"— about four or five hundred in all—"armed in warlike manner with halberds, swords, and pistols." His own royal guardsmen were there, and all his court servants, as well as loyal gentlemen and disbanded army officers, and "divers French men" associated with Henrietta's court.[49]

At about 3 p.m., the party reached Westminster Hall. As the entire body of armed men thronged into the hall, panic-stricken shopkeepers rushed to close their shops, "looking for nothing but bloodshed and desolation." The king's men encountered no opposition. Alarmed at the forces massing at Whitehall that morning, the Commons had asked the City "for four thousand men to be presently sent down to them," but the Lord Mayor remained true to the king's command and none had arrived.[50] So, ordering the bulk of his force to remain in the hall, Charles continued toward the Commons chamber with some eighty men. In the lobby just outside, he ordered the detachment, "on their lives," to go no farther. Here they remained, their cloaks cast off, their hands on their swords, their pistols loaded—at least one was "ready cocked"—cursing and threatening while they forcibly held the chamber door open against the efforts of the Commons' officers. "A pox take the House of Commons: let them be hanged if they will," one said. "I am a good marksman, I will hit sure," said another, as the king entered the Commons, accompanied only by his nephew, Charles Louis, the Elector Palatine.[51]

Charles had never before been in the House of Commons. His speeches to Parliament had always been delivered in the House of Lords. In fact, people said, no English king had ever been inside except, perhaps, King Henry VIII, and he "but once." Straight down the middle of the chamber, bowing to the MPs on either side, who "all bowed again toward him," the king went to stand beside the Speaker's chair, followed by his nephew.[52] There he recited his charges and demanded that the five MPs be handed over. All the while, Charles's eyes searched for his enemies without finding them. So now he asked for Mr. Pym, "whether he were present or not." No answer came, and so he asked for Mr. Holles, and again there was "a general silence." When Charles pressed the Speaker to answer, he fell on his knees, "saying that he could neither see nor speak but by command of the House."

"Well, well," the king replied, "'tis no matter; I think my eyes are as good as another's." Then, after he had looked around "a pretty while,"[53] he observed: "I see all the birds are flown. . . . I cannot do what I came for."[54]

Watching through the open doors, his thwarted men swore "wicked oaths." "Zounds," said one, "they are gone and now we are never the better for our coming." As Charles exited through the lobby, "discontented and angry," they called out for the watchword, but the king gave them none. Only if the five members were present and the Commons refused to give them up would he have legal justification for calling in his troops. Instead, the cry went up to "make a lane,"[55] and through the opening in the crowd, Charles and his men departed.

The "bold blow" had failed, and ever afterward Henrietta would blame herself. Looking back years later, she vividly remembered those agonizing long minutes that extended on to a quarter of an hour, then half an hour, while she remained in her cabinet, praying and worrying. Often she looked at her watch to see if Charles's hour had passed. Often she listened in case someone might be bringing her news. This day, she knew, "must produce great good or great evil": "either we shall be ruined or the king will be in absolute control." At last, convinced that it was all over, she could keep silent no longer. When her old favorite, Lucy, Countess of Carlisle, arrived, Henrietta greeted her ebulliently. "Rejoice, for at this time the king is, as I hope, master of his state": Pym and the others "are without doubt arrested."[56]

Until now, Lucy's connections in the opposition camp had benefited Henrietta. Back in the autumn, Lucy had even brought Henrietta an incriminating document obtained from Viscount Mandeville—the peer whom Charles had just accused of treason with the five MPs.[57] But now Lucy felt bound to save her friends. Concealing her surprise and anxiety, she left Henrietta's presence and wrote a hurried warning note to one of the five MPs. Meanwhile, en route to Parliament, Charles had been held up in the streets by petitioners bringing "supplications of little consequence," but he had stopped to hear them and to talk, so as not to reveal his haste. A coach accompanied by hundreds of marching men could only move slowly anyway. So as he approached Parliament, the five members managed to flee.

It was a "notable fault" that Henrietta had committed, she acknowledged, but Charles, when she confessed, did not reproach her. It was not totally clear that she was the one to blame. Despite Henrietta's belief that the plan was "an important secret between the king and the queen, and very few people were in their confidence," the court had been leaking like a sieve.[58] Already the night before, the five MPs had heard "of this intended design." And today, as Charles and Henrietta dined, the Earl of Essex, Charles's Lord Chamberlain, had sent a message to warn the threatened members "that the king intended to come to the House of Commons to seize upon them there, and that they should absent themselves." Yet still the five MPs returned to the Commons after their midday meal, having had as yet "no direct assurance that the said design should certainly be put in execution."[59]

But at around 2:30 p.m., the news finally arrived, borne by a Frenchman, Captain Hercule Langres. Going past Whitehall as Charles and his entourage were already marching toward Parliament, he met the French ambassador, who told him "of the design of the king's going to the House of Commons . . . to take out those five members by violence."[60] Four of the five were friends of the ambassador: the divisions between the king and Parliament were actively supported by the French, in order to keep Britain weak. So now the ambassador asked Langres to hurry to the Commons and warn the endangered men "to withdraw their persons." Langres had squeezed right through the middle of Charles's troop, with its halberds and swords and pistols, and reached the Commons first.[61] Four of the accused departed immediately. Only William Strode remained—"a firebrand," "one of the fiercest men of the party"—who, "being a young man and unmarried, could not be persuaded by his friends for a pretty while to go out." Half an hour passed, and still Strode protested "that knowing himself to be innocent, he would stay in the House though he sealed his innocency with his blood." At last, as the first of Charles's troop entered Westminster Hall, a friend grabbed Strode by the cloak and pulled him out.[62]

At Whitehall that night, Charles was still determined to get his men, but it would be no easy matter. The five had gone into hiding in the City, where the whole population was up in arms. "The cavaliers were coming to fire the city," people shouted; "the king himself was in the head of them." Lord Digby, now the royal couple's most hot-blooded adviser, offered to go into the City himself, "with a select company of gentlemen." He knew the house where the five had taken refuge; he and his men would "seize upon them, and bring them away alive, or leave them dead in the place." But

Charles refused, still too worried about his precious conscience to countenance such an illegal deed.[63] Instead, the next morning he drove into the City to meet the Lord Mayor and his government. Charles laid the flattery on thick. He buttered up the aldermen with "some familiar discourse"; he invited himself to dinner with one of the sheriffs. With "a gracious speech" to the assembled worthies, he tried to win them over "as much as in him lay," promising to redress all his subjects' grievances. But still there was strident heckling. "Parliament! Privileges of Parliament!" many councillors called out. Charles answered mildly: "I have and will observe all privileges of Parliament, but no privileges can protect a traitor from a legal trial." If the five members could prove their innocence, "he should be glad of it," he said, but if they were guilty, they were not fit to sit in Parliament, which was called "to make good laws and to reform abuses, and not to betray their king." But even as Charles went out, the crowds continued to cry, "The privileges of Parliament!" following him all the way back to Whitehall, "some of them pressing very near his own coach," so that "the good king . . . was glad when he was at home."[64]

In the meantime, the Commons reconvened. After orders "that the door be locked, and the key brought up," the opposition leaders stirred the MPs into a fury. Charles's coming to their domain "in a warlike manner" with "desperate ruffians" was "a high breach of the rights and privilege of Parliament." And not only that. If the five members had been present, the entire Commons would have been forced to defend them "for the preservation of the privileges of our House," and they would have been massacred. Convinced that they were no longer safe at Westminster, the MPs voted to adjourn for a week. In the interim, they would meet once again as a committee, safe in the Guildhall, "to consider and resolve all things that may concern the good and safety of the City and Kingdom."[65]

There, attended by "a great number" of MPs, the committee fell to its work with a will. The king's impeachment of the five members had been "unjust and illegal," they voted; his arrival at the Commons with "soldiers, papists, and others" had been "a traitorous design." The warrants Charles had since issued for the five members' arrests were also illegal. Any person arresting any member of either House of Parliament without that House's consent "should be declared a public enemy of the Commonwealth."[66] On Saturday, January 8, John Pym and the other wanted men joined the Guildhall committee in triumph, guarded by two companies of the City's militia "and multitudes of other citizens of account," amid "universal acclamations."[67] All of London, it seemed, was preparing for war. Six cannons had been brought in. Weapons were stockpiled in private houses—some contained as many as "twenty to forty muskets with ammunition"—while "all the trained bands stand to arms." Shops remained closed, "as if an enemy were at their gates ready to enter and to plunder them."[68] One night, a rumor spread that Charles was coming with his "soldiers and ruffians" "to enter the City armed, to sack it." "Arm, arm!" The cry went up throughout London and its suburbs, and in little more than an hour "forty thousand men in complete arms" turned out, "and near upon a hundred thousand more that had halberds, swords, clubs, and the like."[69]

The rumor soon proved false, but a steady stream of printed "libels," full of allegations of papist plotting, kept the population on constant alert.[70] Henrietta bore the brunt of the blame. Charles himself, the pamphlets proclaimed, was "a good Protestant in his heart": it was "the persuasions of the queen's majesty, and the advice of the Catholic Lords and other gentlemen," that would bring these plots to fruition. "The queen does all," people said. "She is the one who has always advised the king ill."[71] She allegedly had refused the French ambassador's offer of mediating with the Parliamentarians. She had advised Charles to make his attempt on the five members. And she was the one who had stirred up the revolt in Ireland "for the advancement of popery."[72] Granted, people said, the king intended to use the rebels afterward "so as to recover his lost authority in this kingdom." But it was Henrietta who was the "principal author" of what many now called "the queen's insurrection."[73] Henrietta was fast becoming the villain she would remain in Protestant English history: "a papist, a French lady of a haughty spirit"[74] who, "more powerful" even than Laud and Strafford, had applied "her great wit and parts" to stir the king's "violent purpose" against his subjects, producing "sad desolations." Charles "was enslaved in his affection only to her, though she had no more passion for him than what served to promote her designs," wrote the Puritan memoirist Lucy Hutchinson. "Nothing but the mercy of God prevented the utter subversion of Protestant-ism in the three kingdoms."[75]

On Sunday, January 9, the most fearsome news reached White-hall: the MPs were preparing "to accuse Her Majesty of high treason." Already there were articles ready to "be put into Parliament against her" when the Commons returned to Westminster in two days' time.[76] And resistance would be impossible. Determined to come with "strong and sufficient guards," the MPs had already resolved that it was legal for the local sheriffs "to raise the *posse comitatus* for that purpose." In fact, the entire population was required, by "their duty to God, the king, and their country," to turn out to defend Par-liament "from all force and violence whatsoever."[77] On Monday, the Guildhall committee finalized the arrangements. Any citizens who chose to come, mounted and armed, would be welcome. And they accepted the offer of a thousand sailors on the Thames "to defend the Parliament by water with muskets and other ammunition." The six members of Parliament accused of treason would go by river, surrounded by a flotilla of longboats mounted with artillery. In addi-tion, eight companies of the militia were ordered to turn out by 8 a.m., bringing eight cannons with them.[78] This was no mere guard for Parliament, but rather the triumphal procession of a conquering army. In all, some twenty thousand people were expected, "compris-ing countrymen, citizens, and sailors" and outnumbering the king's few hundred gentlemen and army officers many times over.[79]

The news threw Henrietta into "extreme apprehension," but Charles's feelings were of "shame more than fear." What particularly weighed on him was the disgrace he would suffer from the "barba-rous rudeness" of the people, who would come with "the boldness to demand anything, and not leave either myself, or the Members of Parliament, the liberty of our reason and conscience to deny them anything"—an "intolerable oppression," reducing Charles to slavery.[80] He and Henrietta could afford to remain at Whitehall no longer.

It was a sorry party that rode out of the palace gates that Monday evening, January 10, 1642. The king and queen were accompanied by just "thirty or forty" of their bodyguard; the rest, "so poor that they had no horses," were forced to remain behind. Of Charles's courtiers, there were only "some few" who were truly "devoted to him."[81] "Whither we go, and what we are to do, I know not," wrote one; "my duty and loyalty have taught me to follow my king and master, and by the grace of God nothing shall divert me from it."[82] Secretary of State Sir Edward Nicholas was there, as was Henrietta's new favorite, George, Lord Digby: it was he who had warned her of the Guildhall committee's plans to impeach her for treason. Charles's nephew, the Elector Palatine, rode with them, as did three of the royal children: eleven-year-old Charles, Prince of Wales; Mary, age ten; and James, now eight. The two younger children remained behind at St. James's Palace.[83] Also left behind, as prisoners in the Tower of London, were Archbishop John Williams and his eleven loyal bishops, as well as Archbishop Laud.

Out through the suburbs of Westminster rode the royal party, past Hyde Park, where Charles and Henrietta had driven so often on happy Maying expeditions. Then they continued west and south toward Hampton Court. Peasants with carts carried their baggage—clothes and other necessities, valuables such as gold and silver plate and jewelry, and even some of the Crown jewels—but there was no ready money to pay their drivers. It was a difficult journey. The rivers that barred their route were swollen with floodwaters after the recent rains, and crossing them was dangerous. At Hampton Court, nothing was ready, and the three royal children "were obliged to the inconvenience of sleeping in the same bed beside their Majesties."[84] The next day, while the MPs made their triumphant return to Westminster as planned, Charles's army officers—quartered in Kingston, just over the Thames from Hampton Court—were busy with "warlike preparations." The cavalry under Colonel Lunsford's command mustered some two hundred strong. Loads of ammunition were brought in, and war saddles came by water from London. In response, the MPs ordered the local militia to be called out "for the suppressing of these assemblies."[85] Clearly, the royal family was not safe at Hampton Court, "an open place" with no military defenses, so they moved on to Windsor Castle, where again, after "the dangerous crossing of divers rivers," they found "scant convenience."[86]

They were in a "sad condition," Charles and Henrietta realized, seeing how far the king had fallen in just ten days: "from a height and greatness that his enemies feared to such a lowness that his own servants dared hardly avow the waiting on him." Henrietta was especially angry at the disloyalty of old friends such as the Countess of Carlisle and the Earl of Holland, who were now firmly within the Parliamentarian camp. Even her confidant, Lord Digby, soon fled abroad, when the Commons accused him of involvement in the mobilizations at Kingston. But neither Charles nor Henrietta was even remotely inclined to compromise.[87]

Instead, they threw themselves into a new round of military preparations. Utterly alone now, having "no one in whom we could trust, everyone having betrayed us," as Henrietta wrote, she and Charles had to do everything themselves. "I had so many affairs for the service of the king . . . that I am astonished that I did not lose my mind, not having even the time to sleep."[88] At Windsor, the couple's bodyguard was reinforced with "divers several troops of horse." Men and ammunition were sent off to Portsmouth, where George Goring had returned to royal favor. Other wagons arrived at Windsor, laden with ammunition from the Tower of London, where Sir John Byron was under orders to blow up everything rather than surrender it to Parliament.[89] Meanwhile, Charles had already ordered the Earl of Newcastle to take command of Hull and its royal arsenal, which had even more arms than the Tower of London. Then, Charles hoped, he could just "sit still" and wait for his opponents to "come to reason." There would be no need for open military conflict.[90]

But Parliament had spies at court. On the same day that Charles wrote to the Earl of Newcastle, they ordered their own man, Sir John Hotham, to go north, where he seized Hull for them. They also placed a guard around the Tower of London "by land and by water": no "ordnance, ammunition, or other provisions whatsoever" were to be allowed out, nor any "extraordinary provision of victuals, or men" to come in.[91] Every day, it seemed, there was "some committee or

The royal family grew rapidly in the 1630s. This 1637 Van Dyck portrait shows (left to right) Mary, James, Charles, Elizabeth, and Anne. The eldest two are in adult clothes here. Seven-year-old Charles is the little man of the family, his hand extended authoritatively over the giant dog beside him. Mary at six is a pert little miss, with curled hair, pearls, and a long silk dress like her mother's. Between them, four-year-old James is still in a toddler's gown and apron. On Prince Charles's other side are the two new arrivals: Elizabeth, not yet two, holds chubby baby Anne, a classical putto figure draped in white, yearning adoringly toward her eldest brother. This painting hung over Charles's breakfast table at Whitehall, a daily reminder of family life when his children were away at other palaces.

William Laud, Archbishop of Canterbury, was Charles's religious soulmate.
Laud's zealotry in reforming the Anglican Church stirred up Puritan
opposition throughout the nation and sparked war with the Scots.
Henrietta disliked Laud for his anti-Catholic policies.

Earl of Strafford.

Thomas Wentworth, Earl of Strafford, was an ambitious politician whom
Charles summoned to rescue him after his first, failed war against the Scots.
Henrietta at first distrusted Strafford but soon came to admire
him for his political loyalty as well as his courtly graces.
"He had the most beautiful hands," she remembered.

Henrietta Maria's mother, Marie de' Medici, a stern, authoritative figure, arrived to live with her daughter in 1638, to the "unspeakable annoyance" of everyone except Henrietta herself. Henrietta's and Marie's enthusiastic Catholicism only further enflamed Puritan public opinion against the royal government.

*Charles I at his trial in 1649—aged by his misfortunes
but still elegant and unbowed.*

The king's trial in Westminster Hall. Charles sits alone in his box, wearing his hat in defiance of the court. To his right stand the parliamentary prosecutors. Facing him from the head of the hall are the court's commissioners: "high-flown Parliament-men" who acted as both judge and jury.

The execution of King Charles I outside Whitehall Palace. Soldiers with pikes held back the crowds filling the street. As the king's head fell, there came "such a groan by thousands then present as I never heard before, and desire I may never hear again," recalled an eyewitness.

DIEV ET MON DROIT

After Charles's death, Henrietta wore mourning dress for the remaining twenty years of her life—this small, thin woman was bitterly disillusioned by her husband's "barbarous" fate.

other" coming out from the Commons to Windsor "with petitions and expostulations." The Prince of Wales must not be allowed to leave the country: anyone assisting his departure would be guilty of "high treason." Charles must make "a public declaration and promise in Parliament" that he would not receive any political or religious advice from his wife, while Henrietta must "take a solemn oath . . . that she will not . . . at all intermeddle in any of these affairs." Her Catholic servants and all her priests were to be dismissed, her sons and all future royal princes would be forbidden to take Catholic brides.[92]

At first the Lords were reluctant to pass the Commons' more extreme measures, but at the beginning of February, with angry crowds mobilized again at Westminster, they caved in. They joined the Commons in petitioning the king that the kingdom's militia forces be entrusted to "such hands as the Parliament may confide in." After months of inaction, they finally passed the bill depriving the Anglican bishops of their seats in the Lords. Throughout London, there was "great joy": church bells rang and bonfires flamed. Three days later, "after four denials" previously, they voted to join the Commons in asking Charles to remove Sir John Byron from his command of the Tower of London.[93]

Unready to provoke an open confrontation, and hoping still to win back popular support, Charles accepted Byron's resignation and appointed the Commons' man in his place. He also abandoned his prosecution of the six MPs accused of high treason: "For the full contentment of all his loving subjects," he would grant them a "free and general pardon."[94] But on the militia he would not back down. Supreme command of the nation's armed forces was the king's absolute prerogative, the heart of his power; if he abandoned this, he would be left with "nothing but the title of king." He could see that Parliament was bent on "high ways of destruction": "their purpose was by degrees to get so much power into their hands that they need not care for what was left in his."[95] On the bishops, too, he was determined not to yield. It was a matter of conscience: "How shall I remove the bishops, having sworn at my coronation to maintain them in their privileges and pre-eminences?" Already he had conceded too much, he confessed to the Dutch ambassador:

234 · A ROYAL PASSION

> At the beginning I was told that, if I would agree to the death of the
> Deputy [Strafford], my kingdom would be at peace; afterward if I
> allowed a triennial Parliament; and then if I would permit the pres-
> ent Parliament to remain assembled as long as they wished; now that
> I must place the ports, the militia, and the Tower in their hands; and
> . . . remove the bishops. You see how far their intentions go.[96]

But to Parliament Charles made conciliatory noises. He would allow
them to recommend military commanders, under certain conditions. As for the bishops, he would "send an answer in convenient
time." Such weak replies, "more prudent than spirited," encouraged
his enemies: the Commons already believed "themselves even pos-
sessed of the whole militia of the kingdom."[97] But in fact, Charles
and Henrietta were almost ready to put new plans into action.

They agreed that it was not safe for Henrietta to remain in England, facing an imminent treason charge. "Parliament's violence was
so great against me that I had to flee to be sure of my own life," Henrietta told her sister Christine, Duchess of Savoy:

> they said publicly that a queen was merely a subject and that she
> could be punished like any other. Yet it is not the fear of death that
> has made me leave, but of a prison separating me from the king
> which I avow would have been more insupportable than death, for
> that would have ruined all our affairs.[98]

So Henrietta would go to the Netherlands. The Dutch had been
pressing Charles to send Mary to join her new husband ever since
their marriage. Now he agreed that Henrietta would accompany her.
That was the public reason for the queen's journey, announced to
Parliament.[99] But in reality, the royal couple had ambitious plans.
Henrietta would take the couple's jewels with her: everything from
Charles's pearl buttons and her own "great chain" of pearls and "that
cross . . . from the queen my mother" to important Crown jewels such
as Charles's "ruby collar," and a selection of rich coronets, diadems,
and circlets.[100] In the great mercantile cities of the Netherlands, she
would pawn or sell them all, for the benefit of Charles's war effort.

In personal talks with the Dutch government, she might persuade them to send military assistance, or at least to put diplomatic pressure on Parliament. Then she could always go on to France, where she had "very extensive designs."[101]

Meanwhile, Charles would remain in England. After bidding Henrietta farewell at the coast, he would head north in the utmost secrecy. There lay the heartland of his party: in Yorkshire, Henrietta told the Dutch ambassador, the whole population supported the king. At York, Charles would find "a safe place" where he could muster supporters such as Lord Digby, who were currently too afraid of the "rage and violence" of Parliament to join him. Then he would secure some seaport, opening a safe route for correspondence with Henrietta and for receiving the supplies she would send. Newcastle and Berwick were options, but best of all would be Hull, where the king's magazine still lay. Even though the Earl of Newcastle had been turned away, the royal couple hoped that Charles might be admitted to the town when he arrived in person. Then, perhaps, he might consider going to Scotland or Ireland, to gather yet more support.[102]

As the moment of parting approached, both he and Henrietta suffered greatly. Her husband, Henrietta recalled, was

> touched by a lively sadness to see himself in the state he was in, devoured by his own subjects and constrained to separate from his wife whom he loved dearly, without knowing what their fate would be.

She, too, grieved at their misfortunes, which "forced me to leave the king and my children." She would be the most

> wretched creature in this world . . . separated far from the king my lord, from my children, out of my country, and without hope of returning there, except at imminent peril—abandoned by all the world, unless God assist me.[103]

But stronger than her sadness was her fear—not so much of Parliament itself, for she would be out of their reach now, but rather of what her husband might do without her. Henrietta was the one who truly believed in the need for war. "To settle affairs, it was necessary to unsettle them first," she said. It would be "impossible to re-establish her husband's authority in any other way." "You have already shown your goodness sufficiently," she told Charles, which "has been very ill repaid"; there could be no more negotiation until "your people . . . apply themselves to their duty." But her husband, she knew, was more inclined toward a waiting game. He was going into Yorkshire "not to take up arms," he said, but to see what his opponents would do. Once they saw his threat of force, "he did not doubt that they would be more pliable." An "honorable" agreement would be reached, and then Henrietta would "soon return."[104]

In Henrietta's eyes, her husband seemed unrealistic, too indecisive, timid and changeable, too reluctant to insist on his unquestionable rights. He was, she feared, utterly unfitted to deal with the crisis they now faced—an assessment that many of the king's followers would come to share.[105] Henrietta hardly dared to leave him alone. Her friends at court, "much agitated," urged against it. "I am risking all we have left in the world to get money," she told him. If he failed in his part, everything she did would be "rendered ridiculous." Their jewels would be lost, "and we too; for we should have nothing left to help ourselves with."[106]

"Continue your resolution, and do not change"; "lose no time, it is too dear," "you have lost enough already": these would be her constant refrains in the following months. "If you wait . . . you will be ruined altogether." "To begin, and then to stop, is your ruin—experience shows it": "you must dare."[107] Her desperation and frustration were palpable:

> this is no longer a mere play. You must declare yourself; you have testified your gentleness enough, you must show your justice. Go on boldly: God will assist you. You see what you have got by not following your first resolutions, when you declared those of the Parliament traitors. Let that serve you as an example; do not delay longer now in consultations, it is action which must do the work at this hour—it is time.

But even as she reproached her husband, she was ashamed of herself. "My dear heart," she begged,

> pardon me if I have written a little too much on this subject. . . . My whole hope lies only in your firmness and constancy, and when I hear anything to the contrary, I am mad. Pardon once again my folly and weakness: I confess it.[108]

Yet still she could not help herself. It all mattered too much. If Charles failed in his tasks, she feared, she might never see him again; it would only be safe for her to return to England when "his original authority" was restored.[109] If he could not achieve that—if he gave up his command of the militia, as she feared he might— then he would be lost, "and I too." At that point, when "you are no longer capable of protecting anyone, not even yourself," she would "retire into a convent" and bid him, "Adieu, my dear heart."[110]

On February 9, the disheartened royal party left Windsor. Charles and Henrietta—more divided on their plans and expectations than either cared to admit—saw their hour of parting approaching ever nearer. Charles especially suffered "greatly": his love for his wife was "beyond expression." His sons also "grieved at the going-away of their mother and sister."[111] The bodyguard of officers had been dismissed—there was no money to pay for them or for anything else. With Charles's usual income cut off by Parliament, Henrietta had been forced to turn her gold and silver plate into coin just to pay for her "most necessary occasions." Only a small group of courtiers would accompany her abroad. Among them were Father Philip and Jeffery Hudson, the queen's maids of honor, and just three of her great ladies—all of them "much agitated . . . fearful of the object and of the results of this journey."[112]

That night, they stopped at Hampton Court, where, the next morning, the painful family partings began. The princes were left behind, to allay Parliament's fears that they "should be transported beyond the seas."[113] The rest continued on to Greenwich. In the palace where they had passed their early summer months each year so pleasantly, the royal couple now became locked in disagreement.

Charles was still refusing to pass the bill removing the bishops from the House of Lords, but he still had advisers who urged that this one concession would be enough to pacify his opponents. His new Chancellor of the Exchequer, Sir John Colepeper, argued this case at length with the king, but to no avail, so he turned to Henrietta. "Her own safety very much depended upon the king's consent to that bill," Colepeper told her; "if he should refuse it, her journey into Holland would be crossed by the Parliament, and possibly her person in danger."[114]

In fact, Henrietta realized afterward, there was never any danger that the MPs would hinder her journey. They were glad to see her go, believing "perhaps that they would dispose of the king more easily when the queen was not there." But at the time, "terrified with the apprehension of her being hindered from pursuing her purpose," she interceded with the king, as Colepeper had requested. It was no easy matter to persuade Charles against his conscience, but for two days she "gave not over her importunity with the king." At last he yielded for her safety's sake. As for Strafford's attainder, he refused to pass the bill in person, and he appointed a commission of Lords to do the business for him. Then, late in the evening of February 12, the royal party set off for Dover.[115]

At Canterbury, where the younger Charles and Henrietta had spent their honeymoon in "a very Eden or Paradise," the king and queen now heard that the bill had been passed into law. There was rejoicing in London: bonfires flared, and the Members of Parliament sent a message to the king "to express their gratification."[116] But the royal couple saw none of the benefits they had been led to expect. Far from it. That same day, Parliament impeached Attorney General Herbert for treason in "falsely, scandalously, and maliciously" contriving the charge against Lord Mandeville and the five MPs. They also drew up an "ordinance concerning the militia," naming the commanders they wanted the king to appoint. Soon Parliament's messengers reached Charles, pressing him to assent. Concerned for Henrietta's safety, he did not want to refuse directly, so he replied that he would have "to take some time for advisement thereupon."

He promised he would give them "a positive answer" when he returned to London.[117]

By now the royal party was at Dover. Out in the harbor, five royal ships were hurriedly preparing for the voyage. "Things are done in such posthaste that I never heard of the like for the voyage of persons of so great dignity," a harassed navy official complained. Henrietta's "goods and baggage" were being loaded aboard: linen and clothes, money and other personal valuables, her collection of Crown jewels, and "all her vessels for her chapel," which alone were worth tens of thousands of pounds. Last to go aboard were the queen's six coaches, with "about 120 horses of all sorts" and their fodder.[118]

Henrietta was now eager to be gone "without further delay"—to be done with the agonies of parting, to get on with her work in Holland, and then, she hoped, to return to her husband and children.[119] For some days, a contrary wind prevented her from sailing, but on the morning of February 25, down on the seafront, the royal couple said their sad farewells. Charles, "deeply moved . . . did not know how to tear himself away." For a long time, he remained near Henrietta, "conversing with her in sweet discourse and affectionate embraces." Neither could "restrain their tears," lost as they were in "extreme regret and grief." Finally, "after many kisses, many tears," they drew apart.[120] Henrietta stepped into the royal barge and was rowed out to the flotilla's flagship, the *Lion*. She stood on the deck while the sails were hoisted, the anchors weighed, and the ships put out from the harbor. Flying from the mast above her were the royal standard and pennants. Beneath her feet, safe in the hold in heavy locked chests, lay England's Crown jewels. Beside her stood her tiny court, and Princess Mary with her governess, the Countess of Roxburghe. While Henrietta looked back toward England, Charles mounted his horse and followed her ship eastward along the coast, past Dover Castle and out into the country, "for more than four leagues." At last, when Henrietta's figure disappeared from sight, he lifted his hat and "waved it around several times, bidding her a very affectionate but very sad and painful adieu."[121]

Then, bypassing London, the king set off northward to muster his forces. Six months later, atop the Castle Hill in Nottingham, he stood in the rain to see his standard raised. A herald proclaimed England's Parliament traitors to the Crown. Drums and trumpets sounded, and a few companies of wet, wind-battered troops shouted, "God save the King!"[122] The Civil War had begun.

PART THREE

ENDINGS

11

NEWCASTLE,
JANUARY 1647

The town of Newcastle-upon-Tyne was strongly fortified now, "in a condition to resist any army, however powerful." On its high stone walls, Scottish sentries in baggy blue bonnets and red wool coats kept watch, shivering and stamping to keep out the cold. After three years' service, these men were in a "ragged and naked condition." Beside them, their heavy muskets stood ready for use. From the leather bandoliers over their shoulders hung powder horns and pouches of shot. At their sides were swords or dirks. Beneath tall castellated towers, more Scottish troops guarded the town's gates, which were locked every night. No one was allowed to enter without an official pass. On high ground, cannons stood ready, and out in the nearby villages, starved and poor from the Scottish occupation, cavalry regiments kept watch.[1] The Scots had come to Newcastle in 1644, when they joined the English Parliament's war against the king. Now the town was full of Scotsmen of importance: politicians and Presbyterian churchmen, and the army's commander-in-chief, Alexander Leslie, Earl of Leven.

One single man was the reason they were all here. In New House, a grand Elizabethan manor just within the town walls, King Charles I was a changed man—his hair cut short, his face "melancholy, and . . . very grey with cares." Outside the mullioned windows of his chamber lay extensive gardens and grounds, where the Scottish guards had recently been doubled and ordered to "go the rounds continually." Inside, a coal fire burned in the grate, while more Scots guards patrolled his apartments, annoying him with "their continual smoking." Under strict new orders, "eight officers never let him out of their sight."[2] But the king was oblivious to them now. All his attention was focused on what he was about to write: a letter of vital importance for saving his own life. Sitting at his desk that Saturday, January 2, 1647, he dipped his quill into the black ink and set it on the paper. "Dear heart," he began, as he always did when writing to Henrietta,

> I must tell thee that now I am declared what I have really been ever since I came to this army, which is a prisoner . . . the difference being only this, that heretofore my escape was easy enough, but now it is most difficult, if not impossible.[3]

Eight months earlier, Charles had come to the Scots army—alone, disguised, and utterly defeated after five years of war. In those years, he and Henrietta had spent just nine months together after she returned from the Netherlands, having raised some £2,000,000 for her husband's cause. With her she brought an armory of guns, ammunition, and saddles, guarded on her journey through England by a small army of Royalist troops. "Her she-majesty, generalissima," she called herself half-jokingly, telling her husband that she was "extremely diligent, with one hundred and fifty wagons of baggage to govern, in case of battle." Charles was full of admiration and gratitude for the hazards she ran, "in which thou has expressed so much love to me that I confess it is impossible to repay by anything I can do."[4]

On July 14, 1643, the queen was welcomed into Oxford in triumphal style.[5] Church bells rang, crowds cheered, bonfires blazed. Civic authorities and university men turned out in droves to deliver speeches and poems of welcome. Oxford was Charles's headquarters throughout the war. Here he held court in the great hall at Christ Church. Here his own Royalist Parliament met, the law courts heard cases, and the Royal Mint turned out coins to fund his war effort. And here, after Henrietta's return, the delights of the couple's old court life were re-created in miniature. Plays were performed by professional actors forced out of London by Parliament's ordinances against the stage. Portraits of the royal family and their courtiers were painted by William Dobson in his studio on the High Street. Poems were composed by enthusiastic royal followers: William Davenant, Abraham Cowley, and Sir John Denham. There was deer hunting and hare coursing at nearby Woodstock, walks in the college gardens, tennis in the town, and at Christmas masques were put on once more. While Anglican services were held in the cathedral for the king, Henrietta's priests performed Catholic ceremonies in the chapel at Merton College: Henrietta's own base, with a private passageway leading to Charles's apartments at Christ Church. In the queen's bedchamber one night, a new royal baby was conceived.

But still there was the business of war. Bitter factions divided the court. On one side were the professional soldiers, trained in the wars on the Continent. Foremost of these was Charles's twenty-three-year-old nephew, Prince Rupert, now general of the king's cavalry. Henrietta had no doubt of his loyalty, but she distrusted his hotheadedness. "Believe me, he is yet very young and self-willed," she advised Charles. "He is a person capable of doing anything that he is ordered, but he is not to be trusted to take a single step of his own head." On the other side were men such as Sir Edward Hyde, the future Earl of Clarendon: politicians who favored negotiating with the enemy for a peaceful settlement. These, too, Henrietta profoundly distrusted: "Persons . . . who, at the bottom of their hearts, are not well disposed for royalty." Former Parliamentarians who had defected to the king's side out of loyalty to the Anglican Church,

Hyde's party had no wish for Charles to be an absolute monarch: "Their counsels plainly show the contrary," she felt.[6]

Henrietta's own faction was drawn largely from her old court favorites, chief among whom was "Harry Jermyn," as she affectionately called him. He had labored with her in the Netherlands—even entrusted with the secret cipher she and Charles used in their correspondence—then returned to England "as colonel of my guards," commanding her troops on their march to Oxford. Implicated in the court's plots against Parliament before the Civil War, Jermyn and the rest were adamant that the war had to be won and Charles had to be reestablished with all his former authority, so as to secure their own safety from prosecution by Parliament. And Henrietta shared their desperate determination. Action, courage, resolution, no compromise, no delay: these were her constant watchwords to her husband.[7]

No one could fault Charles's courage in battle. "He was very fearless in his person," and his physical strength and fitness stood him in great stead, for he was never ill "throughout all the fatigues of the war." But in his decision-making, his followers lamented, he had a fatal lack of "enterprise": the readiness to undertake difficult or dangerous ventures.[8] That summer, when Henrietta arrived in Oxford, Parliament's army was in disarray, and the queen was determined that Charles and his army should move against London. But, after several days of indecision, he followed more cautious advice and went in the opposite direction: to besiege Gloucester and secure his supply lines from Wales. Henrietta was left behind in Oxford in a state of "no small dissatisfaction." By September, Charles's siege had ended in failure and the strains of the war were taking their toll on Henrietta: "I am so weary, not of being beaten, but of having heard it spoken of."[9]

That winter, her hopes were further dampened when the Scots invaded England. In the South, too, the king's forces were in dire straits, and Henrietta was eager for peace talks with Parliament and the armistice they would bring, even if only temporarily: "The truth is that the king's army here needs it."[10] She herself was in great danger. Back in the previous spring, as her troops marched toward

Oxford, winning victories and taking towns, Henrietta had at last been charged with high treason by the Commons. "The queen hath levied war against the Parliament and kingdom," the MPs voted unanimously; she must "receive a trial and due sentence." Clearly, if she fell into Parliament's hands, Henrietta was likely to suffer the Earl of Strafford's fate. At the very least, she would become a valuable pawn, allowing MPs to "make their own conditions" in negotiating with the king.[11]

By April 1644, Parliamentarian forces were advancing toward Oxford, and the king's army—fewer than ten thousand now—was too small to face them in pitched battle. There was every likelihood that Oxford would be besieged, in which case Henrietta's escape would become impossible. So, unhappily, the royal couple agreed to part. Henrietta was six months pregnant and suffering from "fits of the mother"—breathless panic attacks—"and a violent consumptive cough." Modern assessment of her symptoms suggests she was in the early stages of tuberculosis.[12] It was decided that she would go to Bath to drink the spa waters, while Charles remained to command his troops. On April 17, the royal couple spent a final night together at Abingdon, five miles south of Oxford. The next day, they said their tearful farewells.[13] They did not know it, but they would never see each other again.

From Bath, where rotting corpses from recent warfare lay in the streets and plague was spreading, Henrietta hurried on westward to Exeter—a strongly fortified city commanded by a loyal governor—where she would find safety for the approaching birth. Here she fully expected to die. "My dear heart," she wrote to Charles,

> the cruel pains I have suffered since I left you . . . make me believe that it is time for me to think of another world. If it be so, the will of God be done! . . . Adieu, my dear heart. I hope before I leave you, to see you once again in the position in which you ought to be. God grant it![14]

The birth on June 16 of her daughter, "a lovely princess" named Henrietta, only brought a worsening of her condition. "My disease

. . . is so insupportable," she told Charles, "that if it were not that we ought not to wish for death, it would be too much longed for [by me]." She suffered paralysis and partial blindness, feeling "as though I was so tightly squeezed in the region of the heart that I was suffocating," and her misery was made "complete" by the approach of the Earl of Essex's Parliamentarian army.[15] Overcome with fears "of being shut up" in the city, Henrietta resolved to flee, "even at the hazard of my life," she wrote to Charles.

> I shall show you by this last action, that nothing is so much in my thoughts as what concerns your preservation, and that my own life is of very little consequence compared with that; for as your affairs stand, they would be in danger if you come to help me, and I know that your affection would make you risk everything for that. . . .
>
> Adieu, my dear heart.
>
> The most miserable creature in the world, who can write no more.[16]

Leaving her tiny baby with a little household of caregivers, Henrietta left Exeter in disguise. For more than a week, she was carried in a litter almost to the farthest end of Cornwall, while her physician and a small band of attendants walked or rode beside her. "Here is the woefullest spectacle my eyes yet ever beheld," a Cornish gentleman reported; "the most worn and pitiful creature in the world, the poor queen, shifting for one hour's life longer."[17] On July 14, she sailed for France, even as Charles's northern army was being destroyed in the Battle of Marston Moor.

In Paris that autumn, substantially recovered after drinking the spa waters at Bourbon l'Archambault, Henrietta threw herself into working for her husband's cause. She wrote to Rome, Lorraine, the Netherlands, and the French government, now headed by the queen regent, Anne of Austria, after the death of Louis XIII. Henrietta also approached the Irish rebels, who offered "an army of ten thousand men" if Charles would "condescend to the just demands of his Irish subjects." Further communications went to Charles's military commanders in Scotland and the Southwest of England, where she arranged to export tin from her Cornish dower-lands to France, in return for weapons.[18]

Most of all, she wrote to Charles: letters that were full of love and concern for his safety in the war but also were packed with advice, instructions, and exhortations. As news came that he was entering into negotiations with his enemies, her anxiety increased. "Have a care not to abandon those who have served you, as well the bishops as the poor Catholics," she urged as 1645 began. Charles also needed to retain his military power,

> for if the militia and some of the fortresses are placed in the hands of some of the Parliamentarians, you will only have made war to destroy yourself and your reputation; and as for me, I should be done for, since I could not trust myself to those people.[19]

But all too soon the negotiations failed, and the following June, despite Charles's optimism that "my affairs were never in so fair and hopeful a way," his southern army was defeated at the Battle of Naseby. "Bodies lay slain about four miles in length, the most thick on the hill where the king stood."[20] Almost his entire force was killed or captured, along with the artillery and baggage train. Many of his commanders now talked of abandoning the cause. "There is such a universal weariness of the war," complained Lord Digby to Henry Jermyn in Paris, that

> I do not know four persons living . . . that have not already given clear demonstrations that they will purchase their own and, as they flatter themselves, the kingdom's quiet at any price to the king.

Even the militaristic Prince Rupert advised his uncle to capitulate. But Charles would not hear of it, replying,

> If I had any other quarrel but the defense of my religion, crown, and friends, you had full reason for your advice, for I confess that, speaking either as a mere soldier or statesman, I must say there is no prob-

ability but of my ruin; but as a Christian, I must tell you, that God will not suffer rebels to prosper, or this cause to be overthrown: and whatever personal punishment it shall please him to inflict upon me, must not make me repine, much less to give over this quarrel . . . whatever it cost me.[21]

By December 1645, however, Charles had little choice but to open talks. "His Majesty hath no army at all," wrote Sir Edward Nicholas. Only a few last strongholds still held out, their garrisons unsupplied and unpaid. Meanwhile, Parliament was making preparations to besiege Oxford. Charles faced "the certainty of being blocked up here or in any other place his Majesty can now hie unto." And so again he sent peace proposals to Parliament, offering terms "as low as he can go with preserving of his conscience and honor."[22] He also approached the Parliamentarian army, hoping to exploit differences between them and Parliament. But Henrietta's greatest hope lay with the Scottish Covenanters, whose army was now besieging Newark, about a hundred miles north of Oxford. Back in October, she had opened talks with the Scots envoy in Paris, and by the spring of 1646 she was pursuing this treaty "with all diligence . . . very confident it will succeed." The French government also favored this solution, fearing the power of an English republic if Parliament won the war.[23]

But there remained one great problem: Charles himself, who adamantly rejected the Scots' demand that he establish their Presbyterian religion in England. When the French ambassador, Jean de Montreuil (or Montereul), pressed this point with "many arguments"—"without it, nothing could be done in order to [make] an agreement with the Scots"—Charles still resisted. It was a point inconsistent with "his conscience." Even Henrietta's desperate letters failed to move him. Imagine if their positions were reversed, he asked:

Wouldst thou give ear to him who should persuade thee, for worldly respects, to leave the communion of the Roman church for any other? Indeed, sweetheart, this is my case.

"For God's sake . . . consider that, if I should quit my conscience, how unworthy I make myself of thy love." But as the Parliamentarian army advanced to besiege Oxford, Charles had "neither force enough to resist nor sufficient [force] to escape to any secure place." "Mere necessity" was now his master, he told Henrietta.[24]

Desperately he asked Parliament to allow him to go to London to negotiate, and again he sent separate messages to their army commanders, but to no avail. Only the Scots remained, and Charles wrote to their commissioners in London asking for assurances "that we shall be secure in your army both in conscience and honor." In return, Charles offered:

> as soon as I come into the Scots army, I shall be very willing to be instructed concerning the presbyterial government: whereupon they shall see that I shall strive to content them in anything that shall not be against my conscience.

Conscience and honor were still Charles's supreme principles. "If I cannot live as a king," he wrote to one of his followers, "I shall die like a gentleman, without doing that which may make honest men blush for me."[25]

On April 1, with the authorization of the Scottish commissioners in London, as he thought, Ambassador Montreuil signed a guarantee

> that if the King of Great Britain shall put himself into the Scots' army, he shall be there received as their natural Sovereign . . . and that they shall employ their armies and forces to assist his Majesty . . . in recovery of his Majesty's just rights.

The Royalists were delighted at the "excellent news."[26] While Montreuil went on ahead to Newark to arrange for the king's reception there, Charles prepared to follow, "I having resolved (by the grace of God) to begin my journey thither upon Monday or Tuesday next," he wrote to Henrietta on Thursday, April 2. There was still no formal peace treaty with the Scots, he admitted. The issues of "the [English] militia, Ireland, and my friends" would have to be thrashed out in person when he came to the army. "As for church business, I hope to manage it so as not to give them distaste and yet do nothing against my conscience." But on April 13, Charles was still in Oxford. "It much troubles me that I am not parted from hence," he wrote to Henrietta. "The reason is, because I have not heard one word from Montreuil since he went." And now, "closed upon all sides" by the Parliamentarian armies, he would find escape more difficult than ever. At last a letter came from the French ambassador. It was a bombshell for the king. "The Scots are abominable relapsed rogues," Charles reported to Henrietta, "for Montreuil himself is ashamed of them, they having retracted almost everything which they made him promise me."[27] Their army refused to recognize the agreement made with their commissioners in London. The whole idea of the Scots fighting for the king had vanished. Charles would be allowed to join the army, but only if he pretended to arrive by chance, so as not to offend the English Parliament, and he must establish Presbyterianism in England "as promptly as possible."[28]

His condition was "much worse than ever," Charles wrote to Henrietta, perplexed at "the difficulty of resolving what to do." He had little time to lose. If he remained, he would soon be a captive, so he decided to flee secretly to King's Lynn, on the Norfolk coast. There he might gather enough forces "to procure honorable and safe conditions from the rebels." If that failed, he could sail to Scotland, where the Marquess of Montrose was attempting to raise a new army for him. If Montrose was not ready, then he would flee abroad, to "Ireland, France, or Denmark, but to which of these I am not yet resolved." Yet still Charles dithered. Leaving England was "in no wise counselable," his advisers agreed. It was unbecoming "to quit his party in that faint-seeming way," and there was nothing he could gain by it, for none of these nations had the power to aid him.[29] So Charles settled on a new plan.

As midnight approached on Sunday, April 27, he went secretly to the chamber of John Ashburnham, his groom of the bedchamber, "the person in whom the king of Great Britain has now the greatest confidence." Also present was Dr. Michael Hudson, "his plaindealing chaplain," as Charles called him, "because he told him his mind, when others would or dared not."[30] Hudson had provided horses and an old parliamentary pass, which would permit the party to travel to London. Soon after midnight, while Ashburnham used a knife to cut off the king's long, flowing locks and trim his beard short, Hudson went out to fetch Sir Thomas Glemham, the military commander of Oxford, who unlocked the eastern gate of the city. As the various college clocks chimed 3 a.m., the four men—Glemham, Hudson, Ashburnham, and Charles, now disguised as Ashburnham's roundhead serving man—crossed Magdalen Bridge in pitch darkness and rode out into the fields beyond. Soon Glemham turned back, ready to keep the city gates locked and allow no one to "pass in or out of Oxford, for five days." "Farewell, Harry," he said to Charles, whose face was hidden beneath a woolen soldiers' cap with flaps down over his ears, and a hat on top of that.[31] Then Charles and his two companions rode off southeastward.

Hudson was the ideal man to take charge of the little expedition. During the previous years of war, the clergyman had served as an army scoutmaster, in charge of reconnoitering and gathering intelligence. Around Oxford, he "understood the by-ways as well as the common, and was indeed a very skillful guide." In one village, there was a guard of Parliamentarian dragoons, "which we passed without any difficulty or examination," Hudson recorded. A few miles farther on, they met a party of cavalry. Observing that Hudson and Ashburnham wore pistols in their belts, the enemy troops "asked us to whom we belonged," to which Hudson "answered, 'to the House of Commons,' and so passed." At Henley-on-Thames, they passed again "without any question, only showing the pass to the corporal and giving 12d. to the guards." At Hillingdon, twenty miles west of London, they stopped and went into a tavern "to refresh ourselves." It was now ten or eleven in the morning. They had not slept all night, and decision-making was becoming difficult. For two or three hours, they remained while Charles, "much perplexed," again dithered over "what course to resolve upon—London or northward?"[32]

From Oxford, London had seemed an appealing prospect. Charles and his advisers had been sure that if he could get there safely, Parliament would show "much more moderation" than while he remained "at a distance." It was an action that Parliament feared above all else, expecting that in London the king might well "arouse the respect and affection of the people." But now, so close to London, Charles lost his nerve: the danger of being recognized and arrested en route seemed too great. So he decided to go northward into Norfolk, "where he was least known." There he would wait while Hudson went to the Scots at Newark. If the news from there was bad, he would return to his former plan and "cast himself upon his English [subjects]."[33]

And so they rode north. A mile beyond St. Albans, two horses came "galloping after us very fast," and the trio feared they had been recognized. But it turned out to be merely a gentleman "very drunk" with his servant. Turning off the main road to avoid his company, Charles and his companions stopped for the night and then rode on at dawn. Soon they parted—Hudson bearing northwest for Newark while Charles and Ashburnham rode into Norfolk to stay at the White Swan Inn in Downham Market. Two days later, Hudson rejoined them. The Scots had agreed to all of Charles's demands. They would "secure the king in his person and in his honor," and press him "to do nothing contrary to his conscience." If Parliament refused to restore him, they would "declare for the king; and take all the king's friends into their protection." There was just one problem: they absolutely refused to put anything in writing.[34]

The next morning, concerned about escaping detection, Charles moved to an obscure village alehouse, now disguised as a clergyman in a "black coat and long cassock." Again he considered joining Montrose in Scotland, and Hudson made inquiries "for a ship to go to the North or Newcastle, but could get none." Finally, "destitute of any other refuge," Charles resolved to join the Scottish Covenanters, trusting himself to those who "first began my troubles." Perhaps, despite all, "my rendering my person to them may engage their affections to me, who have oft professed, 'They fought not against me, but for me.'"[35]

Under Hudson's guidance, they traveled by the most secret routes, riding south through the marshes around Ely before turning northward for Newark. The king had another new identity as "the doctor," wearing a freshly purchased hat and a gray coat that Hudson had obtained from a friend. At 6 a.m. on Tuesday, May 5, after eight days on the run, "having passed through fourteen guards and garrisons of the enemies," they reached Southwell, where the French ambassador had his lodgings, a few miles from the Scots army still besieging Newark.[36] Here numerous Scottish lords soon arrived, and the disavowals began. They were delighted to see the king there, they said, but his arrival was totally unexpected. They had heard nothing of any terms settled with their commissioners in London, so they could not honor them. Charles was horrified. All his and Montreuil's arguments had no effect. Instead, before Charles had "drunk, refreshed, or reposed himself," the Scots issued their own demands: Charles must order his garrison in Newark to surrender to the English Parliamentarian army that was also besieging the town. He must sign the Presbyterian Covenant and order the Marquess of Montrose "to lay down his arms."[37]

That night, lodged under strict guard in the midst of the Scottish military headquarters, Charles could see that he was little better than a prisoner. There was nothing of "affection or dependence" in the Scots' behavior. General Leslie never asked him for any orders, and he forbade any army officers to see or speak to him. Meanwhile, a sequence of visitors pressed the king "ungraciously" to "things . . . most averse to his conscience and honor."[38] Briefly, Charles thought of escaping to the Parliamentarian army on the other side of Newark, but he had no messenger to send. So he did what he could to gratify the Scots. The very next day, he sent orders to his men in Newark to surrender "on very hard terms for those who were therein." Then he and the entire Scottish army set out "with much haste" for Newcastle. Fearing an attack by Parliament now that they had the king, the Scots thought they would be safer there. And Charles was willing enough to go. At Newcastle, the Scots suggested, he could meet a new set of their commissioners who might honor the conditions arranged by Montreuil.[39]

But as Charles approached Newcastle, the omens were not good. No crowds came out to cheer. No deputation of civic dignitaries stood ready to welcome him: on Scottish orders, the mayor and aldermen remained at home. The numerous Scottish lords who had recently arrived absented themselves too. Wearing "a sad-colored plain suit," Charles rode between lines of silent soldiers, followed by an escort of three hundred cavalry. As he crossed the River Tyne and passed under Newcastle's great stone walls, not a single ship fired its guns; there were no drums, no trumpets, no bells ringing out from the church towers. Northward Charles continued through the streets, still without any noise or "extraordinary concourse of people"—only more Scottish infantry lining his route. Just before reaching the town walls, he passed under a stone gateway and along an avenue of trees, leading to New House, "one of the bravest houses in the town." This was now to be his home and royal court, and here at last the onlookers raised a shout. Yet it was more a sound of triumph than welcome.[40]

That was more than seven months ago now—months that Charles had passed in disappointment and humiliation. Everything he cared for lay in ruins. In England as well as Scotland, the post of bishop had been abolished, and Presbyterianism had been established as the state religion. Amid scenes of popular fury, stained-glass windows had been smashed, statues of saints beheaded, rood screens torn down, ancient stone churchyard crosses destroyed. His old soulmate, Archbishop Laud, had been tried for treason. Then, when his defense seemed too likely to succeed, he had been condemned by a parliamentary bill of attainder and executed, like Strafford before him. Every last vestige of Royalist military power was gone. On Charles's orders, Montrose's Scottish forces surrendered, as did the last few garrisons holding out in England. From Oxford, James, Duke of York was taken to London, where he joined Elizabeth and Henry in parliamentary custody. Of all the royal children, only Prince Charles still had his freedom. After commanding the last of the king's forces in the southwest of England, he had been forced to set sail—first for the Scilly Isles and then on to the Channel Islands. Repeated letters from his father urged the teenage prince to join his mother in France. "Your going beyond [the] sea is absolutely necessary for me." It was the only "real security" the king could have, and it would "make the rebels harken, and yield to reason," but only if the boy remained constant in his religion: "For all other things, I command you to be totally directed by your mother."[41] By June, the prince was in Paris.

Around New House, Scottish musketeers and "inhabitants of trust" from the local militia kept constant guard. Old men from the town sat "at every passage," ready "to examine and take notice what persons came in or out."[42] The king's few servants were all appointed by the Scottish government. Hudson and Ashburnham had fled to avoid being handed over to the English Parliament. Meanwhile, far from honoring Montreuil's settlement, the Scots only intensified the pressure on the king. Incessantly their lords and Presbyterian ministers demanded his "full concession" to the peace terms the English Parliament had offered him in their "nineteen propositions" back in 1642—demanding, among other things, parliamentary control over both the Church and the militia.[43] On one occasion, when the king retired weeping into his bedchamber, the Scots Lords followed him in to press their demands again. Every Sunday, sermons of "wholesome doctrine" were preached before him at New House or in the churches he attended in the town, advising him "to dispose his spirit to peace and unity." "Thou piece of clay, where thou sittest, think of thy death, resurrection, judgment, eternity," one minister urged, before ending, "in a most compassionate way, with offer of mercy upon repentance." Everyone seemed to be against the king. Even the Newcastle townspeople by and large regarded him as "not only weak but very willful and obstinate; . . . nothing can we see in him tending to a true Christian or the power of godliness."[44]

Charles's sole refuge lay in his correspondence with Henrietta. "All the comfort I have is in thy love," he wrote to her. "Let me hear often from thee," "for seriously, without compliment, thy love preserves my life." As long as she continued to be kind to him, "I care not much for others."[45] Somehow, in the face of his enemies, Charles managed to preserve his usual outward calm: "Never man saw him passionately angry or extraordinarily moved," commented a Presbyterian theologian who often engaged him in debate.[46] To

Henrietta alone did he reveal his true feelings about "the false jug-
gling of the Scots, and the base usage that I have had since I came
to this army." The only people he saw now were "fools or knaves,"
he complained; every day brought "new vexations." "There was never
man so alone as I," he confided; "I never knew what it was to be
barbarously baited before."[47] Within a fortnight of reaching Newcastle, Charles had begun to "expect the worst." Henrietta must not
be deceived by false hopes, he told her, for the new peace proposals
expected from the London Parliament were bound to be "such as
I can never yield to." His one desire was "to go from hence to any
other part of the world." "And, indeed, to deal freely with thee, my
condition is such that I expect never to see thee, except . . . I find
means to quit for a time this wretched country."[48] "If I stay any time,
I am lost." And yet, despite his certainty that escape was impera-
tive, Charles was not prepared to take such a step without his wife's
approval. He begged her to think "seriously and speedily" about his
proposal, "for, upon my word, it will not admit of long delay." But
Jermyn and the rest of Henrietta's men opposed the idea, pointing
out "the danger of the attempt, and the provocation given to the Parliament if successful."[49]

That July, the peace proposals from Parliament were incredibly
severe, and the Scots pressed it all on him mercilessly: "Indeed, it is
almost incredible . . . with what impudence I have been assaulted to
yield," he told Henrietta. Yet still Charles was determined "to make
no concessions."[50] Rather than that, he was ready to face martyrdom
for his rights. "No threatenings, no apprehensions of danger to my
person," no "misplaced pity to me" must make any of them relent
"to the dishonor or prejudice of . . . that kingly authority" that was
Prince Charles's birthright. "I know my cause to be so just that (by
the Grace of God) I shall never faint in it."[51] But Henrietta and her
advisers urged him repeatedly to abandon his commitment to the
bishops and accept Presbyterianism in their place. This might be
enough to satisfy the Scottish Covenanters and the English Presbyterians. Then, allied with them, the king could defeat his irreconcilable enemies, "the Independent and anti-monarchical party," and
restore himself to the throne. It was military power, not the state

of the Church, that needed to be Charles's supreme consideration, they argued. "Keep the militia, and never give up, and by that everything will return," Henrietta wrote.[52]

Charles was appalled: his wife had completely misunderstood the situation. The Presbyterians were just as antimonarchical as the Independents. Their aim was to free the Church entirely from the authority of the Crown, and this would be far more destructive than if he gave up control of the militia, "for people are governed by the pulpit more than the sword in times of peace."

> Believe it, religion is the only firm foundation of all power: That cast loose, or depraved, no government can be stable. For where was there ever obedience where religion did not teach it?[53]

Charles now saw that his negotiations could never gain him acceptable peace terms; he and his enemies were irreconcilably opposed.[54] All he could do was delay them "as long as may be," while Henrietta sought foreign troops for his service. Only with "a strong visible force" against them would the Scots "hear reason," he told her.[55]

But Henrietta knew that no foreign aid would come. There was one stark choice confronting Charles: "Whether you will choose to be a king of presbytery, or no king" at all.[56] To her, his resistance was incomprehensible. Her own father had abandoned his Protestant faith and converted to Catholicism in order to gain the throne of France. "Paris is worth a Mass," was his maxim. What Henrietta now asked of Charles seemed so much less than this: just exchanging one form of Protestantism—one form of heresy, in her eyes—for another. And it would only be temporary, she kept telling him. She was now so fed up with all this, she told Charles, that she desired to retreat into a nunnery. Only her "passion" for him prevented her from doing so, and made her willing to "endure all, if you think it for your service."[57]

Charles was distraught. In "inexpressible grief and astonishment," he begged Henrietta for mercy. "The queen will break my heart if she any more undertake to obtain my consent for Presbyterian government." "For God's sake, leave off threatening me," he implored. Henrietta must promise never to go into a nunnery, "for I assure thee, both I and all my children are ruined, if thou shouldst retire from my business."[58] "There is nothing in this world I love equal to thee." Yet even to his beloved wife he would not yield on this one great "matter of conscience." He had gone against his conscience before, he told her, when he "made that base, sinful concession concerning the Earl of Strafford." Agreeing to that bill of attainder had been the most unhappy event of his life. It had been wrong, he now saw, "to wound a man's own conscience, thereby to salve state sores."[59] And he had been "most justly punished" for it. "No greater calamities" could have come if he had refused to sign that fatal bill. It was this, more than anything else, that made him absolutely determined now to resist all "violent importunities." "A new relapse," he told Henrietta, would only "procure God's further wrath upon me."[60]

For days on end, Charles was occupied entirely at his desk. His earlier pursuits—golf in the countryside around Newcastle, rides along the river to Tynemouth, or games of chess indoors—were a thing of the past.[61] There was a constant round of letters: to Henrietta and her men in Paris, to Parliament in London, and to his enemies and old friends in Scotland. In mid-November, after hearing news from London that an agreement might yet be possible, Charles turned to drafting peace proposals. Henrietta was furious when she heard what he had conceded:

> With the granting [of] the militia [to Parliament's control], you have cut your own throat; for having given them this power, you can no longer refuse them anything, not even my life, if they demand it from you; but I shall not place myself in their hands. . . . Do you think that when I see you so resolute in the affair of the bishops, and so little in that which concerns yourself and your posterity, that I am not in great despair, after having so often warned you as I have done, and it avails nothing? I tell you again, for the last time, that if you grant more you are lost, and I shall never return to England, but shall go and pray to God for you.[62]

As the stresses on the couple intensified, their relationship was approaching breakdown. Driven to desperation by Henrietta's accusations that he was "destroying by my wilfullness all that is dear unto me," Charles even threatened to abdicate: it was a final attempt to force Henrietta to back down on her proposed concessions to Presbyterianism.[63] He was right to think she would be shaken. "I hate it," she replied by return mail. "If any such thing should be made public, you are undone—your enemies will make a malicious use of it. Be sure you never own it again in any discourse." But the king was utterly wrong to think he could browbeat his wife into changing her mind. She insisted that he was the one who was mistaken about the true political situation: he must either "satisfy the Presbyterians" or "leave the work undone."[64]

Charles was at his wits' end when her reply arrived. What did he have to do to make her listen? Henrietta and her advisers would trust "any other information or intelligence" rather than what he said. At last his exasperation broke out:

> Good God, what things are these to try my patience! . . . I could say much more upon this subject; but I will only conjure you, as you are Christians, no more thus to torture me, assuring you that the more ye this way press me, you the more contribute . . . to my ruin.[65]

But the grim reality was that any concessions Charles offered now were irrelevant. For some months, the Scots and the English Parliament had been forging ahead on a peace settlement entirely independent of the king. The Scots would receive money for their services in the war, and then they would withdraw.[66] Charles would be kept by the Scots or handed over to the English, whichever his enemies should decide, but in either case, "I shall be an absolute prisoner," he wrote to Henrietta, when rumors of the arrangements reached him. Again he urged her "to consider well" the idea of escape. Once he was out of Britain, he thought, the Scots and the English Parliament would quarrel "and so give me an opportunity either to join with the weaker party or frame one of my own."[67] And he was well placed to flee. William, Prince of Orange, had sent a warship to Newcastle "to do what the king commands"; some five thousand former soldiers from the Royalist army were also gathering around the town.[68] But at the beginning of December, the king heard back from Henrietta: "Do not think of making any escape from England." A "general peace" was very close on the Continent now, she explained, and then the French were sure to aid him. Their ambassador was already under orders to negotiate a treaty with the Scots to fight jointly against Parliament and restore the king. If Charles fled now, "you would destroy all our hopes": he should leave, she added, only if the Scots declared openly "that they will not protect you."[69] And so, against his better judgment, Charles remained. She was dooming him to imprisonment, he wrote to Henrietta: once the Scots declared against him, it would be impossible to escape. But perhaps she was right, perhaps "it is less ill for my affairs that I should be a prisoner in my own dominions than at liberty anywhere else." Perhaps foreign governments then would be shamed into declaring their support for his restoration. Wearily, he filed away Henrietta's letter with a note on the back, "From my wife, to be kept, being the advice—not stir afore."[70]

Henrietta was astounded when she received her husband's reply. She had never meant him to become a prisoner. If he fell into the hands of the Independents, she would "never be free from the greatest apprehensions." It was "a thing not so much as to be thought on." Instead, Charles must "go along with the Scots into Scotland," or if they refused to take him, he could escape—to Ireland, the Scottish Highlands, or Jersey, "according to your own wisdom, and the conjuncture of affairs."[71]

But long before Henrietta's authorization reached him at Newcastle, Charles had already made his first attempt to escape. It was Christmas Eve 1646 when the news came that the Scottish Parliament had passed "very harsh resolutions." Charles had to approve "all the proposals of peace that have been presented to him by the two kingdoms": until then, his "royal authority will remain suspended."[72] So Charles prepared to escape. Seeing not a single place in Britain "where he could remain in safety," he planned to join Henrietta in France. The new French ambassador, Pierre de Bellièvre, tried desperately to change Charles's mind, arguing especially "the fear I have that it may be very difficult for him to return again." Perhaps he might "retire to the Scottish Highlands" rather than go abroad.[73] But Charles was determined. The Dutch ship waiting on the river was ready: "victualed . . . and new trimmed." That day, her captain was summoned to New House, to meet "in private" with William Murray, one of Charles's grooms of the bedchamber. Later, £100 was carried down to the captain. On Christmas morning, word came back that, if the wind was fair, the captain was happy to sail on the night tide, "notwithstanding any opposition from Tynemouth Castle." Charles was to go in disguise, either in "the habit of a sailor" or as William Murray's servant.[74]

Late that night, Murray went out to reconnoiter. But he soon turned back, whether because his attempt to open one of the town gates had failed—"a key was set fast and broken," one news report claimed—or because the town was too crowded with guards, who regarded him "with suspicion," another report suggested. Returning to New House, Murray gave the Scots guards the night's password, but still he was suspected, being out "at so unusual a time," so he was held in the guardchamber for three hours, "until the governor sent for him."[75] All of Newcastle was in an uproar, "the suspicion was so great, and the stir so great upon it." At once, General Leslie sent his cavalry lifeguards to block the road to Tynemouth. The next day, he ordered the king's guards to "be strictlier posed than they have been hitherto," with a squadron of the Scottish lifeguards to "watch every night."[76]

Through the following week, the king continued his desperate attempts to escape. The Dutch ship was no longer an option: her captain had been summoned for questioning by Newcastle's mayor, and four Parliamentarian warships were approaching the mouth of the Tyne. So, on the last day of 1646, Tobias Peaker, one of Charles's grooms of the privy chamber, was sent off to Hartlepool, twenty-five miles south of Newcastle, to "see what ships were there." But just outside of Newcastle, he lost his nerve. Realizing he would be judged an "accessory to an action which might prove so prejudicial to the kingdom," he turned back to tell the mayor all he knew.[77] That day, the king's guards were doubled, "both within his residence and without, and they go the rounds continually." Extra cavalry was brought in "to keep guard in the neighborhood [i.e., vicinity] of the town."[78]

Realizing his extreme danger, Charles sat down on Saturday, January 2, 1647, to write a letter to Henrietta that he hoped might yet save his life. Gone now were all the arguments, pleadings, and self-justifications of his earlier letters. Instead, he stated his position succinctly: He was truly a prisoner at last, his escape "most difficult, if not impossible." With a tone of striking authority, Charles laid down his last, great request to his wife. She and Prince Charles must "declare publicly" that his offers to his enemies in matters of religion had been most reasonable, and "that neither of you will persuade me to go further, but rather dissuade me, if I had a mind to grant more." This statement, Charles wrote, was "absolutely necessary for my preservation. For if there be the least imagination that Prince Charles will grant more, then I shall not live long after." The Scots, he reckoned, would put him to death so that his son could succeed to the throne and grant them their desires. Now, Charles thought, there was "need to say no more. For I know thy love will omit nothing that is possible for my freedom." Facing the possibility of his own death, he ended by begging his wife "never to despair of a good cause," nor to abandon her labors for Prince Charles, "even as thou loves me, who am eternally thine."[79]

The next day, a train of thirty-six carts entered York, with a "large convoy" of Parliamentarian troops. The journey from London had taken seventeen days, "the ways being very bad." Wagons had overturned and the two hundred or so boxes they carried were filthy and mud-spattered. But inside them, safe still, was £200,000 in "good gold and silver" coins—the first installment of the £400,000 that the English Parliament had agreed to pay the Scots in recompense for all their "pains, hazard, and charges" during the Civil War.[80] In return, the Scots would withdraw from England and deliver the king into English hands as a prisoner. For twelve days, the money remained in York while the English and Scottish treasury officials counted out the coins: several hundred thousand of them at least, and perhaps more than a million if much of the money was in silver. Each £100 was packed carefully into a bag and sealed with both English and Scottish seals. Then, ten bags were placed into each wooden chest, again sealed by both parties. On January 15, the job was finished, and the carts set off northward. Nine days later, the first of the money began to be paid out to the Scots soldiers in Newcastle, "each one reaching out for his share."[81]

In France, Henrietta was distraught. She had believed all along that the Scots would never abandon their king. Every day she wept, overcome by "the unhappy case of the king," who "finds himself abandoned by all and before the gates of a prison." In desperation, she talked of going to Ireland to raise support for Charles, or of retiring into a nunnery, but she could not make up her mind to do either. Instead, she went to see her sister-in-law, Anne of Austria, complaining "with bitter tears" of "the conditions of herself and her husband" and laying the blame on France. The French ministers had led her on with promises "of the great things they would do" once peace came in Europe, and these "long-delayed hopes" had reduced her and Charles "to the utmost extremity."[82]

At Newcastle, meanwhile, Charles remained calm, at least on the surface. When a commission of three Lords and six MPs arrived from Parliament, he was all charm, holding out his hand "with affability" for each of them to kiss. Carefully the commissioners told him they had come "to receive the person of the king from the Scots army," according to the orders of Parliament, "and to serve him during the journey" to Holdenby House, sixty miles north of London.[83] At this, Charles "seemed very well pleased." They were all "very welcome," he said. "None of them were strangers to him," and their business was "no less welcome" than they: he was eager now "to remove jealousies and distrusts, and establish a right understanding betwixt him and his Parliament." He even managed to make some jokes with the deputation's head, the Earl of Pembroke, who had so often entertained Charles at Wilton back in the 1630s.[84]

Still, it was not too late for Charles to avoid being handed over to the English. If he accepted Presbyterianism, the Scots urged, they might take him with them when they left England. Otherwise, they warned, he would have to endure the "strictness" of the English Independents, who, they said, would deprive him "of the consolation of receiving the queen's letters and of the visits of his friends," and treat him like a criminal, with a parliamentary verger deputed "to sleep in his bedroom" at night. But still Charles replied "that he would never give his consent": "what was asked of him was equally opposed to his peace of conscience and to the welfare of his people."[85] With quiet confidence, he expected it would all turn out well in the end. His subjects surely could never manage without him. "Without my establishing [as king], there can be no peace": "the two nations must needs fall out." Once he was in English hands, he felt, the Scots would back down and "do for him . . . what they have refused to do when they had him with them." He also had great hopes from "the power of France," and some of his servants assured him that, although they had failed to get him out of Newcastle, they would certainly "deliver him from Holdenby."[86]

So Charles hurriedly prepared for his English captivity. He destroyed all his papers that "he could not without some risk of harm carry away with him." He wrote to the Marquess of Ormonde in Ireland, the last place where the king's men still had power, ordering him "to follow the queen's and prince's direction," and not to hesitate or scruple "for want of legal power from the king." There was a last letter for Henrietta, too. She must believe no future message from him, he told her, unless it came via a person of unquestionable loyalty. And she must not allow Prince Charles to go to England, whatever "threats or entreaties" Parliament might make and whatever her fears for him.[87]

On the morning of Saturday, January 30, the Scots paraded their entire cavalry through the center of Newcastle, past New House, and out into the countryside. By afternoon, there were just five hundred soldiers left in the town, ready to make the final handover to the five hundred English soldiers who arrived around 2 p.m. It was a "friendly and brotherly parting" on the Scottish side, with the troops under strict orders not "to plunder any houses, drive away any goods, nor exact . . . any moneys or provision."[88] But popular feeling among the townspeople was running high against their former occupiers. The Scots were "nothing but Jews"—"people who had sold their king and their honor," just as Judas had sold Christ to his enemies. The newly arrived English officers were forced to use "blows and threats, to prevent the women of this town from following the Scottish troops and throwing stones at them while they were leaving." Meanwhile, inside New House, the commissioners from the Scottish Parliament were taking leave of the king. Some of them had tears in their eyes as they told him "that as he refused to sign the proposals and treaties, they were obliged to hand him over to the English." But Charles's patience was at last exhausted. Their refusal to receive him in Scotland was of no importance, he replied sharply, "as even if he had been at liberty, he would rather have gone to those who bought [him] than to those who sold him." As the Scots withdrew, their English counterparts entered the king's presence and "at once set their guards."[89]

This was the moment that Charles and Henrietta had dreaded for so long. The king was to be attended now only by servants "appointed by Parliament," with orders not "to allow any letter or paper to be given to him that they had not previously seen." It was the end, at last, of the correspondence the couple had somehow managed to maintain through five years of war and its aftermath. The English government was in no mood for compromise or negotiation. "They have informed their king of what he will have to do," the MPs said; now Charles had to stay at Holdenby House "until he has granted everything." But, knowing that the king was unlikely to give in, they expected that he would remain "always at Holdenby," a perpetual prisoner.[90]

In fact, Charles would spend less than four months at Holdenby before the turmoils of English politics carried him elsewhere. Snatched out of Parliament's hands by their own army, he stayed five months at Hampton Court, negotiating with Oliver Cromwell and the other commanders. From there he fled to the Isle of Wight, where he found only another, stricter imprisonment. Seized once again by the angry army, he was carried to London for trial. Finally, at 2 p.m. on Tuesday, January 30, 1649, two years almost to the hour after his delivery into English hands at Newcastle, the king stepped out of the Banqueting House at Whitehall to be beheaded as a traitor to his country and his people.

12

COLOMBES,
AUGUST 1669

T wenty years after her husband's death, Henrietta Maria reached her own last day on earth—at Colombes, the country retreat outside Paris where she now spent most of her time. In her little chateau, the fifty-nine-year-old queen lived amid the greatest luxury once more. The house was laid out as a royal court, with black-liveried guardsmen standing at the entrance to a suite of sumptuous apartments. Rich wall hangings matched the finely upholstered furniture: crimson brocade patterned with gold and silver thread in Henrietta's grand privy chamber, elegant gray silk in her bedchamber. Tables and cabinets were inlaid with tortoiseshell, or decorated in Chinese lacquerwork, or painted with veins to look like marble. Gilded mirrors hung in every room. Carpets—most of them Persian "of gold, silver, and silk of several colors"—were draped over beds and tables. Innumerable *objets d'art* were scattered throughout the rooms: a pot carved from rock crystal with a silver gilt lid, "an Indian teapot, garnished with gold," "an Indian box lined with rubies." There were fine clocks, rare books, an amber statuette of the Virgin Mary. Henrietta ate from gilded plates with gilded cutlery; twelve gilded candlesticks guided her to bed; her chamberpot was solid silver.

Paintings lined the walls of every room. There were numerous religious pictures, and fine old masters from her 1630s collecting, confiscated by Parliament but since restored to her: works by Correggio, Tintoretto, Giulio Romano, Titian, and others. But pride of place was given to portraits of her family. Facing the queen every day were images of the children she never saw now. There was her youngest son, Henry, dressed in sky blue: the "little cavalier" who had delighted his mother when he joined her in Paris after his release by Parliament—only to depart, estranged, eighteen months later.[1] There was her eldest daughter, Mary, Princess of Orange. Widowed before she was twenty, she had brought up her baby son, William, alone. She died of smallpox in 1660, amid the celebrations of King Charles II's restoration. The portrait of Charles II himself stood over the fireplace in Henrietta's privy chamber, "a tall black[-haired] man, over two yards high," in soldier's buffcoat and arms.[2] He was married now to the Portuguese Infanta, Catherine of Braganza—a Catholic match that delighted his mother. For three years, Henrietta had lived with them in England, until ill health forced her return to France, leaving her second son behind her, too. James, Duke of York, was now Lord Admiral in command of his brother's navy, as his father had intended thirty years earlier. Dressed in armor, he looked down on the queen from above the door of her bedchamber. The only child Henrietta Maria still saw regularly was her youngest, Henrietta Anne, who lived in France as the wife of Louis XIV's younger brother, Philippe, Duc d'Orléans. Her portrait as a girl hung in Henrietta's dressing room, along with that of her baby son, the Duc de Valois, in his swaddling clothes, fourth in line to the French throne.[3]

Beneath all these imposing figures, Henrietta herself was diminutive—slight and frail, in somber widow's weeds, with the black cap and veil she had worn ever since her husband's death. Chronic illness dogged her final years: her old bronchial complaints had become a lingering, wasting disease, with the queen growing ever weaker "in a consumption." Her return to the "much purer" air of France had brought only a partial alleviation.[4] Still she was "continually subject to fainting fits, sleeplessness, and other bodily ailments," and often passed the day in great pain, confined to the crimson-brocade four-poster bed that was set up in her privy chamber, contrary to normal royal etiquette. In her bedchamber was a caddy of gilt cutlery, for meals when she was too ill to move at all. But Henrietta did not whine. "Complaints in illness were useless," she said, "or, if they served for anything, it was to show the great weakness and the little resolution of the persons who complained."[5]

Every day she spent hours alone in the little cabinet or anteroom that opened off her bedroom. Even more than the rest of the house, this room was crammed with luxuries: carved agates and rock crystal, statuettes, intricate pieces of gold and silver filigree work, curiosities from India, a large collection of Chinese porcelain. All these things "of great value" stood atop the tables and the mantelpiece or were tucked away in the little cupboards and drawers of lavishly ornate cabinets. Exquisite little boxes were crammed with jewelry and portrait miniatures; a collection of twenty-two medals "of gold, great and small," was stored in a purse. But Henrietta paid them no heed. To her, this room was like a nun's cell, where she would "commune more quietly and more ultimately with God." The walls were covered with religious pictures, eighty or so in all, with just a few family portraits among them. Beneath them, Henrietta knelt in prayer, while her watch, hung on a gold-filigree hook, ticked away the passing hours. Henrietta's life at Colombes was strictly ordered. Every hour of the day was assigned "to some particular employment": public prayers in her chapel, private "mental prayer, the Mass, meals, company, recreations, business."[6]

Her cabinet was a bright and airy place, with wall hangings and curtains in white damask, matching the couch where Henrietta sat to read after taking her spectacles from their gold-filigree case. Always it was the same book: Thomas à Kempis's *Imitation of Christ*, a guide to leading a perfect religious life in "contempt of all the vanities of the world." She read a chapter every day; when the book was finished, she started again from the beginning, "saying that it was her daily bread and that she would never tire of it." Sometimes she sat at her table made of Jamaican braziletto wood, writing in her little leather-bound notebook or going through her household accounts: a religious mortification that she offered to God "in atonement for the human pride which always attends on crowned heads."[7] Henrietta was content in her quietness and solitude, "for she was undeceived about the world and perfectly acquainted with the worthlessness of Earth's grandeurs." "For some time now, she had felt entirely devoted to God," she said. Yet still, twenty years on, her love for her husband "always occupied her mind." Not a single portrait of Charles hung on her walls: it would be too painful to encounter his face continuously. But hidden away among the seeming infinity of treasures in her cabinet was "a little Indian box," containing a single miniature portrait of her dead husband, along with the betrothal and wedding rings he had given her.[8]

On that February midday back in 1649, when Henrietta first heard the news of Charles's death, she had been stunned. Despite the warning signs from England, despite Henry Jermyn's attempts to prepare her for the worst, still she had not believed it could happen. To us it is no surprise. In the intervening centuries, other European monarchs have come to similar fates: Louis XVI condemned for high treason and guillotined; Tsar Nicholas II forced to abdicate, then shot by the Soviet revolutionaries. But to Henrietta's contemporaries, Charles's fate—tried by a court of law in his own realm and condemned to die publicly "in the face of his people"—was monstrous and unnatural, a "barbarous" act "without precedent": "no age ever heard the like."[9] A king was a sacred person, "God's vicegerent upon earth," set up by divine authority to rule His people. Charles himself, on the day before his trial, had still thought his enemies merely "aimed at his deposing and confinement in the Tower, or some suchlike place." Even the Parliamentarian commissioners who sat in judgment over him had not fully foreseen the end. When it came time, many were unwilling to sign the king's death warrant and were forced to it only by Cromwell's violence.[10]

At the Palace of the Louvre, when Jermyn finished his dreadful tale about Charles, Henrietta had remained silent, lost in her own shock. The man she had loved beyond all others was gone forever—a man she knew to have been "good, just, wise, worthy of her affection and his subjects' love." It was "the most cruel and shameful death that ever [a] king died," beheaded as a traitor to his own country "in the presence of an innumerable concourse of people, by the hand of an executioner, that is to say, of the vilest of men."[11] She knew the place so well, outside the Banqueting House where she and Charles had spent some of their happiest evenings in feasts and plays and masques: the formal ranks of rectangular windows with their classical pediments forming a backdrop of royal grandeur that mocked the horrific events in front. In all this bitter scene was just one consolation: Charles's calm and courage. The French ambassador in London paid special attention to this in his report to Saint-Germain, knowing it would reach Henrietta. On the scaffold, Charles

> saw the preparations for such a fatal act with tranquillity, spoke always with the same freedom, undressed himself and laid himself on the ground, and suffered the greatest violence ever seen with a resignation without example.

But what had Charles really felt? As Henrietta sat silently, did she try to imagine what was going through her husband's head as he spread out his arms in signal to the executioner? Had he been afraid at that last moment, or angry? Had he felt any pain as the axe struck home? Perhaps she tried to picture him now—a lifeless corpse, denied a place in Westminster Abbey with his royal predecessors and laid in the earth "without ceremony."[12] Or perhaps she looked back to the last time she had seen him, at Abingdon in 1644, when they had kissed each other farewell in tears. Now, with hindsight, did she wish she had done it differently, perhaps spent longer or said more, or even stayed on in Oxford through the war to share her husband's fate? Perhaps she still hoped, beyond all hope, that

Charles was not truly dead. Just a few days earlier, she had heard the false report that Charles had been rescued from the scaffold. Might not this latest news also be premature, exaggerated? But she could not keep this hope for long: the news had come from the French ambassador in London himself.

Gone forever were those years of bliss when she had been "the happiest princess in the world."[13] There would be no more idyllic summers in the country, riding, hunting, and partying with their friends; no more shared winter pleasures in London, with dances, masques, and plays; no more spring jaunts out Maying in Hyde Park; no annual move to Greenwich in May to begin their seasonal round all over again. What would become of her now—exiled, dispossessed, penniless, stateless, a queen rejected and detested by her own subjects? And what of her children? Her son Charles, already proclaimed King Charles II by his followers at The Hague, was a monarch without a realm. James, his younger brother, had nothing in the world but what his mother could send him from her own, long-unpaid allowance from the French government. Henrietta Anne was just four years old, sharing her mother's destitution at the Louvre. And still in England were Elizabeth and Henry, whom she had not seen for almost seven years. Would they grow up never knowing their own mother? Would Henry be placed on the throne, a puppet king in the hands of his father's enemies, as the news from England suggested? One thing she knew for certain. Charles's death had made her "the most wretched woman in the world"; "for the rest of her life, this separation would be a perpetual torment."[14]

Amid Henrietta's grief there was anger, too—not only at the Parliamentarian enemies who had brought about her husband's downfall but also at the European powers, her native France included, that had done nothing to help during all the years of war. Perhaps she was even angry with Charles himself. Over and over during the Civil War, she had told him to be more resolute, more ruthless and bold. But always he had shrunk from doing what was necessary. And, imprisoned by the Scots, when the time had come for subtlety and cunning, Charles had refused to follow her advice and accept Presbyterianism to save himself and his throne. Or maybe Henrietta was more angry with herself. She had egged Charles on to arrest the five leading opposition MPs in 1642, precipitating the Civil War. She had persuaded him not to escape from the Scots while he still had the chance.

Probably something of all these thoughts went through Henrietta's mind as she sat beside her dinner table, "quite overwhelmed, without words, without action, without motion, like a statue."[15] Her courtiers tried to rouse her. Her chaplain, Father Cyprien de Gamache, brought all his armory of religious arguments to bear. He reminded her that death was followed by God's judgment, when Christ would take away our sins and lead us to salvation. She must "resign herself to the will of God." Clearly, Providence had overturned her power so she might outlive all worldly attachments and "sentiments of pride": purified by her experiences, she would be able to come nearer to God.[16] But to all such urgings Henrietta seemed "deaf and insensible." Still she could not stir, nor weep, nor speak, nor even hear, it seemed. "Small cares speak out, greater ones are dumb," Gamache wrote in his memoirs, quoting the ancient Roman moralist Seneca: a perfect description of the condition now known as psychological shock. At last her companions could do no more, but they remained standing around her, "all in profound silence, some weeping, others sighing, all with dejected countenance, sympathizing in her extreme grief." Hours passed. Then, as it began to grow dark, the Duchess of Vendôme arrived, wife of Henrietta's illegitimate half-brother, César; Henrietta was "much attached" to her. In tears, the duchess took Henrietta's hand, "kissed it very affectionately, and then talked to her," until at last she roused her from her stupor.[17]

But Henrietta remained in the bitterest grief. The next day, when Madame de Motteville arrived at the Louvre, she found Henrietta in bed. Weeping, the queen held out her hand to be kissed, then talked to her friend as best she could amid "a thousand sobs, which often interrupted her discourse." "The people were a ferocious beast which could never be tamed; the king her lord had proved it," Henrietta warned the French court, which was still locked in civil war with the Paris Parliament. She had lost "a king, a husband, and a friend, whose loss she could never sufficiently mourn"; she was only surprised that she "had been able to survive this misfortune." From this moment, she would wear "a perpetual mourning both on her person and in her heart."[18]

Henrietta was only thirty-nine years old, but she had no more desire for living; the world seemed "disgusting."[19] Her one wish was to spend the rest of her days in religious retirement. But with her little daughter, Henrietta Anne, to look after, she knew she could afford only a temporary withdrawal from the world. Leaving the child at the Louvre, the queen mounted into her carriage and drove eastward along the River Seine, then over the Pont Notre-Dame and south, beyond the city walls, to the Faubourg Saint-Jacques: a line of houses stretched along the road amid gardens, vineyards, and orchards. Here, just beyond the modern Boulevard de Port-Royal, stood the Carmelite Convent of the Incarnation, where Henrietta had often retreated in childhood. Mother Madeleine was still the prioress, and in the last few years Henrietta had often come here to observe the principal holy days of the Catholic calendar. Now, "with some of her ladies and bedchamber women," she devoted herself "to prayer, to mortification, [and] to meditation."[20]

But she could not remain long in private mourning. Duty, in the person of Father Gamache, soon called her back to the world. In England, Parliament had appointed a Council of State to govern the country, which now was "a republic, without king or House of Lords." As they prepared to confiscate all the royal family's possessions to fund the navy and the army, Gamache warned Henrietta that affairs "were in a very bad state, and required her attentions, her counsels, and her efforts."[21] This was what her husband had wanted, she knew. "Though the worst should come," he had written to her from Newcastle, "yet I conjure thee to turn thy grief into a just revenge upon mine enemies, and the repossessing of Prince Charles into his just inheritances." And so, early in March, Henrietta returned to the Louvre, where she threw herself into political work for the sake of her son, King Charles II.[22]

To many people, Henrietta seemed her normal self once more: energetic, authoritative, full of hopes and plans for her cause. But she was a changed woman. Her wit and fun were gone, and in their place was a deep well of bitterness and anger. Her husband's fate had convinced her of the worthlessness and injustice of the world, its unpredictability, the real misery she could expect to find there. God was determined to try her to the last extreme, "to afflict our family" and "to humiliate kings and princes": these were her constant refrains.[23] Disappointments flooded over her. In England, her fourteen-year-old daughter, Elizabeth, whom Henrietta had not seen for eight years, died in Parliamentary captivity in September 1650, "far from doctors and medicines." She was fortunate "to be out of the hands of those traitors," Henrietta told herself, but still "I do not fail to be very touched by it." Two months later, Mary's husband, William, Prince of Orange, died of smallpox, leaving Henrietta weeping for the "wretched condition" of her children, who had "obtained powerful support from the rich resources of that house."[24] Ten months after that, her eldest son, Charles, was a fugitive. The Scots had invited him to come to Edinburgh as their king; from there, he hoped, he could recapture the rest of Britain. But instead his army was destroyed by Oliver Cromwell and his forces at the Battle of Worcester. For a month, Henrietta was in agony, not knowing whether her son was a prisoner or dead—so anxious that it "renders me unfit for anything." "Pray to God for the king, my son," she begged her friends. Then Charles himself arrived in Paris. With his hair cut short and his beard grown, disguised as a servant in "a most extraordinary costume," he was so changed that Henrietta did not recognize him. "Very melancholy," Charles remained with his mother in Paris, lacking money or scope for action.[25]

In these years, Henrietta's religion became an obsession. "Wearied of the world," she often withdrew for weeks or even months at a time, first to the Carmelite convent outside Paris, then to the nunnery she herself founded at Chaillot, "her beloved and most delicious retiring place."[26] Here, in rolling countryside close to the Seine just west of Paris, she had bought a grand country house, financed by the Convent of the Visitation in Paris. An abbess and twelve nuns from that convent were soon installed, and Henrietta sent her own goods and furniture for them to use. She went to Chaillot for every major Catholic festival of the year and at other times besides, sharing as much as possible the order's strict rules of life and finding some peace, "shut up" from all worldly affairs among the nuns, "her inestimable friends."[27]

But back at the Louvre, Henrietta's religion took on a militant tone. With Father Philip dead, her chief religious adviser was Walter Montagu, who devoted himself to his priestly calling "with great austerity." Under his "very passionate" urgings, Henrietta mounted a relentless campaign against Protestantism at her court. The Anglican chapel ceremonies held for her courtiers were abolished as a "scandal." When Charles II's advisers objected that this would alienate the British people, Montagu merely replied that Protestant support was "of no importance to the king's restoration." Soon the queen went further, announcing that her ladies would be dismissed "unless they would come over to the Romish Mass."[28]

Her eldest son was long gone now. In 1654, he was forced to leave, as the French government formed a new alliance with Cromwellian England. Henrietta wept as they parted: "The king is as low now as . . . he can be."[29] And still no real aid came in from foreign powers. The few small Royalist rebellions in Britain were easily crushed. In Cologne, Charles merely existed as best he could, while Henrietta suffered bouts of deep, debilitating depression.[30] But there was one great solace in Charles's departure. His youngest brother, fourteen-year-old Henry, was left behind with their mother. Charles ordered Henry to obey her "in all things, religion only excepted"; and Henrietta promised "never to attempt to work a change" in his religion. But secretly she was determined "to do some good with him, if I can."[31] A few months later, she set to work, and every weapon in her armory was brought to bear. Henry was a penniless exile with no prospects, she pointed out, but through the Church he might rise to be a cardinal one day. He owed obedience not to his brother but to her, both "by the articles of [her] marriage and by the right of a mother." And his conversion would aid his eldest brother's restoration, which was "impossible except by Catholic help." When Henry still proved difficult, she packed him off to the monastery at Pontoise, where Walter Montagu was the abbot.[32]

Charles was appalled when he heard; Henry's conversion "would be the greatest misfortune that ever befell him," he wrote to his mother. She was ruining all his chances of returning to England, for Protestants were bound to believe her attempt to convert Henry was "done with his consent," while any action he would take now to prevent her would "disoblige all Catholics" and end all hopes of aid from abroad. If she did not desist, he threatened, it would "cause a breach between them which will never be made up." And Charles warned Henry that if he converted he would be "not only the cause of ruining a brother who loves you so well, but also your king and country," and then, "you must never think to see England or me again."[33]

To ensure that his orders were carried out, Charles sent one of his most trusted counselors, the Marquess of Ormonde, to Paris. But his interview with the queen only served to open the floodgates on Henrietta's rage and frustration. She cared nothing for the opinion of Charles, who, her courtiers freely said, was a "fainthearted," worthless, and dissolute character, living scandalously with loose women who bore him illegitimate children—a king who came up far "short . . . of his predecessors."[34] Rather, she told Ormonde, she was determined "to fulfill her first duties, which are far above the consideration of consequences." There was too great an "obligation that lay upon her in conscience to have her son reformed of his errors." Her promises had extended only to "using no violence." Even if her husband were alive, she would not have listened to him either. As for Charles's threats of "a breach between them," she could assure him for her part "that he can never so far displease her as to reach that point . . . notwithstanding all the cause he has given her for complaint in the past, and all that he can add in the future."[35]

Next Ormonde traveled to Pontoise to see Henry. There, after several days' assurances of "the disloyalty and the invalidity" of Henrietta's arguments, the boy was convinced. Returning to Paris, he informed his mother that he would obey his brother's wishes, which were "more suitable to his inclinations and his duty." At this, Henrietta's long-pent-up bitterness exploded. "She would no more own him as her son," she said; she "commanded him out of her presence,

[and] forbade him any more to set his foot into her lodgings." When Henry knelt and asked her blessing as he left, she refused to give it. If he wanted to join his brother, she said, "she would not hinder him from doing what he pleased." Before leaving Paris, he made a last attempt to heal the rift, writing her "a very dutiful letter." But his mother refused even to receive it.[36] She never saw Henry again.

The only child left to her now was Henrietta Anne. From the start, the little girl had received a thoroughly Catholic upbringing. Henrietta was "passionate on the point," and Charles II had not insisted otherwise: a royal daughter did not have the political importance of her brothers. At Chaillot, she was instructed by her mother's nuns, as well as Father Gamache, who emphasized her great good fortune in being "called to the Catholic religion." Of all her siblings, he said, she was "the only one . . . to possess that ineffable felicity to see herself happily in the way to heaven, whither the princes and princesses of her family could not come, while heresy made them walk in other tracks."[37] His words would fire the girl's lifelong labors for her brothers' conversions. But for the moment, she saw nothing of them.

Henrietta's attempt to change Henry's religion left her utterly alienated from her sons. In 1656, Charles moved to the Netherlands, where his brothers joined him, commanding three thousand English Royalists fighting under Spanish command against the combined Cromwellian and French armies. Henrietta, in Paris, remained on the political sidelines—unheeded, frustrated, and powerless. She hated Charles's advisers, especially Sir Edward Hyde, whose "arts," she believed, were turning her son against her.[38] And Hyde and his party distrusted Henrietta in return, regarding her influence as "pernicious and destructive." Some even saw her as having been responsible for the Civil War and all its "bloodshedding, with the destruction of the most Christian and orthodox church in the world."[39] Henrietta knew she was being deliberately excluded from the king's counsels, but her pleas for "a fairer communication" between them fell on deaf ears, and when she tried to intervene in his court politics, she merely roused Charles to new ire.[40] All she could do was send weekly assurances of her goodwill, praying to God to make her son "the most happy person in the world." Sometimes, overcome by her powerlessness, Henrietta sank into dejection and gave up altogether on the correspondence: she was "useless" to Charles, she said, and so "I avoid importuning you with my letters." Worst of all was when word of battles came, and weeks or even a couple of months passed "in the greatest possible apprehensions" without news of her sons' safety.[41]

By 1658, Henrietta was "so wrapped up in melancholy" that even Oliver Cromwell's death left her incapable of "any very great rejoicing." But at last there was a rapprochement with Charles. As France's alliance with England crumbled, Charles sought aid from the French court, and Henrietta became his chief negotiator, putting "urgent pressure" on them for her son's "restoration . . . to his dominions."[42] At the end of 1659, mother and son met once more. After five years' separation, King Charles "was joyfully received by his mother." He also met his sister, Henrietta Anne, grown in his absence to a "pretty princess," fifteen years old. For twelve days, Charles remained at Colombes in happy domesticity. She was "satisfied with the king," Henrietta Maria pronounced: there would be "no future misunderstanding" between them. And for his part, Charles went so far as to make Lord Jermyn Earl of St. Albans "at the queen's entreaty."[43] Then Charles left to join James and Henry in Brussels.

Finally, after months of frantic politicking on both sides of the Channel, the long-desired news came: England's Parliament had voted to restore the monarchy, "according to the ancient and fundamental laws of this kingdom." In May 1660, Charles returned to England, greeted everywhere with "shouting and joy."[44] To Henrietta, it seemed a miracle. After "so many enterprises and so many exertions," all of them "useless," Charles had been restored "without war, without battle, without drawing a sword."[45] "We must, amid all this, praise God," she wrote to him. "All this is from His hand; you can see that it is." At Colombes, she ordered bonfires lighted, then went to Chaillot "to hear the 'Te Deum' sung" in celebration and thanksgiving. "You cannot imagine the joy that prevails here," she wrote to Charles from Paris. "I do not have a scant minute to myself, for all the visits and business that I have."[46]

After sixteen years of exile, her way was at last clear to return to

England. Charles was pressing her to do so, and Henrietta herself was full of hope "to see yet before I die all my family together, who will no longer be vagabonds." But that wish would not be granted. In London, Henry died suddenly of smallpox at the age of twenty. Charles wept "bitterly," having "loved his brother tenderly." Henrietta, who had been looking forward to a reconciliation after six years' separation, felt the loss as "a most painful blow."[47] And soon there was more bad news: James had "married a girl in England . . . who was pregnant before his marriage." Henrietta was aghast. The match was utterly "unbecoming": the girl was the mere daughter of an English knight. And worse: that knight was her old opponent, Sir Edward Hyde. The birth was very near, but still, as Henrietta arrived in England, she was determined to break up the marriage.[48]

On Friday, November 2, 1660, the fifty-year-old queen entered London, "acclaimed with the utmost affection and joy, all the city bells being rung and bonfires lighted at every corner." Her apartments at Whitehall had been "richly decorated to receive her," and there she and Henrietta Anne held court for London society: Henrietta in her widow's weeds—"a very little plain old woman," thought the diarist Samuel Pepys, though the young princess was "very pretty."[49] At first Henrietta was delighted with Charles: "The king, my son, has received me with all testimonies of love which could be." But she was soon dismayed to find him taking James's side against her. In "a great passion," she declared that if James's new wife ever set foot in Whitehall, she would leave the palace at once "and never come into it again."[50]

The quarrel simmered on into Christmas, when Henrietta suffered a new blow. Just three months after Henry's death, Mary also died of smallpox, "to the intense grief of the whole court and especially of the king, who loved her most tenderly." Henrietta felt the loss "severely."[51] Just three of the nine children she had borne were still alive. She could bear England no longer. Planning to return to France in January 1661 for Henrietta Anne's wedding, she was now "counting the moments" until she could go. At last, on the day before her departure, she agreed to see James's wife. After all her fears, she found the new Duchess of York "a woman of much spirit and worth," with "an air of grandeur in all her actions" and "a great deal of wit." Henrietta said she "heartily forgave the duke and her, and was resolved ever after to live with all the affection of a mother toward them."[52] Then she returned to Paris, where her youngest daughter married Philippe, Duc d'Orléans, younger brother of King Louis XIV. "I wish it much," Henrietta wrote. The match made Henrietta Anne the "second lady" in France and secured close relations between the two countries. But when it came to the moment of parting, both mother and daughter wept. At Colombes that summer, Henrietta Maria felt profoundly alone: "I have here much silence."[53]

For a time she found comfort with her two remaining sons. On Charles's pressing invitation, she returned to England in 1662 in the grandest style. Somerset House was now thoroughly repaired and refurnished after the depredations of the Interregnum. Her chapel there was reopened and her Capuchins once more began to make conversions, which Henrietta regarded "with great joy."[54] Once more she maintained a vast royal household in which many of her old servants held posts. She spent lavishly on building work at Somerset House, constructing a new range of royal reception rooms, "in every respect . . . magnificent and costly."[55] Here she received London's fashionable society, regaling them with stories of her adventures "during the rebellion and war in England." Hers was soon the most popular of all London's royal courts. Often, in the evenings, the whole royal family gathered here: Charles with his new wife, Catherine of Braganza; James and his duchess and the young Duke of Monmouth; the first of Charles's many illegitimate children, "a most pretty spark of about fifteen years old"; as well as Charles's favorite mistress, Lady Castlemaine.[56]

Henrietta often went out to join London's social whirl: dining at the Lord Mayor's house with the king and his wife, or driving in Hyde Park, "the king, duke, and others . . . a-horseback and the two queens in the queen mother's coach," or walking of an evening in Pall Mall on Henry Jermyn's arm.[57] At Christmas, there were ballets at Whitehall, which Charles pressed Henrietta to see. "I am the happiest woman in the world," she wrote, "the king my son showing me so much affection and confidence that I could not have wished for more."[58] Despite all their differences over the years, Charles was devoted to his "Mam," as he called her: "Never any children had so good a mother as we have," he wrote to Henrietta Anne.[59] And Henrietta adored her son's new queen: a zealous Catholic and "the best creature in the world, from whom I receive so much affection." Henrietta even found that she had regained some of her old political importance. As Charles began to have difficulties with Parliament, he was ready to listen to her advice, recognizing her long experience with English politics. It was in Henrietta's lodgings at Somerset House that he now held his weekly political "secret conferences."[60]

But Henrietta's high-profile Catholicism and her obvious influence raised popular resentment. When Charles acted to exclude Puritan ministers from the Church of England, all "London was highly discontented." People were also angry at high taxes and "at the king's neglect of government for his mistresses," and Henrietta received the blame. "All was carried on by the queen [mother] and her cabal at Somerset House." Salacious rumors about Henrietta's relations with Henry Jermyn made the rounds: "For certain the queen mother is married to my Lord St. Albans." At first, Henrietta was unconcerned,[61] but gradually her high spirits sank. The damp English climate exacerbated her ill health, and by 1664, she was also heavily in debt. That winter, she withdrew from the glamorous social rounds to spend her evenings quietly with Queen Catherine. At Christmas, papers appeared around London "menacing the extirpation of popery and Mass in her chapel." When a sore throat confined her to bed, rumors circulated that she was pregnant. Really afraid now, Henrietta planned to retreat to France. There she might recover her health, and she would also see Henrietta Anne once more. She promised it would be only a temporary absence. But the English, noting her vast train of wagons containing all the fine furniture, paintings, and other possessions from Somerset House, thought that "she did not intend ever to return into England."[62]

Henrietta spent most of her remaining four years at Colombes, where her visitors were few. Henry Jermyn was one of the most frequent guests. Now he was Charles II's ambassador to France, wealthier, more overweight and gout-ridden than ever—"full of soup and gold," as the poet Andrew Marvell put it. Walter Montagu came, too. But most valued of all was Henrietta Anne, who visited sometimes by herself and sometimes with her husband. Henrietta Maria, however, had little conversation to entertain them with. "As she advanced in piety, so also she held back from speaking on almost all things," Madame de Motteville recalled. "The last years of her life she had become scrupulous on this, she weighed her words and appeared very detached from life."[63]

Gradually Henrietta was preparing for death. In the past, when she had thought of it as "far distant, still the bare idea of it made her shudder; so she did not like any one to talk of that doleful subject." But by the end of 1668, impelled by ill health, she was facing up to it. She had already made a general confession of all her sins, "with great application and very firm designs to apply herself to the care of her salvation." Now she often said "that she saw clearly that it was necessary to think of leaving."[64] March brought "a dangerous illness"—with a high fever, she was coughing up blood. Her recovery was slow, and in June she was again "very ill" with diarrhea, which "made her extreme[ly] weak."[65] Her one desire now was to move to Chaillot, "to pass the rest of her life in this place of solitude and retirement," especially since Charles II had cut her allowance by a quarter, making it impossible for her to maintain her old court. She was fed up with doctors and medicines, she said: she would think of them no more, "but only of her salvation."[66]

But still, at Henrietta Anne's insistence, France's leading physicians descended on Colombes before she managed to arrange her departure. Their examination, on Saturday, August 28, was promising. All the queen's symptoms—the fainting fits, insomnia, recurring fevers, and chest infections—were "painful, but without danger of death," pronounced Antoine Vallot, first physician to Louis XIV. He prescribed a regime of opiates and purges, culminating in a grain of the opiate laudanum on Monday night. This would help Henrietta sleep and allow "the quieting of the humors in her body, from whence they conjectured the great disorder came." Henrietta was reluctant. She knew from experience that laudanum "disagreed with her": "the famous English physician, Monsieur de Mayerne, had warned her never to take any." But Vallot persisted, seconded by the personal physicians of both Henrietta Anne and her husband. So, unwillingly, Henrietta agreed.[67]

All the next day, Henrietta was occupied with religious observances, it being Lady Day, "the festival of the nativity of the most blessed Virgin," a time of special devotion for her. That night, she took her "usual remedy," and on Monday morning she was purged "with a certain opiate designed for that purpose."[68] That day was also tiring, as the queen received "several visits" from friends and spent hours in "long spiritual conversations" with her confessor, preparing to receive Communion the next day. By suppertime, she was feeling "something indisposed": "if she continued so ill the next day she would see nobody," she said. But still she "ate heartily, [and] amused herself agreeably after her repast, laughing as if nothing ailed her."[69] When she retired to bed, she was rather feverish, so her physician, Antoine d'Aquin, decided not to give her the laudanum after all. On Henrietta's orders, the curtains were drawn around her bed and her courtiers departed. But Henrietta could not sleep, so around 11 p.m. she summoned d'Aquin and demanded the dose. Reluctantly, he gave it to her, mixed into a raw egg yolk. At once the queen fell asleep. But d'Aquin, sitting by her bedside and observing her shallow, sighing breaths and irregular pulse, realized that she was sleeping "too profoundly." Desperately, he "endeavored by all the means he could to wake her," but "all the several remedies used in such cases" had no effect.[70] Her *valets de chambre* were sent rushing to summon more doctors and Henrietta's priests, who begged her to confess her sins or at least "to give some sign that she understood." But they met only "a mortal silence." The doctors gave hopes that Henrietta's incapacity was due merely "to certain vapors which had ascended to the brain, . . . which, when dispelled, would leave the patient capable of speaking." But after a while, "seeing that there was no abatement of her malady," Father Gamache gave orders for the queen to receive Extreme Unction. Through the dark night, the village curé of Colombes "came in haste" bearing holy oil, with which he anointed the queen's eyes, ears, nostrils, lips, hands, and feet. Between three and four in the morning of Tuesday, August 31,

"without violence, without the slightest convulsion, with great seren-
ity, and a sweet expression of countenance," the fifty-nine-year-old
queen slipped away into death.[71]

None of the earthly remains of the royal couple who had loved
each other so dearly were ever reunited. On the orders of Louis XIV,
Henrietta's body lay in state for five weeks in the Abbey of St. Denis,
just outside Paris, before being buried there among the French
royal graves dating back more than a thousand years. Charles's body
remained three hundred miles away across the English Channel, at
Windsor Castle, where it had been interred after Parliament refused
it admittance to Westminster Abbey.[72] "My dear heart," they had
called each other so often, but after twenty years of widowhood,
Henrietta's piety and world-weariness had the stronger claim. On
her instructions, her heart was cut from her dead body and laid to
rest in the chapel of her convent at Chaillot. The queen's life had
been, her funeral sermon that day proclaimed, "one of those fearsome examples" that proved the world's "utter vanity." She had seen
"all the extremes of things human: happiness without bounds, as
well as miseries."[73]

Notes

FOREWORD

1. Petrie, *Letters*, 242. See also ibid., 118, 147, 161, 162, 164.
2. Petrie, *Letters*, 241.
3. Gardiner, *Constitutional Documents*, c. 88.
4. Gardiner, *Constitutional Documents*, c. 87.

PROLOGUE: WINTER 1649

1. For Henrietta's apartments, see Evelyn, *Diary*, II, 103n1. For the date, see Petitot, ed., *Mémoires*, ser. 2, XXXVIII, 204. This and all other dates given in this book are in the old-style Julian calendar used in England in the seventeenth century. The Gregorian calendar now in use differs by ten days.
2. Bossuet, *Oraison*, 74.
3. Motteville, *Memoir*, 19. See also Montpensier, *Mémoires*, part 1, chap. 3; Reresby, *Memoirs*, 28. Charles also had reckoned himself the happiest king in Christendom: see Wedgwood, *King's Peace*, 19–20.
4. Petitot, ed., *Mémoires*, ser. 2, XXXVIII, 205, 207; Motteville, *Memoir*, 19.
5. Clarendon, *History*, I, 94; Clarendon, *Life*, I, 36; Carew, *Works*, 95. See also Motteville, *Mémoires*, I, 184, 186; *CSPV 1632–1636*, 362.
6. Green, *Letters*, 248, 249.
7. Motteville, *Memoir*, 26; Bossuet, *Oraison*, 115.

8. Motteville, *Mémoires*, I, 222. See also Montpensier, *Mémoires*, part 1, chap. 3.

9. Sophia, Electress of Hanover, *Memoirs*, 13.

10. Motteville, *Mémoires*, I, 223, 222; Sophia, Electress of Hanover, *Memoirs*, 13. See also Motteville, *Memoir*, 28.

11. Motteville, *Memoir*, 26, 27; Petitot, ed., *Mémoires*, ser. 2, XXXVII, 414.

12. BL Add. MS 12,186, ff. 8v, 10v.

13. Sources for courtly dinner etiquette: Society of Antiquaries, *Collection of Ordinances*, 341–42; *Charles and Henrietta Dining in Public*, painted by Houckgeest; *The Babees' Book*, passim; Comenius, *Orbis Sensualium Pictus*, 226–27.

14. Ellis, *Original Letters*, ser. 2, vol. 3: 344; Madame de Motteville, as quoted in Strickland, *Lives*, V, 351.

15. Green, *Letters*, 337–38; *CSPV 1643–1647*, 320. See also ibid., 314; Fea, *Memoirs*, 80; Green, *Letters*, 344–45.

16. *Eikon Basilike*, chap. 7.

17. *CSPV 1643–1647*, 305. See also Fea, *Memoirs*, 80, 130–31.

18. See *Eikon Basilike*, chap. 24.

19. Clarendon, *History*, I, 109.

20. Clarendon, *State Papers*, II, 274; Harrison, ed., *Jacobean Journal*, 103; Clarendon, *State Papers*, II, 274.

21. *CSPV 1643–1647*, 306. See also ibid., 305; Montereul, *Correspondence*, I, 441; *Calendar of Clarendon State Papers*, I, 363.

22. Fea, *Memoirs*, 107.

23. Fea, *Memoirs*, 96, 80; *Eikon Basilike*, chap. 24. See also Fea, *Memoirs*, 94, 127.

24. Charles I, *Reliquiae*, 290. See *Eikon Basilike*, passim, for many expressions of these sentiments.

25. Clarendon, *State Papers*, II, 273; Warwick, *Memoires*, 328. See also Ashley, *Charles I and Oliver Cromwell*, 178; Clarendon, *State Papers*, II, 213.

26. As quoted in Ashley, *Charles I and Oliver Cromwell*, 178. See also ibid., 177.

27. Warwick, *Memoires*, 297; Fea, *Memoirs*, 97.

28. As quoted in Green, *Lives*, VI, 355.

29. Clarendon, *History*, IV, 251, 252–53.

30. Green, *Lives*, VI, 358.

31. Clarendon, *History*, IV, 281; *CSPV 1647–1652*, 39. See also Underdown, "Parliamentary Diary," 155.

32. As quoted in Green, *Letters*, 345–46.

33. Petrie, *Letters*, 239. For Charles's offer, see Gardiner, *History of the Great Civil War*, IV, 220.
34. Warwick, *Memoires*, 326.
35. As quoted in Gardiner, *History of the Great Civil War*, IV, 119–20.
36. *CJ*, VI, December 13, 1648.
37. Clarendon, *History*, IV, 471.
38. Green, *Letters*, 349; Dauncey, *History*, 127; Green, *Letters*, 350. For Henrietta's lack of firewood, see Green, *Lives*, VI, 413.
39. BL Add. MS 12,186, f. 12r. See *CSPV 1647–1652*, 86, for the news arriving at last.
40. *Life and Death*, 44.
41. *CSPD 1648–1649*, 346; *CSPV 1647–1652*, 86; Ellis, *Original Letters*, ser. 2, vol. 3: 344.
42. *CSPV 1647–1652*, 86. For the commissioners, see Gardiner, *History of the Great Civil War*, IV, 293.
43. Petitot, ed., *Mémoires*, ser. 2, XXXVIII, 204.
44. BL Add. MS 12,186, f. 3v.
45. Birch, *Court and Times of Charles*, II, 381.
46. Lockyer, *Trial*, 81; Fea, *Memoirs*, 133; Warwick, *Memoires*, 336.
47. Lockyer, *Trial*, 81. See also Fea, *Memoirs*, 132–33; Jusserand, *Recueil*, XXIV, 69–70; Warwick, *Memoires*, 336; Gardiner, *History of the Great Civil War*, IV, 297–99.
48. Petrie, *Letters*, 241–43.
49. Petrie, *Letters*, 244–46; Fea, *Memoirs*, 134; Petrie, *Letters*, 247–50.
50. Petrie, *Letters*, 249–55. For Charles's stammer, see Warwick, *Memoires*, 339.
51. Fea, *Memoirs*, 132; Lockyer, *Trial*, 102.
52. Quotes are from Lockyer, *Trial*, 101–16; Petrie, *Letters*, 255–58.
53. Warwick, *Memoires*, 94; *Oxford DNB*: William Juxon. See also Panzani, as quoted in Albion, *Charles I*, 413, for a similar character description.
54. Warwick, *Memoires*, 94; *Eikon Basilike*, chap. 2; Prideaux, *History*, 360.
55. Warwick, *Memoires*, 340; Fea, *Memoirs*, 136, 137.
56. Fea, *Memoirs*, 138. See also ibid., 141. Prince Charles's letter is printed in Charles I, *Reliquiae*, 303.
57. Fea, *Memoirs*, 139–40.
58. Charles I, *Reliquiae*, 300–302.
59. Fea, *Memoirs*, 140, 141–42.
60. Fea, *Memoirs*, 74.

61. Fea, *Memoirs*, 142–43, 140. See also ibid., 122–23, 129, 132; Warwick, *Memoires*, 341–42.
62. As quoted in MacGregor, *Late King's Goods*, 272. For illustrations of the clothing and jewels worn by Charles for the execution, see Fea, *Memoirs*, passim.
63. Fea, *Memoirs*, 145.
64. *CJ*, VI, January 30, 1649. See also Fea, *Memoirs*, 145; *King Charls His Speech*.
65. *True Discourse*, 35.
66. *King Charls His Speech*.
67. Pepys, *Diary*, I, 280. See also ibid., 265.
68. Ellis, *Original Letters*, ser. 2, vol. 3, 346. See also ibid., 342, 345; Warwick, *Memoires*, 344.
69. Charles I, *Reliquiae*, 304.
70. All quotes are from *King Charls His Speech*.
71. Fea, *Memoirs*, 45; Ellis, *Original Letters*, ser. 1, vol. III, 323; Fea, *Memoirs*, 45. For the troops, see *King Charls His Speech*.
72. *King Charls His Speech*. See also Jusserand, *Recueil*, XXIV, 70.

1. STRANGERS

1. King James to Parliament, as quoted in Gregg, *King Charles I*, 109. James's appearance is based on portraits, and on Wilson, *History,* 289–90; W[eldon], *Court and Character*, 177–89.
2. *CSPD 1623–1625*, 521; *Cabala*, 292. For the court in Cambridge, see Birch, *Court and Times of James*, II, 484–86; *CSPD 1623–1625*, 405, 411, 412; *CSPV 1623–1625*, 515, 521–22; *HMC Mar and Kellie*, 216; Brienne, *Mémoires* (1824), 389–90; BL King's MS 135, ff. 167v–172v; *Hardwicke State Papers*, I, 547.
3. For the marriage treaty and other documents signed along with it, see *HMC Salisbury MSS,*197–98; *CSPD 1623–1625*, 405; BL King's MS 135, ff. 65v–72r, 186r–188v, 204r; *Hardwicke State Papers*, I, 546; BL MS Add. 37028, ff. 8, 9; *CSPV 1623–1625*, 523–25.
4. *CSPD 1623–1625*, 166. See also Ellis, *Original Letters*, ser. I, vol. III, 181; ibid., ser. II, vol. III, 243; *Cabala*, 288; Patterson, *King James VI and I and the Reunion of Christendom*.
5. As quoted in Gregg, *King Charles I*, 27.
6. *CSPV 1623–1625*, 201, 405. For the history of the French and Spanish marriage proposals, see Ellis, *Original Letters*, ser. II, vol. III, 227 (1612); Herbert of Cherbury, *Autobiography*, 199, 200; Richelieu, *Lettres*, VII, 938; Albion, *Charles I*, 1–12.

7. *CSPV 1623–1625*, 492 (for "angry"); *CSPD 1623–1625*, 412.

8. Clarendon, *History*, I, 11.

9. As quoted in Bowle, *Charles the First*, 7; *CSPV 1621–1623*, 452.

10. *CSPD 1623–1625*, 156. For Buckingham's "supreme influence," see also *CSPV 1623–1625*, 462; *CSPD 1623–1625*, 93, 231, 238, 413. For the French match as Buckingham's brainchild, see *Cabala*, 282, 296. Principal sources for the Duke of Buckingham are Lockyer, *Life*; Clarendon, *History*, I, 10–13, 38–43.

11. Ellis, *Original Letters*, ser. I, vol. III, 92. For Charles's character and early life, see Ellis, *Original Letters*, ser. I, vol. III, 92–96; Heylin, *Short View*, 1–34; Clarendon, *History*, III, 197–99; Warwick, *Memoires*, 64–75; *CSPV 1621–1623*, 450–54; Bowle, *Charles the First*; Carlton, *Charles I*; Gregg, *King Charles I*.

12. *CSPV 1623–1625*, 452, 500.

13. Ellis, *Original Letters*, ser. I, vol. III, 158; Fraser, *King James*, 121; Carlton, *Charles I*, 22.

14. Ellis, *Original Letters*, ser. I, vol. III, 147; Clarendon, *History*, I, 10.

15. Clarendon, *History*, I, 12. The figure of £80,000 comes from Bowle, *Charles the First*, 45.

16. As quoted in Bowle, *Charles the First*, 48.

17. *CSPV 1621–1623*, 451. See also Heylin, *Short View*, 15.

18. Carlton, *Charles I*, 22.

19. Clarendon, *State Papers*, II, Appendix, xxv; Petrie, *Letters*, 4.

20. *CSPV 1621–1623*, 451; Petrie, *Letters*, 7.

21. McClure, ed., *Letters of Chamberlain*, II, 434. See also Birch, *Court and Times of James*, II, 313–14; *CSPV 1623–1625*, 75, 386–87; *CSPD 1623–1625*, 231; Petrie, *Letters*, 4–15, 17–30, 33–34, 40–45, 50–57; Ellis, *Original Letters*, ser. I, vol. III, 145–48; BL Harleian MS 6,988, f. 74.

22. Clarendon, *History*, I, 14. See also Wotton, *Reliquiae*, 80–81.

23. Clarendon, *History*, I, 14–19.

24. *CSPV 1623–1625*, 37; the Spanish minister Olivares, as quoted in Bowle, *Charles the First*, 69. See also *CSPV 1623–1625*, 76, 189.

25. *CSPV 1623–1625*, 136.

26. Shorney, *Protestant Nonconformity and Roman Catholicism*, 58–60.

27. As quoted in Gregg, *King Charles I*, 87.

28. *CSPV 1623–1625*, 232. See also *CSPV 1623–1625*, 269.

29. *CSPV 1623–1625*, 114, 185. Principal sources for the Spanish match and the subsequent Parliament are Albion, *Charles I*, 11–48; *CSPV 1621–1623*, passim; *CSPV 1623–1625*, passim; Bowle, *Charles the First*; Carlton, *Charles I*; Gregg, *King Charles I*.

30. *CSPD 1623–1625*, 191; *CSPV 1623–1625*, 249. See also *CSPD 1623–1625*, 169.
31. *CSPV 1623–1625*, 242; *CSPD 1623–1625*, 192. See also ibid., 191; *CSPV 1623–1625*, 254.
32. *CSPV 1623–1625*, 280. See also ibid., 295, 300–302, 303; *CSPD 1623–1625*, 196, 212.
33. *Cabala*, 281. See also ibid., 274, 279.
34. Clarendon, *History*, I, 78. See ibid., 76–79, for full characters of Kensington and Carlisle. Principal sources for the French marriage negotiations are Clarendon, *State Papers*, II, Appendix; *Cabala*, 274–97; *Hardwicke State Papers*, I, 523–72; *CSPV 1623–1625*, passim; *CSPD 1623–1625*, passim; Albion, *Charles I*, 49–77.
35. *CSPV 1623–1625*, 377; *Hardwicke State Papers*, I, 535; *CSPV 1623–1625*, 434.
36. *CSPV 1623–1625*, 365; Birch, *Court and Times of James*, II, 470.
37. *CSPV 1623–1625*, 455–56; Birch, *Court and Times of James*, II, 466.
38. Clarendon, *State Papers*, II, Appendix, x.
39. Charles to the Earl of Carlisle, October 19, 1624: as quoted in Carlton, *Charles I*, 57; *CSPV 1623–1625*, 394. See also *CSPV 1623–1625*, 478, 479.
40. *CSPV 1623–1625*, 496, 492.
41. *CSPD 1623–1625*, 383; *CSPV 1623–1625*, 503. See also ibid., 492, 497, 504; *CSPD 1623–1625*, 393, 400; Nichols, *Progresses*, IV, 1007.
42. *Cabala*, 292; *CSPV 1623–1625*, 496. For Charles's "great joyfulness," see ibid., 504.
43. *Cabala*, 277.
44. Petrie, *Letters*, 8, 9. See also Bassompierre, *Mémoires*, III, 431.
45. *Life and Death*, 10. See also Clarendon, *State Papers*, II, Appendix, vi.
46. Clarendon, *State Papers*, II, Appendix, vi, iii, vi. See also ibid., xvi.
47. Ellis, *Original Letters*, ser. I, vol. III, 178; Clarendon, *State Papers*, II, Appendix, xii.
48. Ellis, *Original Letters*, ser. I, vol. III, 179; *Hardwicke State Papers*, I, 528.
49. Bodleian Library Clarendon MS 97 contains Charles's draft of this letter, printed (without indicating his amendments) in *Calendar of Clarendon State Papers*, I, Appendix II. For Charles's mode of signature, see *Calendar of Clarendon State Papers*, I, Appendix I, 5; Toynbee, "Two Letterbooks," 358. For the date of the letter, see *CSPV 1623–1625*, 504, 510; *CSPD 1623–1625*, 400.

50. BL King's MS 135, ff. 164r–165r. For Marie de' Medici's apartments and etiquette there, see Batiffol, *Vie Intime*, I, 70–75, 85–86, 102–3, 116. For Carey, see *CSPV 1623–1625*, 504, 510, 520; *CSPD 1623–1625*, 400; Clarendon, *State Papers*, II, Appendix, xiii, xvii; Clarendon, *Calendar of State Papers*, I, Appendix I, 5; BL King's MS 135, f. 159r.

51. Birch, *An Historical View*, 492.

52. My principal sources for Henrietta's parents and childhood are Batiffol, *Vie Intime*, chaps. 1–5, 7; Strickland, *Lives*, V; Dupuy, *Henriette Marie*; Hamilton, *Henrietta Maria*; Marshall, *Henrietta Maria*; Plowden, *Henrietta Maria*. Motteville, *Mémoires*, I, 223–24, describes Henrietta's character.

53. BL MS Royal 16 E XLI is Henrietta's collection of Henri's "reparties, rencontres, et autres dits memorables."

54. Tillières, *Mémoires*, 57. See also *Cabala* 276.

55. *Cabala*, 282. For Henrietta's great expectations, see ibid., 286; *CSPV 1623–1625*, 486, 559; Clarendon, *State Papers*, II, Appendix, xii, xiv. For Marie's orders, see ibid., xii.

56. *Cabala*, 280; Clarendon, *State Papers*, II, Appendix, ii, xii. See also ibid., v; *Cabala*, 276, 280.

57. *Cabala*, 280.

58. Clarendon, *State Papers*, II, Appendix, ii, iv. See also ibid., vi; *CSPD 1623–1625*, 360.

59. Clarendon, *State Papers*, II, Appendix, iii, iv.

60. Clarendon, *State Papers*, II, Appendix, ix; Ellis, *Original Letters*, ser. I, vol. III, 175. This letter is also printed in *Cabala*, 288–91.

61. *CSPV 162–1625*, 486; Clarendon, *State Papers*, II, Appendix, xi. See also *Calendar of Clarendon State Papers*, I, Appendix I, 5.

62. BL King's MS 135, f. 165r.

63. Clarendon, *State Papers*, II, Appendix, xvii. For Henrietta's reception of Charles's letter, see also Howell, *Epistolae*, I, 222; *Life and Death*, 9–10; Heylin, *Short View*, 35. For the date of her reply, see BL King's MS 135, ff. 224r–v, 227v–228r.

64. Ellis, *Original Letters*, ser. I, vol. III, 180; *CSPV 1623–1625*, 539. See also Birch, *Court and Times of James*, II, 494.

65. Clarendon, *State Papers*, II, Appendix, xx; *Cabala*, 296.

66. *Life and Death*, 10; Clarendon, *State Papers*, II, Appendix, xxi. See also *CSPV 1623–1625*, 559.

67. Clarendon, *State Papers*, II, Appendix, xxii, xxi; *Calendar of Clarendon State Papers*, I, Appendix II, 11 *bis*.

68. *CSPV 1623–1625*, 576; *Calendar of Clarendon State Papers*, I, Appendix II, 11.

69. *Calendar of Clarendon State Papers*, I, Appendix II, 11, Appendix I, 6; *Hardwicke State Papers*, I, 558. See also *Calendar of Clarendon State Papers*, Appendix II, 11.
70. *CSPV 1623–1625*, 610; *Calendar of Clarendon State Papers*, I, Appendix II, 12. See also *CSPV 1623–1625*, 615; Birch, *Court and Times of James*, II, 506–7; *HMC Mar and Kellie*, 224.
71. *CSPV 162–1625*, 625, 627; Fuller, *Church History*, X, 113; *CSPV 1623–1625*, 627. For James's illness, see also ibid., 623; Birch, *Court and Times of James*, II, 504, 508; *CSPD 1623–1625*, 505, 507, 509; *Hardwicke State Papers*, I, 562, 565; Ellis, *Original Letters*, ser. I, vol. III, 182.
72. *CSPD 1625–1626*, 1. See also Laud, *Works*, III, 158.
73. Ellis, *Original Letters*, ser. II, vol. III, 244; *HMC Skrine MSS*, 5, 4; Ellis, *Original Letters*, ser. II, vol. III, 244.
74. *CSPD 1611–1618*, 273; *CSPV 1625–1626*, 26–27.
75. Warwick, *Memoires*, 65; *HMC Skrine MSS*, 6; *CSPD 1625–1626*, 10.
76. *CSPD 1625–1626*, 10; Birch, *Court and Times of Charles*, I, 5, 12. See also *HMC Skrine MSS*, 10; *CSPV 1625–1626*, 4, 11, 34; Birch, *Court and Times of Charles*, I, 17.
77. *Calendar of Clarendon State Papers*, I, Appendix I, 7. See also *HMC Skrine MSS*, 7.
78. *CSPD 1625–1626*, 25.
79. *CSPV 1625–1626*, 44.
80. *CSPV 1625–1626*, 10; BL King's MS 135, ff. 123v–124r; Strickland, *Lives*, V, 205. Chevreuse was related through Charles's great-grandmother, Mary of Guise, mother of Mary, Queen of Scots. For the wedding, see also BL King's MS 136, ff. 463–99v; Strickland, *Lives*, V, 203–6; *CSPV 1625–1626*, 44; *True Discourse*.

2. FIRST IMPRESSIONS

1. Clarendon, *State Papers*, II, Appendix, xxiii; BL King's MS 136, f. 499r. See also *CSPV 1625–1626*, 44.
2. Birch, *Court and Times of Charles*, I, 20; BL King's MS 136, f. 257v. See also Birch, *Court and Times of Charles*, I, 18; *CSPV 1625–1626*, 51.
3. Clarendon, *State Papers*, II, Appendix, xxiv.
4. Petrie, *Letters*, 39.
5. Laud, *Works*, III, 162; *CSPV 1625–1626*, 59. For Buckingham's journey, see also Birch, *Court and Times of Charles*, I, 22; *HMC Skrine MSS*, 14, 17; Laud, *Works*, III, 162; *CSPD 1625–1626*, 22; BL Add. MS 12,528, f. 21v.

6. Rushworth, *Historical Collections*, I, 170. See also *Mercure françois*, XI, 365.

7. *CSPV 1625–1626*, 65; BL King's MS 136, f. 499v; BL King's MS 136, f. 499v.

8. *HMC Skrine MSS*, 19; Clarendon, *History*, I, 47. See also Ellis, *Original Letters*, ser. I, vol. III, 189n.

9. Motteville, *Mémoires*, I, 14; Petitot, ed., *Mémoires*, ser. 2, XXXV, 403; "Mémoires de P. de La Porte," in Michaud and Poujoulat, *Mémoires*, VIII, 7.

10. Motteville, *Mémoires*, I, 14–15; Tillières, *Mémoires*, 61. See also ibid., 59–62; "Mémoires de La Rochefoucauld," in Michaud and Poujoulat, ed., *Mémoires*, V, 381; D'Ewes, *Autobiography*, I, 386, 389.

11. Tillières, *Mémoires*, 61; *HMC Skrine MSS*, 19; *CSPV 1625–1626*, 88. For French aid to the Elector Palatine, see Clarendon, *State Papers*, II, Appendix, xxv; *CSPV 1625–1626*, 67–68; *HMC Skrine MSS*, 17.

12. Houssaye, *Cardinal de Bérulle*, 8–9.

13. *CSPV 1625–1626*, 68, 81.

14. *Mercure françois*, XI, 373.

15. For Henrietta's domestic personnel, see Petitot, ed., *Mémoires*, ser. 2, XXXV, 408; BL King's MS 136, ff. 416v–423; PRO SP 16/3/113–14. For her religious household, see BL King's MS 135, f. 75r; King's MS 136, f. 429v; Houssaye, *Cardinal de Bérulle*, 22.

16. BL King's MS 135, f. 40v; Richelieu, *Lettres*, II, 18–19. For Bérulle's career, see Dagens, *Bérulle et les Origines*; Dagens, *Correspondance du Cardinal*; Houssaye, *Cardinal de Bérulle*.

17. As quoted in Albion, *Charles I*, 13.

18. Houssaye, *Cardinal de Bérulle*, 9–11.

19. BL King's MS 135, f. 527v.

20. BL King's MS 136, f. 52r.

21. As quoted in Albion, *Charles*, 77. See also *The Catholic Encyclopedia*, "Golden Rose"; Isaiah xi, 1–7; Romans xv, 12.

22. *CSPV 1625–1626*, 84.

23. For Charles wanting Buckingham and Henrietta present, see *CSPV 1625–1626*, 63; *HMC Skrine MSS*, 17, 19. For Charles delaying Parliament, see *CSPV 1625–1626*, 62, 70; Ellis, *Original Letters*, ser. I, vol. III, 192; Birch, *Court and Times of Charles*, I, 21, 22; *HMC Skrine MSS*, 17, 19; Laud, *Works*, III, 162, 163.

24. *CSPV 1625–1626*, 62. See also ibid., 63, 70, 83.

25. Birch, *Court and Times of Charles*, I, 32. See also *CSPV 1625–1626*, 69, 81.

26. See *CSPV 1625–1626*, 69–70; Birch, *Court and Times of Charles*, I, 27; Toynbee, "Wedding Journey," 78–81.

27. *HMC Skrine MSS*, 20. See also *CSPV 1625–1626*, 69; Birch, *Court and Times of Charles*, I, 27.

28. Clarendon, *State Papers*, II, Appendix, xix; Finet, *Finetti Philoxenis*, 152. See also *CSPV 1625–1626*, 87; Brienne, *Mémoires*, 407.

29. *CSPD 1625–1626*, 37. See also Finet, *Finetti Philoxenis*, 152; *CSPV 1625–1626*, 81.

30. Clarendon, *State Papers*, II, Appendix, xix. See also Birch, *Court and Times of Charles*, I, 28; Toynbee, "Wedding Journey," 79; *CSPV 1625–1626*, 81; *HMC Skrine MSS*, 21.

31. *CSPV 1625–1626*, 83; BL King's MS 136, ff. 316v–318r. See also ibid., ff. 315r–v; *HMC Skrine MSS*, 14, 21; Finet, *Finetti Philoxenis*, 153.

32. See Petitot, ed., *Mémoires*, ser. 2, XXXV, 403–4; BL King's MS 136, f. 306r.

33. Tillières, *Mémoires*, 70–78; Houssaye, *Cardinal de Bérulle*, 3–8.

34. *CSPV 1625–1626*, 81.

35. *CSPD 1625–1626*, 41; *HMC Skrine MSS*, 19. See also Birch, *Court and Times of Charles*, I, 24; Rushworth, *Historical Collections*, I, 170.

36. *Cabala*, 253.

37. See *CSPV 1625–1626*, 81; Rushworth, *Historical Collections*, I, 170; Pett, *Autobiography*, 135; Petitot, ed., *Mémoires*, ser. 2, XXXV, 406.

38. Henrietta's trousseau is detailed in BL King's MS 136, ff. 412r–461v.

39. See *CSPV 1625–1626*, 811; BL King's MS 136, ff. 310v, 313r; *HMC Skrine MSS*, 13; Howell, *Epistolae*, I, 238.

40. BL King's MS 136, ff. 323r–324v; *A True Discourse*, 25 bis. See also Toynbee, "Wedding Journey," 83; *HMC Skrine MSS*, 21; *CSPV 1625–1626*, 70, 81; BL King's MS 136, ff. 323–324v; Petitot, ed., *Mémoires*, ser. 2, XXXV, 407; Finet, *Finetti Philoxenis*, 153.

41. Tillières, *Mémoires*, 89–90; Petitot, ed., *Mémoires*, ser. 2, XXXV, 407; BL King's MS 136, ff. 335v, 343v.

42. BL King's MS 136, ff. 324v–325r; *HMC Skrine MSS*, 21. See also ibid., 14; Finet, *Finetti Philoxenis*, 153; BL King's MS 136, ff. 323v–324r; *CSPV 1625–1626*, 87.

43. Birch, *Court and Times of Charles*, I, 30; *A True Discourse*, 26.

44. *A True Discourse*, 27, 26. See also BL King's MS 136, ff. 343v, 335v–336r.

45. *CSPV 1625–1626*, 87; Heylin, *Short View*, 37.

46. *Cabala*, 278; Clarendon, *State Papers*, II, Appendix, xxv.

47. Birch, *Court and Times of Charles*, I, 31, 30.
48. Ludlow, *Memoirs*, III, 306.
49. Birch, *Court and Times of Charles*, I, 30. For green sickness, see Eccles, *Obstetrics and Gynaecology in Tudor and Stuart England*, 20, 74.
50. Birch, *Court and Times of Charles*, 31. See also *CSPV 1625–1626*, 87.
51. *CSPV 1625–1626*, 288, 515.
52. BL King's MS 136, ff. 335v–337v, 343v–345r.
53. Petitot, ed., *Mémoires*, ser. 2, XXXV, 407–8; Tillières, *Mémoires*, 90–91.
54. BL King's MS 136, f. 337v.
55. *A True Discourse*, 27, 28; Rushworth, *Historical Collections*, I, 170. See also Carlton, *Charles I*, 64.
56. Howell, *Epistolae*, I, 238.
57. Finet, *Finetti Philoxenis*, 153; BL King's MS 136, f. 336r; Howell, *Epistolae*, I, 238. See also *Calendar of Clarendon State Papers*, I, Appendix I, 8; BL King's MS 136, f. 344r; *CSPV 1625–1626*, 87; *A True Discourse*, 27–28; Finet, *Finetti Philoxenis*, 153; Petitot, ed., *Mémoires*, ser. 2, XXXV, 408–9.
58. Petitot, ed., *Mémoires*, ser. 2, XXXV, 409; BL King's MS 136, ff. 336r–v, 344r–v.
59. *HMC Skrine MSS*, 19; *CSPV 1625–1626*, 87. See also Finet, *Finetti Philoxenis*, 152; Birch, *Court and Times of Charles*, I, 31.
60. Petitot, ed., *Mémoires*, ser. 2, XXXV, 408.
61. Birch, *Court and Times of Charles*, I, 31; Petitot, ed., *Mémoires*, ser. 2, XXXV, 409; *True Discourse*, 28–29. See also Petitot, ed., *Mémoires*, ser. 2, XXXV, 409.

3 · QUARRELING

1. Sources for the entry to London are: Birch, *Court and Times of Charles*, I, 29–31; *CSPV 1625–1626*, 87; D'Ewes, *Autobiography*, I, 272; Finet, *Finetti Philoxenis*, 154; Heylin, *Short View*, 37; *HMC Skrine MSS*, 21–22; Laud, *Works*, III, 163; *Life and Death*, 13; *True Discourse*, 30–33.
2. Magalotti, *Travels of Cosmo the Third*, 367.
3. Birch, *Court and Times of Charles*, I, 30. For Whitehall, see Colvin, *King's Works*, IV, 301–34.
4. See Birch, *Court and Times of Charles*, I, 32; *True Discourse*, 35.
5. Petitot, ed., *Mémoires*, ser. 2, XXXV, 410 *bis*; Birch, *Court and Times of Charles*, I, 35. See also *CSPV 1625–1626*, 99; Finet, *Finetti Philoxenis*, 155–56; *HMC Skrine MSS*, 22–23.

6. Birch, *Historical View*, 435.

7. Tillières, *Mémoires*, 91; Birch, *Court and Times of Charles*, I, 18. See also BL King's MS 136, f. 337v; *CSPV 1625–1626*, 88, 606; Clarendon, *State Papers*, II, Appendix, xix.

8. *HMC Skrine MSS*, 20; Tillières, *Mémoires*, 92. For the plague deaths, see Birch, *Court and Times of Charles*, I, 28.

9. *HMC Salisbury MSS*, 198. For the English appointments, see *CSPV 1625–1626*, 98; Birch, *Court and Times of Charles*, I, 39; *HMC Skrine MSS*, 25.

10. Birch, *Court and Times of Charles*, I, 33; *CSPV 1625–1626*, 34; *HMC Skrine MSS*, 23.

11. Birch, *Court and Times of Charles*, I, 33.

12. Clarendon, *State Papers*, I, 33; Bossuet, *Oraison*, 85; BL King's MS 136, f. 274r. See also *HMC Skrine MSS*, 24; Tillières, *Mémoires*, 92; *CSPV 1625–1626*, 98; Clarendon, *State Papers*, I, 33.

13. Birch, *Court and Times of Charles*, I, 36.

14. *HMC Skrine MSS*, 25; *CSPV 1625–1626*, 107. For hopes on Henrietta's arrival, see Birch, *Court and Times of Charles*, I, 31.

15. *HMC Skrine MSS*, 25. See also *CSPV 1625–1626*, 98.

16. Tillières, *Mémoires*, 93, 95; *HMC Skrine MSS*, 31. See also ibid., 3, 6; *CSPV 1625–1626*, 129, 144; Houssaye, *Cardinal de Bérulle*, 36, 40.

17. *HMC Skrine MSS*, 3. See also ibid., 6.

18. Letter from Richelieu to Bérulle, as quoted in Houssaye, *Cardinal de Bérulle*, 35; *CSPV 1625–1626*, 129. See also Houssaye, *Cardinal de Bérulle*, 34; Petitot, ed., *Mémoires*, ser. 2, XXXV, 416; Tillières, *Mémoires*, 94.

19. *CSPV 1625–1626*, 129; *HMC Mar and Kellie*, 230. See also Petitot, ed., *Mémoires*, ser. 2, XXXV, 414–20; Birch, *Court and Times of Charles*, I, 39; Tillières, *Mémoires*, 94.

20. Cousin, *Madame de Longueville*, 432.

21. Houssaye, *Cardinal de Bérulle*, 29–30; Cousin, *Madame de Longueville*, 432.

22. Houssaye, *Cardinal de Bérulle*, 33–36, 42. See also *HMC Skrine MSS*, 28.

23. *CSPV 1625–1626*, 146. For the Privy Council meeting, see ibid., 143; BL King's MS 137, ff. 37v–38r.

24. For the French belief that Buckingham was responsible for Charles's anti-Catholic policies, see Richelieu, *Lettres*, II, 137–40; Houssaye, "L'Ambassade de M. de Blainville," 181. For their hatred of Buckingham at this date, see *HMC Skrine MSS*, 31; *HMC Mar and Kellie*, 230; Tillières, *Mémoires*, passim.

25. BL King's MS 137, ff. 23r–v; Tillières, *Mémoires*, 97. See also *HMC Mar and Kellie*, 233.

26. See *HMC Mar and Kellie*, 233; MS letter quoted in Houssaye, *Cardinal de Bérulle*, 40.

27. *CSPV 1625–1626*, 143; Gardiner, *History*, V, 429; *CSPV 1625–1626*, 6.

28. See Birch, *Court and Times of Charles*, I, 47. For the plague, see *CSPD 1625–1626*, 90; *HMC Skrine MSS*, 28, 32; *CSPV 1625–1626*, 149.

29. Birch, *Court and Times of Charles*, I, 47; PRO SP 16/7/85, ff. 118v–119r; Tillières, *Mémoires*, 99; Ludlow, *Memoirs*, III, 305, 307.

30. PRO SP 16/7/85.

31. Tillières, *Mémoires*, 99–100.

32. As quoted in Houssaye, *Cardinal de Bérulle*, 42.

33. Birch, *Court and Times of Charles*, I, 52. For Sancy, see ibid., 34; Houssaye, *Cardinal de Bérulle*, 10, 42; *HMC Skrine MSS*, 86.

34. Birch, *Court and Times of Charles*, I, 50; Tillières, *Mémoires*, 101; *HMC Skrine MSS*, 38; Tillières, *Mémoires*, 101. See also *CSPV 1625–1626*, 177.

35. *CSPV 1625–1626*, 177, 204. See also Birch, *Court and Times of Charles*, I, 50; *HMC Skrine MSS*, 38; Tillières, *Mémoires*, 101–4.

36. Petrie, *Letters*, 41 (where this letter is wrongly dated December 1625); PRO SP 16/8/29; PRO SP 16/7/85. See also Tillières, *Mémoires*, 104.

37. Petrie, *Letters*, 41; *CSPV 1625–1626*, 177; *HMC Skrine MSS*, 52. See also ibid., 37, 38; *CSPV 1625–1626*, 607.

38. Tillières, *Mémoires*, 105. The principal work on Blainville and his embassy is Houssaye, "L'Ambassade de M. de Blainville."

39. *CSPV 1625–1626*, 212; Houssaye, "L'Ambassade de M. de Blainville," 185; *HMC Skrine MSS*, 36. See also ibid., 34; *CSPV 1625–1626*, 198.

40. As quoted in Houssaye, *Cardinal de Bérulle*, 69.

41. As quoted in Houssaye, *Cardinal de Bérulle*, 45, 70. See also ibid., 46n2.

42. Motteville, *Mémoires*, I, 223; *Life and Death*, 14.

43. *CSPV 1625–1626*, 607; Ludlow, *Memoirs*, III, 306. For the maids being excluded from Henrietta's privy chamber by Charles's regulations, see Society of Antiquaries, *Collection of Ordinances*, 341.

44. Tillières, *Mémoires*, 108; *CSPV 1625–1626*, 271; Ludlow, *Memoirs*, III, 306–7. This incident can be dated between November 11 and 25,

when Charles and Henrietta were both staying at Hampton Court. Tillières says it was roughly a couple of weeks after Charles left Salisbury.

45. Petrie, *Letters*, 40; Ludlow, *Memoirs*, III, 305.

46. Petrie, *Letters*, 40–41; Ludlow, *Memoirs*, III, 305–6.

47. Petrie, *Letters*, 40.

48. *CSPV 1625–1626*, 289. For Richelieu's threat, see Houssaye, "L'Ambassade de M. de Blainville," 184.

49. *CSPV 1625–1626*, 269; Petrie, *Letters*, 41; *CSPV 1625–1626*, 272.

50. *CSPV 1625–1626*, 271, 275. See also *CSPD 1625–1626*, 183; Tillières, *Mémoires*, 108.

51. Birch, *Court and Times of Charles*, I, 68; BL King's MS 138, f. 162v. See also PRO SP 16/12/4.

52. *CSPD 1625–1626*, 561; *CSPV 1625–1626*, 292. The gift was made early in the New Year, although the official grant was not made until February 14.

53. Rous, *Diary*, 1. See also Lockyer, *Buckingham*, 281–83.

54. *CSPV 1625–1626*, 292, 299, 333. See also Houssaye, *Cardinal de Bérulle*, 108.

55. *CSPV 1625–1626*, 288; Tillières, *Mémoires*, 64. See also *HMC Skrine MSS*, 42.

56. *CSPV 1625–1626*, 272; Tillières, *Mémoires*, 129; *CSPV 1625–1626*, 318.

57. *CSPD 1625–1626*, 187; Houssaye, "L'Ambassade de M. de Blainville," 189–91.

58. *CSPV 1625–1626*, 276, 309. See also ibid., 300.

59. Laud, *Works*, III, 179–80; *CSPD 1625–1626*, 243; *CSPV 1625–1626*, 275.

60. BL King's MS 136, ff. 274v–275r, 276v. See also Birch, *Court and Times of Charles*, I, 72; *CSPV 1625–1626*, 311; Richelieu, *Lettres*, II, 124–36.

61. *CSPV 1625–1626*, 311, 326, 311.

62. Ellis, *Original Letters*, ser. I, vol. III, 218. Principal sources for the coronation ceremonies are: Rushworth, *Historical Collections*, I, 200–201; Ellis, *Original Letters*, ser. I, vol. III, 213–19; *CSPV 1625–1626*, 320–21; Laud, *Works*, III, 180–81; Wordsworth, *The Manner of the Coronation*.

63. Birch, *Court and Times of Charles*, I, 78. See also ibid., 79; *CSPV 1625–1626*, 321; *CSPD 1625–1626*, 246.

64. *CSPV 1625–1626*, 326.

65. As quoted in Albion, *Charles I*, 83; *HMC Skrine MSS*, 44.

66. See Finet, *Finetti Philoxenis*, 171; *CSPV 1625–1626*, 327; Tillières, *Mémoires*, 118–20, 122; Houssaye, "L'Ambassade de M. de Blainville," 193–96.

67. *CSPV 1625–1626*, 327. See also Houssaye, "L'Ambassade de M. de Blainville," 195–96.

68. See *CSPV 1625–1626*, 327–28; Finet, *Finetti Philoxenis*, 171; Ludlow, *Memoirs*, III, 307.

69. Tillières, *Mémoires*, 120–21; *CSPV 1625–1626*, 329; Houssaye, "L'Ambassade de M. de Blainville," 199–200.

70. See Houssaye, "L'Ambassade de M. de Blainville," 196–97; Tillières, *Mémoires*, 121–22.

71. Tillières, *Mémoires*, 122. See also *CSPV 1625–1626*, 329.

72. *HMC Skrine MSS*, 49. See also ibid., 47; *CSPV 1625–1626*, 329.

73. McClure, ed., *Letters of John Chamberlain*, II, 630; Birch, *Court and Times of Charles*, I, 85; *CSPV 1625–1626*, 346.

74. *HMC Skrine MSS*, 47; *CSPV 1625–1626*, 346; *HMC Skrine MSS*, 47. For the performance details, see Colvin, *King's Works*, IV, 261; Orgel and Strong, *Inigo Jones* (1973), I, 383–88.

75. See *CSPV 1625–1626*, 300; BL Add. MS 22,474, f. 11; Rushworth, *Historical Collections*, I, 217.

76. Rushworth, *Historical Collections*, I, 216–17; Birch, *Court and Times of Charles*, I, 93. See also BL Add. MS 22,474, f. 19; Rushworth, *Historical Collections*, I, 220, 226–27.

77. *CSPV 1625–1626*, 605; PRO SP 16/32/91.

78. Tillières, *Mémoires*, 135. For Lucy's love life, see the *Oxford DNB* article on her.

79. *CSPV 1625–1626*, 494. See also ibid., 498; Tillières, *Mémoires*, 134; Birch, *Court and Times of Charles*, I, 122, 134.

80. *CSPV 1625–1626*, 497.

81. Ludlow, *Memoirs*, III, 308; Tillières, *Mémoires*, 137–38.

82. *CSPV 1625–1626*, 388; *HMC Skrine MSS*, 94.

83. Birch, *Court and Times of Charles*, I, 121; *CSPV 1625–1626*, 545; PRO SP 16/32/91.

84. *HMC Skrine MSS*, 77. See also Houssaye, *Cardinal de Bérulle*, 120–21. For the pope's letters to Henrietta on the Jubilee, see BL Add. MS 15,389, ff. 150r–152v, 153r–155v; *CSPV 1625–1626*, 388.

85. BL Add. MS 39,288, f. 6; Birch, *Court and Times of Charles*, I, 121; BL Add. MS 39,288, f. 6. See also Birch, *Court and Times of Charles*, I, 132; *CSPV 1625–1626*, 531; *Life and Death*, 16. Only in France was it denied that this visit to Tyburn had been a deliberate pilgrimage: see *CSPV 1625–1626*, 517; Tillières, *Mémoires*, 148.

86. *CSPV 1625-1626*, 517. See also ibid., 531; *Life and Death*, 16.
87. PRO SP 16/32/91; Ludlow, *Memoirs*, III, 305-6; PRO SP 16/32/91. See also Ludlow, *Memoirs*, III, 308.
88. *CSPV 1625-1626*, 466. See also ibid., 482.
89. *CSPV 1625-1626*, 515; Vatican Library, Codices Barberini, 8,616, f. 35, as quoted in Albion, *Charles I*, 85. See also BL MS Royal 18 A XXVIII; *HMC Skrine MSS*, 93.
90. *CSPV 1625-1626*, 506; Birch, *Court and Times of Charles*, I, 134; *CSPV 1625-1626*, 506. See also Tillières, *Mémoires*, 144, 251.
91. *CSPV 1625-1626*, 506. See also ibid., 495, 498; PRO SP 16/33/30; Howell, *Epistolae*, I, 242; *HMC Skrine MSS*, 82.
92. Tillières, *Mémoires*, 252, 144.
93. PRO SP 16/32/91. See also Tillières, *Mémoires*, 145, 251; Birch, *Court and Times of Charles*, I, 119-20; PRO SP 16/33/30; *HMC Skrine MSS*, 82; *CSPV 1625-1626*, 506.
94. Tillières, *Mémoires*, 144. See also Birch, *Court and Times of Charles*, I, 120; Howell, *Epistolae*, I, 242.
95. Birch, *Court and Times of Charles*, I, 120. See also Tillières, *Mémoires*, 145.

4 · NEW BEGINNINGS

1. See PRO SP 16/33/30; Tillières, *Mémoires*, 146, 249, 252; Birch, *Court and Times of Charles*, I, 137; *CSPD 1625-1626*, 396.
2. Ellis, *Original Letters*, ser. I, vol. III, 244.
3. Tillières, *Mémoires*, 253; *CSPV 1625-1626*, 542. See also *Life and Death*, 17.
4. Tillières, *Mémoires*, 253; *CSPV 1625-1626*, 520. See also ibid., 525.
5. Baillon, *Henriette-Marie*, 349-50, 348.
6. *CSPV 1625-1626*, 515; Tillières, *Mémoires*, 67. See also *CSPV 1625-1626*, 507, 515.
7. *CSPV 1625-1626*, 571, 561. See also ibid., 530; Tillières, *Mémoires*, 66-67.
8. *CSPV 1625-1626*, 544. See also ibid., 566; *HMC Skrine MSS*, 84; Tillières, *Mémoires*, 67; Houssaye, *Cardinal de Bérulle*, 181-83.
9. Baillon, *Henriette-Marie*, 349. See also Birch, *Court and Times of Charles*, I, 145; *CSPV 1625-1626*, 526, 539, 546-47.
10. Bassompierre, *Journal*, III, 259-60. See also *CSPV 1625-1626*, 559-60, 565, 573; *HMC Skrine MSS*, 84-86; Birch, *Court and Times of Charles*, I, 151; Bassompierre, *Journal*, III, 257.

11. Bassompierre, *Négociation*, 283; Bassompierre, *Journal*, III, 264–65. See also ibid., 263; *CSPV 1625–1626*, 575–76, 582; *HMC Skrine MSS*, 88.

12. Tillières, *Mémoires*, 255.

13. *HMC Skrine MSS*, 86; *CSPV 1625–1626*, 547. See also Bassompierre, *Journal*, III, 264–69; Tillières, *Mémoires*, 255; Birch, *Court and Times of Charles*, I, 157–58; *HMC Skrine MSS*, 89.

14. Bassompierre, *Journal*, III, 266–67. See also *CSPV 1625–1626*, 592.

15. See Bassompierre, *Journal*, III, 269–70; *CSPV 1626–1628*, 8–9, 21, 615; Bassompierre, *Négociation*, 56, 246–47, 271; Bassompierre's letter, as translated in Strickland, *Lives*, V, 239–42; *HMC Skrine MSS*, 91–92.

16. See Bassompierre, *Journal*, III, 271; *HMC Buccleuch*, III, 310.

17. Bassompierre, *Journal*, III, 272–73; *CSPV 1626–1628*, 9.

18. Bassompierre, *Journal*, III, 274; *HMC Skrine MSS*, 95. See also *CSPV 1626–1628*, 22; Bassompierre, *Journal*, III, 274; Birch, *Court and Times of Charles*, I, 166, 168.

19. Bassompierre, *Journal*, III, 277. See also *HMC Skrine MSS*, 91, 96; Finet, *Finetti Philoxenis*, 192.

20. *HMC Skrine MSS*, 91; *CSPV 1626–1628*, 92, 82. See also ibid., 80, 88, 92, 97, 199, 615.

21. *CSPV 1626–1628*, 62. See also ibid., 9, 63, 97.

22. *CSPV 1626–1628*, 206, 40, 97.

23. See *HMC Skrine MSS*, 100, 103, 104; Birch, *Court and Times of Charles*, I, 186.

24. *HMC Skrine MSS*, 103–4; *HMC Skrine MSS*, 101. See also *CSPD 1625–1626*, 582.

25. *HMC Skrine MSS*, 102–3; *CSPV 1626–1628*, 107. See also *HMC Skrine MSS*, 104, 105.

26. Birch, *Court and Times of Charles*, I, 185.

27. As quoted in Houssaye, *Cardinal de Bérulle*, 188–89.

28. *HMC Skrine MSS*, 104. See also ibid., 107; *CSPV 1626–1628*, 97–98; Birch, *Court and Times of Charles*, I, 186.

29. *Hardwicke State Papers*, II, 22.

30. Birch, *Court and Times of Charles*, I, 202.

31. Birch, *Court and Times of Charles*, I, 141.

32. Clarendon, *History*, V, 167–68. For Philip, see *Oxford DNB*; Bellesheim, *History*, IV, 51; Batterel, *Mémoires*, I, 222–24; Houssaye, *Cardinal de Bérulle*, 9; McMillan, "Robert Philip."

33. See *CSPV 1625–1626*, 515; *HMC Skrine MSS*, 83.

34. Johnson et al., eds., *Proceedings in Parliament*, IV, 163; Clarendon, *History*, III, 509; *CSPV 1626–1628*, 167.

35. *CSPV 1629–1632*, 316.

36. *CSPD 1627–1628*, 222. For Hudson's life and character, see *Oxford DNB*.

37. *HMC Skrine MSS*, 84. See also Society of Antiquaries, *Collection of Ordinances*, 340–46.

38. Birch, *Court and Times of Charles*, I, 206.

39. *CSPV 1626–1628*, 177. See also Green, *Letters*, 11 (this letter is misdated there).

40. *CSPV 1626–1628*, 247–48. See also ibid., 155, 195, 202, 229; Birch, *Court and Times of Charles*, I, 224, 225.

41. *CSPV 1626–1628*, 180. See also ibid., 105, 127, 177, 239; Clarendon, *History*, I, 48.

42. As quoted in Lockyer, *Buckingham*, 367. See also Birch, *Court and Times of Charles*, I, 164; *CSPD 1627–1628*, 252.

43. Birch, *Court and Times of Charles*, I, 209. See also ibid., I, 219; *CSPV 1626–1628*, 68–69, 617.

44. *HMC Skrine MSS*, 116; Birch, *Court and Times of Charles*, I, 209. See also *HMC Skrine MSS*, 116.

45. Birch, *Court and Times of Charles*, I, 246. See also Lockyer, *Buckingham*, 373; *CSPD 1627–1628*, 209.

46. Birch, *Court and Times of Charles*, I, 241, 240. For Buckingham's entertainments, see *CSPV 1626–1628*, 239; Birch, *Court and Times of Charles*, I, 226; *HMC Skrine MSS*, 118.

47. *HMC Skrine MSS*, 121, 120. See also ibid., 119; Birch, *Court and Times of Charles*, I, 247.

48. PRO SP 16/67/105; *CSPV 1626–1628*, 298.

49. *CSPV 1626–1628*, 144; *HMC Skrine MSS*, 122; *CSPV 1626–1628*, 297.

50. Petrie, *Letters*, 53, 52.

51. See Birch, *Court and Times of Charles*, I, 223, 250; Petrie, *Letters*, 50.

52. PRO SP 16/75/83; *CSPV 1626–1628*, 342.

53. Petrie, *Letters*, 52.

54. PRO SP 16/82/42, as quoted in Gardiner, *History*, VI, 189; PRO SP 16/75/22, as quoted in Gardiner, *History*, VI, 189–90.

55. Petrie, *Letters*, 54–55.

56. Birch, *Court and Times of Charles*, I, 286; Clarendon, *History*, I, 50. See also Strafford, *Letters*, 41.

57. *CSPV 1626–1628*, 485; *HMC Skrine MSS*, 133.

58. BL Harleian MS 6,988, f. 76, as quoted in Lockyer, *Buckingham*, 402.

59. Birch, *Court and Times of Charles*, I, 289; *CSPV 1626–1628*, 499.
60. Birch, *Court and Times of Charles*, I, 281. See also ibid., 291; *CSPV 1626–1628*, 528; *HMC Skrine MSS*, 133.
61. *CSPV 1626–1628*, 497. See also Birch, *Court and Times of Charles*, I, 303.
62. *CSPV 1626–1628*, 570, 587. For Bérulle's angry stories, see Nuncio Guidi di Bagno's letter to Barberini, January 28, 1628, as quoted in Hibbard, "Translating Royalty," 27; *CSPV 1626–1628*, 528. For Tillières, see ibid., 558.
63. Birch, *Court and Times of Charles*, I, 328. See also *CSPV 1628–1629*, 37.
64. *CSPD 1628–1629*, 198. See also ibid., 31, 214, 215; *CSPD 1627–1628*, 573.
65. Nichols, ed., *Discovery*, preface, 13; *CSPV 1628–1629*, 171, 173.
66. *HMC Skrine MSS*, 155–56; *CSPV 1628–1629*, 156. See also ibid., 173, 168; *HMC Skrine MSS*, 157.
67. *CSPV 1628–1629*, 242.
68. PRO SP 16/101/43. See also *CSPD 1628–1629*, 219.
69. *CSPV 1628–1629*, 261.
70. Rous, *Diary*, 28. See also *CSPD 1628–1629*, 271.
71. D'Ewes, *Autobiography*, I, 381; Ellis, *Original Letters*, ser. 1, III, 256.
72. D'Ewes, *Autobiography*, I, 381; *CSPD 1628–1629*, 271; *HMC Salisbury MSS*, 244; *CSPV 1628–1629*, 262. Other sources for the murder are: Ellis, *Original Letters*, ser. 1, III, 254–60; *HMC Mar and Kellie*, 244–45; Birch, *Court and Times of Charles*, I, 389, 391–93; Rous, *Diary*, 25–28; Wotton, *Reliquiae*, 112; *HMC Skrine MSS*, 161–63; PRO SP 16/114/20.

5. NO OTHER FAVORITES

1. Clarendon, *History*, I, 37. See also *CSPV 1628–1629*, 262; Birch, *Court and Times of Charles*, I, 390.
2. *HMC Skrine MSS*, 162; Clarendon, *History*, I, 37; *HMC Skrine MSS*, 163. See also *CSPD 1628–1629*, 265; *CSPV 1628–1629*, 262, 283, 295; Lockyer, *Buckingham*, 461.
3. *CSPD 1628–1629*, 310, 268; *CSPV 1628–1629*, 283.
4. Ellis, *Original Letters*, ser. 1, III, 256–60.
5. Birch, *Court and Times of Charles*, I, 388; Clarendon, *History*, I, 37; Birch, *Court and Times of Charles*, I, 388. See also ibid., 394; *HMC Skrine MSS*, 162; *HMC Mar and Kellie*, 245.

6. Birch, *Court and Times of Charles*, I, 396. See also ibid., 389; *CSPV 1628–1629*, 283; *CSPD 1628–1629*, 277. For the fleet, see *CSPD 1628–1629*, 323–24; Birch, *Court and Times of Charles*, I, 396, 398.
7. Birch, *Court and Times of Charles*, I, 397; *CSPV 1628–1629*, 337. See also Birch, *Court and Times of Charles*, I, 389, 399.
8. *HMC Skrine MSS*, 165.
9. *HMC Skrine MSS*, 165; Birch, *Court and Times of Charles*, I, 396. See also ibid., 408.
10. *CSPV 1628–1629*, 310–11. See also *CSPD 1628–1629*, 343; *HMC Skrine MSS*, 165.
11. Birch, *Court and Times of Charles*, I, 419. See also ibid., 451–52.
12. PRO SP 16/121/47; *CSPD 1628–1629*, 413. See also ibid., 393.
13. *CSPV 1628–1629*, 518; *CSPD 1628–1629*, 527. For the first news of the pregnancy, see Birch, *Court and Times of Charles*, II, 4. For its dating, see *CSPD 1628–1629*, 548. For Charles's pleasure, see also *CSPV 1628–1629*, 540, 593. For the penal laws, see Albion, *Charles I*, 104.
14. Laud, *Works*, III, 102. See also *CSPV 1628–1629*, 593; *CSPD 1628–1629*, 534.
15. Laud, *Works*, III, 102; *CSPV 1628–1629*, 600. See also Birch, *Court and Times of Charles*, II, 13.
16. Rous, *Diary*, 11; *CSPD 1628–1629*, 539. For other talk against Henrietta, see ibid., 526; *HMC Mar and Kellie*, 248; Rous, *Diary*, 39.
17. *CSPD 1628–1629*, 517–18.
18. Birch, *Court and Times of Charles*, I, 448; *CSPV 1628–1629*, 379–80. For another instance of Henrietta's protection of Catholics, see *CSPD 1628–1629*, 451.
19. *CSPV 1628–1629*, 310.
20. *CSPV 1628–1629*, 311.
21. Birch, *Court and Times of Charles*, I, 422. For Charles's earlier unwillingness, see *CSPV 1628–1629*, 288, 359; *HMC Skrine MSS*, 168, 169.
22. Birch, *Court and Times of Charles*, I, 424, 425; *HMC Skrine MSS*, 171.
23. *CSPV 1628–1629*, 315. See also ibid., 340, 396.
24. *CSPV 1628–1629*, 374–77. See also ibid., 340.
25. Birch, *Court and Times of Charles*, II, 20; Finet, *Ceremonies*, 61.
26. *CSPV 1629–1632*, 69. See also BL Add. MS 27,962E, f. 282v.
27. D'Ewes, *Autobiography*, I, 412; Birch, *Court and Times of Charles*, I, 355. See also BL Add. MS 27,962E, f. 282v.
28. D'Ewes, *Autobiography*, I, 411; BL Add. MS 27,962E, f. 283r.
29. *CSPV 1629–1632*, 21. See also ibid., 65; Birch, *Court and Times of Charles*, I, 356.

30. *CSPV 1629–1632*, 70; Birch, *Court and Times of Charles*, I, 356. See also D'Ewes, *Autobiography*, I, 412.
31. Birch, *Court and Times of Charles*, I, 356; BL Add. MS 27,962E, f. 283r. For normal midwifery equipment, see Rueff, *Expert Midwife*, 44, 78, 81.
32. *Oxford DNB*.
33. BL Add. MS 27,962E, f. 284r; *CSPV 1629–1632*, 70.
34. BL Add. MS 27,962E, f. 284r.
35. *Life and Death*, 18.
36. BL Add. MS 27,962E, f. 283r; Birch, *Court and Times of Charles*, I, 355; *CSPD 1628–1629*, 548. See also *CSPV 1629–1632*, 70.
37. *CSPV 1629–1632*, 70; *CSPD 1628–1629*, 548, 585.
38. Birch, *Court and Times of Charles*, I, 356.
39. *CSPV 1629–1632*, 156. For the couple at Greenwich, see ibid., 83, 85.
40. As quoted in Hibbard, "Translating Royalty," 27.
41. Chateauneuf's dispatches, as quoted in Gardiner, *History*, VII, 106.
42. *CSPV 1629–1632*, 350, 388.
43. As quoted in Gardiner, *History*, VII, 106–7.
44. See Birch, *Court and Times of Charles*, II, 47; Gardiner, *History*, VII, 106.
45. *CSPV 1628–1629*, 287, 340. See also ibid., 293, 314, 315, 374, 396.
46. Chateauneuf's letters to Richelieu that summer, as cited in Gardiner, *History*, VII, 106–7.
47. As quoted in Houssaye, *Cardinal de Bérulle*, 483n. See also Birch, *Court and Times of Charles*, II, 296–99; Hibbard, *Charles I*, 56, 261n77.
48. *CSPV 1629–1632*, 205.
49. *CSPV 1629–1632*, 136; Birch, *Court and Times of Charles*, I, 417. See also *CSPV 1629–1632*, 168.
50. Birch, *Court and Times of Charles*, II, 41; *CSPV 1629–1632*, 228; Birch, *Court and Times of Charles*, I, 417.
51. *CSPV 1629–1632*, 281.
52. *CSPD 1629–1631*, 185; *CSPV 1629–1632*, 315–16. See also Laud, *Works*, III, 103; *CSPV 1629–1632*, 272, 277, 281; Hamilton, *Henrietta Maria*, 98; Birch, *Court and Times of Charles*, II, 70.
53. Birch, *Court and Times of Charles*, II, 301, 295.
54. Birch, *Court and Times of Charles*, II, 301–2, 67, 302–3.
55. *CSPV 1629–1632*, 304; Birch, *Court and Times of Charles*, II, 63, 68.
56. Birch, *Court and Times of Charles*, II, 67, 76. See also *CSPV 1629–1632*, 315, 337.

57. Rous, *Diary*, 49. For Charles releasing Catholics, see *CSPV 1629–1632*, 315, 337; *CSPD 1629–1631*, 233.
58. Green, *Letters*, 14–15, 15–16.
59. *CSPV 1629–1632*, 316. See also *CSPD 1629–1631*, 217; Birch, *Court and Times of Charles*, II, 69.
60. Ellis, *Original Letters*, ser. 2, III, 259–60.
61. BL Add. MS 27,962F, f. 110v. See also *CSPV 1629–1632*, 348.
62. Ellis, *Original Letters*, ser. 2, III, 262; *CSPD 1629–1631*, 268. See also *CSPV 1629–1632*, 370.
63. BL Add. MS 27,962F, f. 107v; *CSPV 1629–1632*, 350. See also Ellis, *Original Letters*, ser. 2, III, 262.
64. As quoted in Gardiner, *History*, VII, 140; *CSPV 1629–1632*, 350–51. For the callers, see also BL Add. MS 27,962F, f. 107v; Finet, *Ceremonies*, 87.
65. BL Add. MS 27,962F, fff. 105r–v. See also *CSPV 1629–1632*, 373.
66. Ellis, *Original Letters*, ser. 2, III, 262. For the celebrations, see also *CSPV 1629–1632*, 349; BL Add. MS 27,962F, f. 107v; *CSPD 1631–1633*, 218. For the procession and the new star, see BL Add. MS 27,962F, f. 107v; *CSPD 1629–1631*, 314; *Life and Death*, 20.

6. THE COURT OF LOVE

1. For the date of Henrietta's churching, see Finet, *Ceremonies*, 88. Details of the ceremony come from *The Catholic Encyclopedia*, "The Churching of Women."
2. Finet, *Ceremonies*, 88. See also Birch, *Court and Times of Charles*, II, 306; *CSPD 1629–1631*, 283.
3. For the treaty article, see *HMC Salisbury MSS*, 199; BL King's MS 135, f. 70r; *CSPV 1623–1625*, 525. For the priests' protests, see Birch, *Court and Times of Charles*, II, 306; *CSPV 1628–1629*, 540–41; *CSPV 1629–1632*, 369. Recent historians include Hutton, *Charles II*, 4; Hibbard, *Charles I*, 39.
4. See Finet, *Ceremonies*, 89.
5. Heylin, *Cyprianus Anglicus*, 198; Rous, *Diary*, 54.
6. See PRO SP 16/172/81; *CSPD 1629–1631*, 548.
7. BL King's MS 136, ff. 52r, 53v. For the Dorset couple, see Hibbard, *Charles I*, 39; Smith, "Catholic, Anglican or Puritan?"
8. See Laud, *Works*, III, 212; *CSPD 1629–1631*, 369.
9. PRO SP 16/171/42; *CSPD 1629–1631*, 329, 334. See also ibid., 330; *CSPV 1629–1632*, 388.

10. Green, *Letters*, 17, 18 (where this last letter is misdated). See also Ferrero, ed., *Lettres*, 35.
11. Birch, *Court and Times of Charles*, II, 82. See also Green, *Letters*, 19; *CSPV 1629–1632*, 431.
12. *CSPV 1629–1632*, 431. See also *CSPV 1628–1629*, 589; *CSPV 1629–1632*, 75, 177; *CSPD 1629–1631*, 372.
13. *CSPV 1628–1629*, 593.
14. Ben Jonson, *Chloridia* and *Love's Triumph through Callipolis*.
15. *CSPV 1629–1632*, 457; as quoted in Green, *Lives of the Princesses*, VI, 101.
16. *CSPV 1629–1632*, 562; as quoted in Green, *Lives of the Princesses*, VI, 101. For the birth and christening, see also Birch, *Court and Times of Charles*, II, 140; Laud, *Works*, III, 215.
17. *CSPD 1633–1634*, 251; *CSPV 1636–1639*, 174. See also *CSPV 1632–1636*, 157.
18. *CSPD 1633–1634*, 196. See also *CSPV 1632–1636*, 144; *HMC Cowper MSS*, II, Appendix II, 18, 22; Green, *Letters*, 22.
19. See *CSPV 1636–1639*, 143; BL Add. MS 15,390, ff. 86v–87r; Birch, *Court and Times of Charles*, II, 265, 266; *CSPV 1636–1639*, 143; *HMC Denbigh MSS*, V, 47.
20. Green, *Letters*, 34; *CSPV 1632–1636*, 163; *HMC De L'Isle and Dudley MSS*, VI, 98.
21. See BL Harleian MS 7,623, f. 11v; BL Harleian MS 3,791, ff. 113v, 114v, 116r; *HMC Cowper MSS*, II, Appendix II, 12; *CSPD 1635*, 80.
22. *CSPV 1636–1639*, 128. See also Finet, *Ceremonies*, 128, 169.
23. *CSPV 1636–1639*, 288. See also ibid., 416, 418; Gregg, *King Charles I*, 251.
24. Ellis, *Original Letters*, ser. 1, III, 288–89. See also BL Harleian MS 6,988, ff. 97, 99.
25. Camden, *Camden's Britannia*, 155 (note e). For St. James's, see Strong, *Renaissance Garden*, 188; MacGregor, *Late King's Goods*, 23; Colvin, *King's Works*, IV, 241–52.
26. Colvin, *King's Works*, IV, 225, 227. For Richmond, see also ibid., 222–34; MacGregor, *Late King's Goods*, 29.
27. BL Add. MS 15,389, ff. 356r–v. See also *CSPV 1636–1639*, 128.
28. *HMC Cowper MSS*, II, Appendix II, 12, 26.
29. *The King and Queenes Entertainement at Richmond*.
30. Mayor, *Nicholas Ferrar: Two Lives*.
31. Ferrero, *Lettres*, 40.
32. BL Harleian MS 6,988, f. 95.
33. See, e.g., *CSPV 1632–1636*, 445, 447.

34. *HMC Cowper MSS*, Appendix II, 11, 12.

35. *HMC Cowper MSS*, Appendix II, 18. See also *CSPD 1633–1634*, 85.

36. Nicolson, ed., *Conway Letters*, 27; Robert Herrick, *Poetical Works*, 223; Nicolson, ed., *Conway Letters*, 27. Other memories in this paragraph come from Herrick, *Poetical Works*, I, 198–200; Cavendish, *Poems, and Fancies*, 110, 113, 116–18, 160–61.

37. *CSPV 1632–1636*, 116.

38. Pepys, *Diary*, VIII, 338; ibid., III, 221; *HMC Skrine MSS*, 161.

39. *CSPV 1632–1636*, 486.

40. Aubrey, *Aubrey's Brief Lives*, 145.

41. *CSPD 1637–1638*, 49; BL Add. MS 15,389, ff. 173r–174v.

42. *CSPD 1631–1633*, 141. See also *CSPD 1635*, 237; *CSPD 1634–1635*, 213.

43. *CSPV 1632–1636*, 280, 287; *CSPV 1636–1639*, 46; *CSPV 1632–1636*, 486.

44. See, e.g., Hamilton, *Henrietta Maria*, 120; *CSPV 1632–1636*, 15–16; Finet, *Ceremonies*, 166.

45. Finet, *Ceremonies*, 167; Townshend, *Poems and Masques*, 13.

46. Clarendon, *History*, I, 104; Cavendish, *Life of William, Duke of Newcastle*, 103–4. For that summer's itinerary, see *CSPD 1634–1635*, 149.

47. *CSPV 1632–1636*, 570. See also *CSPV 1636–1639*, 44, 61.

48. *CSPD 1636–1637*, 91, 92.

49. *CSPD 1636–1637*, 477. See also ibid., 92; Birch, *Court and Times of Charles*, II, 266. Laud, *Works*, III, 227; V, 149–54; *CSPV 1636–1639*, 77.

50. Birch, *Court and Times of Charles*, I, 379.

51. *CSPD 1631–1633*, 590, 551.

52. *CSPV 1632–1636*, 117. See also Clarendon, *History*, I, 104

53. *CSPD 1633–1634*, 107; *HMC Cowper MSS*, Appendix II, 17, 22.

54. As quoted in Gardiner, *History*, VII, 285. See also *The Entertainment of . . . Charles into his ancient city of Edinburgh*.

55. *CSPV 1632–1636*, 122, 123, 125.

56. *CSPV 1632–1636*, 127.

57. *CSPV 1632–1636*, 132, 131; *HMC Cowper MSS*, II, Appendix II, 26. See also Laud, *Works*, III, 218; *CSPV 1632–1636*, 137.

58. *CSPD 1635*, 122, 401; Cruickshanks, *Stuart Courts*, 103. See also PRO LR 5/63, Establishment List for 1629: "master of the bowes and hounds" paid "for keeping of hounds."

59. *CSPD 1635*, 318. See also *CSPD 1631–1633*, 128; Clarendon, *History*, IV, 489. For the liberty, see *CSPD 1634–1635*, 505. For Charles returning late, see *CSPD 1631–1633*, 128; *CSPD 1635*, 420.

60. *CSPV 1632–1636*, 363; *CSPV 1626–1628*, 409; Laud, *Works*, III, 154. See also *CSPV 1636–1639*, 1; *CSPD 1623–1625*, 346, 349; Laud, *Works*, III, 183.
61. *CSPV 1636–1639*, 64. See also Birch, *Court and Times of Charles*, II, 249–50.
62. *CSPD 1633–1634*, 220; Jonson, *The Works*, VIII, 20.
63. Birch, *Court and Times of Charles*, II, 205, 202, 205 *bis*; *CSPD 1631–1633*, 454.
64. *CSPV 1632–1636*, 367. See also Carlton, *Charles I*, 124.
65. *CSPV 1632–1636*, 251, 572. For Henrietta's conversation and wit, see Evelyn, *Diary*, 442; Motteville, *Memoir*, 28.
66. *CSPD 1635*, 368; *CSPD 1627–1628*, 155; Birch, *Court and Times of Charles*, II, 123.
67. See *CSPD 1631–1633*, 484; Steele, *Plays and Masques at Court*; Carlton, *Charles I*, 147; Marshall, *Henrietta*, 63; Dickens, *Courts of Europe*, 198.
68. *CSPV 1632–1636*, 491. See also Birch, *Court and Times of Charles*, II, 265, 107; *CSPD 1633–1634*, 455.
69. Bassompierre, *Journal*, III, 271. For the birthdays, see Finet, *Ceremonies*, 75; BL Add. MS 15,389, ff. 355v–356r.
70. Birch, *Court and Times of Charles*, II, 214; *Deep Sigh*, sig. A3v. See also Cavendish, *The Blazing World*, 12.
71. Cavendish, *The Blazing World*, 9.
72. See Orgel and Strong, *Inigo Jones*, passim; Strong, *Tudor and Stuart Monarchy*; Harris, Orgel, and Strong, *King's Arcadia*.
73. *CSPD 1631–1633*, 482; *CSPV 1632–1636*, 334. For earlier illnesses, see *CSPV 1629–1632*, 605; *CSPD 1633–1634*, 504.
74. *CSPV 1632–1636*, 334, 28. See also ibid., 63.
75. *CSPV 1632–1636*, 86. See also Birch, *Court and Times of Charles*, II, 95; *CSPD 1629–1631*, 509; *CSPV 1629–1632*, 592.
76. See Birch, *Court and Times of Charles*, II, 176, 187, 216; Montagu, *The Shepherds' Paradise*; Sarah Poynting, "'In the name of all the sisters': Henrietta Maria's Notorious Whores."
77. *CSPD 1631–1633*, 270; As quoted in Strong, *Tudor and Stuart Monarchy*, 196.
78. Petrie, *Letters*, 83; *CSPV 1632–1636*, 323. See also *CSPD 1633–1634*, 64.
79. Finet, *Ceremonies*, 56, 216.
80. Birch, *Court and Times of Charles*, II, 244.
81. Finet, *Ceremonies*, 199.
82. As quoted in Ralph, *Sir Humphrey Mildmay*, 43.

83. For some of these expenses, see *CSPD 1631–1633*, 589; Smuts, "Art and the Material Culture of Majesty," 88–96, 103–10.

84. La Serre, *Histoire*, sig. K. For Henrietta's gardening, see also *CSPD 1628–1629*, 16; Green, *Letters*, 19; Colvin, *King's Works*, and Strong, *Renaissance Garden*.

85. See Carlton, *Charles I*, 142.

86. As quoted in Carlton, *Charles I*, 142. See also MacGregor, *Late King's Goods*, 76.

87. Panzani, *Memoirs*, 251; Wittkower, "Inigo Jones," 50–51.

88. As quoted in Strong, *Tudor and Stuart Monarchy*, 196.

89. Motteville, *Mémoires*, I, 223 *bis*; BL Add. MS 15,389, ff. 196r–197v.

90. Warwick, *Memoires*, 65, 66.

91. See Summerson, *Inigo Jones*, 122–31.

92. Principal sources for these royal building works are Colvin, *King's Works*, IV, and Summerson, *Inigo Jones*.

93. See Summerson, *Inigo Jones*, 68–70; Colvin, *King's Works*, IV, 263–66.

94. *CSPV 1629–1632*, 298; BL Harleian MS 3,888, f. 107; Birch, *Court and Times of Charles*, II, 307. See also ibid., 35.

7 · QUESTIONS OF FAITH

1. Birch, *Court and Times of Charles*, II, 343. For the state of Catholics in this period, see Albion, *Charles I*; Hibbard, *Charles I*.

2. *CSPD 1633–1634*, 464; Birch, *Court and Times of Charles*, II, 211; *CSPD 1633–1634*, 349.

3. Clarendon, *State Papers*, I, 353. See also *CSPD 1631–1633*, 424; *CSPD 1633–1634*, 66.

4. Birch, *Court and Times of Charles*, I, 410; Motteville, *Mémoires*, I, 188–90. See also Panzani, *Memoirs*, 138–39.

5. Clarendon, *State Papers*, I, 355; Panzani, *Memoirs*, 135. See also Albion, *Charles I*, 168–73.

6. Albion, *Charles I*, 412–14; Panzani, *Memoirs*, 161. For Henrietta's frivolity, see Albion, *Charles I*, 148.

7. See, Panzani, *Memoirs*, 190, 206–7; Clarendon, *State Papers*, I, 354–57; II, 217, 249–50.

8. Panzani, *Memoirs*, 188. See also Albion, *Charles I*, 152.

9. *CSPV 1636–1639*, 303; Panzani, *Memoirs*, 204, 234.

10. Panzani, *Memoirs*, 206. See also ibid., 205–6, 211–14; Albion, *Charles I*, 116–43, 164, 288–98.

11. Warwick, *Memoires*, 68.

12. BL Add. MS 15,389, f. 180v; as quoted in Green, *Letters*, 31.

13. BL Add. MS 15,389, ff. 190r *bis*, 196r–v *bis*.

14. BL Add. MS 15,389, ff. 197r–v.

15. As quoted in Green, *Letters*, 34, 30. See also *CSPV 1636–1639*, 69–70; MacGregor, *Late King's Goods*, 95.

16. As quoted in Green, *Letters*, 31; Panzani, *Memoirs*, 251.

17. As quoted in *Oxford DNB*. For Juxon, see Albion, *Charles I*, 160–62; Hibbard, *Charles I*, 56.

18. My translation of Con's Italian, as quoted in Albion, *Charles I*, 162; as quoted in Hibbard, *Charles I*, 54; BL Add. *MS 15,390, f. 65v.*

19. Green, *Letters*, 32. See also *Oxford DNB*; Hibbard, *Charles I*, 34, 53–56.

20. Batterel, *Mémoires*, I, 227; as quoted in Hibbard, *Charles I*, 52.

21. Panzani, *Memoirs*, 165. See also *CSPV 1636–1639*, 150.

22. *CSPV 1636–1639*, 97; Birch, *Court and Times of Charles*, II, 315–16, 432–33.

23. Motteville, *Memoir*, 20. See also *CSPV 1636–1639*, 69.

24. As quoted and translated in Green, *Lives of the Princesses*, VI, 104–5.

25. BL Add. MS 15,389, f. 356r.

26. See MacGregor, *Late King's Goods*, 66; Albion, *Charles I*, 395–96.

27. BL Add. MS 15,390, ff. 249r–250v.

28. As quoted in Albion, *Charles I*, 233.

29. Warwick, *Memoires*, 65; as quoted in Albion, *Charles I*, 233.

30. See BL Add. MS 15,390, f. 15r; Albion, *Charles I*, 402–5.

31. *CSPV 1636–1639*, 120. See also Hibbard, *Charles I*, 49; BL Add. MS 15,390, ff. 10v–14v; Albion, *Charles I*, 258–80, 417–19.

32. Birch, *Court and Times of Charles*, II, 314.

33. Birch, *Court and Times of Charles*, II, 343; *CSPV 1636–1639*, 149–50.

34. Panzani's letter of 24 April/4 May 1635, PRO 31/9/17B (unfoliated); BL Add. MS 15,389, f. 129v.

35. *CSPV 1636–1639*, 149–50. See also BL Add. MS 15,389, ff. 129v–130r, 190v.

36. Warwick, *Memoires*, 73. For Con's realization, see Albion, *Charles I*, 248.

37. Laud, *Works*, III, 407–8.

38. Clarendon, *History*, I, 132. See also Warwick, *Memoires*, 90; Fuller, *Church History*, XI, 217–19; Gardiner, *History*, VII, 317. For contemporary reports of Laud's reforms, see Panzani, *Memoirs*, 138–39; *CSPV 1636–1639*, 125, 217.

39. As quoted in Dickens, *Courts of Europe*, 196; Laud, *Works*, III, 407.

40. *CSPV 1636–1639*, 300, 301, 304, 300–301, 300, 305, 242. See also ibid., 12, 217, 272; *CSPD 1634–1635*, 22.

41. *CSPV 1636–1639*, 125. See also ibid., 136; Laud, *Works*, VII, 319.

42. *CSPV 1636–1639*, 205, 308. See also ibid., 299, 315, 335.

43. *CSPV 1636–1639*, 124–25.

44. Petrie, *Letters*, 95; *CSPV 1636–1639*, 124. See also ibid., 309–10; *CSPV 1632–1636*, 6, 131, 140, 366–67, 491.

45. Birch, *Court and Times of Charles*, II, 278; *CSPV 1636–1639*, 154.

46. *CSPV 1636–1639*, 304, 242; Laud, *Works*, III, 228.

47. *CSPV 1636–1639*, 304 *bis*, 246. For Charles's happiness, see Wedgwood, *King's Peace*, 19.

48. Clarendon, *History*, I, 114.

49. *CSPV 1636–1639*, 259, 273, 277.

50. *Hardwicke State Papers*, II, 95; *CSPV 1636–1639*, 350.

51. See *CSPV 1636–1639*, 272; Hibbard, *Charles 1*, 90, 275n1.

52. Strafford, *Letters*, II, 74; BL Add. MS 15,390, ff. 283r, 251r. See also *CSPV 1636–1639*, 273.

53. As quoted in Hibbard, *Charles I*, 58; BL Harleian MS 3,888, f. 146r. See also BL Add. MS 15,390, f. 283v; Albion, *Charles I*, 218.

54. Strafford, *Letters*, II, 128.

55. Laud, *Works*, III, 229; Strafford, *Letters*, II, 128, 125.

56. Laud, *Works*, VII, 379; ibid., III, 230; ibid., VII, 380.

57. BL Add. MS 15,390, ff. 469v–470r; *CSPV 1636–1639*, 319, 324.

58. *CSPV 1636–1639*, 324; BL Add. MS 15,390, ff. 470v–471r.

59. BL Add. MS 15,390, ff. 477r, 473v; *CSPV 1636–1639*, 324. See also BL Add. MS 15,390, f. 471r–v.

60. BL Add. MS 15,390, f. 486v; Strafford, *Letters*, II, 125. See also Albion, *Charles I*, 213; BL Add. MS 15,390, f. 472r–v; Strafford, *Letters*, II, 128; Albion, *Charles I*, 212.

61. *CSPV 1636–1639*, 359, 358; Albion, *Charles I*, 227. See also ibid., 225–26.

62. The proclamation, as printed in Albion, *Charles I*, 415–16. See also Albion, *Charles I*, 226.

63. BL Add. MS 15,391, f. 2r.

64. As quoted in Hibbard, *Charles I*, 260n72. See also BL Harleian MS 3,888, ff. 119v, 146r–v; Albion, *Charles I*, 226.

65. Strafford, *Letters*, II, 165. See also BL Add. MS 15,390, ff. 472v–473r; Albion, *Charles I*, 163, 212.

66. See Albion, *Charles I*, 203.

67. *CSPD 1637–1638*, 14, 259; *CSPV 1636–1639*, 376. See also *CSPD 1637–1638*, 14, 259.

68. *CSPV 1636–1639*, 377, 379, 387. See also Gardiner, *History*, VIII, 327–28.

69. As quoted in Gardiner, *History*, VIII, 330–32.

70. *CSPV 1636–1639*, 389, 395, 400 *bis*.

71. *CSPV 1636–1639*, 407, 436. See also ibid., 403.

72. Petrie, *Letters*, 107.

73. *CSPV 1636–1639*, 393. See also *CSPD 1637–38*, 524–25.

74. As quoted in Albion, *Charles I*, 243. See also Hibbard, *Charles I*, 90–91, 94–98; Albion, *Charles I*, 302; *CSPV 1636–1639*, 392; *CSPD 1637–1638*, 534.

75. Petrie, *Letters*, 108, 109, 107.

76. *CSPV 1636–1639*, 436, 435, 377.

77. *CSPV 1629–1632*, 544; *CSPV 1636–1639*, 275; *CSPV 1629–1632*, 580; *CSPV 1636–1639*, 460.

78. See *CSPV 1628–1629*, 539; Estrades, *Lettres*, I, 4.

79. *CSPV 1636–1639*, 278; *HMC Denbigh MSS*, V, 56.

80. *CSPV 1636–1639*, 385, 410; Laud, *Works*, VII, 425.

81. *CSPV 1636–1639*, 424, 410.

82. Laud, *Works*, VII, 453. See also Green, *Lives of the Princesses*, VI, 105.

83. *CSPV 1636–1639*, 460, 446, 449.

84. See *CSPD 1638–1639*, 87, 91, 103; *CSPV 1636–1639*, 463, 467; La Serre, *Histoire*, sigs. I1r–K1r.

85. *CSPD 1638–1639*, 48; *CSPV 1636–1639*, 467; Laud, *Works*, VII, 496.

86. La Serre, *Histoire*, sig. F2v; Ferrero, *Lettres*, 54.

87. La Serre, *Histoire*, sig. L1r.

88. La Serre, *Histoire*, sig. K1v; Ferrero, *Lettres*, 55.

89. La Serre, *Histoire*, sig. L1r. See also ibid., sig. O2r; *CSPD 1638–1639*, 65; *CSPV 1636–1639*, 468; Finet, *Ceremonies*, 253–54.

90. *CSPV 1636–1639*, 471; La Serre, *Histoire*, sig. O2r.

91. Birch, *Court and Times of Charles*, II, 432–33, 343. See also La Serre, *Histoire*, sig. M2r; BL Add. MS 15,391, f. 304r.

92. See Petrie, *Letters*, 100–101; Gardiner, ed., *Hamilton Papers*, 62; BL Add. MS 15,391, ff. 329r–330r; *CSPV 1636–1639*, 477, 479.

93. Birch, *Court and Times of Charles*, II, 330; *CSPV 1636–1639*, 495. See also Green, *Lives of the Princesses*, VI, 396; *CSPD 1638–1639*, 362.

94. *CSPV 1636–1639*, 497, 502.

95. *CSPV 1636–1639*, 507. See also Birch, *Court and Times of Charles*, II, 330–31; Hibbard, *Charles I*, 104–7.

96. Clarendon, *State Papers*, II, 20. See also ibid., 26–31; *Calendar of Clarendon State Papers*, I, 168; Hibbard, *Charles I*, 104–7, 277n66.

97. See *CSPV 1636–1639*, 480, 493, 497, 516; *CSPD 1638–1639*, 161.

98. *CSPD 1638–1639*, 506, 367, 506. See also ibid., 377–78; *CSPV 1636–1639*, 494, 496–97, 500–501.

99. *CSPD 1638–1639*, 575; Laud, *Works*, III, 232. For the household's departure, see *CSPD 1638–1639*, 506; *CSPV 1636–1639*, 515.

8. LIBERTY AND RELIGION ALIKE

1. *CSPV 1636–1639*, 533. See also *CSPD 1638–1639*, 626, 628; *CSPD 1639*, 47–48.

2. *CSPD 1639*, 248, 146. For Charles's army, see ibid., 49–50, 52, 58, 59.

3. *CSPD 1639*, 162.

4. *CSPD 1639*, 341–42. See also ibid., 72, 162.

5. *CSPD 1639*, 221, 250.

6. *CSPD 1639*, 270, 281–82, 269.

7. *CSPD 1639–1640*, 632, 536, 246. For Henrietta at Whitehall, see Green, *Lives of the Princesses*, VI, 107; *CSPD 1638–1639*, 607, 621.

8. *CSPD 1639–1640*, 246. See also ibid., 621.

9. *CSPD 1639*, 3. See also *CSPD 1638–1639*, 623; *CSPV 1636–1639*, 536.

10. *A Coppy of the Letter*, 3, 1, 3, 1. See also *CSPD 1639*, 3; *CSPV 1636–1639*, 335; Albion, *Charles I*, 335, 421; Hibbard, *Charles I*, 103.

11. *CSPV 1636–1639*, 506; *CSPD 1639*, 73–74. See also *CSPV 1636–1639*, 539.

12. *CSPD 1639*, 73. See also Gardiner, *History*, IX, 26; Hibbard, *Charles I*, 122–23; Albion, *Charles I*, 336.

13. See Hibbard, *Charles I*, 121; Albion, *Charles I*, 359; *CSPV 1636–1639*, 547.

14. As quoted in Hibbard, *Charles I*, 120; *CSPD 1639*, 294. See also *CSPD 1639*, 288.

15. *CSPV 1636–1639*, 548.

16. *CSPV 1640–1642*, 294. For the talks, see *CSPD 1639*, 330.

17. Clarendon, *State Papers*, II, 56.

18. *CSPD 1639*, 349. See also *Calendar of Clarendon State Papers*, I, 180.

19. *CSPV 1636–1639*, 559; Petrie, *Letters*, 104. For Charles at Berwick, see *CSPV 1636–1639*, 559; Finet, *Ceremonies*, 261; *Hardwicke State Papers*, II, 141.

20. *CSPV 1636–1639*, 554. See also ibid., 563; Finet, *Ceremonies*, 261; Laud, *Works*, III, 233.

21. Clarendon, *History*, I, 165, 164.

22. *CSPV 1636–1639*, 497.
23. Laud, *Works*, III, 361–62.
24. As quoted in Smuts, "Puritan Followers," 31–32.
25. Laud, *Works*, VII, 550. See also *CSPD 1639*, 105.
26. As quoted in Smuts, "Puritan Followers," 30; as quoted in Hibbard, *Charles I*, 146. See also Laud, *Works*, VII, 442, 570–71; *HMC De L'Isle and Dudley MSS*, VI, 158–59.
27. Motteville, *Mémoires*, I, 223; *HMC De L'Isle and Dudley MSS*, VI, 204. See also Hibbard, *Charles I*, 133.
28. Warwick, *Memoires*, 109–10. See also Clarendon, *History*, I, 341.
29. Warwick, *Memoires*, 109. For the state of Ireland and Wentworth's achievements there, see Wedgwood, *Thomas Wentworth*; *Oxford DNB*.
30. Petrie, *Letters*, 96. For Laud and Wentworth, see Laud, *Works*, VII, passim.
31. Petrie, *Letters*, 104.
32. Petrie, *Letters*, 104. For Laud and Con, see Gardiner, ed., *Hamilton Papers*, 62; *CSPV 1636–1639*, 572; Albion, *Charles I*, 304, 312, 315.
33. As quoted in Wedgwood, *Thomas Wentworth*, 267.
34. Laud, *Works*, VII, 508; *HMC De L'Isle and Dudley MSS*, VI, 182 *bis*. See also ibid., VI, 179–80, 182, 208–9; Laud, *Works*, VII, 506, 509, 510, 537–38.
35. *CSPV 1636–1639*, 592. See also ibid., 595; Wedgwood, *Thomas Wentworth*, 267.
36. CSPV 1636–1639, 574. See also ibid., 567, 570, 578, 590, 599; Laud, *Works*, III, 233.
37. *CSPV 1636–1639*, 568; Laud, *Works*, III, 283; *CSPV 1636–1639*, 576.
38. *CSPV 1636–1639*, 592. See also ibid., 595; Laud, *Works*, III, 233; *CSPD 1639–1640*, 158.
39. *CSPV 1636–1639*, 601. See also Warwick, *Memoires*, 110; Clarendon, *History*, I, 341–42.
40. Clarendon, *History*, I, 171. See also Laud, *Works*, III, 233, 282–83.
41. *CSPV 1636–1639*, 601; *CSPD 1639–1640*, 148–49. See also Laud, *Works*, III, 283.
42. Clarendon, *History*, I, 172; *CSPV 1636–1639*, 602; as quoted in Pastor, *History of the Popes*, XXIX, 323. See also *CSPD 1639–1640*, 158.
43. *CSPD 1639–1640*, 321. See also ibid., 158; Wedgwood, *Thomas Wentworth*, 273; *CSPV 1636–1639*, 602.
44. *CSPV 1640–1642*, 23; *CSPV 1636–1639*, 605. See also *CSPV 1640–1642*, 4.
45. See, *CSPD 1639–1640*, 365; Finet, *Ceremonies*, 272.

46. Davenant, *Dramatic Works*, II, 310–26.
47. *CSPD 1639–1640*, 459; *HMC De L'Isle and Dudley MSS*, VI, 231.
48. See MacGregor, *Late King's Goods*, 221, 225; Albion, *Charles I*, 396–97.
49. For the purchase, see *HMC Denbigh MSS*, V, 68; *CSPD 1639–1640*, 157; *HMC De L'Isle and Dudley MSS*, VI, 212. For the design, see Strong, *Renaissance Garden*, 191–97.
50. *CSPV 1640–1642*, 8, 12. For the ministers opposing the war, see also ibid., 17.
51. *CSPV 1640–1642*, 35. See also ibid., 37; *CSPD 1639–1640*, 608; *CSPD 1640*, 6.
52. *CSPV 1640–1642*, 27, 30. See also *CSPV 1640–1642*, 25; Hibbard, *Charles I*, 148; Gardiner, *History*, IX, 159.
53. Evelyn, *Diary*, 14; *LJ*, IV, April 13, 1640. See also Cope, *Proceedings*, 95; *CSPD 1640*, 25.
54. As quoted in Smuts, "Puritan Followers," 34; *LJ*, IV, April 13, 1640.
55. Cope, *Proceedings*, 138; as quoted in Gardiner, *History*, IX, 101.
56. *CSPV 1640–1642*, 40. See also *CJ*, II, April 17, 1640.
57. See Hibbard, *Charles I*, 148; *CSPD 1640*, 88, 102.
58. Laud, *Works*, III, 283. See also *CSPD 1640*, 115.
59. *LJ*, IV, May 6, 1640.
60. Laud, *Works*, III, 234; *HMC De L'Isle and Dudley MSS*, VI, 262.
61. *CSPD 1640*, 115; *HMC De L'Isle and Dudley MSS*, VI, 262.
62. *CSPD 1640*, 112–13.
63. *HMC De L'Isle and Dudley MSS*, VI, 262.
64. *CSPD 1640*, 155; as quoted in Gardiner, *History*, IX, 130.
65. Motteville, *Mémoires*, I, 196; as quoted in Smuts, "Puritan Followers," 42. See also Warwick, *Memoires*, 112; Motteville, *Mémoires*, I, 194.
66. *CSPD 1640*, 117; Laud, *Works*, III, 284; *CSPV 1640–1642*, 47. See also Gardiner, *History*, IX, 133; Laud, *Works*, III, 234.
67. Clarendon, *History*, I, 188; *CSPV 1640–1642*, 47. See also Laud, *Works*, III, 284; *CSPV 1640–1642*, 47; Gardiner, *History*, IX, 133.
68. Laud, *Works*, III, 284; *CSPV 1640–1642*, 47. See also BL Add. MS 35,331, f. 77r.
69. Clarendon, *History*, I, 188; *CSPV 1640–1642*, 47. See also *CSPD 1640*, 150, 167.
70. *CSPV 1640–1642*, 48. See also Gardiner, *History*, IX, 134–35.
71. *CSPV 1640–1642*, 48, 49. See also Gardiner, *History*, IX, 135.
72. *HMC De L'Isle and Dudley MSS*, VI, 272. See also ibid., 270; *CSPV 1640–1642*, 49; Gardiner, *History*, IX, 135–36.

73. See Laud, *Works*, III, 236; *CSPV 1640–1642*, 52; Clarendon, *History*, I, 188; Gardiner, *History*, IX, 141.

74. *CSPD 1640*, 174, 192.

75. *CSPV 1640–1642*, 49. See also Albion, *Charles I*, 339–40.

76. Pastor, *History of the Popes*, XXIX, 324. See also Gardiner, *History*, IX, 141–42; *CSPV 1640–1642*, 52; Pastor, *History of the Popes*, XXIX, 327; Albion, *Charles I*, 338.

77. *CSPV 1640–1642*, 52. See also *HMC De L'Isle and Dudley MSS*, VI, 276.

78. *CSPD 1640*, 272, 293–94. See also Albion, *Charles I*, 339; *CSPD 1640*, 528.

79. *CSPV 1640–1642*, 53. See also BL Harleian MS 3,791, f. 114v; *CSPD 1640–1641*, 172; Albion, *Charles I*, 339.

80. As quoted in Albion, *Charles I*, 359.

81. See Gardiner, *History,* IX, 175; Birch, *Court and Times of Charles*, II, 286; *CSPV 1640–1642*, 59, 66; *CSPD 1640*, 451.

82. *CSPV 1640–1642*, 60. See also *CSPD 1640*, 497, 554.

83. *CSPV 1640–1642*, 71. For mutinies, see Gardiner, *History*, IX, 186.

84. See *CSPD 1640*, 278; *Oxford DNB*.

85. *CSPV 1640–1642*, 52, 65. See also *CSPD 1640*, 516, 563, 571.

86. *CSPV 1640–1642*, 71; *Hardwicke State Papers*, II, 147–50. See also *CSPD 1640*, 587–88, 590–91.

87. *CSPD 1640*, 601. See also *CSPV 1640–1642*, 71.

88. *CSPD 1640*, 507.

89. *CSPV 1640–1642*, 70. See also Gardiner, *History*, IX, 187.

90. *CSPD 1640*, 609; *CSPV 1640–1642*, 73.

91. *CSPD 1640*, 645, 649; as quoted in Gardiner, *History*, IX, 195.

92. *CSPD 1640–1641*, 7; Motteville, *Mémoires*, 194.

93. *CSPV 1640–1642*, 75; *CSPD 1640,* 612. See also *CSPV 1640–1642*, 70–72; *CSPD 1640*, 648; Laud, *Works*, III, 291–92.

94. As quoted in Hibbard, *Charles I*, 156; *CSPD 1640*, 602; Clarendon, *State Papers*, II, 116.

95. Laud, *Works*, III, 237; *CSPD 1640*, 617. See also Albion, *Charles I*, 340; *CSPV 1640–1642*, 73.

96. *CSPV 1640–1642*, 73, 74. See also *CSPD 1640*, 633, 634.

97. *Hardwicke State Papers*, II, 157. See also *CSPD 1640*, 652; Clarendon, *State Papers*, II, 92, 95, 96.

98. *CSPV 1640–1642*, 76; *Hardwicke State Papers*, II, 164.

99. *Calendar of Clarendon State Papers*, I, 204. For other councillors' fears, see *CSPD 1640–1641*, 7.

100. *Hardwicke State Papers*, II, 168–70.

101. *CSPD 1640–1641*, 8.
102. *CSPV 1640–1642*, 79.
103. *CSPD 1640–1641*, 47, 23. See also ibid., 80; *CSPV 1640–1642*, 80.
104. Clarendon, *State Papers*, II, 114, 112; *CSPD 1640–1641*, 46. See also ibid., 1.
105. See Clarendon, *History*, I, 202.
106. *CSPD 1640–1641*, 69. See also ibid., 67, 68.
107. *CSPD 1640–1641*, 92, 91; Clarendon, *History*, I, 202.
108. *Calendar of Clarendon State Papers*, I, 208; *CSPV 1640–1642*, 89.
109. *CSPV 1640–1642*, 90–92. See also *CSPD 1640–1641*, 191.
110. *CSPV 1640–1642*, 86; Clarendon, *History*, I, 203–6.
111. *CSPD 1640–1641*, 246–47.
112. *CSPD 1640–1641*, 104–5; *CSPV 1640–1642*, 97, 91. See also *CSPD 1640–1641*, 111.
113. *CSPV 1640–1642*, 93, See also ibid., 84, 87; *CSPD 1640–1641*, 246.
114. *CSPV 1640–1642*, 94, 79, 94.
115. *CSPV 1640–1642*, 93. See also ibid., 94.

9. EVIL COUNSELORS

1. *CSPV 1640–1642*, 89, 92.
2. See Motteville, *Mémoires*, I, 194–95.
3. D'Ewes, *Journal*, ed. Notestein, 14; *CSPV 1640–1642*, 95, 94.
4. D'Ewes, *Journal*, ed. Notestein, 8, 11n84.
5. *CSPV 1640–1642*, 95; D'Ewes, *Journal*, ed. Notestein, 14.
6. D'Ewes, *Journal*, ed. Notestein, 533.
7. *LJ*, IV, November 13, 1640. See also ibid., November 11, 1640; *CJ*, II, November 11, 1640.
8. See *CSPV 1640–1642*, 98, 112; *CJ*, II, November 30, 1640, December 1, 1640; *CSPV 1640–1642*, 102.
9. *CSPV 1640–1642*, 102; Laud, *Works*, III, 297, 279; *CJ*, II, December 16, 1640.
10. *HMC De L'Isle and Dudley MSS*, VI, 346.
11. D'Ewes, *Journal*, ed. Notestein, 24–25.
12. *CSPV 1640–1642*, 97.
13. Parts of this letter of Henrietta's, Vatican Library, Codices Barberini 8,615, ff. 84–86, are printed in Bellesheim, *History of the Catholic Church*, III, 493, and Albion, *Charles I*, 360. See also PRO 31/9/19, f. 187; Gardiner, *History*, IX, 244, 251–52; *CSPV 1640–1642*, 100; *CJ*, II, November 23, 1640.

14. *CSPV 1640–1642*, 103.

15. As quoted in Albion, *Charles I*, 346.

16. D'Ewes, *Journal*, ed. Notestein, 78; *CJ*, II, December 1, 1640. See also *CSPD 1640–1641*, 312; *CSPV 1640–1642*, 105.

17. *CSPV 1640–1642*, 105.

18. *CJ*, II, December 1, 1640; *CSPV 1640–1642*, 107. See also *CSPV 1640–1642*, 111; *Oxford DNB*, article on John, Baron Finch; Albion, *Charles I*, 346–47.

19. *CSPV 1640–1642*, 111–12.

20. As quoted in Green, *Lives of the Princesses*, VI, 394. Salvetti's report of December 11/21, BL Add. MS 27,962I, dates Anne's death to December 6, 1640.

21. *CSPV 1640–1642*, 106; *HMC De L'Isle and Dudley MSS*, VI, 350; *CSPD 1640–1641*, 326.

22. For Elizabeth, see *True Effigies*, 12; Green, *Lives of the Princesses*, VI, 337. For the negotiations, see *CSPV 1640–1642*, 25, 52, 103; *CSPD 1640–1641*, 278, 291.

23. As quoted in Geyl, *Orange and Stuart*, 7; *CSPV 1640–1642*, 109.

24. *CSPV 1640–1642*, 107, 117.

25. See Gardiner, *History*, IX, 265; *CSPV 1640–1642*, 119.

26. *LJ*, IV, January 1 and 23, 1641. See also ibid., January 25, 1641; D'Ewes, *Journal*, ed. Notestein, 279, 285.

27. As quoted in D'Ewes, *Journal*, ed. Notestein, 321n24.

28. D'Ewes, *Journal*, ed. Notestein, 291. See also ibid., 295, 301.

29. *CSPV 1640–1642*, 123.

30. *LJ*, IV, February 4, 1641. See also D'Ewes, *Journal*, ed. Notestein, 321.

31. *HMC De L'Isle and Dudley MSS*, VI, 376. See also D'Ewes, *Journal*, ed. Notestein, 333.

32. *A Coppy of the Letter*, 11–12. See also D'Ewes, *Journal*, ed. Notestein, 323–24.

33. *CSPV 1640–1642*, 123; D'Ewes, *Journal*, ed. Notestein, 324–25.

34. D'Ewes, *Journal*, ed. Notestein, 357–60.

35. *CSPV 1640–1642*, 111, 126. See also *LJ*, IV, February 15, 1641; *CJ*, II, February 15, 1641.

36. D'Ewes, *Journal*, ed. Notestein, 393. See also ibid., n12.

37. Motteville, *Mémoires*, I, 194–96.

38. See Albion, *Charles I*, 365; Gardiner, *History*, IX, 288.

39. *CSPV 1640–1642*, 125. See Wedgwood, *Thomas Wentworth*, 306.

40. *CSPD 1640–1641*, 461. See also *LJ*, IV, February 16, 1641.

41. *CJ*, II, February 16, 1641; *CSPV 1640–1642*, 127. See also *CSPD 1640–1641*, 462.

42. *HMC Cowper MSS*, II, Appendix II, 272. See also Gardiner, *History*, IX, 259–60.

43. *CSPV 1640–1642*, 128; D'Ewes, *Journal*, ed. Notestein, 247.

44. D'Ewes, *Journal*, ed. Notestein, 393. *LJ*, IV, February 23, 1641, dates these speeches to the Lords' first debate on this issue, on February 22.

45. D'Ewes, *Journal*, ed. Notestein, 488 and n10. For a similar suggestion by Lord Digby on February 4, see D'Ewes, *Journal*, ed. Notestein, 325.

46. D'Ewes, *Journal*, ed. Notestein, 494. See also ibid., 493; *LJ*, IV, March 17, 1641.

47. Warwick, *Memoires*, 112.

48. This scene is based on Wenceslaus Hollar's engraving of the trial and on Wedgwood, *Thomas Wentworth*, 337–38; Motteville, *Mémoires*, I, 196.

49. Chief sources throughout the trial are *LJ* and Wedgwood, *Thomas Wentworth*.

50. Warwick, *Memoires*, 110.

51. *CSPV 1640–1642*, 138. See also Laud, *Works*, III, 440.

52. Motteville, *Mémoires*, I, 196; Clarendon, *History*, I, 289; *Life and Death*, 32. See also *CSPV 1640–1642*, 138.

53. Motteville, *Mémoires*, I, 196–97; *CSPV 1640–1642*, 136. See also *Life and Death*, 32; *CSPD 1640–1641*, 547–48.

54. Motteville, *Mémoires*, I, 196; *CSPV 1640–1642*, 128.

55. Clarendon, *History*, III, 445. For the fortifications, see *HMC Cowper MSS*, II, Appendix II, 280–81.

56. See Russell, "First Army Plot," 99–100; *Calendar of Clarendon State Papers*, I, 204; Gardiner, *History*, IX, 343; Green, *Letters*, 38; *CSPV 1640–1642*, 127; Hibbard, *Charles I*, 180; D'Ewes, *Journal*, ed. Notestein, 484.

57. *LJ*, IV, March 17, 1641; *CSPD 1640–1641*, 510. See also *CSPV 1640–1642*, 140.

58. As quoted in Russell, "First Army Plot," 89. See also *CSPD 1640–1641*, 507.

59. *HMC Portland MSS*, I, 22.

60. As quoted in Gardiner, *History*, IX, 343. Principal sources on the army plot are Motteville, *Mémoires*, I, 197–201; Rossetti's recollections printed in Gardiner, *History*, IX, 343; Russell, "First Army Plot." Extra details come from *CSPD 1641–1643*, 7–8; *CSPV 1640–1642*, 163–64; Verney, *Verney Papers*, 98.

61. Motteville, *Mémoires*, I, 198–99. See also ibid., 197.

62. As quoted in Russell, "First Army Plot," 91. See also Verney, *Verney Papers*, 94–95, 98; *HMC Portland MSS*, I, 22–23; *CSPD 1641–1643*, 18.

63. Verney, *Verney Papers*, 87. See also Russell, "First Army Plot," 93.

64. As quoted in Russell, "First Army Plot," 94; *HMC De L'Isle and Dudley MSS*, VI, 397–98; as quoted in Russell, "First Army Plot," 93.

65. *CSPV 1640–1642*, 138. See also Wedgwood, *Thomas Wentworth*, 346–50.

66. As quoted in Wedgwood, *Thomas Wentworth*, 353; *LJ*, IV, April 10, 1641.

67. *CSPD 1640–1641*, 540.

68. *CSPD 1640–1641*, 540. See also *CSPD 1640–1641*, 560.

69. See Rushworth, *Trial*, 50–53; *CJ*, II, April 21, 1641; *CSPD 1640–1641*, 555.

70. Petrie, *Letters*, 115; *CSPD 1640–1641*, 555.

71. As quoted in Wedgwood, *Thomas Wentworth*, 368; *CSPD 1640–1641*, 560.

72. *CSPV 1640–1642*, 145, 141.

73. *CSPV 1640–1642*, 142. See also Albion, *Charles I*, 365.

74. *CSPV 1640–1642*, 145, 142. See also *HMC Cowper MSS*, Appendix II, 280–81; Russell, "First Army Plot," 97.

75. See *LJ*, IV, April 29, 1641; Wedgwood, *Thomas Wentworth*, 370; Russell, "First Army Plot," 95–96.

76. *CSPV 1640–1642*, 145, 141.

77. *CSPD 1640–1641*, 559.

78. Clarendon, *History*, I, 318–21.

79. *CSPD 1640–1641*, 567.

80. *True Effigies*, 6. See also BL Harleian MS 6,988, f. 101; Mayor, *Nicholas Ferrar: Two Lives*, 154; *CSPD 1640–1641*, 158.

81. *True Effigies*, 10–11.

82. *CSPV 1640–1642*, 142. For William's reception, see also Finet, *Ceremonies*, 309.

83. *CSPV 1640–1642*, 141. See also ibid., 139.

84. *CSPV 1640–1642*, 145. See also Green, *Lives of the Princesses*, VI, 113.

85. As quoted in Green, *Lives of the Princesses*, VI, 112; *True Effigies*, 8; *CSPV 1640–1642*, 145.

86. See Van Dyck's wedding portrait.

87. *CSPV 1640–1642*, 147; my translation of the text quoted in *CSPV 1640–1642*, 147. See also Green, *Lives of the Princesses*, VI, 117.

88. Laud, *Works*, III, 444; *CSPV 1640–1642*, 147; Clarendon, *History*, I, 337; *CSPV 1640–1642*, 148.

89. Clarendon, *History*, I, 336; as quoted in Gardiner, *History*, IX, 351–52; *CJ*, II, May 3, 1641.

90. Russell, "First Army Plot," 92; Clarendon, *History*, 445. See also Verney, *Verney Papers*, 98; Motteville, *Mémoires*, I, 200. Goring's whitewashing of himself is not supported by Percy, who named Goring as a chief plotter: see *CSPD 1641–1643*, 18.

91. *CJ*, II, May 5, 1641; as quoted in Gardiner, *History*, IX, 363.

92. *CJ*, II, May 5, 1641; *LJ*, IV, May 5, 1641; *CJ*, II, May 5, 1641; *CSPV 1640–1642*, 150. See also *CJ*, II, May 6, 1641.

93. See Motteville, *Mémoires*, I, 199–200; *LJ*, IV, May 6, 1641.

94. *LJ*, IV, May 6, 1641; *CJ*, II, May 6, 1641.

95. *CSPV 1640–1642*, 150.

96. Motteville, *Mémoires*, I, 201. See also *CSPV 1640–1642*, 150.

97. *CSPD 1640–1641*, 571. See also Pastor, *History of the Popes*, XXIX, 332.

98. See Russell, "First Army Plot," 97.

99. *CJ*, II, May 7, 1641.

100. *HMC Egmont MSS*, I, 134; as quoted in Hibbard, *Charles I*, 195; *HMC Egmont MSS*, I, 134. See also Gardiner, *History*, IX, 363.

101. As quoted in Gardiner, *History*, IX, 363. See also ibid., 356; *CSPV 1640–1642*, 150.

102. *CJ*, II, May 7, 1641. See also *LJ*, IV, May 7, 1641.

103. Clarendon, *History*, I, 337. See also *Oxford DNB*; Wedgwood, *Thomas Wentworth*, 377, 379 n45; Clarendon, *History*, I, 337; *CSPD 1640–1641*, 571.

104. *LJ*, IV, May 7, 1641.

105. See *CSPV 1640–1642*, 142; *Oxford DNB* entries for the Earls of Holland, Bristol, and Hertford; Wedgwood, *Thomas Wentworth*, 377, 379n45; *CSPD 1640–1641*, 571.

106. *HMC Egmont MSS*, I, 134.

107. Rushworth, *Strafford's Trial*, 743, as quoted in Gardiner, *History*, IX, 362; Motteville, *Mémoires*, I, 202.

108. *HMC Egmont MSS*, I, 134; *LJ*, IV, May 8, 1641.

109. *LJ*, IV, May 7, 1641; *LJ*, IV, May 8, 1641. See also *CSPV 1640–1642*, 151.

110. Clarendon, *History*, I, 337–38; Laud, *Works*, III, 441.

111. *CSPV 1640–1642*, 150. See also PRO 31/9/20, ff. 193–95.

112. *CJ*, II, May 11, 1641.

113. *CSPV 1640–1642*, 150.

114. Clarendon, *History*, I, 338–39.

115. Prideaux, *History*, 360.

116. See *CSPD 1640–1641*, 567; Wedgwood, *Thomas Wentworth*, 376–77.

117. Clarendon, *History*, I, 339.

118. As quoted in Gardiner, *History*, IX, 366–67; Strafford, *Letters*, II, 432.

119. *LJ*, IV, May 10, 1641; *CSPD 1640–1641*, 573.

120. As quoted in Wedgwood, *Thomas Wentworth*, 380; *CSPD 1640–1641*, 574.

121. *LJ*, IV, May 11, 1641.

122. As quoted in Gardiner, *History*, IX, 368; as quoted in Wedgwood, *Thomas Wentworth*, 383. See also Laud, *Works*, III, 442.

123. As quoted in Wedgwood, *Thomas Wentworth*, 386. See also *CSPV 1640–1642*, 151.

124. As quoted in Gardiner, *History*, IX, 369.

125. As quoted in Wedgwood, *Thomas Wentworth*, 386–88.

126. As quoted in Wedgwood, *Thomas Wentworth*, 388; Clarendon, *History*, I, 341.

127. *CSPV 1640–1642*, 151; as quoted in Wedgwood, *Thomas Wentworth*, 389.

128. Motteville, *Mémoires*, I, 202; my translation of the Italian quoted in Pastor, *History of the Popes*, XXIX, 328.

129. *CSPV 1640–1642*, 151, 153, 152. See also Motteville, *Mémoires*, I, 202–3.

10. SHAME AND FEAR

1. *CSPV 1640–1642*, 152. See also ibid., 175.

2. Gardiner, *Constitutional Documents*, 163–66; *CSPV 1640–1642*, 174.

3. As quoted in Hibbard, *Charles I*, 206. See also *CSPV 1640–1642*, 163.

4. *CSPV 1640–1642*, 152, 174, 166. See also ibid., 153, 160, 163, 166.

5. *LJ*, IV, July 14, 1641. See also *CSPD 1641–1643*, 47, 48; *CSPV 1640–1642*, 179; Verney, *Verney Papers*, 106.

6. *CSPV 1640–1642*, 183, 187. See also *CJ*, II, July 21, 1641.

7. Ferrero, *Lettres de Henriette-Marie*, 57–59.

8. As quoted in Russell, *Fall*, 304; *CSPV 1640–1642*, 194.

9. *CSPV 1640–1642*, 200.

10. *CSPD 1641–1643*, 101; Evelyn, *Diary and Correspondence*, IV, 50. See also *CSPV 1640–1642*, 205.

11. *Nicholas Papers*, I, 25; *CSPV 1640–1642*, 208.

12. See *Nicholas Papers*, I, 7; Evelyn, *Diary and Correspondence*, IV, 75.

13. Evelyn, *Diary and Correspondence*, IV, 75; Motteville, *Mémoires*, I, 205. See also *CSPV 1640–1642*, 213, 225.

14. *CSPV 1640–1642*, 250–51, 236. See also Motteville, *Mémoires*, I, 205; Evelyn, *Diary and Correspondence*, IV, 77.

15. *CSPV 1640–1642*, 236–37; *CSPD 1641–1643*, 148.

16. *CJ*, II, November 1, 1641; *CSPD 1641–1643*, 168.

17. *CSPV 1640–1642*, 250. See also *Oxford DNB*: John Pym; *CSPV 1640–1642*, 243–45.

18. *LJ*, IV, November 2, 1641. See also ibid., November 15, 1641.

19. *CSPD 1641–1643*, 171.

20. *CSPV 1640–1642*, 254; Motteville, *Mémoires*, I, 205.

21. *CSPD 1641–1643*, 177; *CSPV 1640–1642*, 254, 250–51. See also Gardiner, *Constitutional Documents*, 201; *Ovatio Carolina*; Motteville, *Mémoires*, I, 205.

22. See D'Ewes, *Journal*, ed. Coates, 200n6, 202–3, 213.

23. Gardiner, *Constitutional Documents*, 202ff. See also *CJ*, II, December 2, 1641.

24. D'Ewes, *Journal*, ed. Coates, 261.

25. *CSPD 1641–1643*, 194; *LJ*, IV, December 14, 1641. See also D'Ewes, *Journal*, ed. Coates, 244.

26. Gardiner, *Constitutional Documents*, 233. See also *CSPV 1640–1642*, 263.

27. D'Ewes, *Journal*, ed. Coates, 345, 344; *CJ*, II, December 24, 1641.

28. *CSPD 1641–1643*, 217. See also *CSPD 1641–1643*, 215, 216, 218; *CSPV 1640–1642*, 271; Gardiner, *History*, X, 112.

29. As quoted in Gardiner, *History*, X, 117.

30. For Godfrey Goodman's conversion, see Hibbard, *Charles I*, 150.

31. See D'Ewes, *Journal*, ed. Coates, 347.

32. *CSPD 1641–1643*, 217. See also Gardiner, *History*, X, 117; *CSPV 1640–1642*, 272.

33. *CSPD 1641–1643*, 218, 214–15.

34. *CSPV 1640–1642*, 272. See also *CSPD 1641–1643*, 217.

35. *CSPD 1641–1643*, 215; *CSPV 1640–1642*, 272. See also *CSPD 1641–1643*, 216, 217.

36. *CSPD 1641–1643*, 216, 241.

37. *LJ*, IV, December 30, 1641. See also *CSPD 1641–1643*, 216, 217, 241, 242; D'Ewes, *Journal*, ed. Coates, 376; *CSPV 1640–1642*, 275.

38. *CSPD 1641–1643*, 216; *LJ*, IV, December 30, 1641; *CSPV 1640–1642*, 273.

39. D'Ewes, *Journal*, ed. Coates, 366–67; *CJ*, II, December 31, 1641.

40. *CJ*, II, December 31, 1641. See also D'Ewes, *Journal*, ed. Coates, 366–67.

41. My translation of the Italian quoted in Gardiner, *History*, X, 128n1; *CSPV 1640–1642*, 275–76. See also D'Ewes, *Journal*, ed. Coates, 373n18.

42. See Gardiner, *History*, X, 128n1.

43. As quoted in D'Ewes, *Journal*, ed. Coates, 395; Clarendon, *History*, IV, 489; Bossuet, *Oraison*, 96. See also Clarendon, *History*, IV, 492.

44. *LJ*, IV, January 3, 1642; *CJ*, II, January 3, 1642. See also *CSPD 1641–1643*, 239.

45. *Eikon Basilike*, chap. 3; Motteville, *Mémoires*, I, 205. See also *CSPD 1641–1643*, 239.

46. D'Ewes, *Journal*, ed. Coates, 379; *CJ*, II, January 3, 1642; *CSPD 1641–1643*, 236.

47. *CSPD 1641–1643*, 242; D'Ewes, *Journal*, ed. Coates, 394, 382–83. See also ibid., 379, 393–94.

48. Motteville, *Mémoires*, I, 205–6.

49. Gardiner, *Constitutional Documents*, 237ff.; D'Ewes, *Journal*, ed. Coates, 395. See also ibid., 378, 382n; *CSPD 1641–1643*, 242.

50. D'Ewes, *Journal*, ed. Coates, 393; *CSPD 1641–1643*, 242.

51. D'Ewes, *Journal*, ed. Coates, 382n, 393, 394.

52. *CSPD 1641–1643*, 242; D'Ewes, *Journal*, ed. Coates, 381. See also *CSPD 1641–1643*, 239.

53. D'Ewes, *Journal*, ed. Coates, 381.

54. As quoted in Gardiner, *History of England*, X, 138.

55. Gardiner, *Constitutional Documents*, 237ff.; D'Ewes, *Journal*, ed. Coates, 383, 382, 393.

56. Motteville, *Mémoires*, I, 205; As quoted in Gardiner, *History*, X, 134n3; Motteville, *Mémoires*, I, 205.

57. See Evelyn, *Diary and Correspondence*, IV, 75.

58. Motteville, *Mémoires*, I, 206, 205.

59. D'Ewes, *Journal*, ed. Coates, 383–84.

60. D'Ewes, *Journal*, ed. Coates, 395.

61. As quoted in D'Ewes, *Journal*, ed. Coates, 383n19. See also ibid., 384.

62. D'Ewes, as quoted in Forster, *Arrest of the Five Members*, 220; as quoted in *Oxford DNB*; D'Ewes, *Journal*, ed. Coates, 384.

63. Clarendon, *History*, I, 485. See also *CSPD 1641–1643*, 244.

64. Sources for this incident are: *CSPD 1641–1643*, 240–44; *CSPV 1640–1642*, 277; Clarendon, *History*, I, 485–86.

65. For this Commons debate, see D'Ewes, *Journal*, ed. Coates, 382–87; *CJ*, II, January 5, 1642.

66. Principal sources for the committee's work are: *CSPD 1641–1643*, 243; D'Ewes, *Journal*, ed. Coates, 386–96; Verney, *Verney Papers*, 140.

67. D'Ewes, *Journal*, ed. Coates, 399n9; *CSPV 1640–1642*, 280.

68. *CSPD 1641–1643*, 237; *CSPV 1640–1642*, 277; Clarendon, *History*, I, 505. See also *CSPD 1641–1643*, 242.

69. D'Ewes, *Journal*, ed. Coates, 392; *CSPV 1640–1642*, 279; D'Ewes, *Journal*, ed. Coates, 392. See also *CSPD 1641–1643*, 245, 249.

70. *CSPD 1641–1643*, 243. See also D'Ewes, *Journal*, ed. Coates, 392; *CSPV 1640–1642*, 280.

71. As quoted in Hibbard, *Charles I*, 222; *CSPD 1641–1643*, 276; BL Add. MS 27,962I, f. 345r. See also ibid., f. 345r; *CSPV 1640–1642*, 277.

72. Clarendon, *History*, I, 399. See also *CSPV 1640–1642*, 277; BL Add. MS 27,962I, f. 342r.

73. BL Add. MS 27,962I, f. 338v.

74. Hutchinson, *Memoirs*, 85.

75. Hutchinson, *Memoirs*, 88–89.

76. *LJ*, IV, January 20, 1642; Coates et al., *Private Journals*, I, 117.

77. As quoted in D'Ewes, *Journal*, ed. Coates, 397n; *CSPD 1641–1643*, 248.

78. D'Ewes, *Journal*, ed. Coates, 398. See also ibid., 400–401; *CJ*, II, January 11, 1642; Verney, *Verney Papers*, 141–43.

79. *CSPV 1640–1642*, 280. See also *CSPD 1641–1643*, 252.

80. Clarendon, *History*, I, 555; *Eikon Basilike*, chap. 6.

81. Clarendon, *History*, I, 507, 519, 507; *CSPV 1640–1642*, 281. See also *CSPD 1641–1643*, 254.

82. *CSPD 1641–1643*, 256.

83. See *CSPV 1640–1642*, 285; BL Add. MS 27,962I, f. 343r.

84. *CSPV 1640–1642*, 281. See also BL Add. MS 27,962I, ff. 343r–345r.

85. Verney, *Verney Papers*, 144; *CJ*, II, January 12, 1642. See also Clarendon, *History*, I, 515.

86. *CSPV 1640–1642*, 282; BL Add. MS 27,962I, f. 343r. See also Clarendon, *History*, I, 520; *CSPD 1641–1643*, 252.

87. Clarendon, *History*, I, 524. See also Prinsterer, *Archives*, ser. 2, IV, 6–7; *CSPV 1640–1642*, 283.

88. Ferrero, *Lettres de Henriette-Marie*, 59.

89. *CJ*, II, January 14, 1642. See also *CJ*, II, January 12, 1642.

90. Clarendon, *History*, I, 554–55. See also ibid., 523; Rossetti's letter quoted in Gardiner, *History*, X, 157n1.

91. *CJ*, II, January 12, 1642. See also *CJ*, II, January 11, 1642; Clarendon, *History*, I, 523–24; *CSPD 1641–1643*, 253, 256; *CSPV 1640–1642*, 284.

92. Clarendon, *History*, I, 515; Coates et al., *Private Journals*, I, 130. See also *CSPV 1640–1642*, 288; *CJ*, II, February 19, 1642.

93. *LJ*, IV, February 1, 1642; Laud, *Works*, III, 457; *CSPD 1641–1643*, 277.

94. *LJ*, IV, February 7, 1642.

95. *CSPV 1640–1642*, 285; Clarendon, *History*, I, 529, 554.

96. Prinsterer, *Archives*, ser. 2, IV, 22.

97. *LJ*, IV, February 7, 1642; ibid., February 8, 1642; *CSPV 1640–1642*, 293; Clarendon, *History*, I, 558.

98. Ferrero, *Lettres de Henriette-Marie*, 59–60.

99. Coates et al., *Private Journals*, I, 305, 306, 307; *CJ*, II, February 7, 1642; *LJ*, IV, February 7, 1642.

100. Green, *Letters*, 64. See also Ferard, *Law of Fixtures*, 158n.

101. *CSPV 1640–1642*, 294. See also ibid., 13, 21.

102. Clarendon, *History*, I, 572. See also Prinsterer, *Archives*, ser. 2, IV, 7; Motteville, *Mémoires*, I, 207–8; Green, *Letters*, 52–70, passim; *CSPD 1641–1643*, 306, 310–11.

103. Motteville, *Mémoires*, I, 208; Ferrero, *Lettres de Henriette-Marie*, 59; Green, *Letters*, 72.

104. *CSPV 1640–1642*, 295; Green, *Letters*, 75; Prinsterer, *Archives*, ser. 2, IV, 23.

105. See Gardiner, *History*, IX, 403–4; Clarendon, *History*, IV, 490, 492; Laud, *Works*, III, 440–41.

106. *CSPV 1640–1642*, 295; Green, *Letters*, 65, 68–69, 65.

107. Green, *Letters*, 57, 58, 65, 60, 65. See also ibid., 52, 55, 59, 61, 68, 80, 85.

108. Green, *Letters*, 70, 61.

109. *CSPV 1640–1642*, 294. See also ibid., 295; Gardiner, *History*, X, 163.

110. Green, *Letters*, 56, 69, 56, 61, 69. See also ibid., 55–56.

111. *CSPV 1640–1642*, 296.

112. Clarendon, *History*, I, 556; *CSPV 1640–1642*, 295. See also *CSPD 1641–1643*, 282; Green, *Letters*, 50.

113. Clarendon, *Life of Edward*, I, 53.

114. Clarendon, *History*, I, 567. See also ibid., 565–66; Clarendon, *Life of Edward*, I, 51.

115. Motteville, *Mémoires*, I, 207; Clarendon, *Life of Edward*, I, 51. See also *LJ*, IV, February 14, 1642; *CSPV 1640–1642*, 296; Clarendon, *History*, I, 567; *CSPD 1641–1643*, 282.

116. *A True Discourse*, 28–29; *CSPV 1640–1642*, 297.

117. *LJ*, IV, February 14, 1642; ibid., February 21, 1642. See also Clarendon, *Life of Edward*, I, 52.

118. *CSPD 1641–1643*, 283, 288, 294, 286. See also ibid., 286, 293; *CSPV 1642–1643*, 13; Birch, *Court and Times of Charles*, II, 349.
119. *CSPV 1640–1642*, 296.
120. *CSPV 1642–1643*, 5; Birch, *Court and Times of Charles*, II, 349. For the date, see *CSPV 1642–1643*, 4, 5, 13; Laud, *Works*, III, 244; *HMC Cowper MSS*, II, Appendix II, 308; Clarendon, *Life of Edward*, I, 52; Coates et al., *Private Journals*, I, 449, 450, 455, 461, 463, 470.
121. Motteville, *Mémoires*, I, 208; Birch, *Court and Times of Charles*, II, 349. See also *CSPD 1641–1643*, 284, 285.
122. *A True and Exact Relation*.

11. NEWCASTLE, JANUARY 1647

1. *CSPV 1640–1642*, 96; as quoted in Terry, "Visits," 122. See also ibid., passim. Information on the equipment of the troops comes from Reid, *Scots Armies*.
2. As quoted in Terry, "Visits," 111, 140n310, 140; *CSPV 1643–1647*, 301. See also Ellis, *Original Letters*, ser. 2, III, 328.
3. Bruce, ed., *Charles I*, 99.
4. Green, *Letters*, 222; *King's Cabinet Opened*, 38. For the money Henrietta raised, see Strickland, *Lives,* V, 290.
5. For wartime Oxford, see Roy and Reinhart, "Oxford and the Civil Wars"; Roy, "The City of Oxford"; Varley, *The Siege of Oxford*; Wood, *Life and Times*, I, 67–103.
6. Green, *Letters*, 97, 144.
7. Green, *Letters*, 222. See also Clarendon, *Life of Edward*, I, 185.
8. Clarendon, *History*, IV, 490; Warwick, *Memoires*, 64; Clarendon, *History*, IV, 490.
9. Green, *Letters*, 225, 227–28. For Henrietta's advice for London, see Hamilton, *Henrietta Maria*, 203; *Life and Death*, 37–38.
10. Green, *Letters*, 235.
11. *CJ*, III, May 23, 1643; *LJ*, VI, May 23, 1643; as quoted in Green, *Letters*, 165–66. See also *HMC Cowper MSS*, II, Appendix II, 334.
12. Ellis, *Original Letters*, ser. 3, IV, 303. See also Marshall, *Henrietta*, 114; *Oxford DNB*.
13. See Dugdale, *Diary*, 65.
14. Green, *Letters*, 244–45.
15. Green, *Letters*, 246, 247.
16. *CSPD 1644*, 318; Green, *Letters*, 248–49.
17. Polwhele, *Traditions and Recollections*, I, 17. See also Ellis, *Original Letters*, ser. 3, IV, 303.

18. Green, *Letters*, 271. See also BL Add. MS 12,184, f. 318r; *Life and Death*, 40; Strickland, *Lives*, V, 332–33.

19. Green, *Letters*, 283, 287–88. See also ibid., 279.

20. *King's Cabinet Opened*, 14; as quoted in Warburton, *Memoirs of Prince Rupert*, III, 111n1.

21. As quoted in Kenyon, *Civil Wars*, 150; as printed in Clarendon, *History*, IV, 74.

22. Evelyn, *Diary and Correspondence*, IV, 179–81; Clarendon, *State Papers*, II, 196–97.

23. *HMC Portland MSS*, I, 327. See also *CSPV 1643–1647*, 196.

24. Clarendon, *State Papers*, II, 209; Bruce, ed., *Charles I*, 19, 21, 28.

25. Evelyn, *Diary and Correspondence*, IV, 175; Petrie, *Letters*, 176.

26. Clarendon, *State Papers*, II, 220; *Calendar of Clarendon State Papers*, I, 310.

27. Bruce, ed., *Charles I*, 31, 33, 34, 36.

28. Montereul, *Correspondence*, I, 180–81.

29. Bruce, ed., *Charles I*, 37–38; Fea, *Memoirs*, 201.

30. Montereul, *Correspondence*, I, 195; as quoted in *Oxford DNB* article on Michael Hudson.

31. Fea, *Memoirs*, 70n1. For cutting Charles's hair and beard, see also Terry, "Visits," 111.

32. Clarendon, *History*, IV, 192; Fea, *Memoirs*, 70.

33. Fea, *Memoirs*, 205; *CSPV 1643–1647*, 254; Fea, *Memoirs*, 70–71.

34. Fea, *Memoirs*, 72. See also Montereul, *Correspondence*, I, 192–93.

35. Fea, *Memoirs*, 72n1; Clarendon, *History*, IV, 191; *Eikon Basilike*, section 22.

36. Fea, *Memoirs*, 72n1, 206.

37. As quoted in Kaplan, "Charles I's Flight," 217. See also Clarendon, *History*, IV, 190, 193; Fea, *Memoirs*, 206.

38. Clarendon, *History*, IV, 193–94; Montereul, *Correspondence*, I, 194; Fea, *Memoirs*, 207.

39. Montereul, *Correspondence*, I, 193–94; Fea, *Memoirs*, 75. See also ibid., 208, 209.

40. Terry, "Visits," 109–11.

41. Clarendon, *History*, IV, 110; Petrie, *Letters*, 175. See also ibid., 180; Clarendon, *History*, IV, 78, 97.

42. As quoted in Terry, "Visits," 113.

43. Fea, *Memoirs*, 209–10. See also Montereul, *Correspondence*, I, 194; Bruce, ed., *Charles I*, 40.

44. As quoted in Terry, "Visits," 122, 116, 118; as quoted in Howell, *Newcastle-upon-Tyne*, 204. See also ibid., 224n8; Terry, "Visits," 117.

45. Bruce, ed., *Charles I*, 46, 47, 50, 46.
46. As quoted in Ashley, *Charles I and Oliver Cromwell*, 177.
47. Bruce, ed., *Charles I*, 41, 44, 46, 45.
48. Bruce, ed., *Charles I*, 44, 50, 44, 42.
49. Bruce, ed., *Charles I*, 51, 42; *Calendar of Clarendon State Papers*, I, 326.
50. Petrie, *Letters*, 199; Bruce, ed., *Charles I*, 54.
51. Petrie, *Letters*, 200; Clarendon, *State Papers*, II, 247. For Charles's willingness to suffer martyrdom, see also *Calendar of Clarendon State Papers*, I, 268, 322.
52. *Calendar of Clarendon State Papers*, I, 333; Green, *Letters*, 326. See also Clarendon, *State Papers*, II, 246–48, 261–64, 268–69, 273–75, 301–2; Green, *Letters*, 325–27; Bruce, ed., *Charles I*, 57–62; Petrie, *Letters*, 203–7.
53. Petrie, Letters, 200, 204. See also ibid., 205–6.
54. Clarendon, *State Papers*, II, 246.
55. Bruce, ed., *Charles I*, 51; Clarendon, *State Papers*, II, 246; Bruce, ed., *Charles I*, 57. See also ibid., 55, 62.
56. Clarendon, *State Papers*, II, 263.
57. Bruce, ed., *Charles I*, 69. See also Clarendon, *State Papers*, II, 270.
58. Petrie, *Letters*, 206; Bruce, ed., *Charles I*, 62, 76–77, 69.
59. Bruce, ed., *Charles I*, 70, 80; *Eikon Basilike*, section 2.
60. Bruce, ed., *Charles I*, 80; *Eikon Basilike*, section 2; Bruce, ed., *Charles I*, 80–81.
61. See Gardiner, *Hamilton Papers*, 113–14; Terry, "Visits," 126.
62. Green, *Letters*, 335–36. See also Bruce, ed., *Charles I*, 76.
63. Bruce, ed., *Charles I*, 81.
64. Green, *Letters*, 334, 333.
65. Clarendon, *State Papers*, II, 314.
66. See *CJ*, IV, May 19, 1646, for the first suggestion.
67. Bruce, ed., *Charles I*, 64; Petrie, *Letters*, 210. See also Bruce, ed., *Charles I*, 66; *CSPV 1643–1647*, 292; Clarendon, *History*, IV, 211–12.
68. As quoted in Terry, "Visits," 132. See also ibid., 133.
69. Green, *Letters*, 331. See also *Calendar of Clarendon State Papers*, I, 346.
70. Bruce, ed., *Charles I*, 83; Green, *Letters*, 331. See also Bruce, ed., *Charles I*, 84.
71. Clarendon, *State Papers*, II, 312–13.
72. Montereul, *Correspondence*, I, 374, 365. See also Gardiner, *History of the Great Civil War*, III, 181–82.

73. Montereul, *Correspondence*, I, 401, 375, 366. See also ibid., 387, 393.

74. As quoted in Terry, "Visits," 134; *LJ*, VIII, January 11, 1647; Ellis, *Original Letters*, ser. 2, III, 327. See also ibid., 328.

75. As quoted in Terry, "Visits," 137; Ellis, *Original Letters*, ser. 2, III, 328.

76. Gardiner, *Hamilton Papers*, 140; Ellis, *Original Letters*, ser. 2, III, 328. See also ibid., 327; Terry, "Visits," 139.

77. *LJ*, VIII, January 11, 1647. See also *LJ*, VIII, January 11, 1647; *CSPV 1643–1647*, 299, 302; Montereul, *Correspondence*, I, 402.

78. Montereul, *Correspondence*, I, 390.

79. Bruce, ed., *Charles I*, 99–100. See also Montereul, *Correspondence*, I, 387–88.

80. *CSPV 1643–1647*, 296; as quoted in Terry, "Visits," 140; *CJ*, V, December 15, 1646.

81. As quoted in Terry, "Visits," 144.

82. *CSPV 1643–1647*, 299, 301, 299, 301. See also Clarendon, *State Papers*, II, 332.

83. Fea, *Memoirs*, 77; Montereul, *Correspondence*, I, 440–41.

84. Fea, *Memoirs*, 77, 78.

85. Montereul, *Correspondence*, I, 425–26, 401.

86. Petrie, *Letters*, 210; Montereul, *Correspondence*, I, 442, 426, 423.

87. Montereul, *Correspondence*, I, 443; *Calendar of Clarendon State Papers*, I, 358; Montereul, *Correspondence*, I, 443.

88. *CSPD 1645–1647*, 517. See also Montereul, *Correspondence*, I, 444; *CJ*, V, December 15, 1646.

89. Montereul, *Correspondence*, I, 445; *CSPV 1643–1647*, 304.

90. *CSPV 1643–1647*, 305; Montereul, *Correspondence*, I, 411–12.

12. COLOMBES, AUGUST 1669

1. Ferrero, *Lettres de Henriette-Marie*, 104. This portrait may now be in the Royal Collection: RCIN 400962.

2. As quoted in *Oxford DNB*: Charles II.

3. For Henrietta's possessions at Colombes, see PRO SP 78/128, ff. 190r–202v.

4. Pepys, *Diary*, VI, 142; Birch, *Court and Times of Charles*, II, 453. See also *CSPV, 1661–1664*, 246.

5. Birch, *Court and Times of Charles*, II, 465. See also PRO SP 78/128, ff. 191r, 194r.

6. Birch, *Court and Times of Charles*, II, 470, 467. The cabinet's contents are detailed in PRO SP 78/128, ff. 200r–202r.

7. Motteville, *Memoir*, 27–28.

8. Motteville, *Memoir*, 29, 30; PRO SP 78/128, f. 201v.

9. Fea, *Memoirs*, 131; *Nicholas Papers*, I, 113, 109. See also *CSPV 1647–1652*, 87.

10. As quoted in *OED* under "vicegerent"; Fea, *Memoirs*, 131. See also Fraser, *Cromwell*, 286–87.

11. Petitot, ed., *Mémoires*, ser. 2, XXXVIII, 205; *Responce de la Reine d'Angleterre*, 4; Birch, *Court and Times of Charles*, II, 380.

12. Jusserand, *Recueil*, XXIV, 70.

13. Motteville, *Memoir*, 19.

14. Petitot, ed., *Mémoires*, ser. 2, XXXVIII, 205–7. For news of Henry, see ibid., LVIII, 162.

15. Birch, *Court and Times of Charles*, II, 382.

16. *Les Sanglots Pitoyables de l'Affligée Reyne*, 6; Bossuet, *Oraison*, 115.

17. Seneca, *Hippolytus*, ii. 3, 607; Birch, *Court and Times of Charles*, II, 382.

18. Petitot, ed., *Mémoires*, ser. 2, XXXVIII, 207, 205–6.

19. Birch, *Court and Times of Charles*, II, 382.

20. Birch, *Court and Times of Charles*, II, 382. See also Cousin, *Madame de Longueville*, 433; Ellis, *Original Letters*, ser. 2, III, 344; Hurtaut and Magny, *Dictionnaire Historique de la Ville de Paris*, II, 45–46, 51.

21. Gardiner, *Constitutional Documents*, chap. 87; Birch, *Court and Times of Charles*, II, 383.

22. Bruce, ed., *Charles I*, 56. See also ibid., 38–39; Green, *Letters*, 358–59; *Nicholas Papers*, I, 116–18.

23. Ferrero, *Lettres de Henriette-Marie*, 99, 100. See also ibid., 106, 112, 115; Montpensier, *Mémoires*, part 1, chap. 6; Motteville, *Memoir*, 29.

24. Ellis, *Original Letters*, ser. 2, III, 330; Ferrero, *Lettres de Henriette-Marie*, 89–90; *CSPV 1647–1652*, 159.

25. Green, *Letters*, 372–73; Montpensier, *Mémoires*, part 1, chap. 11; Thurloe, *State Papers*, I, 311–24. See also *CSPV 1647–1652*, 202; Green, *Letters*, 373.

26. *CSPV 1647–1652*, 145; Green, *Letters*, 371. See also Ferrero, *Lettres de Henriette-Marie*, 70–71.

27. *Calendar of Clarendon State Papers*, IV, 169; Strickland, *Lives*, 471. See also Green, *Letters*, 371–72; Chaillot engraved after Lantara; Bordes, "Personnages," 78–79; PRO SP 78/122, f. 181r.

28. Clarendon, *Life*, II, 120–21; Evelyn, *Diary*, 308: October 1, 1651.

29. *Oxford DNB*: Edward Hyde, Earl of Clarendon, citing Clarendon, *State Papers*, II, 381. See also *CSPV 1653–1654*, 190, 235.

30. Thurloe, *State Papers*, I, 676–93.

31. *Calendar of Clarendon State Papers*, II, 383; Ferrero, *Lettres de Henriette-Marie*, 110.

32. *Calendar of Clarendon State Papers*, II, 429. See also ibid., 414; *Nicholas Papers*, II, 113.

33. *Calendar of Clarendon State Papers*, II, 425, 419, 425; Thurloe, *State Papers*, I, 661–75.

34. *Nicholas Papers*, II, 110–11, 113.

35. *Calendar of Clarendon State Papers*, II, 424, 428, 425.

36. *Calendar of Clarendon State Papers*, II, 429, 434, 436.

37. As quoted in Green, *Lives of the Princesses*, VI, 417; Birch, *Court and Times of Charles*, II, 411.

38. Thurloe, *State Papers*, I, 676–93. See also *Calendar of Clarendon State Papers*, III, 45.

39. *Nicholas Papers*, I, 116; *Calendar of Clarendon State Papers*, II, 183.

40. *Calendar of Clarendon State Papers*, IV, 53. See also ibid., 54; II, 348.

41. Thurloe, *State Papers*, I, 676–93; Green, *Letters*, 385, 388.

42. Green, *Letters*, 388–89; *CSPV 1659–1661*, 23.

43. *Calendar of Clarendon State Papers*, IV, 459, 474.

44. *CJ*, VIII, May 1, 1660; Pepys, *Diary*, I, 158.

45. Bossuet, *Oraison*, 123; Birch, *Court and Times of Charles*, II, 415.

46. Green, *Letters*, 399, 398; Ferrero, *Lettres de Henriette-Marie*, 121–22.

47. Ferrero, *Lettres*, 121; *CSPV 1659–1661*, 198; Ferrero, *Lettres*, 123.

48. Ferrero, *Lettres*, 124; *CSPV 1659–1661*, 217. See also *CSPV 1659–1661*, 269.

49. *CSPV 1659–1661*, 215, 214; Pepys, *Diary*, I, 299.

50. Green, *Letters*, 407; Clarendon, *Life of Edward*, II, 36.

51. *CSPV 1659–1661*, 235.

52. Montpensier, *Mémoires*, part 2, chap. 4; as quoted in *Oxford DNB*: Anne Hyde; Clarendon, *Life of Edward*, II, 40.

53. Green, *Letters*, 403, 409. See also *Calendar of Clarendon State Papers*, V, 51; Birch, *Court and Times of Charles*, II, 423.

54. Birch, *Court and Times of Charles*, II, 437. See also ibid., 400, 431, 459; Pepys, *Diary*, V, 63.

55. Pepys, *Diary*, V, 63. See also ibid., VI, 17. See also *Life and Death*, 61–67; *Calendar of Clarendon State Papers*, V, 291.

56. Evelyn, *Diary*, 446: October 21, 1662; Pepys, *Diary*, III, 191. See also ibid., III, 299, 303; IV, 48.
57. Pepys, *Diary*, IV, 216. See also ibid., 193–94, 229–30.
58. Ferrero, *Lettres de Henriette-Marie*, 126. See also ibid., 127, 128.
59. Norrington, *My Dearest Minette*, 151, 174, 57.
60. Ferrero, *Lettres de Henriette-Marie*, 126; *CSPV, 1661–1664*, 217. See also ibid., 212, 217; Ferrero, *Lettres*, 128.
61. *Calendar of Clarendon State Papers*, V, 278–79; Pepys, *Diary*, III, 263. See also Ferrero, *Lettres*, 127; Reresby, *Memoirs*, 29.
62. Clarendon, *Life of Edward*, II, 263. See also *HMC Hastings MSS*, II, 146; Birch, *Court and Times of Charles*, II, 453; *CSPV 1664–1666*, 125; Pepys, *Diary*, VI, 142.
63. As quoted in *Oxford DNB*: Jermyn; Motteville, *Memoir*, 29.
64. Birch, *Court and Times of Charles*, II, 467; Motteville, *Memoir*, 28, 29.
65. *CSPV 1669–1670*, 39; PRO SP 78/126, f. 233r. See also Green, *Letters*, 415; *CSPV 1669–1670*, 42.
66. Birch, *Court and Times of Charles*, II, 470; Motteville, *Memoir*, 31.
67. Birch, *Court and Times of Charles*, II, 465–66; Green, *Letters*, 416; Birch, *Court and Times of Charles*, II, 466.
68. Green, *Letters*, 416.
69. PRO SP 78/127, f. 95r; Birch, *Court and Times of Charles*, II, 466; PRO SP 78/127, f. 95r; Birch, *Court and Times of Charles*, II, 466.
70. Green, *Letters*, 417. See also *OED*: palpitation, oppression.
71. Birch, *Court and Times of Charles*, II, 468. See also Green, *Letters*, 417.
72. See *HMC Buccleuch MSS*, I, 439; *Life and Death*, 66; *CSPD 1668–1669*, 469; Fea, *Memoirs*, 49, 147–51.
73. Bossuet, *Oraison*, 73–74. See also Birch, *Court and Times of Charles*, II, 470–71; Green, *Letters*, 418; *Life and Death*, 91; Motteville, *Memoir*, 9.

Bibliography

MANUSCRIPTS

BODLEIAN LIBRARY, OXFORD

Clarendon MS 97. State papers collected by Edward Hyde, Earl of Clarendon.

BRITISH LIBRARY, LONDON

BL Additional MSS 12,184–12,186. Despatches of Sir Richard Browne, English Resident at Paris, from August 1641 to November 1651.

BL Additional MS 12,528. Sir Sackville Crowe's Book of Accompts, containing the receipts and disbursements on behalf of the Duke of Buckingham from January 1622 to June 1628.

BL Additional MSS 15,389–15,391. Transcripts from the Papal Registers: correspondence of Gregorio Panzani and George Con.

BL Additional MS 22,474. "Speaches, Passages, and other Obseruations at the Parliament begun and holden at Westminster vjo Febr. 1625[6]."

BL Additional MS 24,023. Original letters of Royal and other personages, principally English; 1596–1844.

BL Additional MSS 27,962E–27,9621. Transcripts from the public archives at Florence of the correspondence of the Florentine ambassadors to England.

BL Additional MS 35,331. Autograph Diary of Walter Yonge, of Colyton, co. Devon. (M.P. for Honiton in the Long Parliament) from 1627 to April, 1642.

BL Additional MS 39,288. Transcripts of State letters and papers, 1521–1631.

BL Harleian MS 3,791.

BL Harleian MS 3,888. "Evangelicall Fruict of the Seraphicall Franciscan Order. . . . Elucubravit P N Archibold, Capuccinus."

BL Harleian MS 6,424. Parliamentary Diary of John Warner, Bishop of Rochester.

BL Harleian MS 6,988. Royal letters.

BL Harleian MS 7,623. "A Copie of the Booke (assigned by his Majestie) of Diet, Wages, &c. for Prince Charles his Highness, & the rest of his Majesties Royal Children. Anno xiiii. Rs. Caroli."

BL King's MSS 135–136. "Recueil de Lettres, de Memoires, d'Actes. d'instructions et de Contracts, faits pour parvenir le Traité de Mariage d'entre Madame Henriette Marie soeur du Roy, et Charles Premier Roy de la Grande Bretagne" 1624–1625.

BL King's MSS 137–138. Négociation de Monsieur de Blainville, Ambassadeur en Angleterre en l'année 1626.

BL MSS Royal 16 E XLI. "Recueil des reparties, rencontres, et autres dits memorables du roy Henry le Grand": a collection of sayings, &c. of Henry IV of France, addressed to his daughter, [Henrietta Maria] Queen of Great Britain, by Gaultier Quinne, i.e., Walter Quin, formerly tutor to Charles I as prince.

BL MS Royal 18 A XXVIII. Political tract, in form of a letter addressed to Charles I, by Henry Cock, on the fortunate dismissal of Queen Henrietta Maria's French attendants and of "those who are communely called the fathers of the Oratory, who lately were chapleins to the Queenes Majesty" and on the machinations of "Fisher the Jesuite" [John Fisher, al. Percy, d. 1641] and [William Smith] "Bishop of Chalcedon, superior of the English Romane clergy," who were concealed "in the very palace," and of "Father Phillips, the Queenes Majestyes Confessor" [Robert Philips, d. 1650?] and others.

BL Sloane MS 1,679. Sir Thomas Mayerne's Receipt Book.

PUBLIC RECORD OFFICE, LONDON

PRO 31/9/17B. Transcripts of Gregorio Panzani's Letters from England, 1634–1637.

PRO 31/9/19–20. Transcripts of Carlo Rossetti's Letters from England, 1639–1641.

PRO E 403. Exchequer of Receipt: Issue Rolls and Registers.

PRO LR 5/63. Documents subsidiary to the accounts of the Treasurer and Receiver General, 1629–1639.

PRO SP 16. State Papers Domestic, Charles I.

PRO SP 78/122. SP Foreign, France, 1666.

PRO SP 78/126. SP Foreign, France, 1669 January–June.

PRO SP 78/127. SP Foreign, France, 1669 July–October.

PRO SP 78/128. SP Foreign, France, 1669 November–December.

PUBLICATIONS

Albion, Gordon, *Charles I and the Court of Rome: A Study in 17th Century Diplomacy* (London, 1935).

Ashley, Maurice, *Charles I and Oliver Cromwell: A Study in Contrasts and Comparisons* (London, 1987).

Ashmole, Elias, *The Institution, Laws and Ceremonies of the Most Noble Order of the Garter* (London 1672).

Aubrey, John, *Aubrey's Brief Lives*, ed. Oliver Lawson Dick (London, 1968).

The Babees' Book: Medieval Manners for the Young, trans. by Edith Rickert and L. J. Naylor (Cambridge, Ontario, 2000).

Baillon, Charles, Comte de, *Henriette-Marie de France, Reine d'Angleterre: Etude Historique par le Comte de Baillon, Suivie de ses Lettres Inédites* (Paris, 1877).

Bassompierre, François de, *Journal de ma Vie: Mémoires du Maréchal de Bassompierre*, ed. Marie Joseph Audoin de La Cropte, marquis de Chantérac, 3 vols., Société de l'Histoire de France Publications 153, 162, 173 (Paris, 1870–75).

———, *Négociation du Mareschal de Bassompierre, Envoyé Ambassadeur Extraordinaire, en Angleterre . . . l'an 1626* (Cologne, 1668).

Batiffol, Louis, *La Vie Intime d'une Reine de France au XVIIe Siècle: Marie de Médicis*, 2 vols. (Paris, n.d.).

Batterel, Louis, *Mémoires Domestiques pour Servir à l'Histoire de l'Oratoire*, 5 vols. (Paris, 1902–11).

Beddard, Robert A., "Six Unpublished Letters of Queen Henrietta Maria," *British Library Journal* 25 (1999), 129–43.

Bellesheim, A., *History of the Catholic Church in Scotland*, trans. David Hunter-Blair, 4 vols. (Edinburgh, 1887–90).

Birch, Thomas, *The Court and Times of Charles the First*, 2 vols. (London, 1848).

———, *The Court and Times of James the First*, 2 vols. (London, 1849).

———, *An Historical View of the Negotiations between the Courts of England, France, and Brussels: From the year 1592 to 1617* (London, 1749).

Bordes, Hélène, "Les Personnages de la Famille Royale Britannique d'après l'Année Sainte," in C. Smith and E. Dubois, eds., *France et Grande-Bretagne de la Chute de Charles Ier à celle de Jacques II (1649–1688)*, (Norwich, 1990), 77–89.

Bossuet, Jacques-Bénigne, *Oraisons funèbres* (Paris: Garnier, 1961).

———, *Oraisons funèbres*, ed. Alfred Rébelliau (Paris : Hachette, 1906).

Bowle, John, *Charles the First* (London, 1975).

Brienne, Henri Auguste de Loménie de, *Mémoires . . . contenant les évenements les plus remarquables du Règne de Louis XIII. et de celui de Louis XIV. jusqu'à la mort du Cardinal Mazarin*, ed. J. F. Bernard ([S.l.], 1824).

Britland, Karen, *Drama at the Courts of Queen Henrietta Maria* (Cambridge, 2006).

———, "Fairy-tale Marriage: Charles and Henrietta Maria's Romance," in Alexander Samson, ed., *The Spanish Match: Prince Charles's Journey to Madrid, 1623* (Aldershot, 2006), 123–38.

Bruce, John, ed., *Charles I in 1646: Letters of King Charles the First to Queen Henrietta Maria*, Camden Society, ser. 1, 63 (1856).

Cabala: Sive Scrinia Sacra: Mysteries of State & Government: In Letters of Illustrious Persons, and Great Agents; in the Reigns of Henry the Eighth, Queen Elizabeth, K: James, and the late King Charls (London, 1654).

Calendar of Clarendon State Papers Preserved in the Bodleian Library, ed. H. O. Coxe et al., 5 vols. (Oxford, 1869–1970).

Camden, William, *Camden's Britannia: Newly Translated into English, with Large Additions and Improvements*, ed. Edmund Gibson (London, 1695).

Carew, Thomas, *The Works of Thomas Carew* (Edinburgh, 1824).

Carlton, Charles, *Charles I: The Personal Monarch* (London, 1995).

The Catholic Encyclopedia: An International Work of Reference, ed. Charles G. Herbermann et al., 16 vols. (New York, 1907).

Cavendish, Margaret, Duchess of Newcastle, *The Blazing World and Other Writings* (Harmondsworth, 1994).

———, *The Life of William Cavendish, Duke of Newcastle*, ed. C. H. Firth (London, 1886).

———, *Poems, and Fancies* (London, 1653).

Charles I, *The Papers which Passed at New-castle bewixt His Sacred Majestie and Mr Al: Henderson: concerning the Change of Church-Government. Anno Dom. 1646* (London, 1649).

———, *Reliquiæ Sacræ Carolinæ: Or the Works of that Great Monarch and Glorious Martyr King Charls the I* (The Hague [i.e., London], 1651).

CJ: *Journal of the House of Commons*. URL: http://www.british-history.ac.uk/subject.aspx?subject=6&gid=43.

Clarendon, Edward Hyde, Earl of, *History of the Rebellion and Civil Wars in England*, ed. W. D. Macray, 6 vols. (Oxford, 1888).

———, *The Life of Edward, Earl of Clarendon, Written by Himself*, 2 vols. (Oxford, 1827).

———, *State Papers collected by Edward, Earl of Clarendon: Commencing from the year MDCXXI*, 3 vols. (Oxford, 1767–86).

Coates, Willson H., Anne Steele Young, and Vernon F. Snow, eds., *The Private Journals of the Long Parliament*, 3 vols. (New Haven, 1982).

Colvin, H. M., *The History of the King's Works*, 6 vols. (London, 1963–82).

Comenius, Johann Amos, *Orbis Sensualium Pictus: English & Latin* (London, 1659).

Cope, Esther S., and Willson H. Coates, eds., *Proceedings of the Short Parliament of 1640*, Camden Society, 4th ser., 19 (London, 1977).

A Coppy of 1. The Letter sent by the Queenes Majestie concerning the Collection of the Recusants Mony for the Scottish Warre, Apr. 17. 1639 . . . (London, 1641).

Cousin, M. Victor, *Madame de Longueville: Etudes sur les Femmes Illustres et la Société du XVIIe siècle: La Jeunesse de Madame de Longueville* (Paris, 1859).

Cruickshanks, Eveline, ed., *The Stuart Courts* (Stroud, 2000).

CSPD: *Calendar of State Papers, Domestic Series, of the Reign of James I*, ed. Mary Anne Everett Green, 5 vols. (London, 1857–72); *Calendar of State Papers, Domestic Series, of the Reign of Charles I*, ed. John Bruce, 23 vols. (London, 1858–97); *Calendar of State Papers, Domestic Series, of the Reign of Charles II*, ed. Mary Anne Everett Green et al., 28 vols. (London, 1860–1938), URL: http://www.british-history.ac.uk/period.aspx?period=7&gid=103.

CSPV: *Calendar of State Papers and Manuscripts, relating to English Affairs, existing in the Archives and Collections of Venice*, ed. Rawdon Brown, 38 vols. (London, 1864–1947). URL: http://www.british-history.ac.uk/catalogue.aspx?type=3&gid=140.

Cust, Richard, *Charles I* (London, 2007).

Dagens, J., *Bérulle et les Origines de la Restauration Catholique* (Paris, 1952).

———, *Correspondance du Cardinal Pierre de Bérulle*, 3 vols. (Paris, 1936–39).

Dauncey, John, *The History of the Thrice Illustrious Princess Henrietta Maria de Bourbon, Queen of England* (London, 1660).

Davenant, Sir William, *Dramatic Works*, ed. J. Maidment and W. H. Logan, 5 vols. (London, 1872–74).

A Deep Sigh Breath'd through the Lodgings at White-hall, Deploring the Absence of the Court, and the Miseries of the Pallace (London, 1642).

D'Ewes, Sir Simonds, *The Autobiography and Correspondence of Sir Simonds D'Ewes, Bart: during the Reigns of James I and Charles I*, ed. James Orchard Halliwell, 2 vols. (London, 1845).

———, *The Journal of Sir Simonds D'Ewes: From the Beginning of the Long Parliament to the Opening of the Trial of the Earl of Strafford*, ed. Wallace Notestein (London, 1923).

———, *The Journal of Sir Simonds D'Ewes: From the First Recess of the Long Parliament to the Withdrawal of King Charles from London*, ed. Willson Havelock Coates (London, 1942).

Dickens, A. G., ed., *The Courts of Europe: Politics, Patronage and Royalty, 1400–1800* (London, 1977).

Dugdale, William, *Monasticon Anglicanum*, 6 vols. (London, 1846).

Dupuy, Micheline, *Henriette Marie, Reine d'Angleterre* (Paris, 1994).

Eccles, A., *Obstetrics and Gynaecology in Tudor and Stuart England* (London, 1982).

Eikon Basilike, or the King's Book, ed. E. Almack (London, 1904). URL: http://anglicanhistory.org/charles/eikon/3.html.

Ellis, Henry, *Original Letters, Illustrative of English History: including numerous royal letters: from autographs in the British Museum and one or two other collections*, 3 series, 11 vols. (London, 1824–46).

The Entertainment of . . . Charles into his ancient city of Edinburgh (London, 1633).

Estrades, Godefroi Louis, comte d', *Lettres, Mémoires et Négociations de Monsieur le Comte d'Estrades*, 9 vols. (Londres [i.e., La Haye], 1743).

Evelyn, John, *Diary and Correspondence of John Evelyn . . . To which is subjoined The Private Correspondence between King Charles I and Sir Edward Nicholas, and between Sir Edward Hyde, afterwards Earl of Clarendon, and Sir Richard Browne*, ed. William Bray, 4 vols. (London, 1859).

———, *The Diary of John Evelyn*, ed. E. S. de Beer (London, 1959).

Fea, Allan, *Memoirs of the Martyr King (Being a Detailed Record of the Last Two Years of the Reign of His Most Sacred Majesty, King Charles the First, 1646–9)* (London, 1904).

Ferard, Joseph, *The Law of Fixtures, and Other Property: Partaking Both of a Real and Personal Nature*, ed. William Hogan (New York, 1855).

Ferrero, Hermann, ed., *Lettres de Henriette-Marie de France, Reine d'Angleterre, à sa sœur Christine, Duchesse de Savoie*, Estratto dalla Miscellanea di Storia Italiana, ser. II, vol. V (Turin, 1881).

Finet, Sir John, *Ceremonies of Charles I: The Notebooks of John Finet 1628–1641*, ed. Albert J. Loomie (New York, 1987).

———, *Finetti Philoxenis: Som Choice Observations of Sir J. F., . . . touching the Reception and Precedence, the Treatment and Audience, the Puntillios and Contests of Forren Ambassadors in England* (London, 1656).

Forster, John, *Arrest of the Five Members by Charles the First* ([S.l.], 1860).

Fraser, Antonia, *King James VI of Scotland and I of England* (London, 1977).

Fuller, Thomas, *The Church-History of Britain: From the Birth of Jesus Christ, untill the year MDCXLVIII* (London, 1655).

Gardiner, Samuel Rawson, *Constitutional Documents of the Puritan Revolution, 1628–1660* (Oxford, 1899). URL: http://www.constitution.org/eng /conpur_.htm.

———, *The Hamilton Papers, being Selections from Original Letters in the Possession of His Grace the Duke of Hamilton and Brandon relating to the Years 1638–1650*, Camden Society, new ser., 27 (London, 1880).

———, *History of England 1603–1642*, 10 vols. (London, 1884).

———, *History of the Great Civil War, 1642–1649*, 4 vols. (London, 1897–98).

Geyl, Pieter, *Orange and Stuart 1641–1672* (London, 2001).

Gower, Lord Ronald Sutherland, *The Tower of London*, 2 vols. (London, 1902).

Green, Mary Anne Everett, ed., *Letters of Queen Henrietta Maria: Including her Private Correspondence with Charles the First* (London, 1857).

———, *Lives of the Princesses of England*, 6 vols. (London, 1849–1855).

Gregg, Pauline, *King Charles I* (London, 1981).

Hamilton, Elizabeth, *Henrietta Maria* (London, 1976).

Hardwicke, Philip Yorke, 2nd Earl of, *Miscellaneous State Papers from 1501 to 1726*, 2 vols. (London, 1778).

Harris, John, Stephen Orgel, and Roy Strong, *The King's Arcadia: Inigo Jones and the Stuart Court: A Quatercentenary Exhibition Held at the Banqueting House, Whitehall, from July 12th to September 2nd, 1973* ([London], 1973).

Harrison, G. B., ed., *A Jacobean Journal* (London, 1941).

Herbert of Cherbury, Edward Lord, *The Autobiography of Edward, Lord Herbert of Cherbury*, ed. Sidney Lee (London, [1906]).

Herrick, Robert. *Works*, ed. Alfred Pollard, 2 vols. (London, 1891).

Heylin, Peter, *Cyprianus Anglicus: or, the History of the Life and Death, of the Most Reverend and Renowned Prelate William, by Divine Providence, Lord Archbishop of Canterbury* (London, 1671).

———, *A Short View of the Life and Reign of King Charles (The second monarch of Great Britain), From his Birth to his Burial* (London, 1658).

Hibbard, Caroline, *Charles I and the Popish Plot* (Chapel Hill, 1983).

———, "Henrietta Maria in the 1630s: Perspectives on the Role of Consort Queens in Ancien Regime Courts," in Ian Atherton and Julie Sanders, ed., *The 1630s: Interdisciplinary Essays on Culture and Politics in the Caroline Era* (Manchester, 2006), 92–110.

———, "Translating Royalty: Henrietta Maria and the Transition from Princess to Queen," *Court Historian* 5 (2000), 15–28.

HMC Buccleuch MSS: Royal Commission on Historical Manuscripts, *Report on the Manuscripts of the Duke of Buccleuch and Queensberry, K.G., K.T., preserved at Montagu House, Whitehall*, 3 vols. in 4 (London, 1899–1926).

HMC Cowper MSS: Royal Commission on Historical Manuscripts, *The Manuscripts of the Earl Cowper, K.G., preserved at Melbourne Hall, Derbyshire*, 3 vols. (London, 1888–89).

HMC Denbigh MSS: Royal Commission on Historical Manuscripts, *Report on the Manuscripts of the Earl of Denbigh preserved at Newnham Paddox, Warwickshire*, Part V (London, 1911).

HMC De L'Isle and Dudley MSS: Royal Commission on Historical Manuscripts, *Report on the Manuscripts of Lord de l'Isle & Dudley preserved at Penshurst Place*, 6 vols. (London, 1925–66).

HMC Egmont MSS: Royal Commission on Historical Manuscripts, *Report on the Manuscripts of the Earl of Egmont*, 2 vols. in 3 (London, 1905–09).

HMC Hastings MSS: Royal Commission on Historical Manuscripts, *Report on the Manuscripts of the late Reginald Rawdon Hastings, Esq., of the Manor house, Ashby de la Zouche*, 4 vols. (London, 1928–47).

HMC Mar and Kellie: Royal Commission on Historical Manuscripts, *Report on the Manuscripts of the Earl of Mar and Kellie preserved at Alloa House*, II (London, 1930).

HMC Ninth Report, House of Lords MSS: Royal Commission on Historical Manuscripts, *Calendar of House of Lords Manuscripts* (London, 1884).

HMC Portland MSS: Royal Commission on Historical Manuscripts, *Report on the Manuscripts of His Grace the Duke of Portland*, 10 vols. (London, 1891–1931).

HMC Salisbury MSS: Royal Commission on Historical Manuscripts, *Calendar of the Manuscripts of the Most Hon. the Marquis of Salisbury: preserved at Hatfield House, Hertfordshire* (London, 1971).

HMC 16 Skrine MSS: Royal Commission on Historical Manuscripts, *The Manuscripts of Henry Duncan Skrine, Esq: Salvetti Correspondence* (London 1887).

Houssaye, M., "L'Ambassade de M. de Blainville à la Cour de Charles Ier, Roi d'Angleterre," *Revue des Questions Historiques* 23 (1878), 176–204.

———, *Le Cardinal de Bérulle et le Cardinal de Richelieu, 1625–1629* (Paris, 1875).

Howell, James, *Epistolae Ho-Elianae: The Familiar Letters of James Howell*, ed. Joseph Jacobs, 2 vols. (London, 1892).

Howell, Roger, *Newcastle-upon-Tyne and the Puritan Revolution: A study of the Civil War in North England* (Oxford, 1967).

Hurtaut, Pierre-Thomas-Nicolas, and Magny, *Dictionnaire Historique de la Ville de Paris et de ses Environs,* 4 vols. (Paris, 1779).

Hutchinson, Lucy, *Memoirs of the Life of Colonel Hutchinson, Governor of Nottingham Castle and Town* (London, 1899).

Hutton, Ronald, *Charles II: King of England, Scotland, and Ireland* (Oxford, 1991).

Johnson, Robert C., et al., eds., *Proceedings in Parliament, 1628*, 6 vols. (New Haven, 1977–83).

Jonson, Ben, *Chloridia. Rites to Chloris and Her Nymphs, Personated in a Masque at Court. By the Queenes Majesty and her Ladies* (London, 1631).

———, *Love's Triumph through Callipolis. Performed in a Masque at Court 1630. By his Majestie with the Lords, and Gentlemen assisting* (London, 1630 [i.e., 1631]).

———, *The Works of Ben Jonson*, ed. W. Gifford, 9 vols. (London, 1816).

Jusserand, J. J., *Recueil des Instructions Données aux Ambassadeurs et Ministres de France depuis les Traités de Westphalie jusqu'à la Revolution Française: Angleterre*, vols. 24, 25 (Paris, 1929–1965).

Kaplan, Lawrence, "Charles I's Flight to the Scots," *Albion* 11 (1979), 207–23.

Kenyon, John, *The Civil Wars of England* (London, 1988).

The King and Queenes Entertainement at Richmond. After their departure from Oxford: In a Masque, Presented by the Most Illustrious Prince Charles. Sept. 12. 1636 (Oxford, 1636).

King Charls His Speech, Made upon the Scaffold At Whitehall-Gate, Immediately before his Execution, On Tuesday the 30 of Jan. 1648 (London, 1649). URL: http://anglicanhistory.org/charles/charles1.html.

The Kings Cabinet Opened: or, Certain packets of secret letters & papers, written with the Kings own hand, and taken in his cabinet at Nasby-field, June 14. 1645, by victorious Sr. Thomas Fairfax . . . published by speciall order of the Parliament (London, 1645).

La Fayette, Madame de, *Fatal gallantry: Or, The Secret History of Henrietta Princess of England*, trans. Ann Floyd (London, 1722).

La Serre, M. de Jean-Puget, *Histoire de l'Entree de la Reyne Mere du Roy tres Chrestien, dans la Grande-Bretaigne* (London, 1639).

Lacey, Andrew, *The Cult of King Charles the Martyr* (Woodbridge, 2003).

Laud, William, *The Works of the Most Reverend Father in God, William Laud, D.D. sometime Lord Archbishop of Canterbury*, ed. William Scott and James Bliss, 7 vols. (Oxford, 1847–60).

The Life and Death of Henrietta Maria de Bourbon, Queen to that Blessed King & Martyr, Charles I (London, 1685).

LJ: Journal of the House of Lords. URL: http://www.british-history.ac.uk/sub ject.aspx?subject=6&gid=44.

Lockyer, Roger, *Buckingham: The Life and Political Career of George Villiers, First Duke of Buckingham, 1592–1628* (London, 1981).

————, ed., *The Trial of Charles I: a contemporary account taken from the memoirs of Sir Thomas Herbert and John Rushworth* ([S.l.], 1959).

Ludlow, Edmund, *Memoirs of Lieutenant General Ludlow*, 3 vols. (Vevey, Switzerland, 1699).

McClure, Norman Egbert, ed., *The Letters of John Chamberlain*, 2 vols. (Philadelphia, 1939).

MacGregor, Arthur, ed., *The Late King's Goods: Collections, Possessions and Patronage of Charles I in the Light of the Commonwealth Sale Inventories* (London, 1989).

McMillan, W. "Robert Philip, Father Confessor to Henrietta Maria," *Records of the Scottish Church History Society* 9:2 (1946), 83–96; 9:3 (1947), 142–54.

Madan, Francis Falconer, *A New Bibliography of the Eikon Basilike of King Charles the First* (London, 1950).

Magalotti, Lorenzo, *Lorenzo Magalotti at the Court of Charles II: His Relazione d'Inghilterra of 1668*, ed. and trans. William Edgar Knowles Middleton (Waterloo, 1980).

————, *Travels of Cosmo the Third, Grand Duke of Tuscany, through England, during the Reign of King Charles the Second (1669)* (London, 1821).

Marshall, Rosalind K., *Henrietta Maria: The Intrepid Queen* (London, 1990).

Mayor, J. E. B., *Nicholas Ferrar: Two Lives, by his Brother John and by Doctor Jebb* (Cambridge, 1855).

Le Mercure françois (Paris, 1609–).

Michaud, Joseph François, and Jean Joseph François Poujoulat, *Nouvelle Collection des Mémoires pour Servir à l'Histoire de France depuis le XIIIe siècle jusqu'à la fin du XVIIIe*, 34 vols. (Paris, 1850).

Millar, Oliver, *The Age of Charles I: Painting in England 1620–1649* (London, 1972).

Montagu, Walter, *The Shepherds' Paradise*, ed. Sarah Poynting (Oxford, 1997).

Montereul, Jean de, *The Diplomatic Correspondence of Jean de Montereul and the Brothers de Bellièvre, French Ambassadors in England and Scotland 1645–48*, ed. J. G. Fotheringham, 2 vols., Publications of the Scottish History Society 29–30 (Edinburgh, 1898–99).

Montpensier, Anne Marie Louise d'Orléans, Duchesse de, *Mémoires de Mademoiselle de Montpensier: petite-fille de Henri IV*, ed. A. Chéruel, 4 vols. (Paris, 1858–68). URL: http://penelope.uchicago.edu/mlle/.

Motteville, Françoise de, *Memoir by Madame de Motteville of the Life of Henrietta Maria*, ed. M.G. Hanotaux, Camden Miscellany 8, Camden Society, N.S. 31 (1863).

————, *Mémoires de Madame de Motteville sur Anne d'Autriche et Sa Cour*, 4 vols. (Paris, 1904–11).

Nelson, Karen L. "Negotiating Exile: Henrietta Maria, Elizabeth of Bohemia, and the Court of Charles I," in Carole Levin, Jo Eldridge Carney, and Debra Barrett-Graves, ed., *"High and Mighty Queens" of Early Modern England: Realities and Representations* (Basingstoke, 2003), 61–76.

The Nicholas Papers: Correspondence of Sir Edward Nicholas, Secretary of State, ed. George F. Warner, 4 vols., Camden Society, new ser., 40, 50, 57, third ser., 31 (1886–1920).

Nichols, J. ed., *The Progresses, Processions, and Magnificent Festivities of King James I the First*, 4 vols. (London, 1828).

Nichols, John Gough, ed., *The Discovery of the Jesuits' College at Clerkenwell in March 1627–8*, Camden Miscellany II (1854).

Nicolson, Marjorie Hope, ed., *Conway Letters: The Correspondence of Anne, Viscountess Conway, Henry More, and Their Friends, 1642–1684* (London, 1930).

Norrington, Ruth, *My Dearest Minette: The Letters between Charles II and his Sister Henrietta, Duchesse d'Orléans*, (London, 1996).

Orgel, Stephen, and Roy Strong, *Inigo Jones: The Theatre of the Stuart Court: including the complete designs for productions at court for the most part in the collection of the Duke of Devonshire*, 2 vols. (London, 1973).

Ovatio Carolina: The Triumph of King Charles, or the Triumphant Manner and Order of receiving His Maiesty into his City of London, on Thursday the 25th. day of November, Anno Dom. 1641 (London, 1641).

Oxford DNB: Oxford Dictionary of National Biography. URL: http://www.oxforddnb.com/.

OED: Oxford English Dictionary. URL: http://dictionary.oed.com/.

Panzani, Gregorio, *The Memoirs of Gregorio Panzani, giving an Account of his Agency in England, in the years 1634, 1635, 1636. Translated from the*

Italian original, and now first published, ed. Joseph Berington (Birmingham, 1793).

Pastor, Ludwig, *The History of the Popes from the Close of the Middle Ages: Drawn from the Secret Archives of the Vatican and other Original Sources*, ed. Frederick Ignatius Antrobus, 40 vols. (London, 1891–1953).

Patterson, William Brown, *King James VI and I and the Reunion of Christendom* (Cambridge, 1997).

Pepys, Samuel, *The Diary of Samuel Pepys*, ed. Robert Latham and William Matthews, 11 vols. (London, 1995).

Petitot, Claude Bernard, et al., eds., *Collection des Mémoires Relatifs à l'Histoire de France, depuis l'Avenement de Henri IV jusqu'à la Paix de Paris Conclue en 1763; avec des notices sur chaque auteur, et des observations sur chaque ouvrage*, 1st ser., 52 vols.; 2nd ser., 78 vols. (Paris, 1819–1829). URL: http://visualiseur.bnf.fr/CadresFenetre?O=NUMM-36334.

Petrie, Sir Charles, ed., *The Letters, Speeches and Proclamations of King Charles I* (London, 1935).

Pett, Phineas, *Autobiography*, ed. W. G. Perrin, Publications of the Navy Records Society, 51 (1918).

Plowden, Alison, *Henrietta Maria: Charles I's Indomitable Queen* (Stroud, 2001).

Polwhele, Richard, *Traditions and Recollections, Domestic, Clerical and Literary; in which are included letters of Charles II, Cromwell, Fairfax, Edgecumbe, Macaulay, Wolcot, Opie . . . and other Distinguished Characters*, 2 vols. (London, 1826).

Poynting, Sarah, "'In the name of all the sisters': Henrietta Maria's Notorious Whores," in *Women and Culture at the Courts of the Stuart Queens*, ed. Clare McManus (Basingstoke, 2003).

Prideaux, Mathias, *An Easy and Compendious Introduction for Reading all sorts of Histories, Contrived in a more Facile Way then Heretofore hath been Published* (Oxford, 1682).

Prinsterer, Gulielmus Groen van, *Archives ou Correspondance Inédite de la Maison d'Orange-Nassau*, 1st ser., 9 vols.; 2nd ser., 6 vols. (Leiden, 1835–96).

Ralph, Philip Lee, *Sir Humphrey Mildmay: Royalist Gentleman: Glimpses of the English Scene, 1633–1652* (New Brunswick, 1947).

Reid, Stuart, *Scots Armies of the Civil War, 1639–1651* (Leigh-on-Sea, 1982).

Reresby, Sir John, *Memoirs of Sir John Reresby*, ed. Andrew Browning (London, 1991).

Responce de la Reine d'Angleterre au Prince de Galles son fils (Paris, 1649).

Richelieu, Armand Jean du Plessis, duc de, *Lettres, Instructions Diplomatiques et Papiers d'Etat du Cardinal de Richelieu*, ed. Denis Louis Martial Avenel, 8 vols. (1853–1877).

Rous, John, *Diary of John Rous: Incumbent of Santon Downham, Suffolk, from 1625 to 1642*, ed. Mary Anne Everett Green, Camden Society, ser. 1, 66 ([London], 1856).

Roy, Ian, "The City of Oxford 1640–1660," in R. C. Richardson, ed., *Town and Countryside in the English Revolution* (Manchester, 1992), 130–68.

———, and Dietrich Reinhart, "Oxford and the Civil Wars," in Nicholas Tyacke, ed., *The History of the University of Oxford*, IV: *Seventeenth-Century Oxford* (Oxford 1997), 687–731.

Les Royales Cérémonies faites en l'édification d'une chapelle de Capucins à Londres en Angleterre (Paris, 1632).

Rueff, Jakob, *The Expert Midwife, or An Excellent and Most Necessary Treatise of the Generation and Birth of Man* (London, 1637).

Rushworth, John, *Historical Collections of Private Passages of State, Weighty Matters in Law, Remarkable Proceedings in Five Parliaments. Beginning the Sixteenth Year of King James, Anno 1618. And Ending the Fifth Year of King Charles, Anno 1629*, 3 vols. (London, 1659–1701).

Russell, Conrad, *The Fall of the British Monarchies, 1637–1642* (Oxford, 1991).

———, "The First Army Plot of 1641," *Transactions of the Royal Historical Society* 38 (1988), 85–106.

Les Sanglots Pitoyables de l'Affligée Reyne d'Angleterre du Trepas de son Mary (Paris, 1649).

Shorney, David, *Protestant Nonconformity and Roman Catholicism: A Guide to Sources in the Public Record Office* (London, 1906).

Smith, D. L., "Catholic, Anglican or Puritan? Edward Sackville, fourth earl of Dorset, and the ambiguities of religion in early Stuart England," in *Transactions of the Royal Historical Society*, ser. 6, II (1992).

Smuts, R. Malcolm, "Art and the Material Culture of Majesty in Early Stuart England," in R. Malcolm Smuts, ed., *The Stuart Court and Europe: Essays in Politics and Political Culture* (Cambridge, 1996).

———, "The Puritan Followers of Henrietta Maria in the 1630s," *English Historical Review* 93 (1978), 26–45.

Society of Antiquaries, *A Collection of Ordinances and Regulations for the Government of the Royal Household, made in divers Reigns. From King Edward III to King William and Queen Mary* (London, 1790).

Sophia, Electress of Hanover, *Memoirs of Sophia, Electress of Hanover, 1630–1680*, trans. H. Forester [i.e., Mary Leighton] (London, 1888).

Steele, Mary Susan, *Plays & Masques at Court during the Reigns of Elizabeth, James and Charles* (New Haven, 1926).

Strafford, Thomas Wentworth, Earl of, *The Earl of Strafforde's Letters and Dispatches: with an Essay towards his Life, by Sir George Radcliffe*, ed. William Knowler, 2 vols. (Dublin, 1740).

Strickland, Agnes, *Lives of the Queens of England from the Norman Conquest*, 8 vols. (London, 1851).

Strong, Roy, *The Renaissance Garden in England* (London, 1998).

———, *The Tudor and Stuart Monarchy: Pageantry, Painting, Iconography.* Vol. III: *Jacobean and Caroline* (Woodbridge, 1998).

Summerson, John, *Inigo Jones* (New Haven, 2000).

Terry, C. S., "The Visits of Charles I to Newcastle in 1633, 1639, 1641, 1646–7, with some Notes on Contemporary Local History," *Archaeologia Aeliana*, 2nd ser., 21 (1899), 83–145.

Thurloe, John, *A Collection of the State Papers of John Thurloe, Esq.; Secretary, first, to the Council of State, and afterwards to the two Protectors, Oliver and Richard Cromwell*, ed. Thomas Birch (London, 1742). URL: http://www.british-history.ac.uk/subject.aspx?subject=6&gid=101.

Tillières, Comte Tanneguy Leveneur de, *Mémoires Inédits du comte Leveneur de Tillières: Ambassadeur en Angleterre, sur la Cour de Charles Ier, et son Mariage avec Henriette de France*, ed. M. C. Hippeau (Paris, 1863).

Todd, Henry John, *Letter to His Grace the Archbishop of Canterbury, concerning the Authorship of Eikon Basilike* (London, 1825).

Townshend, Aurelian, *The Poems and Masques of Aurelian Townshend: With Music by Henry Lawes and William Webb*, ed. Cedric C. Brown (Reading, 1983).

Toynbee, Margaret Ruth, "Two Letterbooks of Charles I in the Bodleian Library," *Notes and Queries*, 193 (1948), 358–62.

———, "The Wedding Journey of King Charles I," *Archaeologia Cantiana* 69 (1956 for 1955), 75–89.

A True and Exact Relation of the Manner of his Maiesties Setting up of His Standard at Nottingham, on Munday the 22. of August 1642 (London, 1642).

A True Discourse of all the Royal Passages, Tryumphs and Ceremonies, obserued at the Contract and Mariage of the High and Mighty Charles, King of Great Britaine, and the most excellentest of ladies, the Lady Henrietta Maria of Burbon (London, 1625).

The True Effigies of our most Illustrious Soveraigne Lord, King Charles Queene Mary, with the Rest of the Royall Progenie (London, 1641).

Underdown, David, "The Parliamentary Diary of John Boys, 1647–8," *Bulletin of the Institute of Historical Research* 39 (1966), 141–64.

Varley, Frederick John, *The Siege of Oxford: An Account of Oxford during the Civil War, 1642–1646* (Oxford, 1932).

Veevers, Erica, *Images of Love and Religion: Queen Henrietta Maria and Court Entertainments* (Cambridge, 1989).

Verney, Sir Ralph, *Verney Papers: Notes of Proceedings in the Long Parliament, Temp. Charles I*, ed. John Bruce, Camden Society, ser. 1, 31 (London, 1845).

Warburton, Eliot, *Memoirs of Prince Rupert, and the Cavaliers: including their Private Correspondence*, 3 vols. (London, 1849).

Warwick, Sir Philip, *Memoires of the Reign of King Charles I. Containing the Most Remarkable Occurrences of that Reign* (London, 1701).

Wood, Anthony à, *The Life and Times of Anthony Wood, antiquary, of Oxford, 1632–1695, described by Himself*, ed. Andrew Clark, 5 vols. (Oxford, 1891–1900).

Wordsworth, Christopher, ed., *The Manner of the Coronation of King Charles the First of England, at Westminster, 2 Feb., 1626*, Henry Bradshaw Society 2 (London, 1892).

Wedgwood, C. V., *The King's Peace, 1637–1641* (London, 1966).

———, *Thomas Wentworth: First Earl of Strafford, 1593–1641: A Revaluation* (London, 1988).

W[eldon], Sir A[rthur], *The Court and Character of King James* (2nd ed., London, 1651).

White, Michelle Anne, *Henrietta Maria and the English Civil Wars* (Aldershot, 2006).

Wilson, Arthur, *The History of Great Britain, Being the Life and Reign of King James the First* (London, 1653).

Wittkower, Rudolf, "Inigo Jones—Puritanissimo fiero," *Burlington Magazine* 90 (1948), 50–51.

Wotton, Sir Henry, *Reliquiæ Wottonianæ. Or, A Collection of Lives, Letters, Poems; with Characters of Sundry Personages* (London, 1651).

Index

Galloway, Bishop of, 150
Gamache, Cyprien de, 11, 275, 276, 280, 286
Garnett, Henry, 81
Gascony, 89
Gaston, Duc d'Orléans, 39, 43, 51
Gentileschi, Artemesia, 135
Gentileschi, Orazio, 135
George, Saint, 17
George III, King of England, xvi
Germany, 26n, 32, 34
Glemham, Sir Thomas, 253
Gloucester, 346
Gloucester, 1st Duke of, see Henry, Prince, 1st Duke of Gloucester
Goodman, John, 192, 193
Goring, George, Lord, 127, 168–69, 198, 199, 200, 202, 206, 208, 232
Goutier, Jacques, 89, 90
Graham, James, 1st Marquess of Montrose, 252, 254, 255, 256
Gravesend, 49, 85
Great Britain, 24
Great Council of Peers, 182–83
Greenwich Palace, 104–6, 110, 122, 123, 125, 126, 127, 133, 156, 177, 237–38, 274
    Queen's House at, 96, 135, 171
Greyfriars Church, 155
Guildhall, 218, 222, 228–29, 230, 231
Gunpowder Plot of 1605, 81, 102, 208

Hacket (chaplain), 67
Hague, 215, 274
Hamilton, Marchioness of, 101, 115
Hamilton, Marquess of, 101, 156–57
Hampton Court, 64, 72, 87, 91, 101, 119, 125, 231–32, 237, 267
Hapsburgs, 24, 139
Hartlepool, 263
Harwich, 158
Hay, James, Earl of Carlisle, 32, 46
Henley-on-Thames, 253
Henri IV, King of France, 177
    assassination of, 36, 43

Catholic conversion of, 259
fatherhood of, 36, 80, 86, 207
Henrietta Anne, Duchesse d'Orléans:
    birth of, 247–48
    Catholic instruction of, 280
    childhood and adolescence of, 10, 270, 274, 276, 280, 281
    French exile of, 10, 276, 280
    Henrietta's relationship with, 270, 276, 280, 282, 284–85
    marriage of, 270, 282–83
    motherhood of, 270
    portrait of, 270
Henrietta Maria, Queen of England:
    acceptance of Charles's regulations by, 91, 117
    belief in the need for war by, 235–36, 246
    birthdays of, 72, 88, 102, 130
    birth of, 1
    brown hair and eyes of, 1, 3, 35, 54, 57
    building projects of, 96, 135–36, 171, 283
    burial of, 287
    capture and imprisonment feared by, 3, 230, 248
    Catholic courtiers of, 138, 142, 145, 153, 167, 187
    Catholic faith of, xviii, xx, 5, 7, 42–43, 46–48, 50, 52, 55, 62–74, 80–82, 87–91, 96, 102, 104, 106–9, 111, 115–17, 124, 135–46, 151, 188–89, 245, 271–72, 275, 277–80, 284, 286–87
    character and personality of, xviii, 34, 36, 51, 54, 143
    charged of high treason against, xvii, 10, 247
    Charles urged to accept Presbyterianism by, 258–61, 274
    charm and wit of, 1, 3–4, 34, 36, 51, 63, 91, 129, 229
    childhood and adolescence of, xviii, xix, 1, 34–42, 120, 276
    "churching" of, 115, 119

ABOUT THE AUTHOR

Katie Whitaker grew up in London, England, before gaining a BA in natural sciences at Cambridge University, specializing in history and philosophy of science. She then spent a year in the United States, as a Century Fellow at the University of Chicago, where she received an MA in philosophy. Returning from there to Cambridge, she took a PhD in the history of science. Her PhD thesis, on the emergence of the English Scientific Revolution from gentlemanly culture in the mid-seventeenth century, was awarded the University's Thirlwall Prize and Medal in 1997 for the best original historical work by a Cambridge scholar under thirty. Her first book, *Mad Madge: The Extraordinary Life of Margaret Cavendish, Duchess of Newcastle, the First Woman to Live by Her Pen*, won the Elizabeth Longford Prize for Historical Biography in 2004. Whitaker now lives in Yorkshire, England, with her husband and two children.